D1090901

Lavery Library
EX LIBRIS
ST. JOHN FISHER COLLEGE

Images for Battle

Images for Battle

British Film and the Second World War, 1939–1945

Clive Coultass

An Ontario Film Institute Book
Newark: University of Delaware Press
London and Toronto: Associated University Presses

Associated University Presses
440 Forsgate Drive
Cranbury, NJ 08512

Associated University Presses
25 Sicilian Avenue
London WC1A 2QH, England

Associated University Presses
P.O. Box 488, Port Credit
Mississauga, Ontario
Canada L5G 4M2

The paper used in this publication meets the requirements of the American National Standard for Permanence of Paper for Printed Library Materials Z39.48-1984.

Library of Congress Cataloging-in-Publication Data

Coultass, Clive.
Images for battle.

"An Ontario Film Institute book."
Bibliography: p.
Includes index.
1. World War, 1939–1945—Motion pictures and the war. 2. Motion pictures—Great Britain—History—20th century. I. Title.
D743.23.C68 1989 791.43'09'09358 87-40355
ISBN 0-87413-334-3 (alk. paper)

Printed in the United States of America

Contents

Acknowledgments

Since the major source of this work has been the films themselves, I am especially grateful for the help of Stephen Perry of the Imperial War Museum and Elaine Burrows and Jackie Morris of the National Film Archive for arranging the viewing of them. Kay Gladstone of the IWM guided me through the oral history project initiated by him on Second World War cameramen and official filmmakers; Frances Thorpe of the British Film Institute helped with documentation; and Teresa Silk, who typed the manuscript, showed great patience and perseverance in coping with the considerable number of alterations to it. My thanks also go to Bridget Kinally of the NFA, and Jane Carmichael and Ron Brooker of the IWM, who supplied the stills; to Jeffrey Richards of the University of Lancaster and Charles Barr of the University of East Anglia, who read drafts; and to Anne Fleming and Terry Charman of the IWM, who assisted with many assorted items of information.

Permission has been granted for the reproduction of John Pudney's poem "For Johnny" by David Higham Associates, and for Leonard England's report on *Target for Tonight* by the Trustees of the Mass-Observation Archive, University of Sussex.

Stills from the films *The Gentle Sex, 49th Parallel, Secret Mission, Waterloo Road, In Which We Serve, We Dive at Dawn, The Life and Death of Colonel Blimp, Millions Like Us, The Way Ahead, They Met in the Dark, The Demi-Paradise, A Canterbury Tale,* and *The Way to the Stars,* by courtesy of The Rank Organisation plc; from *The Proud Valley, Convoy, Ships With Wings, The Big Blockade, The Foreman Went to France, Went the Day Well?, Nine Men, The Bells Go Down, Undercover, San Demetrio–London,* and *Johnny Frenchman,* by courtesy of the Weintraub Entertainment Group; from *The Lion Has Wings,* by courtesy of Korda Films/Central Independent Television; from *Pastor Hall,* by courtesy of the Boulting Brothers; from *One of Our Aircraft is Missing,* by courtesy of Republic Pictures Corporation; and from *The First of the Few,* by courtesy of Riverside Productions Limited. Efforts have been made to contact, or find, holders of copyright for *Contraband, The Volunteer,* and *They Came to a City,* without success. All other film stills are official British Crown Copyright, for the reproduction of which permission has been granted by the IWM.

Introduction

The Second World War surpassed in its range and intensity any previous conflict in history. Within the space of a relatively short period it became a vast kaleidoscope of events of many different kinds—military activity on land, sea, and air in almost all continents, invasion and occupation, genocide on an unprecedented scale, national mobilization and involvement of civilian populations in a manner never known before. The political and social consequences of the war have had a lasting influence on the rest of the twentieth century. It continues to inspire a never-ending line of literature as more records become available and as assessments change with further distance from its main incidents. Likewise, no other historical episode has received so much treatment in visual form, from film as it was originally shot and from its extension in later decades through the medium of television.

It happened that the war coincided with the era when the cinema industry was reaching the peak of its development, in terms of technique as well as popularity. More recent years have seen the dominance of the electronic media—the wars in Lebanon and the Falklands, for instance, were both video events—but during the Second World War the main visual medium was still film, almost all of it 35mm black and white and, at its best, crisp and clear in the quality of its images. Many millions of feet were shot by the major combatant nations (in the case of Britain by the service units and the newsreel companies), and preservation of this material has left a unique legacy of record film, available for research or for reissue as basic shots and sequences in further films or television programs about the war.[1]

At the time, though, the newsreels made up only a tiny part of a cinema program. For the British people "going to the pictures" was a major leisure activity and unlike football or racing it was one that was shared equally by both sexes. The public liked to see feature films, and there seems to have been little complaint from them that most of the ones they watched were American. The industry had to struggle so hard in the shadow of Hollywood that in 1927 a quota law was introduced that compelled distributors and exhibitors to show a proportion (eventually rising to about one-fifth of all screenings) of British-made films.[2] Unfortunately the quality of many of these was poor, hidebound as they were by the insularity and class-ridden nature of British society, a liability paralleled to some degree by the isolation of national art and music from the continent and America. In general, Hollywood demonstrated both greater technical finesse in film-making and greater sense of glamor in presentation of the movie stars who were likely to attract the audiences. If, as is often assumed, most people needed the collective experience of cinema-going to take them away to a fantasy world of escape from the routine of their everyday lives, Hollywood in the main would give them what they wanted.[3] The war changed nothing. Indeed, as weekly attendances rose above the twenty million mark (some people going twice a week) it was clear that the cinema was a refuge for the public from the problems of severe rationing, bombing of their cities, general mobilization, civilian and service deaths and injuries, and the very special burden of standing for a period almost alone against the Nazi menace.[4] The quota percentage had been lowered in 1940 because the industry could not produce enough to fulfill it, so Hollywood became more dominant than ever, in terms of quantity at least.[5] Moreover, even after the United States joined the hostilities, most American films continued to have no war content at all, and there has been no evidence to suggest that the public wanted any.

It would be wrong to generalize too far about the nature of the British cinema audience, although its bulk was obviously drawn from the urban working class. Regional and even local differences may have been very pronounced, just as society in the thirties was itself very divided. The depression had fallen heavily on certain areas in Scotland, Wales, and the north of England, as the older industries that had formed the base of Victorian prosperity now began to decline. Most of the southeast, by contrast, had stayed relatively prosperous, and newer industries had sprung up around London and in the midlands. For many the standard of living was moderately comfortable, and the years before the war even saw real improvements for those who were fortunate enough to have employment.[6] Nevertheless, the realities of slum housing, unemployment, and poor health provision for much of the population were sufficient to feed a movement of left-wing feeling that grew stronger as fascism spread throughout central Europe. The British ruling classes for their part remained confident about their own racial and cultural superiority, an attitude that led them to look with condescension toward a youthful nation like America. For that essentially American form, the cinema, many intellectuals expressed contempt. They deplored common public taste, as if their own habits of going to the drama, opera, or concerts were not also part of a quasi-religious function that was itself another kind of escapism.

The British film was an inheritance of the national drama tradition, with actors and actresses almost entirely from the upper-middle-class section of society. The accents of their speech and the expressions they used, common to stage, screen, the BBC, Oxbridge and the establishment in general, were alien to the mass of the population. For many Americans they also confirmed an impression of social rigidity, snobbery, and absence of warmth in personal relationships. However, this did not stop successful British players from moving to Hollywood. American film producers were quick to appreciate the potential appeal of a certain type of English upper-class poise and self-confidence, as expressed by actors like Leslie Howard and David Niven, provided it was in the right context. American films, on the other hand, may have found a responsive audience in Britain because of their earthiness and directness and the classlessness of their idiom. Even so, it is likely also that the deference factor operated among many of the people, so that the characters in British films, remote though most of them were from the grassroots of society, became a part of that dream world which the cinema tried to make the public accept without criticism. Certainly folk figures like George Formby and Gracie Fields were also popular in the thirties, and for purely patriotic reasons a high percentage of the audience may have willed British films to succeed if they were good enough.

In economic terms the British industry had always lived precariously. American films could recover their costs within the United States alone. A large percentage of the profits from British films went to the distributors, and it was difficult for them to secure screenings in America. The Hungarian exile Alexander Korda attempted in the thirties to produce films which would rival the glossier American movies, and, after the success of *The Private Life of Henry VIII* in 1933, he was able to attract a certain amount of investment to the industry. His series of imperial films built upon a sentimental attachment to the idea of the British Empire that had been propagated by educationalists and that was to be reflected, more surprisingly, in some Hollywood productions of the period.[7] Few at that time would have predicted the demise of the Empire within a couple of decades, and in this respect the Korda films may be seen as symbolizing the illusions of British life immediately before the war. By 1937 the boom had collapsed and the industry was in retreat again. The last of the imperial films was *The Four Feathers,* made in 1939 but reissued both during the war and shortly after it. There was still apparently some mileage in what were popularly supposed to be the benevolent and civilizing aspirations of the Empire.

The studios which made British films were scattered about areas to the west and north of London. Korda's financial problems compelled him to sell control of Denham to J. Arthur Rank, the financier who was building up his own huge empire within the production and exhibition sections of the industry. Rank also provided most of the backing for Pinewood Studios, to be used during the war by the official film units. Mobilization of personnel, shortage of materials, and other constraints caused by war contributed to a further decline in the level of production, and by 1943 the number of studios in active use had fallen from twenty-two to nine.[8]

Throughout the thirties there had been a massive silence from the British cinema on political and social questions that might be regarded by the conservative-based National Government as controversial. Direct control of the media is a commonplace in totalitarian societies. In spite of the apparent freedom of democratic Britain, the government was able to exercise a powerful influence on the trade-centered British Board of Film Censors. The major personalities within the industry were almost all right-wing in sympathy to varying degrees, though there were exceptions like Sidney Bernstein, founder of Granada cinemas and a rare exhibitor also in that he had commissioned public opinion polls to find out what films his audiences really did like.[9] Subjects which might conflict with British foreign policy in the era of appeasement were kept firmly off the screen. The newsreels also put forward a bland and self-satisfied image, avoiding for instance any hostile references to Nazi Germany (unlike the American *March of Time* series). In the same way the censors frowned upon scripts that concerned themselves with the internal conflicts created by the effects of the depression.[10]

Just before the outbreak of war there were signs of a slight thaw, allowing, for instance, the production of a couple of films set in mining districts. Carol Reed directed *The Stars Look Down,* an adaptation of an A. J. Cronin novel. Ealing had begun *The Proud Valley,* starring Paul Robeson, the black American singer and actor, later known for his radically left-wing views. Policy at this studio was in the hands of Michael Balcon, a man who had dedicated his career to the establishment of a national style of British film, first with Gainsborough Pictures, which he started in the twenties, and later at Gaumont British. Among the directors encouraged by him was Alfred Hitchcock, maker of a number of successful thrillers, who left for Hollywood in 1939. The young Penrose Tennyson was directing *The Proud Valley* when hostilities began, and, before its eventual issue, the ending of the film had

The Proud Valley. **Miners' delegation march to London, but social conflict gives way to unanimity as war overtakes the nation.**

been altered to show coal owners and miners in Wales forgetting their differences and uniting in the common war effort.[11]

But these examples were rare. The commercial film industry to date had shown little evidence of social awareness. To some extent the gap had been filled by the British documentary movement, which owed its existence initially to the inspiration of John Grierson, who had seen the potential use of film as a mass medium of education and instruction.[12] At first he had been able to attempt this through the Empire Marketing Board Film Unit, established in 1928. The idea of promoting an enclosed protectionist market area within the Empire turned out to be an abortive one, neither British manufacturing interests nor the new dominions being willing to deny themselves the chances of trade with other countries. However, having been able through the enthusiasm of the EMB's secretary Sir Stephen Tallents to set up a government-sponsored group to make documentaries, Grierson succeeded in 1933 in having its functions transferred to the Post Office. The GPO Film Unit was still in existence at the beginning of the war, and its members were unique in British film circles. Although almost all of them were from the public schools,* they became a part of that considerable strand of intellectual opinion in the thirties which was committed to the left. As filmmakers their model was Soviet cinema during its progressive period, as much for its techniques as for its political outlook.[13] It seemed to suggest a methodology for presenting on the screen real people in real circumstances, free of the fantasies of the commercial industry. In fact, of course, what Russian audiences made of many of these complex and allusive films is likely to remain one of the unsolved mysteries of the twentieth century.

The films produced by the GPO started with the concept of postal services, but the unit was also able to spread its wings in other directions. Because it was a body dependent for its existence on the National Government, it could not go very far along the road of social criticism. Indeed much of its output embodies a romantic rather than a realistic view of labor, seen at its most extreme in the notorious example of *Industrial Britain,* which, in spite of its title, made reference to "England" and "English workers" only, in the commentary which had been imposed on it by its distributors, and which still seemed to be describing a craftsman-orientated structure remote from the actualities of factory production in that age. It has become fashionable of late to decry the documentary movement on account of these limitations,[14] but in fairness it was almost all that could be done at the time. Official sponsorship provided some backing for the work of the other independent documentary film units that on occasion, as in *Housing Problems* (made by Arthur Elton and Edgar Anstey for the British Commercial Gas Association) or in *Today We Live* (produced by Strand Films and directed by Paul Rotha for the National Council for Social Service), were able to put forward possible solutions for solving the social evils of the urban slums. The documentaries received only limited distribution and the GPO Film Unit's more daring experiments with sound and image probably made little impression on the public. Nevertheless, the organization and the experience existed at the start of the war for the making of propaganda films if the government needed them.

This essentially middle-class and Oxbridge interest in working people was well intentioned but distanced, as it was also in other contemporary examples like George Orwell's *The Road to Wigan Pier* and the social surveys which were being undertaken under the title of Mass-Observation.[15] This latter group continued in the war to record the reactions of audiences to selected films, a difficult process that was often no more scientific than simply sitting in a cinema and painstakingly writing notes when the people laughed, gasped, or groaned. They discovered that before the war it was normal to laugh at soldiers on the screen and at the beginning of the war to laugh at uniformed civil defense workers—until the blitz started.[16] Such was the extent to which the public was unused to looking at images of people in genuine working environments, confined as it had been to viewing ordinary folk in feature films only as figures of lower-class comedy. Mass-Observation also interviewed members of audiences as they were leaving the cinemas. The problem here, still a valid one, is that instant reactions to a film can differ from more thoughtful verdicts at a later stage. But their work on a very few films, regrettably not enough and almost all from the first half of the war, is the only existing guide to public response, though obviously much also may be deduced from box-office receipts.

In spite of the closure of studios, the commercial film industry in the Second World War was forced to respond in some positive way to the reality of the national crisis, in order to feel that it was making its own contribution to the war effort. With variable success it tried to shake off some of its more superficial aspects, and it managed by the end to produce a

*American readers should note that "public schools" in Britain are actually private schools for privileged teenagers. However, the term has such resonance in British society that it loses its meaning if it is translated to "private schools."

The film industry at war. Leslie Howard behind the camera directing *The Gentle Sex*.

core of films the content of which directly related to the war, its events, and its effects. The official films of course took this path as a matter of policy. Their closeness to the conflict itself gives these productions, features and documentaries alike, a distinctive interest for the present-day observer. To try to recapture this sense of immediacy, we discuss almost exclusively in this survey, in relation to the historical incidents of the war, films made between September 1939 and August 1945, the period of Britain's participation.[17] Brief reference is also included to some later fiction films that have tried to re-enact specific episodes from the war, something the wartime scriptwriters found little time or inclination to do. But, to take a single example, even a conscientiously made action film like *A Bridge Too Far,* a view in perspective of the Arnhem battle, belongs more in style and outlook to the era of thirty years after the war than to 1944 itself. There is something rather extraordinary about the way British films of the time were a reflection of the gradual progression of the war, of changing attitudes to it, and of the lives of the people throughout its course, and, if one forgets their faults, they give us now a more intimate glimpse of actual wartime conditions and appearances than those which have followed them.

A little known film called *Traitor Spy,* directed by Walter Summers and finished at the end of 1939, had the form of a conventional thriller on prewar lines, but its plot now was about an attempt by the German embassy to steal the plans of a secret motor boat being tested by the Admiralty. The "traitor spy" conceals his supposed disappearance by leaving the police with a dismembered body they assume to be his—hence the more vivid American title of *The Torso Murder Mystery.* He is traced by an intelligence agent to a sleazy night club in London. Here we see various performers in different phony ethnic styles, a West Indian band, other black men and women mixing freely with a mainly white clientele, a fight flaring up in a corner unnoticed by most people in the room, a group of obviously lesbian women at a table. Almost everyone, man or woman, wears a hat, even while dancing. It is a short sequence but a fascinating one for anyone interested in social history on the screen, because it looks so much more real and convincing than any similar scene in a later film about the same period.

It is for this kind of view of the twentieth century that film is uniquely qualified. The academic historians may feel that it is not enough, that film does not go beyond the surface of life, and no doubt in a way this is true.[18] But we live in an age of images, and behind the historians there is a legion of amateur observers, members of the broader public who obtain much of their information through television. The medium has made familiar the British record material of the actualities of the Second World War. Many of the feature films have continued to be rescreened. Perhaps only the documentaries have been less well known, but recently a few historical programs also have begun to revive interest in them.[19] It is only by taking account of the whole range of production, from the commercial studios, the newsreel companies, and the official and independent short-film units, that it is possible to understand the totality of the effort that British cinematographers directed to creating a comprehensive portrait of the nation and the people in wartime.

1
The First Months

Britain's part in the Second World War started as soon as Hitler caused Germany to invade Poland in September 1939. The years of appeasement had persuaded the Nazi dictator that the decadent western democracies would not have the will to fight. It turned out to be a miscalculation but only a very narrow one, and in the event neither Britain nor France could do anything to take the pressure off the unfortunate Poles, who were also to be attacked two weeks later by Stalin and the Soviet Union. Poland's territory was split up between the two great tyrannies of west and east, an arrangement determined by the Nazi-Soviet Pact of that summer.[1]

The British had not wanted another war and their prime minister, Neville Chamberlain, had done everything possible to prevent it. They had lost nearly a million dead in the stalemate and misery of the First World War. Everyone wished to avoid a repetition of that terrible catastrophe at almost any cost, and so appeasement had been a popular policy in the thirties, a fact that was soon to be forgotten. The Labour party, which was to gain in the 1945 election from the backwash of public opinion, in fact had been totally against rearmament for most of the interwar period. There seemed no reason in 1939 to expect anything other than a second prolonged and destructive war, though not everyone believed this, especially those who thought that the French army was the most powerful in Europe. The invention of the tank was in practice to break the concept of static war, but advocates of its potential, like Liddell Hart in Britain, had been listened to only by the Germans.[2]

There was one great unknown element at the beginning of the Second World War. Civilians had been bombed from the air in the previous war, a tactic started by Germany in raids by aircraft and airships over England, but the development of the bomber in the thirties appeared to make the possibilities even more frightening than before. It became common gospel that "the bomber will always get through"[3] and it had seemed to do so both in China and in Spain. The Spanish Civil War had polarized ideological differences between right and left and brought volunteers from overseas to help the legitimate government and more powerful intervention by the fascist powers on the side of the rebels. Propaganda perhaps exaggerated the overall effects of the bombing of Spanish cities by German aircraft, but it was sufficient to shock many people in the thirties who expected more civilized standards of behavior than the killing of unarmed civilians. The plight of Spain was not ignored in British film. There was in existence before the war an independent left-wing school of documentary production, started by men like Ralph Bond and Ivor Montagu, and operating outside the normal distribution channels.[4] In the months before the Second

World War it encouraged the making of *Spanish ABC* and *Behind the Spanish Lines,* both in support of the republicans and both directed and edited by Thorold Dickinson and Sidney Cole, who were normally members of the commercial film industry, not the documentary movement.

The British people expected a repeat performance of the previous conflict, not only direct bombing but also the possible use of gas. A feature film made in 1935 by Korda's London Films, *Things to Come,* from the book by H. G. Wells, had forecast the kind of destruction and breakdown that might be caused by mass bombing. Civil defense precautions had been taken and during the summer of 1939 the GPO Film Unit made a short descriptive film for the Home Office, explaining what would happen and who would do what in the event of a raid. Its title was to have been *If War Should Come,* but the real start of hostilities led to it being released as *Do It Now.*[5] The declaration of war brought about a total blackout across the whole country during the night hours. The regulations were vigorously enforced, local wardens in remote areas often delighting in their role of harassing those who struck matches in the dark or released minute chinks of light from their curtains. People learned to find their way around the streets by instinct and habit, as did those who could still use their cars or who were driving military or public vehicles. A scene in the spy thriller *Contraband,* issued early in 1940, gives an impression of the confusion and disorientation of the blackout in London.

The mood of that September of 1939, at least in the capital, was captured in the GPO's documentary *The First Days.*[6] The unit tended to function collectively, almost all of its members beginning as amateurs in the film world and learning each of the individual jobs in a production team as they went along. They worked with limited equipment and in somewhat primitive conditions at a studio in southeast London, where nevertheless they had been able to build up some of their most realistic effects, as in the trawler scenes of Harry Watt's *North Sea,* for which the interiors had been reconstructed. The recruitment of Alberto Cavalcanti to lead them had added a higher degree of expertise, especially an appreciation of the creative use of the sound track. He was not able to stay with them in the same role when in time they became the Crown Film Unit, because he was a native of Brazil, but at the beginning of the war they were ignored by the newly constituted Ministry of Information (MOI), which had plans instead to use the commercial industry.[7] On their own initiative then the unit set out to produce a film about those early days and their effect on Londoners by shooting scenes in the streets and by putting in short pieces of improvised dialogue, for which in some cases it used its own people as players. It was assembled hastily, with contributory material from Harry Watt and Humphrey Jennings, already directors of some experience and also from Pat Jackson, who had made only a single film to date, and given its final shape by Cavalcanti and the unit's senior editor R. Q. McNaughton.[8] No doubt it was hoped that the ministry would be impressed. In spite of its speedy production, *The First Days* turned into an evocative reminder of London as a city forced reluctantly into war, the track skilfully alternating silences with intermittent snatches of music and speech and blending unobtrusively with the film's images.

The opening sequences look back symbolically to the First World War with children playing on an old German artillery piece, then shots of the facade and a gallery of the Imperial War Museum, founded originally as a memorial to the dead of that war. Robert Sinclair's commentary starts, "London is at peace on this Sunday morning." People are going to church, setting out for trips to the country, cycling, strolling by the Serpentine. The sound of Big Ben introduces the voice of Neville Chamberlain, "I am speaking to you from the Cabinet Room. . . ." His sad tone as he talks about "evil things" is reflected in the somber faces of listeners around their wireless sets. The broadcast of the declaration of war on that third day of September goes out over the air waves, "London is calling, London calling to the world, this is London."

Suddenly the air raid warning sounds. The wavering note of the siren was to become familiar nightly during the blitz of 1940–41, but the alarm on that first day was a false one. Briefly Londoners thought their worst fear, an immediate assault from the air, to be confirmed. People are directed by wardens to the shelters and barrage balloons climb slowly into the sky. The wardens wear steel helmets, or "tin hats" as they were more popularly known. The capital had been prepared for the emergency to a degree that varied in different boroughs, but in practice only a small proportion of the population could go to shelters, which in the main were brick structures that might collapse even from the blast of a near miss. The barrage balloons were cylindrical objects supposed to deter dive bombers and make the enemy fly at greater height. The film shows wardens as ordinary citizens, their "principal equipment is friendliness," and awkward jokes are exchanged in the shelters. "People joked but in their hearts was devastation." Out in the streets sandbags are passed from hand to hand.

Newly called-up troops train to a background of Elgarian music as the commentary says, "At that moment Londoners saw a remarkable thing. A genera-

***The First Days.* A sandbag-covered air raid shelter is decorated with symbols of defiance as hostilities commence.**

tion of young men born in the last war and brought up in contempt of militarism and the bogus romance of the battlefield went into uniform willingly and with clear understanding because they found they had grown up in a world where there was no peace. Now they carried arms but they are still our children." City workers are coming out of the tube stations with their gas masks, which had been issued by the authorities to everyone throughout Britain. Shopkeepers paste strips of paper in patterns across windows, a device to prevent glass being blown inwards and causing injury. Some citizens have turned into policemen, girls are driving ambulances, taxicabs are towing trailer fire pumps. There is a glimpse of the major operation of that period, the evacuation of children to the country.

From Waterloo station the British Expeditionary Force is leaving for France, bands playing. A husband and wife buy flowers from a street seller, their actions punctuated by a series of "Goodbyes" on the sound track (the man's part was acted by Jack Lee, himself to become a film director of merit). The National Gallery and British Museum are being emptied of their treasures. Aliens are queuing to register with the authorities ("they are part of London, part of its broad culture, part of its tolerance"). Soldiers in lorries sing, "We're going to hang out the washing on the Siegfried Line." Theaters have been closed on the outbreak of war "but no one has ever stopped the cockney voice of London" and a barrel organ plays in the street as darkness falls. With a new day there is a feeling of hope, "for this is not twilight which has come to England, it is dawn, and dawn for more than England."

The First Days received little attention at the time from the public, for whom its approach was probably too consciously artistic. Sinclair's commentary had referred to Britain as a country where ideals were still cherished. In truth the ideals in question were those of the intellectual group which shared the assumptions of the documentary filmmakers, politically left in aspiration, liberal and middle-class in background. They had a common repugnance for the essential destructiveness of war but were agreed about the need to stand up against Hitler. However, not everyone saw the situation in those terms. Some in more right-wing circles would have preferred Britain to stay out of the conflict altogether in the hope that Germany would stop the march of communism from the east. Many thought that there might still be time for a reasonable settlement without the necessity of heavy fighting and the inevitable casualties that would follow. *The First Days* had made a statement about the reluctance of the British people to go to war again, their obligation to do so as a last resort for the defense of their democracy, but it possibly overemphasized a unity of effort that did not arise until after the crisis of Dunkirk, and that even then did not change the fundamentally divided nature of British society. The "tolerance" of aliens did not survive the besieged state of the country in 1940, although their treatment scarcely approached the paranoia and persecution of the First World War; and during those first months of war organized activities like the evacuation of children from poor districts to more fortunate areas were already putting a strain on the public's sense of responsibility.

The views of the conservative establishment about what Britain was fighting for and how it ought to be presented in film were not very different in some respects from those which had been expressed in the script for *The First Days.* A memorandum produced within the MOI during the winter stressed the desirability of laying emphasis on British traditions of freedom and parliamentary government, something from which the mainstream documentary filmmakers would not have dissented.[9] Where they were to part company was in the need for further social reform after the war, and it is unlikely that those who favored the left would have agreed to the choice, in the same memorandum, of *Goodbye Mr Chips,* a sentimental story of public school life made by MGM-British in 1939, as a representative of all that was best in British character. However, the Conservative party before the war had taken an interest in film propaganda and had used it in its election campaigns. It was not surprising therefore that the man who had been in charge of this aspect of party publicity, Sir Joseph Ball, was selected as the first head of the MOI's Films Division.[10]

Ball had cultivated relationships with some of the major personalities of the film industry in the thirties, in keeping with the government's appreciation that it was the feature type which was the most popular in the cinemas and the most likely, along with the newsreels, to have an influence on people. Alexander Korda, who was also friendly with Winston Churchill, the chief enemy of appeasement, had no difficulty in securing official cooperation for the making of a feature documentary on the Royal Air Force. Planned before the start of hostilities, it was meant to be a reassurance to the public about Britain's ability to brush aside the danger from the feared German bombers. The Air Ministry sent a liaison officer to London Films to advise on the script and the progress of the production.[11] There was no government financial backing for it, though the MOI indicated at first its approval of the film, at least until some of its civil servants had given more time to thinking about its somewhat disjointed nature, a consequence of the haste with which it was finished—before the end of October—and the division of labor between at least three directors (Adrian Brunel, Michael Powell, Brian Desmond Hurst). Korda had been hoping to build up his capital again with a new series of spectaculars and, alongside production of this RAF film, titled *The Lion Has Wings,* he had Michael Powell working at Denham on the color feature *The Thief of Bagdad,* which was eventually to be completed in Hollywood.

For the script of *The Lion Has Wings* Korda chose Ian Dalrymple, an experienced screenwriter and editor who had worked on a number of feature films. With the declaration of war, the original shape of the production was modified, to start with a forthright introductory section that would give an exposition of the basic decencies and achievements of British life and set them against the harsh totalitarianism of Nazi Germany. It was meant to be a justification, in crude propaganda terms, of Britain's intervention in Europe, and it was expressed through a text clearly conditioned by traditional concepts of Tory paternalism. Dalrymple even quotes the Latin tag *mens sana in corpore sano,* incomprehensible to the average cinemagoer, who had not received a public school education. However, the choice for narrator of E. V. H. Emmett, whose hectoring voice was well known to the public from the Gaumont British News, brought the needed kind of didactic force. Rapid crosscutting of the film's images in this opening part also contributed to its hard-hitting style and it is impossible not to observe here the hand of Korda's American supervising editor, William Hornbeck, who later in the war was to provide the same type of emphasis for Frank Capra's official United States series *Why We Fight.*

Britain is shown to be peaceful and progressive in the thirties, slumdwellers being housed in better developments, the country producing new industries, new schools and new hospitals. "Is this to stop because one man wishes to dominate the world?" Exercise and the pursuit of leisure activities are the key to the well-balanced human being, "rowing, running, jumping, or in Scotland throwing heavy things about in a way that only Scotsmen can understand." At least this last reference made the audience laugh, according to a Mass-Observation report.[12] An objective viewer's opinion might have been that Germany also made some material progress at the time, nor were Germans themselves an unathletic race, but the film presents them only as marching soldiers, and the narration refers to Hitler giving his people the choice of "guns or butter." The youth of Britain prefer the arts of peace, going to football matches or the racecourse, using their horses not for cavalry but for exercise, with foxhunting introduced as an example of this idyllic way of living. Hitler's rantings are contrasted with the gestures of bookies at the races—"would you rather hear this going on or this?" George VI appears with his family at a scouts' rally, tapping head and knee to the tune of "under the spreading chestnut tree." Do the British want a ruler like Hitler who is protected by armed guards or "a man who need not fear to walk freely?" The Nazis in fact saw this sequence from a prewar newsreel differently and used it in one of their own issues to deride the British monarchy.[13]

A short historical section next summarizes the takeover of Czechoslovakia and Poland, with Britain's guarantee to the latter country compared with the "scrap of paper" that had been used to defend Belgian independence in the previous war. "Britain must defend her freedom," Emmett says, "the British navy is the greatest in the world and her army always wins the last battle." But the RAF was to be the main subject of the film and Korda now put in a dramatized sequence, beginning with the Hendon air display, watched by German diplomats who are scornful about British resolution and will to fight. Ralph Richardson appears there as a wing commander. As the threat from Germany grows, Britain is seen to be rearming, and sequences showing factory production (with material taken from the GPO Film Unit) are introduced at this point. When at last war is declared, the announcement is heard at Richardson's home by his wife and her friend, the parts played respectively

***The Lion Has Wings*. War is declared and the patriotic upper-middle class ladies of England stand at attention as the national anthem is played on the radio (June Duprez and Merle Oberon).**

by Merle Oberon and June Duprez. Coming in at the end, the wing commander asks, "What was that, are we at war?" The casual, stiff-upper-lip style, to become one of the chief clichés of the British officer class on film throughout the war (and after it), is established at once.

The next substantial part of *The Lion Has Wings* was also unplanned, and it took advantage of the fact that the company was able to shoot a real sequence of aircraft returning from an operation against the German fleet in its own waters. To re-enact the raid, the first British action of that September, was a temptation not missed by Korda. Britain had "drawn first blood of a war that was not of their making," the narrator says. The film accurately reconstructs the briefing of pilots, the takeoff of bombers, and the cramped conditions experienced by aircrews in flight. Korda's RAF liaison officer (Squadron Leader Wright) himself plays a part as leader of the formation. At the climax of the episode, bombs are seen exploding on an obviously studio-created German warship.

The RAF had drawn up a number of plans for possible offensive action against Germany, going as far as strategic bombing of industrial targets, but it had been decided by the Cabinet that the killing of civilians should be avoided. The motivation for this was partly fear of provoking retaliation. The British did not want to be the first to start the bombing of cities, a tactic that might rebound on them with terrible consequences. RAF bomber operations in the first months of war were limited therefore to the dropping of propaganda leaflets by night on German territory and some attempts in daylight to strike at the enemy fleet in the Heligoland Bight.[14]

Although British admirals in general were sceptical about the effectiveness of aircraft against warships, and these early efforts only reinforced their prejudices, they must have welcomed the RAF raids because of the serious potential harm the Germans could cause at sea to British shipping. Experience from the First World War demonstrated that the menace existed not only in the form of German submarines (U-boats), which themselves in sufficient number might spread wide-ranging havoc, but also from individual surface raiders. In 1939 Germany had some warships ideally suited for this task. There is often confusion about the class and nomenclature of these vessels, largely because they did not correspond to the conventional categories of heavy ships in other world navies: the battleship, the most powerful in terms of armament and armor; and the battlecruiser, a ship of equivalent size and with similar guns but lightly protected in order to give it the speed to chase hostile cruisers. British battle-cruisers in fact were vulnerable in a major action, the fragility of their deck armor allowing easy penetration to their magazines. Three of them had blown up at Jutland in 1916, and the *Hood,* the largest of all, was to be lost in 1941 in the same way.

Germany had been forbidden between the wars by international treaty to build beyond certain limits, and this had brought about the construction of three vessels of a special class, known to the British as "pocket battleships" but more correctly called by the Germans "armored ships," linking them to a type of warship that had existed during the First World War. They were armed with six eleven-inch guns and their completion was followed by the building of two larger ships, classed as battleships by the Germans, the *Scharnhorst* and *Gneisenau,* each with nine eleven-inch guns. The British preferred to call them battlecruisers because of their exceptional speed. All of these warships were faster than the British fifteen-inch and sixteen-inch gun battleships, and in theory they could overwhelm any smaller cruisers. The armored ships in particular seemed to be well equipped for commerce raiding, an extra asset being their high fuel-storage capacity.

Reconnaissance had identified the armored ship *Admiral Scheer* at anchor in the Schillig Roads and the *Scharnhorst* and *Gneisenau* in the Elbe. The Blenheims that attacked the *Scheer* on September 4 had been instructed to fly low and to drop delayed-action bombs onto her superstructure. Probably three hits were scored, but the bombs had been in stock for some years and none of them exploded, while five of the British aircraft were lost, one crashing into an enemy cruiser. The raid by Wellingtons over the Elbe was also a failure, and two planes did not return.[15] Certainly audiences knew nothing of the true nature of this fiasco as they watched *The Lion Has Wings,* and dissatisfaction with it, which was recorded by Mass-Observation as a reaction among some people, was probably provoked by its documentary style, not popular with the cinemagoer who wanted straightforward entertainment.[16]

The structure of the rest of the film is very confused. The defensive arm of the RAF now has its turn as the Nazis attempt to bomb London. There was an obvious inconsistency in having a re-enactment of a real action for Bomber Command and then a wholly fictional incident for the fighters, especially as one wave of the attackers is deterred by the sight of the barrage balloons alone and turns away without pressing on to its objectives. This was carrying reassurance to the point of dishonesty. In addition to footage introduced from a prewar instructional film about air defenses called *The Gap,* a clip is cut in from a 1937 feature film about the menace of the Armada, *Fire Over England,* Flora Robson playing Queen Elizabeth and making an appropriately patriotic speech. Ralph Richardson is seen as an RAF ground officer directing operations as the German bombers are chased away from London.

The press had become very curious about this first sizable British war film and they managed to photograph the two stars in uniform, Richardson as a wing commander, Oberon as a nurse, both standing in the grounds at Denham, while they were preparing for the final scene. In this location Merle Oberon has the last lines of dialogue—"We must keep our land, darling, we must keep our freedom, we must fight for what we believe in—truth and beauty and fair play—and kindness." As she speaks, Richardson falls asleep. To the thinking critic, then and now, it is an inept and embarrassing effect, but it may have been a partially unconscious acknowledgment of the fact that the viewers needed to wind down from the gravity of all the sentiments that had gone before.[17] The public school had not trained the British to make propaganda about war aims, and the cinema audience at large did not take kindly to being lectured about them.

The first few months of the war confounded many of the predictions. The expected aerial holocaust did not take place. Apart from minor patrol activity, nothing happened on the Western Front, both sides remaining substantially behind their lines, waiting on events. The casualty of this inaction was Poland, for whose defense Britain and France had supposedly entered the war. Those who wanted German industrial targets to be bombed as a means of helping the Poles were warned about the danger of retaliation and were told anyway by the Secretary of State for Air that armament works were "private property." A plan for burning the Black Forest was also rejected. It was that curious period which has come to be known as the "phony war," when the allies seemed to believe that the longer they waited the more chance they had of winning as their military forces grew in strength.[18] No one understood the unpreparedness and incapacity of the French army, the only major allied instrument that could either win or lose the war on the continent at this stage.

At sea, on the other hand, there was no lack of incident. The U-boats began at once to harass Britain's fleet and merchant shipping, sometimes with spectacular success. One submarine penetrated the defenses of Scapa Flow and sank the old battleship *Royal Oak* with heavy loss of life. An aircraft carrier was lost out of harbor, and there might have been more casualties but for the fact that German torpedoes at that time were frequently defective. In fact the fleet flagship was struck by duds while Winston Churchill, then First Lord of the Admiralty, was aboard her. The number of escorts available to protect convoys was limited, and the navy had to use passenger liners fitted out with guns, though the vulnerability of these "armed merchant cruisers" was demonstrated when the *Rawalpindi* came across the *Scharnhorst* and *Gneisenau* in northern waters and was destroyed by them.

At the beginning of the war Michael Powell's film *The Spy in Black* was still running in the cinemas and, because of its setting in the Orkneys, attracted further attention as a result of the *Royal Oak* tragedy. It starred Valerie Hobson and the exiled German actor Conrad Veidt in a First-World-War spy story. The same pair now took part in Powell's first complete wartime film, *Contraband* (U.S. title: *Blackout*), the script written by his close collaborator, Hungarian-born Emeric Pressburger, and based on the British practice of seizing cargoes from neutral ships that might aid the German war effort. A Danish freighter is intercepted in the English Channel by a British destroyer and forced against her will to go into port for a compulsory inspection. The firm though polite relationship between the British authorities and the skipper, played by Veidt, is shown to be typical of the situation. The cargo is labelled as contraband, but the Ministry of Economic Warfare has to decide whether or not it is intended for Denmark, and in the meantime the ship is delayed overnight.

From this point the film becomes a spy thriller, as two of the passengers, Mrs. Sorensen (Valerie Hobson) and Mr. Pidgeon, (Esmond Knight), abscond without permission to London and the captain sets off in pursuit of them. It is when he catches up with Mrs. Sorensen that we witness the earliest filmed recreation of the blackout and the difficulties it causes in the capital.[19] It turns out that she and her colleague are British agents whose task is to pass information across the Atlantic to the Admiralty about the movements of German shipping—in a rather tortuous fashion, one must say. Both she and the captain fall into the hands of German spies, among them the sinister "brothers Grimm," memorably portrayed by Peter Bull, Stuart Lathan, and Leo Genn. However, they escape and start a hunt for the enemy, calling on the services of the friendly staff of a Danish restaurant, the Three Vikings, owned by the brother of the freighter's chief officer (both parts played by Hay Petrie). In the penultimate scene Raymond Lovell as the chief Nazi chases the captain round a darkened storehouse of plaster casts, knocking off the heads of

***Contraband.* Danish skipper and British secret agent toast each other at the restaurant table (Hay Petrie, Conrad Veidt, and Valerie Hobson).**

some of them as he fires his revolver, until at last the Dane traps him and manages to strike him unconscious with a figure of Neville Chamberlain. It was a smoothly made film in popular style and in spite of its improbable plot was distinguished by its players, with Veidt's handsome strength and Hobson's cool English beauty. Its issue almost coincided with Denmark's loss of neutrality in April 1940.

The most dramatic event of the phony war was the battle of the River Plate in December 1939, and it soon became the main subject of a Gainsborough film called *For Freedom.* For a couple of months the German armored ship *Graf Spee* had pursued a successful career as a roving raider through the Indian Ocean and South Atlantic, sinking a number of merchant ships and transferring some of their crews to the supply vessel *Altmark.* By a stroke of exceptional judgment, Commodore Harwood made a guess that she was heading for the estuary that separates Uruguay and Argentina, and he was able to move up his squadron of three cruisers to bring her to battle. In fact he was heavily outgunned by the German warship and relied in the main on maneuvering behind smokescreens and threatening her with torpedo attacks. His largest ship, the *Exeter,* soon had to withdraw with severe damage. However, although the *Graf Spee* had come through the action relatively unpunished, Captain Langsdorff became anxious about the possibility of being immobilized so far from home and he decided to make for Montevideo and ask the Uruguayan authorities for time to effect repairs. A game of diplomatic bluff played by the British consular authorities in the two South American countries finally persuaded him that an overwhelming force was waiting for him outside the Plate, though the truth was that no heavy British unit was nearer than a thousand miles away. Watched by a horde of excited spectators, the *Graf Spee* moved away from her anchorage, took off her crew by boat, and scuttled herself by flooding the hull and setting off explosions. Two days later, Langsdorff committed suicide in Buenos Aires.[20]

The tale of this first British success of the Second World War was tremendous news for people at home, bored as they had been by the apparent inactivity in hostilities so far. In 1956 Powell and Pressburger made a color epic about the incident with the title *The Battle of the River Plate* (U.S. title: *Pursuit of the Graf Spee*), a workmanlike production which had Peter Finch giving a humane portrayal of Langsdorff and Anthony Quayle as Harwood.[21] In terms of authenticity, it was only marred by the decision to use borrowed warships for shooting at sea and it was unfortunate that the American heavy cruiser "playing" the *Graf Spee* bore no resemblance to her at all. On the other hand, the reproduction of the battle in *For Freedom,* with an admiral explaining the situation and illustrating it with the use of models, was very much less effective. It is often repeated that Finch was the first to play one of the enemy in sympathetic terms. However, this is only a half-truth. The image of the "good German" who was not fully in accord with Hitler had already appeared on British screens in wartime in various films. Even in 1939 there was comment on the fact that Langsdorff had saluted in the naval rather than the Nazi fashion at the last meeting with his comrades and also that he had shot himself while wrapped in the Imperial German flag.[22]

For Freedom was directed by Maurice Elvey, a veteran of the industry with a prolific record of filmmaking, including some silent movies in the previous war. The script, written by Leslie Arliss and Miles Malleson, attempted a mix of documentary method and fictionalized story, with even more muddled results than in *The Lion Has Wings.* It starts again with an outline summary of recent history for the cinema public, but in a more populist style than in the Korda film, using this time the device of a setting in a newsreel production office. E. V. H. Emmett appears once more as the narrator, now playing himself. The staff are seen in September 1938 making a record of the crisis over Czechoslovakia and putting together a history of previous events from the Versailles Treaty onwards. Will Fyffe takes the role of the newsreel boss Ferguson, injecting further animation into the team's account of "the old bullying spirit of Prussia" with his own more vigorous anti-Nazi remarks. The issue is supposed to end on a patriotic note, with a determined national response to German demands, but even as the unit is working on it news arrives of Chamberlain's settlement with Hitler. Made as it was in 1940, it is hardly surprising that the film ignores the genuine relief felt by most British people at the time of the Munich agreement.

The themes of appeasement and pacifism do emerge, however, in the next scene. Their spokesman is Ferguson's son Stephen, who discusses idealistically his vision of a United States of the World. He has assembled the newsreel's representatives from different capitals to have a runthrough of film sequences for a project on international social and cultural achievements, including the "friendly rivalry" of the Olympics (the notorious and very political meeting of 1936 in Berlin).[23] News is heard now of the Nazi occupation of Prague, provoking Ferguson to berate his son over his pointless ideas, and the next we hear of Stephen is that he has been packed off to Rio de Janeiro, far enough away (one imagines) for him to do the least amount of harm with his peaceful views. The film jumps next to the outbreak of war. Actors portray Henderson, the British ambassador in Berlin, and Hitler, played very briefly by Billy Russell in what was probably his earliest screen representation. A newsreel conference breaks up as Ferguson says farewell to his German correspondent, who tells him that they have to be enemies now. The Russian also goes home, and the American leaves to cross the Atlantic—on the liner *Athenia,* sunk by a U-boat within the first day of war. Down in South America Stephen does make himself useful after all, because he manages to send a plane to film the battle of the River Plate. In reality, the only aircraft to witness the action was the one from Harwood's flagship *Ajax,* which was used to spot the fall of shellfire. In *For Freedom* Stephen rushes back to London with the fictional reels and also brings Captain Dove, one of a number of British merchant navy officers rescued from the *Graf Spee.*

During the routine account of the battle that follows, the only real interest for the viewer is the use of actual people who had participated, officers from the *Ajax* and *Exeter* and some of those who were prisoners aboard the *Graf Spee* and *Altmark.* Captain Dove, master of the *Africa Shell,* replays his role well, especially in the part where his ship receives the German boarding party. Dove has put his secret documents through the porthole, offers the Germans whisky when they arrive in his cabin, and writes a protest about being taken, as he alleges, within territorial waters. This able performance in a commercial movie anticipated some better-known amateur acting in later official films.

A final episode of *For Freedom* deals with the sequel to the battle, the fate of the supply ship *Altmark* which was navigating its way back to Germany with British prisoners aboard. Captain Dau, who had made himself detested by his captives, succeeded in reaching Norwegian waters and concealed from the authorities there the fact that he was hiding British merchant seamen below his decks. On Churchill's orders Captain Vian took the destroyer *Cossack* into the fiord, put her alongside the *Altmark,* boarded her, and released the prisoners. In February 1940 this incident broke another period of inertia and created a wave of enthusiasm at home, carried along under the headline "The navy's here!"—words spoken by one of the first men to open the hatches on the *Altmark.* The Norwegians, whose neutrality had been violated, were not so euphoric. *For Freedom* finishes with the sailors from the River Plate marching through London and Churchill making his congratulatory speech at the Guildhall while the newsreel chief Ferguson directs the filming of events.

One newsreel company—Pathé—did in fact produce such an issue, a lengthy explanation of the events leading up to war and culminating with the same River Plate celebration and extracts from the speeches by Churchill and the captains of the *Exeter* and *Ajax.* It was called *The Curse of the Swastika,* and its two narrators (Roy de Groot and R. Danvers-Walker) put across the message in the typically flat, somber style that the newsreels drew upon when they had to make persuasive but unsensational propaganda for the cinema audiences. Chamberlain's Munich settlement with Hitler over Czechoslovakia was seen not as an act of weakness, which it soon was believed to be, but as a sensible postponement of war until the country was strong enough to act—a more charitable judgment than the one implied in the script of *For Freedom,* and one that still finds some support.

The *Altmark* incident was a reflection of the way in which the Scandinavian countries and their neighbors were being drawn reluctantly into the conflict. At the end of November the USSR attacked Finland, having failed to secure territorial concessions from that country. Stalin tried to set up a puppet Finnish government to represent the "people," but it attracted no support at all. The Finns resisted so resolutely that a Russian victory was delayed until March. The western allies had discussed the possibility of intervention to help Finland, although the main British interest in the matter was to find an excuse for cutting off the supplies of Swedish iron ore that were being transported through the ice-free Norwegian port of Narvik to Germany. For a time it seemed as if there was a chance of Britain and France going to war with the USSR as well as Germany and also bringing in Norway and Sweden against their will. The surrender of Finland at least released the allies from such a potentially disastrous commitment, and the Russians for their part had suffered such unexpectedly severe losses that their settlement with Finland was on balance a moderate one.[24]

George Formby's comedy *Let George Do It,* directed for Ealing by Marcel Varnel, had its ukelele-playing hero in Norway first mistaken for a Nazi spy and then helping a British agent, played by Phyllis Calvert, to unmask the real espionage ring.[25] Its choice of location was ominous for the spring of 1940, the time of the film's completion. The question of the iron-ore shipments had remained alive, especially in the mind of Winston Churchill, who wanted to use British sea power in a more effective way than simply as an instrument of blockade. A plan was drawn up to lay mines in Norwegian waters, although Norway would be informed politely of what was happening. The Germans too were concentrating more of their attention in this area. Before the war one of their admirals had written a book that demonstrated the usefulness to them of sheltering their ships in the fiords, using Norway as a forward base for striking at British communications across the Atlantic.[26] Hitler knew of the likelihood of the British intervening to cut off the iron-ore supplies and he was determined to forestall them. Early in April both sides put to sea, intending to break Norwegian neutrality in different ways. The phony war was about to be terminated by a new decisive phase of hostilities.

It had been a period of relative anticlimax for the British people. One of the most noticeable symptoms of this was the partial reversal of the evacuation scheme. Factors like homesickness and the frequent incompatibility of host and evacuee had contributed to it, but the scales were tipped in the end by the knowledge that the children's homes in the cities had not been destroyed. Before the first Christmas of the war, a major drift back was taking place. If any good had come out of it, there was the revelation to some of the more comfortably placed British citizens of the genuinely poor and deprived circumstances of many of the children from the cities.[27]

The MOI was also forced to share the general sense of disillusionment. It had expected there to be mass bombing and nothing had happened. There seemed to be no general call for it to take a lead in sustaining public morale. Indeed, for many it just appeared to be an overlarge bureaucratic body, the "Ministry of Aggravation" of Tommy Handley's popular radio comedy series ITMA ("It's that man again"). There was no clearly defined policy of war aims, partly because the government wanted to put all the blame on Hitler in the hope that the German people would come round to rejecting him. Certainly the Chamberlain cabinet had no concept of the war being fought in order to bring about social improvements within Britain itself, objectives dear to the heart of the documentary filmmakers and expressed in the editorials of their in-house journal *Documentary News Letter.*[28] The radicals of the movement anyway resented being kept out in the cold by the MOI's Films Division. However, by the new year Ball had been replaced by Sir Kenneth Clark, Director of the National Gallery, another curious choice perhaps (whether or not one believes the popular story that it was because he knew about "pictures") but at least a man with some cultural imagination. At the same time Sir John Reith, the founding spirit of the BBC, was persuaded to become Minister of Information, and within the few months of his tenure he attempted some reforms designed to stop an apparent impression of drift—though with only a limited chance of immediate success.[29]

In the meantime Michael Balcon at Ealing had produced for the MOI a trio of dramatized "careless talk" films. A number of posters had been distributed round the country on the same subject, and it remained a major obsession with the authorities throughout most of the war. There was a powerful fear of the dangers of information being given away to the enemy through gossip and idle conversation, and it was exaggerated by widespread misconceptions about the efficiency of German spy activities. In fact both sides in the war gained more by breaking each other's codes, by a long way the most influential part of intelligence operations, though it was an aspect of the conflict that remained secret for a long time afterwards. However, concern with the assumed spy menace was a godsend for the commercial film industry. Spy stories of course made good thrillers and thus good entertainment, and they provided a basis for more wartime British movies than any other single topic.

The three Ealing productions were short pieces directed by John Paddy Carstairs. In *Now You're Talking,* careless chatter in the Red Lion pub discloses that a couple of scientists are working overnight at a local factory to discover the secrets of a weapon that has been retrieved from a crashed German plane.[30] Whatever this is, it is certainly made to have monumental importance. The well-equipped and resourceful spies manage to draw off the police guard, shoot a soldier at the gate, and plant a bomb that destroys the factory. In the second film, *All Hands,* the chief listener is a café proprietress, a spy, or a traitor—the distinction is not made clear.[31] Hearing news of the sailing of a warship from Portsmouth, she passes the message in a darkened cinema to someone else who in his turn phones a man living in a cottage on the coast. This individual is an apparently harmless butterfly collector, the moral of course being that the most unlikely people might be secret Nazis. He is able to send a signal to sea and guide a U-boat to a position where it can sink the British vessel, presumably with "all hands." The sailor whose conversation in the café with his fiancee had started the chain of betrayal was played by John Mills.

The final film, *Dangerous Comment,* varied the formula slightly by having the spies caught at the end.[32] Perhaps too much pessimism would be bad for the public. Even so, it is put forward as a cautionary tale being narrated by the spy-catchers to a young man in their office who leaves them with the words that it will be quite a story to tell to his father! "You see what we're up against?" the officer says in despair. A conversation in a bar about an RAF raid on the Bender Dam is heard by the barman Charlie who goes on to meet his contact, the man who empties the money from the machines in a pin-table hall. He passes the information to him under the cloak of the popular slang expression "bender," meaning a drinking bout. Their dialogue here is indeed wonderful:

> "Hello, Charlie."
>
> "Evening, guv'nor."
>
> "Having a night off?"
>
> "That's right. Thought I'd like to go on a—*bender!"*
>
> "A bender, eh?"
>
> "That's right" (The pinball rolls) *"Damn!"*
>
> "Ha, ha, it's all in the game, you know."
>
> "The time I spend in here you owe me more than I get."
>
> "Ah well, come along some other time, we'll see what we can do for you."
>
> "I'd rather make it—*tonight."*

Back in the bar, Charlie has just to knock over a glass when someone asks him, "Been on a bender since we saw you last?" The film does not make clear how the spies give themselves away, the raid being recalled in time, but in the context of this ludicrous plot it hardly matters.

Although the GPO Film Unit was not finally transferred to the MOI until the summer of 1940, its relationship with the ministry during the phony war period was exactly the same as that of any documentary company. The films produced by Cavalcanti were all developed in cooperation with Kenneth Clark's department. One of these, *Spring Offensive,* was not to

***Dangerous Comment*. A cocktail cherry dropped into a glass by a careless talking lady at the bar stands for a bomb falling on the Bender Dam.**

be issued until late in the year and then under the title of *Unrecorded Victory*.[33] Its theme was the government-sponsored program to encourage farmers to plough up grassland and increase the amount of national arable production. The script was written by A. G. Street, a farmer himself as well as a popular author; and the director was Humphrey Jennings.

In many documentary and travel films the essence of rural life had been presented in an idyllic form, the familiar image of the thatched cottage and the contented countryman serving as a romantic representation of the heart of Britain (or more particularly perhaps, England). *Spring Offensive* went only a small way to reverse this idea, even a derelict farm appearing in it rather as an aberration. In fact farming had been in a depressed state during the interwar years, profits from cereal products being so low that the keeping of livestock had seemed to be the only solution. Farm laborers were badly paid and lived in primitive conditions. Farms themselves were often in a state of disrepair and neglect. With the coming of war, a nation deprived of imports needed more basic food from the land. Fortunately the Ministry of Agriculture had made plans in advance. Farmers were to be paid two pounds for each acre of grassland they ploughed up during the winter of 1939–40.[34] The film shows the representatives of a War Agricultural Executive Committee in East Anglia informing and sometimes persuading the farmers, some of whom must have feared that the changeover might cause a loss of milk output, also badly needed. Tractors are made available by the authorities, and land girls (as recruits for the Women's Land Army were called), replace the men who have been enlisted for military service. A tiny subplot of the film features one farmer and his evacuee, a boy from London, all happy and contented, of course—the boy's parents visit him before Christmas. That first winter of the war was unusually cold, and there are shots of the hard, frozen ground. In spite of these difficulties the derelict farm is cleared up and the ministry's goals are achieved in time for the harvest of the spring. The film comments that the land is only looked after properly during periods of war! By 1945 there was more acreage of arable land than grassland in Britain, and citizens throughout the country had become accustomed to double summer time, introduced to give the farmers more daylight working hours.

In his autobiography, Harry Watt gave an entertaining account of his arrest on suspicion of being a spy while making the GPO's *Squadron 992,* a film that had been intended by the RAF to bring some sense of purpose to the territorials who were manning barrage balloons in various parts of the country.[35] The idea for it had been put to the unit by a senior officer, Air Vice-Marshal Boyd, a man who clearly had more enlightened views than many others in the service (unfortunately he was killed before the end of the war). Watt started the film with a training lecture being given to the men, in which the function of the balloons, to inhibit enemy dive bombers, is explained. The Stuka dive bomber had won much notoriety in Poland, almost as much for the noise it made as for the damage it caused, but it was vulnerable to modern fighters, and in the event it was rarely used over Britain. Watt had found the balloon barrage topic uninspiring until he had been able to incorporate into it an account of an attempted German raid over the Firth of Forth. As they were filming fishermen picking up survivors (played by students) from a shot-down German plane, he and his assistants Jonah Jones and Julian Spiro were arrested by the navy, their cameras seized, and they were held in jail for the rest of the day and well into the night. Such was the extent of the mania about German spy activities.

By the time the film was finished, the end of the

***Squadron 992*. Raising the clumsy barrage balloons, intended to deter German dive bombers.**

phony war had made it seem irrelevant and it was not widely released. In style, though, it was one of the most notable documentaries of the war. Watt took pains to identify the RAF men as people, recalling the prewar jobs of some of them, and, forthright Scotsman as he was, he also was able to give convincing if brief sketches of the Scots living in the area. The splendid photography of Jonah Jones illuminates the routines of handling the unmanageable balloons. The raid is simulated by using Blenheims with German markings, and Watt and his editor R. Q. McNaughton cleverly cut between a Spitfire chasing a Nazi plane and a poacher's hound pursuing a hare. A shot with the animals in the foreground and the aircraft behind them is one of its most striking images. In the story the absence of defenses at the Forth leads the balloon squadron to be ordered north, and it embarks on an epic journey, again well paced in the film, which ends with the commandeering of land and the placing of the barrage balloons close to the Forth Bridge. *Squadron 992* was the last film for which music was written by Walter Leigh, killed in Libya in 1942, a composer best remembered for his evocative score for Basil Wright's prewar film *Song of Ceylon.*

The GPO Film Unit also set out in 1940 to make a film about air attacks on lightships, a matter which had been receiving some attention from the press in January. The Trinity House relief vessel *Reculver* had been bombed and machine-gunned for half an hour, causing two deaths and many injuries. This incident, allied to the strafing of fishing vessels, provoked a page-long article in one weekly journal under the title "This is the sort of war Nazi airmen prefer."[36] Three days later, as part of a series of assaults on British shipping along the east coast, the East Dudgeon lightship was attacked, and the last of nine bombs struck her. The crew abandoned ship but, after rowing overnight in difficult conditions, all but one were drowned when their boat capsized near the coast. Indignation about these events was whipped up as a propaganda measure, probably to influence the neutrals who were also dependent on lightships for navigational aid, and a film was planned with a re-enactment of the East Dudgeon example.

The director was to be David MacDonald, who had not previously worked in the documentary field, having made a career in the commercial industry, at one period in Hollywood as an assistant to Cecil B. De Mille. Apparently he offered his services to Cavalcanti at the right moment.[37] Unfortunately production of the film was delayed a couple of months owing to the Air Ministry's crass insistence that a scene had to be inserted to show a German plane being shot down. It would not be good for national morale if it were to be thought that the RAF could not defend our lightships. There was an obvious inconsistency in introducing this fictional element into a factual story, and also it would be an absurdity, because the crew could hardly have been left to their fate if the RAF had been on the scene. The Air Ministry finally gave way after intervention by the MOI. As the film was being made, the Norwegian campaign began and, by the time it was finished, under the title *Men of the Lightship,* neutrality had ended for most of the nations who made use of the North Sea.[38]

True to his industry background, MacDonald had begun by hiring actors until Cavalcanti insisted on the use of real Trinity House men, and the naturalness of their dialogue is one of the strengths of the film. Before the climax, the raid itself, something is shown of the routine of lightship work and also its incidental wartime dangers, in a scene where a drifting mine has to be secured from the lightship's boat before the navy can blow it up by rifle fire. Again the RAF helped by using Blenheims in enemy guise, although there were some shots taken from Nazi newsreels of pilots at the controls and bomb doors opening, the same sequences as were used in a similar context in *Squadron 992.* During the attack the camera concentrates individually on the tense faces of the crew and again in the lifeboat on their weary expressions as they struggle at the oars. *Men of the Lightship* was edited by Stewart McAllister, whose influence on many of these wartime documentaries has been examined in a notable book by Dai Vaughan that gives also a timely corrective to the view, common in critical and educational circles, that the director is necessarily the single person most likely to stamp his own identity on a particular production.[39] At the close of *Men of the Lightship* a narrator says, "Their story is only one episode in a war of unparalleled horror. The Nazis must be stopped. We can, we will stop them." There was reason behind these emphatic sentiments. When the film was completed, the war for democracy was being fought by Britain alone.

Seizing Denmark on the way as a stepping stone, the Nazis invaded Norway in April. The Norwegians put up a gallant resistance, but Anglo-French aid was too slow and too inadequate and was overwhelmed by German air superiority. The one allied success, the capture of Narvik, was negated by enemy advances in the south and center of the country, and in any case the campaign was given up not long after the opening of Hitler's major offensive against France, whose fate became a more vital matter. Nevertheless, the German navy suffered very heavy losses, with even the *Scharnhorst* and *Gneisenau* out of action for a time. The British fleet also did not come out unscathed, but

Men of the Lightship. **Civilian sailor on a lightship under attack by German aircraft.**

it could more easily afford such casualties. However, Hitler had achieved his aim of occupying Norway, securing his iron ore shipments, and gaining bases from which he could threaten British maritime communications. The world became aware of a new word, "quisling," after the name of the principal Norwegian traitor and collaborator.[40]

While the balance of power was changing dramatically in Europe three British feature films, each with widely different war themes, were being prepared for release—MGM's *Night Train to Munich,* Charter Films' *Pastor Hall,* and Ealing's *Convoy.* Taken together as a group, they sum up some of the more obvious illusions of the phony war period for Britain.

The original title for the first of these had been *Gestapo,* but redistribution saw it given its more subtle label of *Night Train to Munich* (U.S. title: *Night Train*). Based on a novel by Gordon Wellesley, the script had been written by Sidney Gilliat and Frank Launder, and the film was directed by Carol Reed. As Prague falls to the Nazis, a Czech scientist, Axel Bomasch, manages to take the last plane to England. Unfortunately his daughter Anna, played by Margaret Lockwood, is arrested before she too can flee, and she is placed in a concentration camp. Here her friendship grows with another prisoner, Karl Marsen, and together they escape and cross the Channel. Anna finds that her father is being kept in hiding, in fear for his safety, but she tracks him down to a south-coast resort where he is under the care of a British intelligence officer known as "Mr Bennett," though his real name is Randall. This part is taken by Rex Harrison. Anna's trust in Karl proves to be ill-founded because in fact he is a Nazi agent, and, having been put on the trail of the Czech scientist (without meeting Randall), he contrives to kidnap both father and daughter by means of a submarine. Bomasch's work is concerned with munitions, and clearly it has great value for both sides, even before war has begun.

Randall determines to attempt a rescue, and, entering Germany, he disguises himself as an army major. The captives are being interrogated at naval high command, and here Randall is able to persuade the authorities that, as an old friend of Anna, he can use some special influence with her to get her father to cooperate. Instructions are received to take them by train to Munich with Karl Marsen and a pair of guards. Randall accompanies them and is recognized by a couple of English travelers, one of whom knew him at Balliol—none other than the famous cricket-loving duo Charters and Caldicott, played by Basil Radford and Naunton Wayne. These two had been seen on screen in Hitchcock's *The Lady Vanishes* and were the heroes of radio serials, continuing after the war, in which they were accustomed to find themselves in a variety of comically dangerous situations. Momentarily they give the game away, but in the end they succeed in helping Randall to overpower the Nazis and escape in a car to the Swiss border. There is a final scene of tension as Randall and Marsen struggle for control of a cable car that carries the fugitives to freedom.

The plot then follows the normal thriller conventions, with Rex Harrison playing the role of the suave and unflappable Englishman. Radford and Wayne embody other kinds of comic bumbling English upper-class stereotypes ("Dickie Randall couldn't be a Nazi—he played for the Gentlemen at Lord's"). However, the Germans are not wholly cardboard figures, not even Raymond Huntley as a Gestapo official, nor the various minor characters who appear in the train journey and on a station platform—none of these latter showing any animosity to the two cricketers even though war is being declared on that day. Perhaps it was assumed that the majority of German people were simple, average human beings who had been drawn reluctantly into war and upon whose support Hitler would in time be unable to rely. Certainly the British authorities hoped that events would turn in that direction. Karl Marsen of course is a dedicated Nazi but, as played by Paul Henreid (himself a refugee and still known at that time as Paul von Hernried), he is an intelligent personality, a long way from the stiff-necked individuals who are introduced as enemy characters in many other films.

The most searching of these productions in terms of its theme was *Pastor Hall,* produced by John Boulting and directed and edited by Roy Boulting. It was based on a play by the exiled writer Ernst Toller, itself inspired by the example of Pastor Martin Niemöller in Germany. The twin Boulting brothers, only twenty-six in 1940, had been able to form their own company to make films before the war. Unlike most of their colleagues in the industry, they were politically left-wing, and their hostility to fascism had caused them to plan an adaptation of *Pastor Hall* for the screen. However, their aims had been thwarted by the censors, who declined to give approval to a script which was so openly anti-Nazi in content. Toller's play had been published in Britain by The Bodley Head in 1939, translated from German by Stephen Spender, but a film was a totally different matter. The restriction could only be removed with the outbreak of war, when the Boultings were able to put their project into production at last.

Martin Niemöller's first career had been in the navy, and he had won fame for himself as a U-boat commander in the First World War. Uncompromising as ever, he refused to take his vessel to surrender at Scapa Flow in 1918. He turned next to the Protestant church, into which he was ordained in 1924 and, after a period doing administrative work, he became pastor at the Berlin suburb of Dahlem in 1931. To this date his main political sympathies had remained nationalist and, like many other Germans who disliked the Weimar Republic, he had voted for the Nazis in the twenties. Even after Hitler's accession to power, he had led a group of clergymen who sent a telegram congratulating the Führer on withdrawing Germany from the League of Nations in 1933, the first step, it seemed, towards reversing the humiliations of the Versailles peace settlement.

Hitler had gained much support within the Protestant community because he had promised to restore the historic links between church and state, broken by the fall of the monarchy in 1918. His most active supporters were a group known as the German Christians, and they were successful in securing the appointment of their own candidate as Reichsbishop. It is likely that Niemöller's dissidence dated from that event. Even before the end of 1933 it became clear that the new regime would require the church to denounce Jewish influence, prohibit the marriage of Christians and Jews, and reject most elements in the Old Testament, thus causing doctrinal and political matters to be entangled with each other The new "people's church" would be based on the concept of "One policy, one Reich, one faith," and Luther would become historically a more specifically nationalist figure. Niemöller's pulpit at Dahlem soon grew to be the center of religious opposition, and perhaps also a meeting place for citizens who disapproved of Hitler's actions.

Niemöller was finally arrested in June 1937. By the time that a court found him guilty of political offences, he had been imprisoned for longer than the sentence imposed. Hitler intervened personally to prolong his detention, and he was sent to Sachsenhausen concentration camp. A number of clergymen became victims of the Nazis, including Dietrich Bonhöffer who was murdered in 1945, but it was Niemöller's case which attracted worldwide attention in 1938. He fell into a special category as a prisoner, and he was spared the extremes of harsh treatment inflicted on most of those in the camps. His life had always been controversial, and in September 1939 he made a curious request to serve again in the navy, on the ground, he said later, that the only effective resistance to Hitler could be organized from within the armed forces. As a Christian, how would he have coped with the personal loyalty oath, which inhibited so many in the services who had anti-Nazi leanings? We shall never know because Niemöller was to be kept for the rest of the war in Dachau concentration camp, in close custody with three Catholic priests who had also opposed Hitler.[41]

The play by Ernst Toller introduces the character of Pastor Friedrich Hall who, like Niemöller, has been making sermons critical of the Nazis. His stance causes argument with his wife Ida, who believes that he is sacrificing the interests of his family to his own principles. There is also some hostility to his ideas within the community. However, he has been protected to some degree by a local SS officer called Fritz Gerte, who is hopeful of becoming engaged to the pastor's daughter Christine. In fact she is planning to marry Werner, the son of General von Grotjahn, a First-World-War hero who is contemptuous of the Nazis. Werner has accepted an invitation to lecture at Columbia University, New York—an act of betrayal to Germany in Gerte's eyes. By using a threat of blackmail over an apparently illegal currency deal, Gerte manages to persuade Ida that the marriage should be broken off. However, Pastor Hall refuses to go along with this, and Gerte contrives to have him thrown into a concentration camp, the setting for the central part of the play. Eventually Hall escapes, with the connivance of an SS man called Heinrich Degan, who had been one of his congregation, and he takes refuge in the house of General von Grotjahn. The engagement has been ended, though by Christine, who has become disillusioned with Werner when he had failed to support her father.

At the climax of the play, flight is being urged upon the Halls, but the pastor decides that, since it is Sunday, he will go down to his church and preach a last sermon. The general resolves to accompany him, and even Ida acknowledges at last her husband's courage. Pastor Hall says, "I will live. It will be like a fire that no might can put out, the meek will tell the meek and they'll become brave again. One man will tell another that the anti-Christ rules, the destroyer, the enemy of mankind—and they will find strength and follow my example." The play *Pastor Hall* was an affirmation of the need to oppose Hitler, a pointer to the way in which resistance might grow among the German people, and it was this theme that the Boultings tried to establish in their film.

Roy Boulting has acknowledged the considerable help given by another exile, the Austrian writer Anna Reiner, in producing a film script, on which Leslie Arliss and Haworth Bromley also collaborated.[42] It was a major modification of the play, the principal change being the introduction of a longer sequence of events before Hall is arrested, in order to put the growth of his dissidence into its historical context. The location had not been specified in the play, but the film identifies it as a small town where the impact of the Hitler regime on a previously harmonious community can be examined in company with Hall's developing awareness of the evils of nazism. The character of Ida is omitted altogether, and Werner aids the pastor's escape from the concentration camp, rather than running away when matters become too hot for him. It is evident also that Pastor Hall is executed by the Nazis at the end of his final sermon, a decisive departure from the Niemöller story. The film was dedicated to the day when it might be shown in Germany, just as the dedication page of Toller's play had expressed a similar hope about its future.

The parts of Hall and Grotjahn were played in the film by two notable stage and screen actors of the time. Wilfred Lawson, who performs the role of the pastor with great conviction, appeared again in few films with relevance to the war, although in 1942 he took the lead as the composer in the period movie *The Great Mr Handel.* Sir Seymour Hicks, equally distinguished as the general, had already been appointed controller of the forces' entertainment organisation ENSA, and in this role he was to travel with them both to France and the Middle East. In conversation at the beginning of *Pastor Hall,* it is Grotjahn who expresses scorn for the Nazis while Hall tends to think that their bad reputation has been exaggerated. The play had Gerte as a local man who has been helped by the Halls in his early life, but the film introduces him as a newcomer, a political leader who has the task of bringing the town's inhabitants into line with the ideals of the Reich. Marius Goring plays Gerte as an orthodox and single-minded but nevertheless credible Nazi. He asks Hall to identify Jews, socialists, and other unsavory elements within the community, a duty that the clergyman resists. Hall also meets a new school head, who requests the pastor to revise his scripture classes so that the Old Testament is avoided, Jews are not referred to as the chosen people, pity as a topic is not enlarged upon, and love is spoken of only in the strictly Nordic sense. Hall's awakening realization of the true nature of the regime is reinforced when he witnesses attacks on Jewish shopkeepers, and he makes his first unavailing protest to Gerte.

Unlike the play, the film script also makes reference to the episode known as the "night of the long knives." Hitler's original supporters had been the brown-shirted SA, the proletarian street stormtroopers of the movement, but in 1934 the growing rival influence of their leader Röhm led him to cut them violently back. With the help of his elite SS forces, he had Röhm and a number of others murdered, an action that also gained for himself the sympathetic concurrence of the army, a move essential for him if he was to assert the new Germany's place in Europe by means of military strength.[43] In the film *Pastor Hall,* the young Erich Kemp had joined the SA, attracted by its superficial glamor, only to fall victim to Hitler's purge. Hall comforts his bereaved mother, already a widow and an invalid, and he buries the young man's remains at night, an action which marks the commencement of coolness toward him from the local bourgeoisie. He hears next that the girl Lina Veit is pregnant after a stay in a youth labor camp (an episode hinted at in the play), and he goes in person to talk to the commandant, whose response is to tell him that the young man who has seduced her is unlikely to marry her and that anyway it is a woman's role to bear children for the Reich. Hearing of malicious gossip about her in the town, Lina commits suicide. Hall determines now to speak out against the Nazis from the pulpit, an action which leads to his

***Pastor Hall.* Artificial concentration camp settings and dejected prisoners place the film in a British theatrical tradition, diminishing the effect of realism.**

being sent to the concentration camp.

The scenes in the camp illustrate some of the brutalities of imprisonment, new inmates forced to run the gauntlet of baton-wielding SS men, a captive strung up by his wrists for ten hours, an old man sentenced to twenty-five lashes. As in the play, one of the prisoners, a convicted criminal, has been appointed to supervise the others. Hall makes friends with a young Jew who had returned to Germany from safety in Paris because he could not believe the stories of Nazi atrocities. Heinrich Degan, the SS man who had been born in the town where the main action is set, is played by Bernard Miles, whose homely style of delivery at first seems to be at odds with the usual image of the black-uniformed camp guards. However, it serves to establish the fact that the Nazis drew their support from the rural communities and that many seemingly ordinary young men joined the movement and went on to commit unspeakable atrocities, though in Degan's case it turns out that his conscience can be awakened, an important point in the context of the film's overall thesis.

Christine (Nova Pilbeam) pleads with Gerte for her father's release, even offering herself to him as one of the conditions. Gerte needs an assurance from the pastor that he will stay silent. Refusing to sign a retraction, Hall bursts out with the words, "I denounce this Hitler, architect of evil." Degan strikes him to the ground. The camp commandant orders solitary confinement and twenty-five lashes a day, and the first of the floggings almost cripples Hall. Rebelling against these cruelties, Degan contrives an escape though he himself is shot. Werner has a car outside the fence, and he brings Hall to the Grotjahn house. Gerte arrives in pursuit, but he is disarmed by the general and shut in the cellar. General von Grotjahn is now wearing his uniform and decorations, and he decides on that Sunday morning to accompany Pastor Hall to his church.

The film has a final scene in the church itself, where Lawson's acting appears at its most dignified. A new pastor is ordered out by the general, and Hall takes his place to preach a sermon based on a text from St Paul ("Put on the whole armor of God"). He tells the congregation that their voices are meant to be used as a sword against evil things, that they can pass on the messages to their children, and he will be with them when they "triumph over the enemies of God."

***Pastor Hall.* Lone resistance from the pulpit, representing a failed hope for the Nazis to be overthrown by their own people (Wilfred Lawson).**

The congregation listens in silence, sympathetically it seems (one man guiltily covers up a swastika armband), but the ejected pastor has summoned the SS, and they wait outside, intending to shoot Hall as he emerges.

As a screen drama, *Pastor Hall* was handicapped by not being able to overcome its theatrical origins, no matter how much the text had been modified. The crude obviousness of the studio sets for the town and the concentration camp only enhanced that impression. Moreover, there was a difficulty, rarely solved with success throughout the war, in having Germans played by West End actors and actresses. In *Pastor Hall* they had chosen to speak with English voices. In other films (*Convoy* was an early example) fake German accents were used, a device that usually created caricatures.

The expectation *Pastor Hall* represented, that opposition to Hitler would grow among ordinary Germans, was not realized. The people had entered the war in 1939 with little enthusiasm, no doubt like their British and French counterparts in fearing a repetition of the carnage of the previous world conflict, but victory over France in the following year produced national celebrations. Pride seemed to have been restored by the overturning of the Versailles settlement. Later in the war, as events turned the scales against Germany, there was continuing solidarity behind the leadership, reinforced by the political effects of the allied demands for unconditional surrender and by the counterproductive influence on morale of the massive bombing of German cities. There was indeed both discontent and opposition, more widespread than was believed at one time, culminating in an attempt in July 1944 by army officers to overthrow Hitler by force, but little prospect of a universally popular rising.[44]

Convoy was directed by Penrose Tennyson, who also wrote most of the script. It was more successful at the box office than any other British film of 1940, perhaps because, up to the Battle of Britain, the navy had seemed to be the only one of the nation's armed services to have had much contact with the enemy. Traditional fondness for the fleet among the people probably also worked in its favor. There is something of the spirit of the *Graf Spee* victory in this story of the cruiser *Apollo* that tackles the German armored ship *Deutschland* in the North Sea, keeping it at bay while a British convoy succeeds in escaping to the Scottish coast. The *Deutschland* was a real vessel, though Hitler renamed her the *Lützow* for fear of loss of face if a ship bearing the name of the Teutonic nation came to be lost. Some shooting for *Convoy* had taken place at sea, and Ealing took pains to secure authenticity in the scenes aboard ship and in the battle that made up the climax of the film.

Unfortunately though, its plot and its characterizations are much less of a triumph. The two principal naval figures, the cruiser's Captain Tom Armitage and Lieutenant David Cranford, are played by Clive Brook and John Clements respectively within the tight-lipped conventions of their class. Cranford, after an affectionate farewell on the quayside to a girlfriend (Penelope Dudley Ward), joins the *Apollo* against Armitage's wishes. It seems that Cranford, in a previous posting, had run off with the captain's wife and then deserted her. The account of his caddish behaviour soon circulates round the wardroom, and he finds himself ostracized. While the cruiser is at sea she receives an SOS message from a merchantman, the *Seaflower*, which has detached itself from the convoy, partly because its stubborn skipper, who had been a gun-runner in the Spanish Civil War, wants to be independent of it. Now she is reporting that she is sinking. Armitage refuses to send assistance because he cannot spare a vessel, and he will not change his mind even when he hears that his former wife Lucy (Judy Campbell) is aboard, returning home from Poland. Cranford, on his own initiative, signals an aircraft to look for the *Seaflower*. It is promptly shot down by the Nazi boarding party from a U-boat that has seized the *Seaflower* and is using her as a decoy by making fake distress transmissions. In fact a destroyer manages to sink the U-boat, and Lucy and the other passengers are temporarily transferred to the *Apollo*. Cranford meanwhile has been arrested and kept under guard in his cabin for his disobedience, but the interlude provides an excuse for Lucy to tell Armitage that it was she who had abandoned her lover, an admission which appears to clear up the relationship between the two men. As the *Apollo* goes into action, Cranford reports for duty again. "David, Lucy told me a lot of things," says Armitage. "I think I overdid it." "I know I did, sir," Cranford replies. His final redemption is to die heroically in action.

The sailors and marines in *Convoy* are mostly comic cockney characters with lines like "Blimey, reminds you of Guy Fawkes' Day, don't it, chums?" as the battle rages. John Laurie plays a Scotsman in the crew and also, more heavily disguised in their roles, Hay Petrie and Mervyn Johns are two other Scots aboard a minesweeper who spend their time fishing over the side, one responding only "aye" to the other's words. Other British character actors, Edward Chapman and Edward Rigby, are captain and mate of the *Seaflower*, the former uncomfortable with a phony northern accent. The Germans are robots, most of their dialogue on the level of "Dot vos good verk" from the

Convoy. **Stiff upper lips in conflict as Royal Navy officers debate a breach of their class code (John Clements and Clive Brook).**

captain of the *Deutschland.* Refusing a tot of rum, a prisoner smashes the mug to the ground, gazes heavenwards, and lifts his arm in a Heil Hitler salute. "With his own lips our Führer has told us how to fight this war," says the leader of the boarding party aboard the *Seaflower* when he tells the crew and passengers that, if they do not have enough boats, they will have to go down with the ship. Lucy and the skipper reply with a recital of Nelson's prayer on the eve of Trafalgar. However, it is unlikely that in the summer of 1940 many people in the audiences were very concerned about these waxwork portraits. It was the last film to be made by Penrose Tennyson, who was himself killed in a flying accident while serving as a naval reserve officer.

The phony war was so relatively short that neither the commercial industry nor the official film had time to adjust to it. None of the films made within the period shows any understanding of the likely course

Convoy. **Members of the less pukka merchant service. The mate tries to summon aid as his skipper dies (Edward Rigby and Edward Chapman).**

of the conflict or of the immense effort and resolution that would be needed to defeat Nazi Germany. In this respect they were simply reflecting both public and official opinion. By the early part of 1940 a mixed mood of boredom and complacency had set in. Even so, confidence in Chamberlain and the government's leadership was still relatively strong.[45] Between those on the right who continued to favor a settlement with Hitler and those on the left who already looked forward to the possibility of a new socialist Britain after the war, there was probably a moderate consensus about the need for democracy to prevail against totalitarianism. It was not necessary for this to be overstated, as it had been in the opening of *The Lion Has Wings,* and belated recognition of the fact contributed to the failure of that film's ending. Elsewhere, the confused approach of official propaganda was to some extent a consequence of the uncertainties inevitable in pluralist and parliamentary societies. But at their best these earlier war films, in spite of their obvious shortcomings, did produce images that convey some sense of the knowledge the British had of what they were fighting for, sufficient for them to set aside their deep-rooted abhorrence of participation in another war in favor of the defense, and possible postwar improvement, of their way of life.

2
Britain at Bay

The events of May and June 1940 took the world by surprise. The heavy fortifications of the Maginot Line along France's frontier with Germany were supposed to be impregnable, and it was reckoned that any invading army which passed through Belgium, as happened in 1914, could be held in a campaign of attrition by the French forces. The attack, the so-called blitzkrieg, started on 10 May and comprised the occupation of the Netherlands as well as Belgium.

The German masterstroke was to move tanks through the supposedly impassable Ardennes and then strike across the Meuse and along the Somme to the coast. Guderian, the architect of victory, did not hesitate to leave the infantry behind at times and, ten days after the attack started, this risky maneuver brought him to the English Channel. The French army had not been defeated so much as bypassed and left in confusion and disorder.[1] The British Expeditionary Force was cut off and, after the fall of Belgium, forced back to the coast, at Dunkirk. The surrender of this professional core of the British army would have been a calamity from which the country, even under the new leadership of Churchill, might never have recovered. Instead, through the efforts of the Royal Navy with some aid from private craft of all sizes, some 330,000 troops, both British and French, were brought back to England. The loss of the army's equipment was serious enough, but loss of the men themselves would have been worse. The French were to complain that they had been left in the lurch by the British withdrawal, but not for the first or the last time in the history of the two countries national self-interest overrode everything else.

The Dunkirk evacuation was the first large-scale episode in which the British had become involved in the Second World War. It was a defeat, but it was also celebrated as a miraculous rescue operation. Psychologically, it had the effect of making the nation aware at last of the full consequences of appeasement of Hitler. Already the setback in Norway had seen off Chamberlain, who only just before the invasion of that country had talked of Hitler "missing the bus." The new government led by Winston Churchill was a coalition. But the reverberations of Dunkirk, the memory of Britain's unpreparedness for war, and the lack of resolution shown by the previous conservative-centered administration went on rumbling until the general election of 1945.[2]

The script for an Ealing re-enactment of the operation, a feature film titled *Dunkirk* and directed in 1958 by Leslie Norman, acknowledged these very issues, even at that distance from the end of the war, by having comments made by those waiting on the beaches about the rotten state of the nation and the debacle it had produced. However, for such a momentous event actual British film coverage had been slight. Only Charles Martin of Pathé was on the scene to photograph lines of exhausted troops struggling

The blitzkrieg starts and Belgian refugees take to the roads. From a Pathé newsreel, shot by Charles Martin.

through the water toward their rescuers. Ronnie Noble of Universal, in his book about his own life as a film reporter, suggested that there might have been more material if Martin had not felt compelled to lend a helping hand himself, but the dilemma is an understandable one and must have been faced throughout the war at times of danger by other film correspondents.[3] All of the newsreel companies, Gaumont British, Pathé, Paramount, Movietone, and Universal, had been represented in France, their cameramen originally based at Arras, but the authorities evacuated them through Boulogne before the German thrust had been completed, and Martin alone was able to return to the beaches, by way of Harwich.[4]

In this pretelevision age, cinema newsreels were the only medium through which the public could see real moving pictures of the war. Immediate information came over the wireless, and the audience for radio news bulletins made up a substantial proportion of the nation, with the newspapers providing the most detailed coverage. By contrast, cinema images were highly selective. The cameramen themselves were not always able to shoot near the front line, which is where the public probably wanted them to be. Some of the military felt that film correspondents were a nuisance and were liable to get in the way when action was taking place. They were handicapped by having to move cumbersome equipment. The cameras were smaller than those in use during the previous war, but the film gauge was still 35mm, and the size of reels allowed for only a couple of minutes' shooting at most before they had to be changed. Moreover, their clockwork mechanisms were not consistently reliable.[5] Cameramen could be exposed to as much danger as the troops themselves, and it is hardly surprising that many of the activities they filmed were actually behind the lines. Even in battle itself, it was more practicable to shoot artillery firing at a distance from the enemy than soldiers in direct contact with their opponents.

Soon the authorities compelled the newsreel companies to work on a shared basis (known officially as the "rota"), so that material shot by any of them could be made available to the others, a situation they resented, and it did not diminish the spirit of competitiveness between the cameramen themselves. Official censorship was undertaken in London, and one of Reith's reforms was to have control of it assumed again by the MOI, after a few months of drift when the task had been undertaken by a separate body.[6] The establishment has always been more sensitive about what appears on film (or television) than in any other media, perhaps out of some belief that its emotive influence is more powerful. There were among the military many who could recognize the value of informing the public as fully as possible in film terms, but others who seemed more intent on the suppression of information for fear of passing on something of value to the enemy. The latter attitude has to be seen in relation to the public's own beliefs, partly fostered by official propaganda, about the reality of the spy menace. Mass-Observation even experienced one instance where a researcher taking notes in a darkened auditorium was reported by a couple of people to the cinema manager, who then sent for a puzzled policeman. Fortunately she was able to convince him that she had not been writing down some vital military information.[7]

There had been two main complaints about the government's attitude to cinema in the early months of the war. First, there was the argument expressed most cogently by the *Documentary News Letter* group, who had their own ideological axe to grind, that Nazi propaganda was not being countered by any comparable attempt on the British part to make a statement of war aims and to put across a blueprint for a postwar society. The second, and even more fundamental, failure was caused by the restrictions placed on combat photography, including the absence of a fully constituted official unit on the German model, so that the world saw images of Nazi triumphs from Poland to France and little or nothing from the other side. It was not even until the summer of 1940 that the MOI put into effect the distribution abroad of British newsreels in the languages of the countries to which they were being sent, and in this respect the crisis in France had produced a new approach at last.[8]

Each newsreel cameraman had to prepare a "dope sheet" of details of what he had shot, the precise location, the type of camera used, and other essential facts. The sheets themselves were blue-penciled by the censors.[9] Film was viewed both before and after completion of the newsreel. Commentaries had to be approved, and it was this circumstance in particular that turned the private newsreels into agents of government propaganda during the war. For the first three years little went right for Britain. The depressing nature of the news, sometimes reflected in the cinema images, had to be balanced by statements on the track that somehow counteracted the gloom. The speed of production of newsreels put them in the forefront of a campaign to sustain and encourage public morale from that critical summer of 1940 to the end of hostilities. Week by week, the public took in the exhortatory tones of the likes of Emmett of Gaumont British and Leslie Mitchell of Movietone. Tom Harrisson of Mass-Observation thought that their words produced "a sort of phonetic nausea in people,"[10] basing that view on surveys suggesting that dislike for the newsreels grew during 1940,[11] maybe because the public was too directly involved in the struggle for survival to need to be reminded of it in the cinemas. The truth is likely to be that reactions varied between individuals and changed at different times, according to how the war was progressing.

The MOI issued its own tiny epitaph to Dunkirk in the form of a short film called *Channel Incident*.[12] Directed by Anthony Asquith, it built a story around one of the legendary "little ships," a yacht sent out to ferry soldiers from the beaches to the deep-water vessels. The owner is himself in the BEF, but the boat is skippered by his wife (Peggy Ashcroft), accompanied by the steward of the yacht club (Gordon Harker) and a young boatman, described as "a bit simple" and played as a well-meaning rustic. A soldier (Robert Newton) also volunteers to go with them and dies behind his Bren gun as the rescuers are attacked by German aircraft. The wife spares few tears for him, however, and back in the Channel port she goes on a search for her missing husband. Eventually she finds him on a stretcher—"I've been looking for you," "Well, here I am." Although it had been meant no doubt as a tribute, the film looked like another piece of upper-class condescension and was justifiably criticized as such.[13] The MOI's attempts at dramatization seemed to have misfired again in this case.

The Universal cameraman Ronnie Noble had taken sequences of refugees being attacked from the air in Belgium, and this aspect of the blitzkrieg made the news headlines in Britain. It was to be reproduced later in the feature *The Foreman Went to France,* issued in 1942, a memory also of those final days of French collapse. In mid-June France was also being invaded, not very effectively, by the Italians. Originally it had been expected that Italy would join the war from the beginning, but Mussolini had waited until the last moment, hoping in the end to snatch something for himself from the defeat of France. Paramount News had produced a film called *Italy Beware,* which was meant to encourage the public to be confident about the strength of allied forces around the Mediterranean, but it was hastily withdrawn from the circuits as

Channel Incident. **Re-enactment of the Dunkirk evacuation, with small private boats taking soldiers out of the war, a gesture which excited national pride.**

soon as it became known that France was about to surrender and was not to continue the struggle from North Africa. An armistice was signed on the twenty-first. The north and west of France were to be occupied by the Germans, and the southern part neutralized and governed by the aged Marshal Pétain from the spa town of Vichy.

The future of a free Europe now lay with the British, who were already sheltering anti-Nazi refugees and military combatants from Poland, Norway, Czechoslovakia, and the Low Countries. They were joined by a remnant of the French, led by General de Gaulle, a renegade in the eyes of the new Vichy government. Offers of peace terms by Hitler were rejected. The cause found its man of the moment in Winston Churchill. He knew well enough that no reconquest of Europe was possible without eventual participation by the United States of America, but in the meantime British territory had to be defended and kept intact as a future base for operations from the edge of the continent. Such was the quality of his determination and his inspirational leadership that the British do not seem to have doubted that they could rise to the task. Within a couple of weeks of French surrender, Churchill had signaled his intentions to the world by initiating one of his most controversial actions, the bombardment by the British navy of French warships at Mers el Kébir in Algeria, to prevent them from falling into German hands, a battle which caused heavy damage and much loss of life on the French side.

Hitler's ultimate aim was a march eastwards against the Soviet Union, but he did not want to fight a war on two fronts and preferred to find a way of dealing first with the troublesome British. For his army to cross the English Channel in safety, and to continue being supplied so that it could defeat the relatively weak British land forces, it was essential to secure command of the air. The Royal Air Force had to be destroyed. But by mid-September the British airmen had inflicted such a scale of losses on their opponent, Goering's Luftwaffe, that the invasion was postponed, eventually to be abandoned forever. It was true also that the RAF had been nearly at its last gasp and might not have survived but for a switch in German tactics from attacks on airfields to the bombing of London. With his main priority remaining the move against Stalin, Hitler was no longer willing to risk the lives of valuable pilots. To date the Luftwaffe had been most devastating when it had acted in support of blitzkrieg, where the Stuka divebomber could come into its own, and it would be needed again for this purpose in Russia.[14]

The Battle of Britain became a legend at once, as soon as Churchill uttered his judgment on it, "Never in the field of human conflict was so much owed by so many to so few." His words were used for the title of *The First of the Few,* about the invention of the Spitfire fighter, a film started during the winter. However, no production about this most decisive single British action was made during the war itself and its only lengthy documentary tribute was to be American, as one of Capra's *Why We Fight* series. When a British feature film was attempted at last, *Angels One-Five,* directed by George More O'Ferrall in 1952, it was weighed down by tight-lipped understatement, as if the subject was too awesome to be approached, with the script putting a kind of plastic language into the mouths of the public schoolboy "types" who flew the Spitfires and Hurricanes. On the other hand, the characters in the 1969 blockbuster *Battle of Britain,* directed by Guy Hamilton, had the appearances and the voices of men of the sixties, and this film is mostly memorable for its scenes of aerial combat, its hectic score (by Ron Goodwin), and for the playing by Laurence Olivier of Dowding, the British commander and victor of the battle.

That summer of 1940 saw major changes within the Films Division at the MOI. Reith had been replaced as minister by Duff Cooper, more experienced as a politician and more likely to follow Churchill's line than his fiercely idiosyncratic predecessor who had no liking for the new prime minister. Kenneth Clark took up a more senior position, though he did not seem to enjoy it very much (if his autobiography is to be believed),[15] and the new films head was Jack Beddington, formerly Director of Publicity at Shell and responsible there for a notable advertising campaign. Among the independent documentary film units, Shell, started originally by Edgar Anstey in 1934, had been one of the most successful, and Beddington's recruitment provided the MOI with the required drive and vision. Sidney Bernstein from the Granada cinema chain became an advisor on marketing and distribution, and shortly afterwards Sir Arthur Elton, an experienced maker of documentaries, was appointed as supervisor of film production. Elton's films had included a number that dealt with industrial and technological processes.[16] The ministry absorbed the GPO Film Unit at last and brought in Ian Dalrymple as its head, and it was soon to be renamed, more appropriately, the Crown Film Unit and operated from Pinewood.[17]

One of the major policy decisions taken was to commission the production, in the main from the independent units, of what were described as "five minute films" because it was felt that shorter pieces would fit more comfortably into the average program.[18] Distributors and exhibitors were known to dislike documentaries, judging that the public went to the cinema primarily for diversion, a perception which was probably broadly right. People often arrived late in their cinema seats, just as the documentary was being screened, and most of them were unlikely to be looking for too much intellectual stimulation from the average program of one or two longer films, a cartoon, and a newsreel. The MOI's five-minute limitation was not literally followed—many films ran over that length—and by the middle period of the war it had become policy to produce again some longer documentaries, as well as those like *Fires Were Started* or *Western Approaches,* which leaned towards the style of features. Even so, many of them still encountered resistance from the cinemas. One exhibitor who was being prosecuted in Manchester for not keeping up his quota of British films said that "educational films depicting the life of a midge or a flower did not go too well in Collyhurst or Hulme," and the same no doubt was true of some of those with more apparent relevance to the war effort.[19] Mass-Observation reported in 1942 that their researchers often found it difficult to see documentaries because cinemas did not advertise them and sometimes did not show the films even when they had them.[20]

Nevertheless, these instances may have been exceptional. There was a chain of "news theaters," usually located in main railway stations to catch among others people waiting for trains (often a frustrating experience in wartime), and these showed only nonfiction films. The MOI also promoted a scheme of nontheatrical distribution of 16mm prints, initially under the supervision of Thomas Baird, to be shown in villages remote from cinemas and in factories where workers were prevented by the shift system from attending cinemas regularly. This was organized on a regional basis, with local film officers working in different parts of the country, and it had definite educational and instructional aims. The films can have reached only a minority through these outlets, and not only is it difficult to estimate in retrospect with certainty how they were received, but also it is unhelpful to generalize about their influence when they covered such a wide variety of topics. However, the film officers did try to gauge public opinion by distributing questionnaires.[21] The nontheatrical scheme might have been more widespread but for the fact that in August 1940 a select committee on public expenditure had expressed doubts about a policy of lavishing large sums of money on the production of documentary films and in particular had recommended that priority should be given to theatrical release. The committee had started its work before the phony war had ended and so reflected many of the attitudes current both in the MOI and the industry within that period.[22] By the time that the report had been published, the reorganization of the Films Division had been completed and the major nonfiction films of the war were yet to come.

Before taking up his new post, Ian Dalrymple's own contribution to the five minute program had been a film called *Sea Fort*, an exposition of the role of the Royal Artillery in manning an offshore fortress.[23] It was produced by Ealing, and Dalrymple both directed and wrote the commentary, the jocular tone of which was intended, one supposes, to reach down to the popular cinema audience. He set out to make a second film, on the Army Pioneer Corps, but it failed to win the approval of the MOI, which used its interventionist authority, as it did on other occasions, to have the film stopped, perhaps because these units at the time included aliens from enemy countries. Dalrymple's appointment to head the GPO Film Unit rescued him from any gloom he might have felt about this incident, and his role thereafter was administrative rather than creative.[24]

The GPO Unit was engaged during that spring and summer in making *Merchant Seamen*, a film about some of the more forgotten men of the war.[25] In fact there had been little relief from danger in the remorseless progress of the Battle of the Atlantic, and the attempt by U-boats to cut off Britain's supplies was to intensify as Hitler gave up his invasion plans. Directed by Jack Holmes and edited by R. Q. McNaughton, the film was not finally released until 1941, apparently because the MOI wanted some changes in it. H. E. (Chick) Fowle was responsible for the photography, and the music was written by Constant Lambert, one of the more interesting figures among that band of composers who contributed to the British wartime film, though, like all the others, he wrote for the screen in a thoroughly orthodox manner, as might seem fitting for a popular medium. This was Lambert's only film score during the war, and it was made into a concert suite that was performed on a number of occasions.[26] Holmes used some real seamen, in documentary tradition, and made a slow-paced and somewhat low-key film. A ship is sunk by an explosive device—the crew argue whether it is a torpedo or a mine—and are rescued by a lifeboat. One young man volunteers for a naval gunnery course and in time joins another ship as one of a small group who can handle the four-inch gun mounted near the stern—a common defensive tactic then although technically merchant seamen were civilians. Almost too easily, a well-aimed shot strikes a U-boat. The amateur acting is a trifle self-conscious, and the convoy procedures were to be looked at in more detail later in the war in Pat Jackson's *Western Approaches.*

Churchill had brought into his government two colorful figures from opposite ends of the political spectrum: the press baron Lord Beaverbrook to administer the vital area of aircraft production and the trade unionist Ernest Bevin to keep organized labor solidly behind the war effort. Both were remarkable men, in frequent disagreement with each other. Bevin had to swallow hard some of the principles to which he had devoted his life: the right of workers to collective bargaining and the freedom of labor from centrally directed regimentation.[27] In his new role he appeared briefly in the GPO Film Unit's *Welfare of the Workers,* talking to assembled factory employees about the job they had to do and how they must do it cheerfully.[28] Industry had already been celebrated in a longer documentary, *Behind the Guns,* made by Merton Park Studios and directed by Montgomery Tully, that went through the various processes in the production of different types of war equipment, accompanied by incisive music written by Francis Chagrin.[29] It used a northern voice for its narrator, in keeping with the straightforward nature of its style. The commentary for *Welfare of the Workers* was written by Ritchie Calder, and it started with an explanation of the kind of improvement the men had gained through their membership of unions and through factory legislation. Now the effects of the blackout sent workers home tired and depressed "but the alternative was the blackout of liberty." Hitler had suppressed trade unions altogether, and the British worker was being asked to give up some of his rights in order to resist. The film was directed by Humphrey Jennings, with photography by Jonah Jones, and they selected scenes showing workers, some of them women now, being resettled and helped by welfare

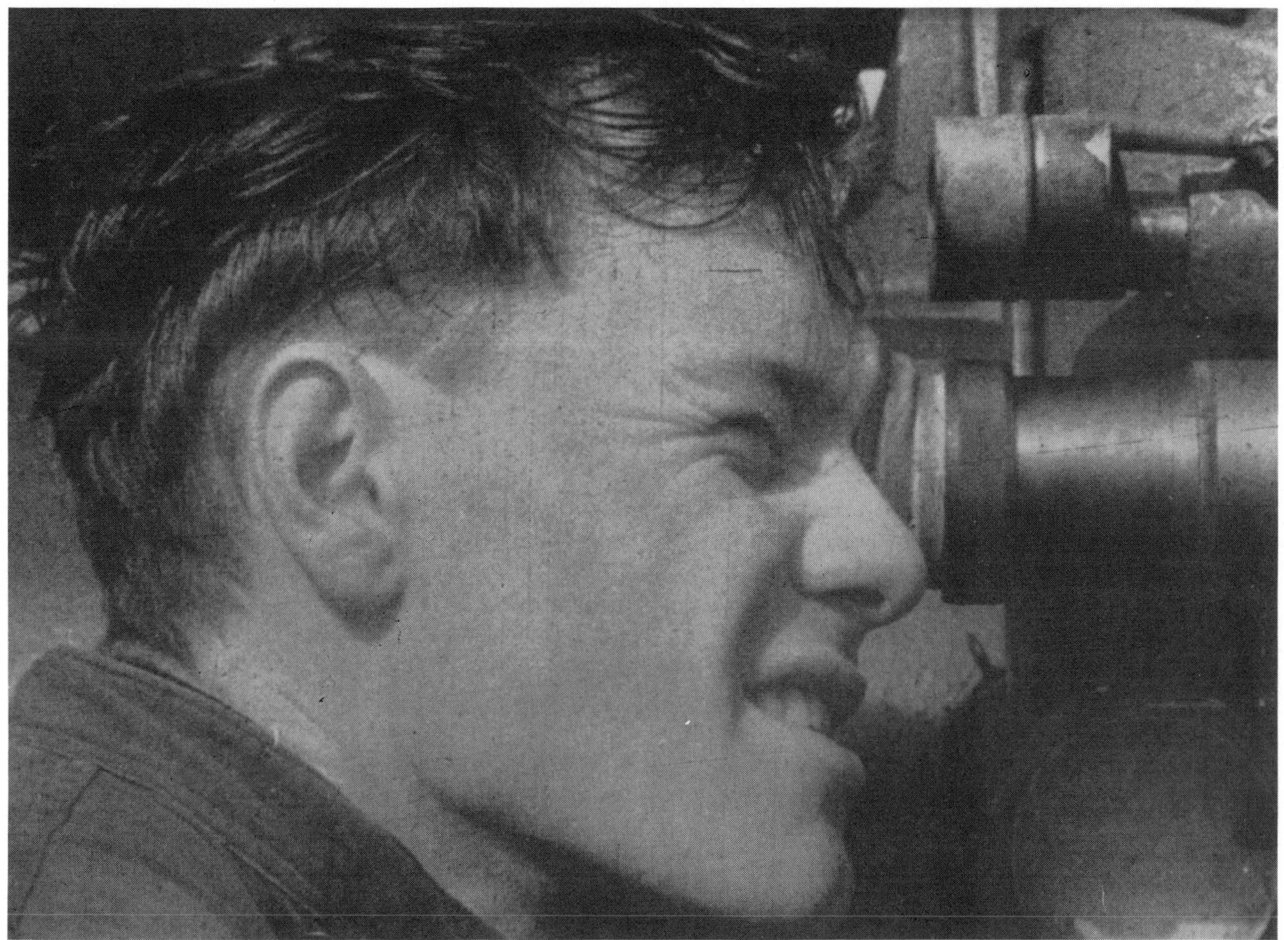

Merchant Seamen. **Merchant Navy gunner aiming his four-inch gun at a U-boat as the war at sea becomes crucial for Britain's survival.**

officers. The points made in the script are interesting ones in the context of the war effort at that time. Clearly workers were not expected to fall into line without some questioning of the need to do so, an inheritance of the conflicts of prewar industrial relationships. Bevin for his part had given in to the inevitable, although the main movement to mobilize labor, including the replacement of thousands of men called up for military service by women workers, only followed the presentation of a report in December by Sir William Beveridge.[30]

The argument for keeping Britain in the war was put across in film at this time by two famous though very different writers. In spite of the scorn he had expressed for the sentiments employed in *The Lion Has Wings,* Graham Greene's own script for Strand's short documentary *The New Britain,* directed by Ralph Keene, lacked very little in patriotism.[31] The film took the form of a pageantry of British achievements in the interwar years, notably in transport, communications, and housing—a second kind of industrial revolution in fact. Employee and employer are shown as working in harmony for the common good. "But we forgot Germany," the narrator says repeatedly. This kind of image of Britain accorded more with the type of resolve needed in 1940 than with the reality of the social situation between the wars. The final line of Greene's script speaks of "the spirit behind the long coastline and among quiet fields, simple, unboastful, and unbreakable."

The voice of the popular author J. B. Priestley was familiar to listeners in 1940 through a series of radio talks he had been giving as postscripts to the Sunday news bulletins. Yorkshire-born Priestley did not speak with the standard BBC accent, and the radical sentiments he expressed soon turned out to be uncomfortable for the government.[32] In July he was used by the GPO Film Unit to write and narrate the commentary for their "five-minute" film *Britain at Bay,* which put forward a staunch front to the reverses of the summer. Within this brief compass, actually eight minutes in length, the concision of the text is admirable. The opening shots, romantic ones of the English landscape, contrasted with others of northern industrial towns, project an image that was to become familiar throughout the war whenever cinema tried to present a notion of the kind of country the audience should be fighting for—an idealized and Arcadian view of England that appeared repeatedly in both documentaries and features.

From this vision the film moves to the enemy, the Germans who cannot live peacefully with their neighbors, seen now concluding their victorious blitzkrieg. "The future of the whole civilized world rests on the defense of Britain. . . . Britain must become an impregnable citadel of free people." There is a call for voluntary aid, most particularly for Local Defence Volunteers, or the Home Guard as they were soon to be renamed. It was intended that the army would be backed up by this body, recruited from men between the ages of fifteen and sixty-five who already had full-time jobs. They were hastily trained and badly equipped and expected to meet the well-publicized menace of Nazi parachute troops. The Home Guard has been immortalized by the most famous of all British war comedy television serials, *Dad's Army,* and it has been easy to laugh at them in retrospect because they were never called on to sacrifice themselves in what must have been a hopeless battle. The Germans indeed had declared that they would treat the volunteers as guerrillas and would shoot them out of hand.[33] In *Britain at Bay,* regular soldiers are seen on guard as Priestley quotes Churchill's famous lines about fighting on the beaches, on the landing grounds, in the fields, and in the hills. The final shot is of landscape again. The film was distributed in America, more wisely perhaps, under the title *Britain on Guard* (apart from Priestley himself and the composer Richard Addinsell no credits are available for it). The popularity of Priestley's broadcasts probably

Miss Grant Goes to the Door. **Disguised German invader finds British rural ladies more than prepared for him (Mary Clare and Martita Hunt).**

helped the reception of it at home.

The way in which the ordinary citizen was expected to do his duty in the event of invasion was illustrated by *Miss Grant Goes to the Door,* a short commercially made film directed by Brian Desmond Hurst.[34] Two middle-aged women (played by Mary Clare and Martita Hunt) discover a dying German airman at the door of their country cottage. Next they are startled to hear the church bells ringing. The bells throughout Britain had been silenced and were meant to be used only as a warning that invasion had begun, a prearranged signal that had been established throughout the nation. When another German, disguised as a British officer, arrives, he betrays himself by asking the way to Jarvis Cross, pronouncing the first word in the Teutonic fashion. One of the women holds him up temporarily with a gun she has taken from the other Nazi, and, though he manages soon to escape from her, he is unable to start a car outside because it has been immobilized by the sensible ladies. Finally he falls into the hands of the local Home Guard. Rural England had triumphed over the foolish Germans all too easily in this film, to which Thorold Dickinson had contributed as a co-writer of the script.[35]

Harry Watt had gone to Dover to supervise the shooting of a GPO Film Unit production titled *The Front Line.*[36] He had been there with his cameraman Jonah Jones while the Dunkirk evacuation was taking place, but permission had been refused for them to cross the Channel.[37] Now that segment of Kent had become popularly known as "Hellfire Corner." The town could be reached by long-range guns from the French side and suffered heavy bombardment, which demolished the buildings along the sea front and many of those further inland. Shipping in the Straits was under air attack, and the whole area was also a grandstand for the Battle of Britain overhead, with barrage balloons frequently being shot down and aircraft falling into the sea and into the fields beyond the cliffs. A well-known impromptu BBC radio commentary by Charles Gardner, in which he gave a vivid account of the dogfights in the skies, had gone out in mid-July.[38] Watt's film was completed by mid-September, and the opening titles announce that Dover has been a frontier town for three months. The actuality shots were intercut with statements by the mayor of Dover and other citizens, all emphasizing how high morale is in the town in spite of the shelling. Hop pickers are still working in the fields amid the wreckage of the destroyed planes. "The Battle of Britain is being won, won by the spirit of the people." Indeed, the Luftwaffe had withdrawn its major daytime effort by the time the film was released.

Another contribution to the MOI's short-film program was being made, with their own company, by the Boulting brothers, who, after *Pastor Hall,* had been waiting for their call-up to the armed services. *Dawn Guard,* which was finally released in January 1941, is an unusual film for that period because it was not content only to emphasize the need to stand up to Hitler, but also took a reformist view of the social outlook for postwar Britain.[39] Its medium of achieving this, in the form of a dialogue between two Home Guards standing by a country windmill, may appear to be somewhat halting. One of them was played by Bernard Miles, who participated with the writer Anna Reiner in the planning of the film. According to Roy Boulting's account, the MOI's Films Division knew nothing of the content of the film until it was previewed. He also recalled that its official reception was cool, the only MOI officer to make brief favorable comment being John Betjeman, although the left-wing aspirations of the script surely sound too mild for serious objection.[40] (Nevertheless, a Realist Film Unit production, directed by John Taylor, *Goodbye Yesterday,* which had a similar message, was more actively opposed. No prints of it seem to have survived).[41]

The argument of *Dawn Guard* fell into two parts. The Home Guards discuss the Nazi menace, one of them (played by Percy Walsh) talking about the ordinary British countryman's life, ploughing, sowing, reaping, playing darts in the evening, his words backed up by complementary shots of the English countryside. The other guard (Bernard Miles) intervenes to say that stopping the Nazis is not enough, they must think about everyone getting together in peacetime. "When it's all over, we've got to make a fine big peace effort, no two ways about it." No one had been unemployed at Dunkirk. The film cuts to images of the urban slums. There must be "no more dirty, filthy back streets and no more half starved kids with no room to play," exactly the kind of sentiments which a film like *The New Britain* had evaded. Unfortunately *Dawn Guard's* social propaganda was self-defeating because the idyllic view of rural Britain once more came out as an overworn cliché, and the impersonation of the Home Guards itself became a parody of hierarchical village society, as one may judge from a couple of snatches of dialogue—

Miles: "I reckon schoolmaster were right about them Nazis. He reckoned they were a sewage burst right over Europe." Walsh talking about Hitler interfering with the British countryman's way of life: "Heaven knows why, it's beyond me. I asked parson but he ain't none too clear neither."

Bernard Miles was to be seen as a Home Guard

The Front Line. The Lord Mayor of Dover, representative of the stalwart citizens of Britain as their homes are bombarded.

Dawn Guard. Members of the citizens' army stay vigilant, but also find time to discuss the needs of a postwar world (Percy Walsh and Bernard Miles).

again, in a Strand film produced by Donald Taylor that dealt with the training of this volunteer force. The original title was *Home Guard,* but a slightly longer version, distributed overseas, was also issued in 1941 as *Citizen's Army,* with a different commentary.[42] Although never called into action, the Home Guard made itself useful throughout the war by relieving soldiers of routine duties like mounting sentries in security areas. George Formby also put on the uniform of the volunteers for a comedy called *Get Cracking,* released in 1943, in which, with the help of his girlfriend, played by Dinah Sheridan, he builds a primitive "tank" in order to gain victory over a unit from a rival village.

The German decision to switch the main weight of their bombing to London took the RAF by surprise on 7 September 1940. The raids started in late afternoon, continuing into the night, and the military objective was dockland on both sides of the river east of the City. In these areas the homes of the workers were closely packed together, near the fringes of the docks and warehouses themselves, and the initial assault fell on them like a thunderclap. Huge fires sprang up, visible for many miles beyond the capital. From stricken Silvertown hundreds fled on the ferry across to Woolwich, where the Arsenal itself had been damaged. Other families moved out to Epping Forest. It was the day when the possibility of universal panic, so often predicted in apocalyptic terms, seemed to be on the point of being realized. Firemen, four-fifths of them auxiliaries for whom this was their first operational experience, struggled for forty hours or more without respite to contain the blaze. Wardens worked throughout the night to move the homeless to prepared rest centers. But nowhere could the emergency services cope with the scale of the disaster. The events of that first calamitous raid have been vividly described, especially as they affected Bermondsey and West Ham, in *The Blitz* by Constantine Fitzgibbon. "Blitz" was an adaptation of blitzkrieg and it became a lasting title for that period of the mass bombing of London and other British cities during the autumn and winter of 1940–41.

A week later the Battle of Britain had turned in the RAF's favor, and the Luftwaffe casualties had been so high that the emphasis was turned now to bombing by night. And it was to cover the whole of London, no longer to concentrate on military objectives. The era of terror bombing had begun in earnest, just as the invasion had been given up. However, most of the bombs fell into open spaces or streets in the metropolitan area, and, though the effects of those that did find targets were terrible enough, they were not so devastating that a serious breakdown was ever threatened again. Perhaps the most famous raid of the winter was the one at the end of December that set ablaze considerable stretches of the older buildings in the City, an episode extensively filmed by the Fire Service for permanent record. Public morale was boosted by the sound of the antiaircraft barrage, even if the guns scored few actual successes, and people in general were able to face the nightly clangor with more stoicism. A small part of the population, those that could afford to do so, had moved out to the country. Of those who stayed, a minority slept in the tube stations, some in "Anderson" shelters sunk into their gardens, others under their stairs, while many just carried on regardless and trusted to luck. The bombing of London has attracted the greatest amount of attention (apart from the single raid which laid Coventry waste), but from November many other cities in Britain also went through their own ordeals until the Nazi effort began to slacken in the spring of 1941. Some forty thousand civilians had been killed and over a million homes damaged.[43]

The most celebrated photograph of the blitz showed the dome of St Paul's rising above the pall of smoke from the burning City in the December fire raid. The survival of St Paul's became the symbol of London's ability to defy the bombers, and it was the cathedral which was used in the opening shots of the GPO Film Unit's *London Can Take It,* first a medium shot with the film's title over it, then a long shot with St Paul's in the distance.[44] It had been intended to send a newsreel compilation to America to present a view of calm and spirited resistance, until Harry Watt intervened with the MOI to have the film made by himself and Humphrey Jennings, with Stewart McAllister as editor.[45] *London Can Take It* was the American title, but a shorter version released at home was called *Britain Can Take It,* a label more likely to placate the feelings of those in the nation who were also under fire and might consider with some justification that only London was being featured in the national press.

The commentary on *London Can Take It* was spoken by the American journalist Quentin Reynolds, who, in Watt's account, had to be persuaded by the sound recordist Ken Cameron to modify his booming tones by sitting down and talking quietly into a microphone. The result is distinctive and unforgettable. The film was made very quickly, to Watt's treatment, with much of the material being shot on the streets by Jennings, but it achieves its impact through the precision of McAllister's editing in synch with Reynolds's words.

The citizens of London, seen queuing at bus stops, go home from their daily work and change into the uniforms of their voluntary services. Dusk falls—"This has been a quiet day for us but it won't be a quiet night. We haven't had a quiet night now for more than five weeks." People move into the shelters as the guns and searchlights prepare for action. As the raid starts, the film cuts between roof shots, searchlights, guns firing, shelter signs, bomb explosions, darts players carrying on, people asleep in the shelters and back to the guns again. "These are not Hollywood sound effects. This is the music they play every night in London, the symphony of war." Fires are tackled by the "people's army." With dawn the raiders, "creatures of the night," pass away. The daylight also reveals the damaged buildings, but people are continuing with their lives as normally as possible, a woman gazing out of a broken window, another retrieving a milk bottle from her doorstep, office workers riding on a horse-drawn cart, shop assistants sweeping out broken glass from the store windows. Shots of the King and Queen visiting bombed areas demonstrate the solidarity of British society at this time of suffering. "They would rather stand up and face death than kneel down and face the kind of existence the conqueror would impose upon them." To sequences of clearing up the rubble Reynolds says that he has seen no panic and no fear in London. The RAF is striking back with its own bombers. Although the raids will continue and will destroy buildings and kill people, they "cannot kill the unconquerable spirit and courage of the people of London. London can take it." These closing words accompany shots of streets, a cab driver lighting a warden's cigarette, a broken window at the Houses of Parliament and the statue there of Richard the Lionheart with uplifted sword.

London Can Take It has become one of the most famous of British war documentaries because it seems to capture a public mood at the right time. However, it should not be forgotten that in its original form it was designed for American consumption, as part of the campaign to awaken people across the Atlantic to the threat from Nazi Germany. In the United States,

***London Can Take It*. Aftermath of the blitz. A woman looks out of her broken window.**

the documentaries to date had made little impact, some like *Squadron 992* and *Men of the Lightship* probably arriving too late, when they had lost their relevance.[46] *London Can Take It,* at least, seems to have been a limited success. It appeared as if Quentin Reynolds were making his own genuine report, instead of presenting the picture of the heroism of the British people that they themselves wanted to put across to the world. The version distributed at home, *Britain Can Take It,* cut out very little of the script, and it was concise enough to appeal to the average audience.

Reynolds continued in London as an active broadcaster, and he was used again by Harry Watt for a second film, *Christmas under Fire.*[47] He is seen at the beginning sitting at a table, on the point, he says, of leaving for New York to take with him this "film dispatch" of London at Christmas 1940. It tried to reach traditional American sentiment by showing how there would be no normal Christmas this year, no room in the shelters for Christmas trees, families separated because husbands and fathers were in the services, presents in short supply. "There is no reason for America to feel sorry for England this Christmas. England doesn't feel sorry for herself. Destiny gave her the torch of liberty to hold and she has not dropped it." Carols are being sung on Christmas Eve by the choir of King's College Cambridge, and the film cuts from their chapel to the tube shelterers settling down for the night.

It is interesting to contrast the cogent relationship of voice and image in *London Can Take It* with their less successful marriage in another GPO/Crown Film Unit production, *The Heart of Britain,* made no doubt to redress the balance of film coverage in favor of London by showing something now of the comparable determination of the people of the north and midlands of England.[48] Here Humphrey Jennings took the sole credit as director, with McAllister editing. The film's title is superimposed on an image of a rock face, to symbolize the solidarity and durability of northern character (to the accompaniment of emphatic Elgar strings). Shots of moorland are succeeded by views of cathedrals—Durham, Liverpool, and Coventry—and then it is "black Sheffield," with a steel worker talking to the camera about coming off his shift and going home to take up his warden's duties. In Lancashire fire watchers stand on the roofs of cotton mills, rescue squads train in a Liverpool school playground, and mill girls are seen going to their shelters. But in Manchester they still "respect the genius of Germany," and Malcolm Sargent and the Hallé Orchestra start Beethoven's Fifth Symphony. The opening "fate knocking at the door" motive of this work coincided with the morse taps of the V (Victory) signal, and it was to be used to introduce the BBC's transmissions to occupied Europe. The lofty sounds of the Fifth Symphony had been heard also in the prewar documentaries *Industrial Britain* and *BBC: The Voice of Britain,* and as a single work it almost came to embody the cultural elitism which the filmmakers of this school found it difficult to disguise in spite of their left-wing sympathies.

As the music is being played, the camera pans across scenes of severe and widespread bomb damage. Eventually we are told it is Coventry. The bombing of this city on 14 November had been a heavily concentrated attack, lasting ten hours. Having previously shot the cathedral for the opening sequence, the crew returned to film the effects of the raid, and Jennings altered the structure of the documentary to accommodate this new material.[49] The city center, including the historic cathedral, had been wiped out, and elsewhere destruction also had been considerable. The immediate impact on morale was shattering, but it was an isolated incident and soon Coventry struggled to life again. Battered though they had been, even the vital aircraft factories recovered production. It was a foretaste of the kind of massive bombing later to be inflicted on Germany, and its failure to cause a lasting collapse could have been a lesson that those who advocated terror bombing to the end might have heeded but chose not to.

In the films with Quentin Reynolds, the easy style of his transatlantic delivery had come across well, even to the British public, used as they were to the broad appeal of the Hollywood film. The commentary for *The Heart of Britain* was written and narrated by Crown's senior producer Jack Holmes, whose upper-middle-class voice sounds incongruous for a film about northern England. The inappropriateness of it strikes one especially when he speaks of the mill girls as "Lancashire lassies," or when he throws in the expression "mates" to describe the workers. From Coventry, and a brief statement by a voluntary worker, the film cuts away to the Huddersfield Choral Society in Handel's *Messiah,* women choristers respectfully wearing hats, all standing to proclaim their unanimity in the uplifting sounds of the Hallelujah Chorus. The final section has RAF bombers leaving for the counterattack, the nation "striking back," and the narrator's pronunciation of "back" rings out with strident Oxbridge clarity (an American version, though, called *This Is England,* had Ed Murrow as narrator).

There has been some debate about whether the sense of national unity that these films project was a true representation of the real situation. Contemporary accounts refute suggestions that class-con-

***Neighbours Under Fire*. Bombed-out women and children wait at a rest center in a dockside London borough.**

sciousness disappeared totally in the face of universal danger. There were reported instances of refugees from the East End receiving grudging treatment at the hands of some of the middle-class occupants of areas to which they had moved. It would be surprising if there had not been considerable discord in a country that, though geographically small, was the home of pronounced cultural differences between its inhabitants and its regions and that anyway had inherited a class structure which the educational system served to perpetuate. On the other hand, it is too cynical a view to lean completely to the other extreme in reaction against the mood of these blitz films. People of all classes undoubtedly did come together and work unsparingly beside each other in the voluntary services. For a time there was certainly a national will to survive that compelled the British to help each other, even if that sense of joint purpose was to rapidly vanish.[50]

In retrospect of course, a scene like the one in Strand's *Neighbours Under Fire* where a jolly rector in a tin hat gets the bombed-out people of Bermondsey to sing the "Old Bull and Bush" is bound now to arouse scepticism, especially when such a preponderately nonreligious community joins him in prayer afterwards.[51] The film was directed by the committed socialist Ralph Bond, and, as well as explaining how improvization was needed to cope with the problems of the homeless, it was intended to demonstrate the feeling of togetherness experienced by those who lived in a dockland borough of this kind. Another film by Bond, *Post 23,* showed air-raid wardens at their duties and developed the theme of their post becoming "more and more a community center." Among those whose civilian jobs are cited are a bus conductor, a clerk, an architect, and a stockbroker, and, in spite of this balance in favour of the middle classes, the expectations of the film sound more convincing than those put forward by *Dawn Guard.* Between clearing bomb damage and taking out the injured, the wardens discuss how for the first time they have come to know almost everyone in a neighborhood where the raids have destroyed many of the old slum dwellings. "That's just the point. We've got to see that the job's done decently this time." If they can work together with this sense of responsibility in wartime, they must be able to clear up the mess in peacetime. The narrator (John Longden, playing a warden) sums up. "The qualities we've learned from comradeship and common suffering are not going to be wasted after this war. It's out of experience like ours that the new world will be built." This theme of anticipating a better postwar era became more common in a number of the films made in subsequent years, and to some extent it was encouraged by the MOI, which gradually responded to the swing in favor of social reform that was being experienced by the public.

The longer film that many would regard as the definitive record of the blitz, *Fires Were Started,* was not completed until 1943, but already by 1941 there had emerged a conscious awareness that it was the official filmmaker's duty to photograph the events of that trying winter for posterity, as one may witness by reading the caption addressed "to the future historian" at the beginning of the Crown Film Unit's *Ordinary People.*[52] This film, directed by Jack Holmes (assisted by Jack Lee), was only distributed abroad. Again the cinematography of Jonah Jones is an outstanding feature, notably in the opening sequence of mud flats and the river at dawn, moving to the Tower of London where the gates are being opened and the flag run up. The morning begins with people coming out of the shelters, mobile canteens serving tea to girls with head scarves, taxi drivers starting work. A number of parallel stories are developed through a single day. A man in a bowler hat goes to a registrars' court, where he puts on the wig of a judge. During the hearing of a case the alert sounds and the court moves down to the basement. A factory worker leaves his home, which has lost its windows, and his wife takes in a neighboring family whose house has been destroyed. At the Bourne and Hollingsworth store, shoppers and assistants go downstairs until the "all clear" sounds. Two GPO workers put on their tin hats

Post 23. **Civil Defence workers at their station, two wardens and a telephonist. A wall poster illustrates the fear of a gas attack.**

as they work down in a hole in the road. As night falls an off-duty cab driver offers his vehicle to a friend who has been unable to get his own taxi out. The factory worker finds the other family still at his home, and, when the siren sounds again, they all move to the shelters where they are joined by others, including the cab driver and a parson. The bombing starts, and everyone joins in together with "South of the border, down Mexico way," one of the most popular songs since the summer of 1939. The overall impression created is of calm, composure, friendliness, and cooperation.

None of these films, understandably for the time they were made, says anything about the muddles and inefficiencies of the days of blitz, the unpreparedness and petty squabbling of some of the local authorities, or the inadequacies of the shelter policy. Original estimates had expected much greater casualties, and they had not forecast homeless uninjured people flooding the rest centers. They had not expected bombing by night, continuing for week after week. Many of the places where the people of the East End sheltered were sordid and disagreeable. There were few gardens where the public could have used Anderson shelters, which had to be dug three feet into the ground with a corrugated iron roof, and the communal brick shelters proved to be fragile and comfortless. There can be no question that some of the population in these working-class areas felt deprived and resentful. Even in the City precautions turned out to be lacking, as the great fire raid at the end of December was to prove, through inexcusable failure to provide sufficient manpower to safeguard empty buildings over the weekend. The regional cities had comparable difficulties. Gradually the situation looked up as the lessons were learned. The "Morrison" shelter was introduced, actually only a portable tiny structure with a steel top and wire-mesh sides in which people could lie down in their own homes. However, many of the benefits of these improvements came too late for the initial blitz.[53]

It might seem, therefore, that some propaganda was wasted on trivialities or even misconceptions. The blackout campaign appears to have produced a fear that showing the most insignificant amount of illumination would instantly bring a bomb directly down on oneself and, this must have been the assumption behind the 20th Century-Fox short *Mr. Proudfoot Shows a Light.* Here a glimmer of light revealed for a moment by a jovial but careless local worthy causes a Nazi plane both to drop an incidental bomb close to his home and to find its main target town, though it hits the hospital there rather than the intended munitions factory. Scripted by Sidney

Mr. Proudfoot Shows a Light. **He pays the penalty as his carelessness causes a bomb to fall close to his home.**

Gilliat, this contribution to the MOI program looks now as silly as the commercial industry's earlier careless-talk films.

It is unfortunate also that, because the film units and their studios were located near London, the documentaries concentrated on the capital, although the newsreels gave more generous coverage of events elsewhere. It is true that London was the most heavily bombed, with two particularly sharp raids in March 1941 to follow a slack period and then the worst of all, in casualties, on 10 May. But Clydebank was virtually destroyed on a couple of nights in March, Plymouth ferociously battered the same month, Merseyside pounded for a week in May, and few urban concentrations throughout Britain escaped some of the havoc, which extended as far as Belfast. These final attacks of the blitz in the spring preceded the German invasion of the USSR, when the bulk of their bomber force was moved eastwards. Even if civilian morale at times had been threatened, the British had refused to back out of the war.

There were considerable movements of people during the bombing, including the phenomenon of "trekking" from some of the regional cities, when thousands marched off into the country, taking some of their belongings with them. Evacuation was restarted, more than a million of all ages being moved away from their homes during the winter blitz, although many returned again after the raids had ceased. An earlier evacuation of children, better organized than the first wave, had been examined in Thorold Dickinson's film *Westward Ho!,* issued in the summer of 1940. It had ended with warnings by mothers from occupied countries about the need to safeguard children in this way. Realist's *Living with Strangers,* directed by Frank Sainsbury, looked at the difficulties experienced by billeting officers in accommodating both parents and children from bombed areas, and it recognized the tension between host and evacuee as they try to cope with each other under the same roof.[54]

The MOI's five-minute program produced films on a great number of topics, many of them purely instructional in nature. In fact the ministry had taken the decision to move away from exhortation, which might be counterproductive if overdone, toward the provision of information for the public. Brief trailers with the same purpose were also added to the newsreels. The period 1940–41 featured subjects that concerned immediate emergencies, like how to deal with incendiary bombs or how to administer first aid. There was a great deal of concentration, as the rationing situation grew worse, on how to use available resources for food and how to make recipes economically, one of the most graphically descriptive of these being the Realist film *When the Pie Was Opened,* directed by Len Lye, an animator of distinction, who here used a number of inventive visual and aural effects to demonstrate the making of a vegetable pie.[55] Recipe programs are a familiar part of modern television programming, but films of this type were something of a novelty in the forties. In cooperation with the Royal Horticultural Society, a series of six films was devised to show people how to develop allotments. In similar fashion, advice was given through the screen on how to maintain standards of health.

Other documentaries distributed by the MOI concentrated attention on the activities of the people as they were mobilized for war. *Night Watch,* a Strand film produced and directed by Donald Taylor, gave an impression of the constant night-long vigilance of wardens, firemen, and policemen by showing them accidentally preventing a soldier on leave and his girlfriend from spending some private time together out of doors (meeting indoors was perhaps too immoral a situation for the film censors of the time).[56] Realist's *They Also Serve* highlighted the role of women left at home by absent husbands and evacuated children. This film was the last directed by Ruby Grierson, who died when the liner *City of Benares,* taking children to Canada, was torpedoed by a U-boat. Women were also the main subject of *Village School,* a Strand film directed by John Eldridge, in which teachers deal with the influx of evacuees joining local children. Shell made *Transfer of Skill,* produced by Arthur Elton and directed by Geoffrey Bell, to pay tribute to skilled craftsmen who were changing their occupations: the watchmaker now producing fuses, the fishing rod maker turning to machine-gun parts, a fisherman creating nets for camouflage, and so forth. Wilfred Pickles, soon to become the first BBC newsreader with a northern accent, narrated the Cooperative Society's film *Machines and Men,* an account of four Yorkshire engineers repairing a corroded American machine unfamiliar to them, with no blueprints to guide them.[57] The operations of the fighting services were also recognized, as in Shell's *Ack-Ack,* produced by Edgar Anstey with Peter Baylis directing, where the manning and firing of an antiaircraft gun was explained, partially in diagrammatic form.[58] A few films took a story line; of these Verity's *Shunter Black's Night Off,* directed by Maxwell Munden, was a good example, a dramatization about a railway shunter who returns to his yard during a raid in order to help his colleagues. Finding that a blaze has spread to an ammunition truck, he manages to have it towed away to a place of safety where the fire can be extinguished. This is only a selection of titles from a wide-ranging area. The appeal of these films for a popular audience may be disputed, but most of them have gained retrospectively in historical interest.

It is possible indeed that many people except the most sophisticated were lost by the Crown Film Unit's *Words for Battle,* a short film which stands outside the categories mentioned above.[59] It is very much a personal statement by its director Humphrey Jennings, the first of his war films to have a totally distinctive identity; but the combination of literary quotations, Laurence Olivier's rhetoric, and the symbolism of the images worked out with the editor Stewart McAllister puts some strain on the coherence of the argument. Apparently it had been intended originally that the title would be *In England Now,* and it would be balanced by a second production called *In Germany Now,* which would place the humanitarian words of German writers against clips from the Nazi propaganda films, but the total project was not completed. The theme, reinforced by lines from the Elizabethan chronicler Camden, and from Milton, Blake, and Browning, is again the unity and determination of England, the clamorous horn calls of Handel's Water

Village School. Schoolmistress behind her desk. Evacuation of children from the cities put a heavy burden on the lives of villagers.

Shunter Black's Night Off. He is called back to his railway yard as bombs set an ammunition truck on fire.

Music giving further weight. Blitz damage is seen to Kipling's words, "It was not part of their blood . . . When the English began to hate." Olivier repeats part of Churchill's "Fighting on the Beaches" speech, and the final extract is from Lincoln's Gettysburg address, a direct appeal to American audiences. Another short film, *An Airman's Letter to His Mother,* had John Gielgud reading the genuine testament of a killed pilot. Its mood was one of high patriotism, and it was produced by Michael Powell after the letter itself had been published in *The Times.*[60]

Outright hard-line propaganda against fascism was missing from all of these films, and more often mockery came to be employed as a weapon, as in the brief film *Germany Calling,* put out through the newsreel companies. Here Charles Ridley used rapid jump cuts to have Hitler and his stormtroopers (in footage taken from Leni Riefenstahl's *Triumph des Willens*) perform antics to the tune of the popular cockney song "Doing the Lambeth Walk." The title had an immediate association for British people because William Joyce ("Lord Haw-Haw") used these words to introduce his English language broadcasts from Berlin that had been heard by many radio listeners in Britain at some time or other. After leaving the GPO Film Unit, Cavalcanti moved to Ealing and produced *Yellow Caesar,* a four-reel mixture of newsreel and staged sequences on the life of Mussolini, linked by a derisory script and commentary that trotted out a number of jokes about Italians (making use of the barrel organ stereotype, for example) while taking the line that they were reluctant followers of the dictator. The script is credited to Frank Owen and Michael Foot, journalists with left-wing views who worked at that time for the *Evening Standard,* part of the Beaverbrook empire. Foot was to be the author (under the pseudonym "Cassius") of *The Trial of Mussolini,* a condemnation of the activities of the fascist leader. Mussolini was a soft target, with so much of the footage of his speaking or acting in public lending itself easily to parody, and the retreat of his army in Libya made up the conclusion of *Yellow Caesar* when it was issued in 1941.

It is unsurprising that the British public, having withstood the blitz, demanded more action from the armed forces. The navy was struggling hard in the Atlantic, and the Italians were being engaged in Africa, but the only instrument available for striking directly at Germany was Bomber Command of the RAF. Churchill was well aware of the propaganda value of retaliation for the raids on Britain. A bombing policy had always been in prospect, in spite of initial reluctance to cause civilian casualties, and the groundwork had been completed that would produce in 1942 a fleet of four-engined aircraft. Specific objectives had been marked out, with oil installations at the top of the list, but the absence of long-range fighter protection compelled the British to follow German practice and to send out the bombers to find their targets by night. In spite of the obvious difficulty of doing this accurately, an intelligence report of December 1940 gave a most misleading impression of the RAF's rate of success, suggesting that Germany's oil resources already had been heavily damaged. Killing a few civilians on the fringes of industrial areas seemed to be a small price to pay in terms of morality, especially as the Nazis were bringing terror bombing to Britain, and, before the end of 1940, it had also been acknowledged that, in cases where specific targets could not be reached, it was permissible to widen the area of the attacks. The pressure was kept up, with the limited resources the RAF possessed at that time, until appeals from the navy in the spring of 1941 diverted the bombing offensive to the French Atlantic-coast ports, sheltering not only U-boats but also the dangerous battleships *Scharnhorst* and *Gneisenau.*[61]

It was in this context that the film *Target for Tonight* was first planned towards the end of 1940 and finally released in the summer of 1941.[62] Harry Watt directed for the Crown Film Unit, and his main collaborators again were Stewart McAllister and Jonah Jones. The RAF gave full cooperation and allowed some location shooting at Mildenhall airfield, the base for a unit of twin-engined Wellington bombers, at the time the most effective aircraft flown by Bomber Command. An aircrew of six, led by Squadron Leader Pickard, was released to work with Watt at the studios outside London, and a new Wellington fuselage was sent round there to be used for intimate shots inside the plane. Although much of *Target for Tonight* was created in the studio, one of the film's chief attributes is its simulation of reality. Only the shots of bombs actually hitting their objectives look contrived.

The story, scripted by Watt himself, had the utmost simplicity. It starts at Bomber Command headquarters, positioned near High Wycombe though this location, naturally enough, was not named in the film, just as Mildenhall was given the pseudonym Millington. Reconnaissance photographs reveal the growth of an oil installation at Freihausen in the Ruhr. The main control room had been reconstructed by Watt with rather more bombing groups listed on the wall than the RAF had in 1941. The commander-in-chief Sir Richard Peirse is seen in person giving out instructions for a maximum-effort attack. One group is asked to divert a squadron to Freihausen. At Millington the station commander

***Target for Tonight.* Briefing the bomber crews for a night raid on Germany, squadron commander standing, station commander sitting right.**

calls for maps and photographs from the intelligence officer, and the ground staff receive their instructions for loading bombs onto the aircraft.

The afternoon briefing is led by the squadron commander, and a change of personnel enables the crew of Wellington F for Freddie to be identified for the camera—the pilot, second pilot, navigator/bomb aimer (the RAF equivalent of bombardier in the USAAF), wireless operator, and two gunners. At this event we witness for the first time the class-based apartheid that was still the rule in the RAF. All noncommissioned aircrew, many of them less than twenty years of age, were automatically given the rank of sergeant. The pilot was captain of the aircraft, and many of these were sergeants, taking on the kind of role originally expected of officers. However, the rank of officer still tended to be reserved for those with public school or university background. Consequently all officers, pilots or not, shared one mess with its own special privileges, and the noncommissioned officers, including sergeant pilots, went to another. Nevertheless, there grew up a genuine comradeship between these men when a plane was airborne. Their dependence on each other for their lives was higher than in any other unit of the armed services.

After the briefing, ending with the station commander's summing up, the crews put on their flying gear and are carried out by lorry to the bombers, to be directed as they take off in the gathering darkness by the squadron commander from his control van. The shots of F for Freddie in flight through cloud are unpretentiously conceived but photographically appropriate to the sober style of the film. Stirring music by Leighton Lucas, played by the RAF Central Band, accompanies the plane as it approaches Germany. The ground appears dimly, ribbonlike waterways shining in silhouette behind a foreground shot of one of the Wellington's engines. Searchlights probe for the raiders, and now Watt slightly shifts the film's point of view with a ground shot of German anti-aircraft gunners opening fire. Planes could maneuver to avoid the flak, which became deadlier in time as guidance techniques improved, but the truly nerve-racking moments for a bomber crew were during the actual run up to the target, when the aircraft had to be held absolutely steady so that the bomb aimer in the nose could direct the pilot to the correct point for releasing the bombs. The film shows bombs falling onto railway sidings and starting a huge fire amid the oil tanks.

The return trip is treated equally unsensationally, with none of the drama one would expect in a commercial feature film. The plane is hit, with injury to the wireless operator, and communication is lost with base. Although one engine is failing, the pilot decides to press on to Millington in spite of heavy fog developing over the English coast ("That, gentlemen, is good old England and I must say I'm damned glad to see it"). Out of doors the station and squadron commanders listen anxiously for the sound of F for Freddie, the only plane yet left to return. Finally the flare path is lit for the landing. An ambulance is summoned for the wounded wireless operator. At the debriefing the second pilot says that their last bomb "caused a hell of a great big fire, buckets of smoke." The unemotional tone is kept to the end. The interrogating officer finishes with, "That seems to be all. Good show. Good night." After reporting by phone to group intelligence he stretches, yawns, says, "Well, old boy, how about some bacon and eggs?" The target fire shot is recapitulated, and the film ends with F for Freddie seen motionless on the ground in the morning mists.

Target for Tonight received an enormous amount of publicity. It had grown from an original Air Ministry concept as a two-reel film to one of fifty minutes in length. One consequence of the blitz had been the shortening of programs so that somewhat longer documentaries than the five-minute type were becoming more acceptable again, alongside of the main feature. The independent distributors who had handled most of the earlier MOI films were disappointed when *Target for Tonight,* intended to reach the maximum audience, was released exclusively on commercial terms to Gaumont British. It was put out as if it were meant to be a West End and national success, and at some cinemas it became the principal feature of the program. The *Daily Express* serialized the story of the film, and also issued it as a separate booklet. Following the Battle of Britain, it appeared to give yet another boost to the reputation of the RAF.

Leonard England, stationed at an army ordnance camp, reported for Mass-Observation—"*Target for Tonight* was probably more looked forward to in Donnington Depot than any other film that has been in Wellington in the last six months. The Depot is not film conscious but a very large percentage, 50 or 60 percent, wanted to see this. When it came to Wellington, it was shown at two out of the three local cinemas in the same week, once as the main feature film, once as a supplementary to Deanna Durbin in *Nice Girl?* Both were more extensively advertised than most films. The film was a complete failure, nine out of every ten people came back disappointed, and actual audience reaction was poor. . . . A documentary was billed twice as vigorously as a normal feature. . . . It just could not stand this weight, plus superb criticism in the papers, plus leading articles. Constant comment took the line of "I was disappointed," "not as good as I had hoped," etc. The blitz scenes, flak from the air, were thought to look unreal, while there was not sufficient action in it for most people."[63]

There was also unfavorable comment in the report on some of the "Oxford" accents. This is perhaps unfair because, although Pickard and his copilot were both officers, their accents do not seem now to be too intrusive, and the rest of the aircrew came from different backgrounds, one of them a Scotsman, while the station commander's voice had a noticeably northern inflexion. The film's original treatment, as written down by Harry Watt, indicates that it was intended to show the RAF as being broadly representative of different classes, regions, and even countries (there is a Canadian officer, for instance). Probably the stricture was directed mostly at the squadron commander, whose upper-class tones were heard at length in the briefing and the take-off sequences, but the fact that it was raised at all says something about the amount of class hostility present in the services.

A single report is too flimsy a piece of evidence on which to gauge general reactions to *Target for Tonight.* The popular press was unlikely to have been completely wrong about the potential appeal of such a film, and it had unusual success in America where demand grew for nontheatrical distribution of it. Nevertheless, the points made by England are considered ones and suggest at least the possibility that the film was oversold so that the public went in expectation of seeing a production with the dramatic appeal of a feature film. At a fairly gloomy period in the war, people would be looking for a means of giving a fillip to their national self-confidence, and some might have felt let down by the starkness of the documentary approach, just as others were impressed by it. The observation about the unreality of the bombing sequence is especially interesting, and one regrets that Leonard England was not able to pursue this question further, to find out if the soldiers actually believed the RAF could operate with such precision. The clear implication of *Target for Tonight* was that they could do so and with minimal casualties.

It must have been a considerable surprise to Churchill to receive, in the same month as this film was being shown, a report initiated by his scientific advisor Lord Cherwell, who had been sceptical for some time about Bomber Command's claims. It was known already that a third of crews did not reach their target area. The report now made out that of the remainder only one-third had dropped their bombs within five miles of their objectives, and in the industrial Ruhr the proportion fell to a tenth. It was doubtful if Germany's industrial capacity had even been faintly diminished. Clearly the bombing offensive to date had been a total failure. With the navy hard pressed at sea and the army needing cover from the air in its North African campaign, the pretensions of the most enthusiastic of the bombing lobby, that they could win the war on their own, might now have been challenged. But during the winter of 1941–42, the RAF was to develop another doctrine, that if the smallest area which they could be sure of hitting by night was a whole town then that should be the target. Blanket area bombing would simultaneously cripple German industry and destroy the people's will to fight.[64]

The RAF formed its own Film Unit in July 1941. Before that date another extended flying film, *Ferry Pilot,* had been turned out by the Crown Film Unit, although its subject this time was the civilian group named the Air Transport Auxiliary, which was responsible for taking finished planes from factories to operational airfields.[65] Its director, Pat Jackson, had made only one previous wartime film, *Health in War,* distributed nontheatrically, basically an account of the preparations made by hospitals for coping with emergencies, but containing also some more altruistic passages that looked back at prewar advances in medicine and linked them to the need for a more centralized health service.[66] Its commentary had been written by Robert Sinclair. Unfortunately, it fell back on the village cricket match cliché for its images of the continuity of English life. The longer film *Ferry Pilot* contained some outstanding aerial photography by Chick Fowle, including a marvelous sequence of a test pilot putting a Spitfire through its paces. It throws some light on a little-known aspect of war operations. Jackson interpolated a dramatic episode in which a Whitley, being flown to the northeast, is almost caught by German aircraft but is rescued in time by RAF fighters. One of the pilots seen briefly in the film is Jim Mollison, famed for his flying partnership with his wife Amy Johnson, the much-loved pioneer of long-distance solo aviation by women. Both of them, divorced by that time, had joined the ATA and Johnson tragically lost her life over the Thames estuary. Their story became the subject of a feature film, *They Flew Alone* (U.S. title: *Wings and the Woman*), with Anna Neagle and Robert Newton, directed by Herbert Wilcox and released in 1942.

After Dunkirk the army also had been persuaded of the desirability of having its own film unit. Originally only a single cameraman, Harry Rignold, had been sent with an assistant to join the BEF in France.[67] The initiative for expansion came from the War Office's public relations section (PR 2), which had responsibility for advertising army activities, among other duties. It had a military director, but the post of publicity officer was a civilian appointment, held by Ronald Tritton, who in peacetime had performed a somewhat similar function for the Savoy Hotel group. One of his responsibilities was that of liaison with the newsreel men, now and again a difficult task because of the rivalries between them and their dislike of the rota, and also liaison with Jack Beddington and the MOI's Films Division. It was under the PR 2 umbrella that a larger War Office unit was set up in November 1940, although at first it was planned as an adjunct to the Crown Film Unit under Dalrymple's leadership, a proposal never finally carried out. David MacDonald was chosen as its head, selected, as Tritton recalled, for his gift for personal relationships in addition to his filmmaking background.[68] Many of the regular members of the documentary movement were known to be antipathetic to the army and not thought to be suitable for this kind of job, and indeed the experienced personnel who joined the service units were mainly from the commercial industry.

By October 1941 it was appreciated that the work of still photographers and cinematographers should be integrated and, although the title Army Film Unit was to survive independently in certain circumstances, particularly at Pinewood (which its production section shared with its RAF and MOI counterparts), the overall designation of this body was now the Army Film and Photographic Unit (AFPU). Its first duty was the shooting of record film, in time to generate production of a massive amount of original unedited material from the army's main fronts. MacDonald himself took an early hand in this when he and the cameraman Walter Tennyson d'Eyncourt climbed to the top of St Paul's on the night of the great London fire raid and shot film of the City burning.

For its second task, the production of its own documentaries, the AFPU lacked at first the professional skills of the more established filmmaking groups. Hitherto the army had depended for publicity on the other units, even the commercial cinema. One of Cavalcanti's first productions after moving to Ealing had been *Young Veteran,* edited by Charles Crichton, with script again by Frank Owen and Michael Foot. The idea of the raw recruit becoming a seasoned soldier was based on the cartoon character "Young Bert" of the *Daily Express,* whose editor, Arthur Christiansen, appeared briefly in the film. Much of it was a retrospect of war events up to the autumn of 1940. The commentary took flight into rhetoric at the point where the defeat of the Luftwaffe was celebrated (the track quoted Norbert Schultze's music for *Feuertaufe,* Goering's propaganda film about the air assault on Poland), and it confidently predicted an ultimate British military victory in Germany as soon as the right weapons were available. This may have sounded comforting to some, but it is doubtful if any informed people believed it to be possible without American support.

The first of the new Army Film Unit's documentaries was called *Northern Outpost,* and it dealt with the establishment of a British garrison in Iceland. Arctic waters were to be featured again in their next major undertaking, a record of the Lofoten raid, and the problems they experienced here were typical of the birth pains of the new organization. The concept of raiding the enemy-occupied coast of Europe, using a new category of soldiers called "commandos," had been enthusiastically endorsed by Churchill. The army establishment was lukewarm about the idea, but, with the Prime Minister's backing, troops were trained under the control of a Combined Operations Command, designed to coordinate the work of the three services. Buccaneering of this kind appealed to the more individualistic of the British. The men-about-town celebrated in Evelyn Waugh's fiction found a fresh sense of purpose in joining the new units, and the commandos themselves were tough and determined, embodying the new spirit of aggression that had followed the Battle of Britain.

The Lofoten Islands, off the coast of Norway, were the site for a number of fish-oil factories, the products of which supplied vitamins and also glycerine for explosives, all used by the German army. Enemy opposition to the raid in March 1941 was slight. Unfortunately, the army cameramen were wrongly placed to shoot all the material they needed, and Rignold's camera anyway developed a fault that put some of his images out of focus. MacDonald took a 16mm color camera, with stock he had obtained from Technicolor, scarce at that time, and some of it was blown up to 35mm black and white for the documentary that was made afterwards (the original color has survived).[69] Tennyson d'Eyncourt had to go down to Wandsworth to shoot a faked sequence of fuses being lit near oil tanks.[70] It was intended to quickly complete and distribute the short film *Lofoten,* with commentary written by Anthony Kimmins, a prewar film director then in the Admiralty's Press Office. The initiative enraged the newsreel companies, who saw the project as a form of competition.[71] The Crown Film Unit was called in, presumably to speed up the production process, and the editor Robert Verrall has recalled that Humphrey Jennings came along to discreetly direct it, although the film has not elsewhere been attributed to him.[72] Taking account of the limited quality of film available, *Lofoten* was a competent production, which finished with shots of happy Norwegians who had volunteered to join the British standing in a group aboard one of the cross-Channel steamers used as assault ships in the raid. The MOI was so concerned about the lack of action that film of the raid seemed to demonstrate that it issued a note to the newsreel companies suggesting they should present it as an example of how the Germans were incapable of defending the territory they were occupying.[73]

The AFPU began to stand more on its own feet as it recruited new members from the industry. Hugh Stewart, who had worked commercially as a film editor, directed a short piece about women in the army *(ATS).* It may be thought that questions of class and accent are more often commented on retrospectively, and it is instructive therefore to look at the review of it in *Documentary News Letter,* which, while praising the film's technique, doubted if it would do much to attract working-class girls to join the forces. Accents are described as "very ladylike, some of them indeed unbearable," girls are dressed to look like "rather terrifying members of another species," they are all "so invincibly masterful and feminist."[74] The last phrase perhaps reveals the writer's own prejudices about women taking over men's roles.

Combined Operations itself moved ahead with the appointment of Lord Louis Mountbatten to command it. There were more raids and army cameramen went out again to the Norwegian coast, shortly after Christmas 1941, in an operation against Vaagso, where shipping and fish-oil factories were once more the targets. Resistance here was stiffer, but the film record of troops advancing in the snow, buildings burning, and prisoners being brought back was one of the best of the war. Rignold went again, under the supervision now of Roy Boulting, who had just joined the unit at MacDonald's request after going through conventional army training. Harry Watt, not to remain with Crown for much longer, also came on the expedition.[75] In spite of the presence of

British commandos in action on Norwegian soil. From AFPU footage of the Vaagso raid.

two distinguished directors, the only documentary product was a leaden-paced naval instructional film, made by Gaumont British with E. V. H. Emmett narrating.

Of all the service departments, the Admiralty had been the most conservative about filming. The naval authorities preferred on the whole to retain the use of filming for strictly internal purposes like training and instruction, and sequences of ships at sea seen by the public in newsreels had been shot by the companies themselves. However, in 1941 the navy promoted from Paramount a film called *The Gun,* to be distributed in the United States, designed to persuade American opinion that Britain urgently needed more supplies of the Oerlikon antiaircraft gun for the protection of vessels in convoy. Real naval personnel and merchant seamen took part in it, and Ed Murrow of CBS narrated the commentary and was also shown on screen making a visit to the Admiralty during an air raid. G. T. Cummins directed this competent piece.[76] However, no actual record film of the war was shot by naval cameramen until the Normandy invasion of 1944. Finally, at the very end of hostilities, a naval film unit accompanied the British fleet sent to assist the Americans in the last stages of action against Japan.

The government at the beginning of the war had thought it unimaginable that cinemas would be able to remain functioning while cities were being bombed. Declaration of hostilities had led to prompt compulsory closure, continuing for the first part of September 1939, but thereafter the cinemas opened again and went on to welcome the public throughout the real blitz of 1940–41. Attendance grew in Christmas week. Guy Morgan recalled one cinema manager running Hollywood's *Destry Rides Again* as bombs were falling on the capital.[77] In defiant spirit, people still came into his cinema from the street, thinking perhaps that one place of refuge was as likely as any other to be either hit or spared. Sidney Bernstein's Granada chain even allowed its London patrons to stay through the night, seeing a succession of films, a circumstance which was remarked on by Angus Calder in his classic study of the British people at war as an indication that in some senses the cinema had become a kind of community center of the time.[78]

It is not surprising that the public most enjoyed those films which took them as far away as possible from the real perils they had to face that winter, in the cities at least. No doubt British comedies like *Sailors Three,* with Tommy Trinder, or *Gasbags,* with Flanagan and Allen, went some way toward meeting what they wanted. Marcel Varnel, who had directed the latter film, also made for Gainsborough *Neutral Port,* in which a Scottish skipper, played by Will Fyffe, takes his own personal revenge on a U-boat for sinking his ship. Its remoteness from any pretense of coming to grips with the actuality of the war situation was perhaps taken too seriously by its critics, but it was not untypical of the British feature film at that stage of the conflict. Even those productions that attempted a less frivolous approach to the crisis of the nation still continued to show slight appreciation of what would be required for survival and victory.

The Two Cities film *Freedom Radio* (U.S. title: *A Voice in the Night*), directed by Anthony Asquith, was finished a year after *Pastor Hall,* but even at that time it reflected the same kind of hopes for an internal resistance movement in Germany. Clive Brook took the lead as the surgeon Karl Roder, who becomes so convinced of the iniquities of Nazism that he conspires with a young engineer named Hans (Derek Farr) to set up a clandestine broadcasting station. Karl's wife Irene (Diana Wynyard) is a famous actress appointed by Hitler to be Director of Pageantry (almost an analogy with the real-life favors granted to the actress and filmmaker Leni Riefenstahl). Unaware

***Freedom Radio*. The brutal SS are impersonated by two of the most English of screen actors (Raymond Huntley and Bernard Miles).**

at first of the full extent of her husband's opposition activities, she nevertheless condemns his general outlook as treasonable, and the couple are estranged from each other. The climax of the film nears with a rally at Templehof, staged by Irene, at which the resisters are determined to interrupt Hitler's speech. Hans penetrates the stadium and interferes with the cables, getting some unexpected help from an SS man, Dressler (Clifford Evans), who reveals himself as also hostile to the Führer. The loyal SS are played by Raymond Huntley and Bernard Miles, already convinced of the surgeon's guilt. Irene finally becomes converted to Karl's viewpoint when she realizes that his prediction of the Nazi invasion of Poland is correct. They are both trapped in a vehicle from which they are trying to transmit a warning to the German people—"act now or your chances are gone forever. Rise up and make a stand for freedom." As Karl dies, his wife takes up the microphone to say "That was the death of a brave man" just before she too is shot. The SS leader is about to phone Hitler to tell him that Freedom Radio is finished when he hears the voice of Hans announcing that the broadcasts will go on as usual. Although the film was released early in 1941, its basic assumptions still belonged in spirit to the phony-war period.

The same is partly true of *Pimpernel Smith,* produced and directed by its principal star, Leslie Howard.[79] Short MOI documentaries could be made rapidly, newsreels almost instantly, but the longer production schedule of a feature film caused a time lag which made the risk unavoidable that it would have outgrown both subject and attitudes by the time it was finished. This was never more true than over the period between the blitzkrieg and the invasion of the USSR, when the direction of the war changed dramatically. The opening caption of *Pimpernel Smith* seemed to recognize that fact by stating that the film is a fantasy, but based on the "exploits of a number of courageous men who were and still are risking their lives daily to aid those unfortunate people of many nationalities who are being persecuted and exterminated by the Nazis."

If one had to select from the early period of the war a single screen player to sum up the kind of impression that the British establishment had of itself and that it wished to project to the world, it would have to be Leslie Howard. Whether or not that image would have been appropriate for the time beyond the years of gallant resistance against odds will never be known because Howard died in 1943 when Nazi planes shot down an aircraft on which he was returning from Lisbon. Although in fact he was of Hungarian origin, he seemed to be everything one could expect of the ideal cultured, sensitive Englishman with a sense of fair play and decency. He had worked both in London and Hollywood, and his last movie before returning home was none other than the most romantically famous of all time, *Gone with the Wind,* which ran for months on end during the war. In England again, Howard had helped to work out for the MOI an idea for a short film in which he encounters in Trafalgar Square three servicemen from the Commonwealth: an Australian, a New Zealander and a Canadian. They have responded politely to the gushing compliments of an upper-class lady on how they have come of their own free will from the Empire to help the motherland, and Howard tries to redress the balance with what he believes to be his own less patronizing version of what they all are fighting for. Nevertheless, it is still England that is the birthplace of the values they have in common, as he explains in some detail. New Zealand is complimented on bringing English equality to the Maoris, Canada on respecting the rights of French Canadians, and even South Africa is mentioned in the same breath, although its particular internal contribution to the democratic ideal is not specified. Called *From the Four Corners,* it promoted the Leslie Howard persona as the champion of British liberalism but fell on stony ground as a statement of war aims.

The title of *Pimpernel Smith* had been inspired by Baroness Orczy's "Scarlet Pimpernel" story, of which a film made by Korda in 1935 had Howard in the lead and was reissued in 1942. The new film gave Howard an opportunity to portray an absent-minded, kindly university professor taking a group of students on an archaeological dig in prewar Germany, while beneath the facade he is in reality a determined patriot who risks his life helping refugees to escape from the regime. The double role symbolized the outward appearance of British decadence in the appeasement era and their latent resolution below the surface. In that sense the film is a representation of the rallying together of the British after Dunkirk, but in other respects, especially in its depiction of the Germans, it looks back to some of the preconceptions of the earlier period. This is seen most clearly in the playing by Francis L. Sullivan of Smith's opponent, the rotund Goering-like figure of a Nazi minister who imagines that Shakespeare was a German poet. It is misleading to think that all of the early feature films caricatured the Nazis, but General von Graum in *Pimpernel Smith* comes across as a particularly charmless and one-dimensional individual given to uttering sentiments like "Power and strength and violence will rule the world."

The screenplay for *Pimpernel Smith,* written by

Anatole de Grunwald, is barely more credible than that of a George Formby comedy. The Pimpernel rescues his refugees with ease, leaving the Nazis only one clue, a whistled version of "There's a Tavern in the Town," over the identification of which they exercise a great deal of musical scholarship. In order to be near one prison work party, Smith disguises himself as a scarecrow, at which a sentry takes a casual pot shot. Blood is seen trickling down the scarecrow's hand. It is the professor's bandage which causes his students to realize his true identity, and they determine to help him, even managing to obtain admission to a concentration camp by masquerading as American journalists. They release a Polish journalist whose daughter Ludmilla (Mary Morris) is being blackmailed by Graum to search for the Pimpernel.

The archaeological dig proves that there was no early Aryan civilization in the country, that the Germans are just barbarians. The party leaves for the border, and the professor manages to get the refugees through as part of a Thomas Cook's group, while the SS are searching his cases of specimens. He is about to follow with Ludmilla, pausing only to quote Rupert Brooke on England, as the "land where men with splendid hearts may go." However, Graum detains the professor, knowing that he is the man being hunted by him. Previous conversations between the two had been about the nature of English humor, which of course the German cannot comprehend. Now Graum tells Smith that they are about to invade Poland: "We shall make a German empire of the world." The professor retorts that they are taking the first step along a dark road, leaving behind a "wilderness of misery and hatred." They will "find no horizon, see no dawn" until their own destruction. "You are doomed, captain of murderers," Smith says. Graum tries to contrive the shooting of the professor while attempting to escape, but the Englishman slips through the barrier into the haze beyond. "Come back!" "Don't worry—I'll be back. We shall all be back." It is indeed a fantasy, sustained by the charm and wit of Leslie Howard's performance, but its message of standing up to Nazi violence by making the most of decent, English public school qualities was soon to become redundant.

RKO-Radio's *Dangerous Moonlight* (U.S. title: *Suicide Squadron*), directed by Brian Desmond Hurst, appeared in the middle of 1941 and is best remembered for the music of Richard Addinsell, a short piece for piano and orchestra (a postwar reissue prolonged the brief familiarity of this pastiche with the title "Warsaw Concerto" in the style of Rachmaninoff). The supposed composer is Polish musician and flyer Stefan Radetzky (Anton Walbrook), who escapes from his country in 1939. He pursues his career as a pianist in America and marries a wealthy reporter, Carole Peters (Sally Gray), whom he had originally met in Warsaw. However, the progress of the war disturbs his conscience, and after the fall of France he crosses the Atlantic to join the RAF, a decision that causes a break with his wife. A crash brings on amnesia, from which he recovers only when Carole rejoins him. The film was coy about crediting the real pianist Louis Kentner with the playing, as if it meant to keep up the illusion of Walbrook performing the music himself.

The spy theme was still popular in both comedies and serious films. Anthony Asquith's next film, *Cottage to Let* (U.S. title: *Bombsight Stolen*), had Nazis trying to steal the secrets of a revolutionary kind of bomb sight—very topically, it would guarantee absolute pinprick accuracy for the RAF—from an eccentric inventor living in Scotland. Alistair Sim plays a sinister-sounding renter of the cottage, and John Mills appears in the guise of a Battle-of-Britain hero who is convalescing there after bailing out from his plane. Inevitably, Mills turns out to be the head spy, and Sim the British intelligence agent. But the most interesting performance, as an evacuee, comes from the young George Cole in his first film, engaging as ever in a cockney role. Trying to escape at the end, the spy is shot and dies in front of a distorting mirror, one of a number of sequences handled with poise by Asquith. In lighter mood spies were featured again in Walter Forde's *The Ghost Train,* with the popular comedy pair Arthur Askey and Richard Murdoch, and in two films with Will Hay playing schoolmaster parts, *The Ghost of St Michael's* in which he and his evacuated pupils have to cope with the enemy in a "haunted" castle, and *Black Sheep of Whitehall,* where he is mistaken by the BBC for an economics expert, the real person having been temporarily kidnapped by the Nazis. John Mills also starred in the latter production.

Britain's main area of struggle against Germany during the autumn and winter of 1940–41 remained the Battle of the Atlantic. For a period the U-boats had a series of spectacular successes, their so-called "happy time," against which the British with their shortage of escorts seemed to be helpless. In fact the early corvettes, specially built antisubmarine vessels planned before the war, were too slow to catch their enemies on the surface, and this became a crucial factor when the Nazis worked out their wolf pack tactics, concentrating a number of U-boats against a single convoy and often attacking by night without taking the precaution of submerging. The carnage they could cause was convincingly depicted in an early episode from Charles Frend's *The Cruel Sea,* an Ealing film made in 1953, after the popular novel by Nicholas Montsarrat. The film version went well both in Britain and America and attracted praise too for the gritty performance of Jack Hawkins as a naval reserve commander.

German surface raiders also rampaged on the high seas. The *San Demetrio* incident, soon to be re-enacted in a film, came about in November 1940 when a convoy protected only by the armed merchant cruiser *Jervis Bay* was trapped by the *Admiral Scheer.* Most threatening of all, the fast battleships *Scharnhorst* and *Gneisenau* found their way to Brest, on the French Atlantic coast, and the RAF's efforts to damage them there bore little fruit. By the beginning of 1941, Germany had ready for sea the new battleship *Bismarck,* which with her sister ship *Tirpitz,* still under construction, was the most powerful vessel afloat in European waters. Two recently completed British battleships, Admiral Tovey's flagship *King George V* and the *Prince of Wales,* could not completely match them because the British had been more scrupulous about keeping the treaty restrictions on their overall displacement weight. Most of the older British capital ships were holding the line in the Mediterranean, and it was clear to the Admiralty that the possibility of the *Bismarck* joining the other two battleships in harbor at Brest represented the greatest challenge to Britain's command of the seas.

In May 1941 the attempt was made, marked at first by stunning success. The *Bismarck* put to sea in company with the cruiser *Prinz Eugen,* and in the Denmark Strait between Iceland and Greenland they encountered the *Prince of Wales* and the old battlecruiser *Hood,* the biggest ship in the British fleet. In a brief action, plunging fifteen-inch shells from the *Bismarck* penetrated to the *Hood's* magazines and blew her apart. There were three survivors. The ill-fated *Prince of Wales* had gone out so hastily that she had dockyard workers still aboard, and some of her guns failed to function. When her bridge was hit she was forced to withdraw from the battle. Luckily for Britain, an attack by naval aircraft from the carrier *Ark Royal* a couple of days later succeeded in crippling the *Bismarck's* steering gear, and she was caught and battered to extinction by the *King George V* and the older *Rodney.* The *Prinz Eugen* escaped to Brest.[80]

The loss of the *Hood* had been an enormous blow to a people used to the traditional superiority of their navy. Churchill was well able to appreciate the extent of the humiliation, and his urgent command "Sink the *Bismarck!*" to the Admiralty was used as the title of a feature film made in 1960, directed by Lewis Gilbert. Action at sea was shot in the studio, using models, but characterization of the Germans was not so very far advanced on that in *Convoy,* and Kenneth More's role as an operations officer at the Admiralty was embarrassingly filled out with an irrelevant romantic interest, conventionally thought to be more likely to get the attention of the public. A decade or two had seen little improvement in the quality of some British war movies, and there is no more misleading assumption than the one, sometimes indiscriminately made, that the Second World War caused the British cinema as a whole to take a great leap forward. In fact much of it moved at the same pace as the society it represented, conservative and divided by class-consciousness, with the war only temporarily pulling the nation together.

Less than a month after the sinking of the *Bismarck,* Hitler turned against the USSR and Britain's isolation was ended. By Christmas 1941 the German failure to take Moscow had doomed the Nazi regime to a slow and protracted collapse, a fact more easily understood in retrospect, for at the time the issue seemed to be far from clear. The British needed, most of all, more active transatlantic support, and it was fortunate that they had a determined American advocate in President Franklin D. Roosevelt, who managed to push through the lend-lease program of aid for Britain in spite of formidable opposition from the isolationist lobby in Washington. He was able also to take further steps, relieving the British garrison in Iceland with an American one and even allowing convoys to go so far into the Atlantic under American escort. The United States gradually arrived at what could be interpreted as a state of undeclared war at sea against Germany. A secret meeting aboard ship off Newfoundland between Churchill and Roosevelt in August 1941 produced the Atlantic Treaty, a declaration of common objectives for a postwar world, the occasion itself later to be made the subject of a special Movietone issue called *Atlantic Charter.*

While crossing the ocean in the *Prince of Wales* Churchill had watched again one of his favorite movies of the year, *Lady Hamilton,* produced in Hollywood by Korda, who had contact in the United States with the British intelligence services and who had aroused the wrath of isolationist American Senators on the justifiable grounds that he was in America to make propaganda for the British cause.[81] In fact *That Hamilton Woman,* as it was titled in the United States, was an uncomplicated and patriotic film, calling to mind contemporary parallels, though it was inevitable that the story of Nelson (Laurence Olivier) and Lady Hamilton (Vivien Leigh) became somewhat sentimentalized. In the meantime British techniques for dealing with the U-boats had improved, and the Americans had transferred to them fifty destroyers of First World War vintage to use as a stopgap, although in the event their usefulness was somewhat limited. The smaller Canadian navy also was taking more responsibility for patrolling the western part of the ocean, and it seemed now as if the key to winning the Battle of the Atlantic was cooperation between the three English-speaking nations of the northern hemisphere.

Promoting and strengthening this kind of affinity was the main motivation for the feature film *49th Parallel,* directed by Michael Powell and originally conceived during the fateful summer of 1940.[82] Its opening sequence had brief vistas of Canada, cities and prairies, accompanied by a narration that referred to the parallel, the line of latitude separating Canada and the United States, as the "only undefended frontier in the world." The film's story begins with a U-boat operating off the Canadian coast. It sinks an isolated tanker and moves then into Hudson's Bay, surfacing to avoid icebergs and to send a party ashore in search of supplies. Suddenly an aircraft swoops on the submarine, and a well-dropped bomb destroys it with no one surviving apart from the six who are already ashore. The saga of their pursuit across Canada makes up the theme of the film, for which Powell had obtained financial backing from the MOI, with help from Kenneth Clark and the producer John Sutro. Powell's friend and collaborator Emeric Pressburger wrote the script. The fact that it was an officially sponsored film was soon leaked to the trade press.[83]

Much of the shooting was done on location in Canada, across the country and up at Hudson's Bay, while a whole replica of a U-boat was assembled and brought offshore the coast of Newfoundland. Freddie Young was responsible for the photography, one of the film's outstanding ingredients, and David Lean was its editor. The music had been commissioned from Ralph Vaughan Williams, the most distinguished of senior British composers. In January the unit was back at Denham for studio work, but a major problem had arisen through the refusal of the exiled Austrian actress Elizabeth Bergner to return to beleaguered Britain, and her part had to be reallocated to Glynis Johns. The need to do some reshooting contributed to the lengthy production schedule of the film, not finally completed until the autumn of 1941, by which time its propaganda value was beginning to lessen, with America's growing involvement in the war. Nevertheless, it proved to be a popular success in 1942. In America it was released under the title *The Invaders.*

The interest of the public in *49th Parallel* was captured by its thrillerlike aspects, the classic plot of chase and suspense, sufficient to divert attention from the more heavily polemical points it tried to make, even though they were presented in a palatable form in line with the director's intentions. From his conning tower the U-boat captain, who dies with his vessel, announces German aims, "Today Europe, tomorrow the whole world, Heil Hitler!" The shore party is led by a couple of lieutenants, Kuhnecke who describes himself as an old party member, a practical man, while his companion Hirth is an idealist and a dreamer. Powell and Pressburger thereafter spare no effort to define the meaning of fascism and to bring the pursued Nazis into conflict with individuals who in different ways represent the ideological standpoints of the Anglo-American democracies.

First of these in fact is a French-Canadian trapper, played by Laurence Olivier with his own wholly characteristic brand of dedication to authenticity of voice and manner, almost to the point of caricature ("Ma foi, I teenk—" and so on). Johnnie knows nothing of the war and cares less, until Hirth tells him that France has surrendered and the Germans are coming to liberate French Canada. They will be able to speak their own language and have their own schools—rights which they possess already, Johnnie says. There is a fracas as a seaplane arrives at the Eskimo settlement; the crew is murdered by the Nazis and Johnnie also is shot. Dying, he asks for a crucifix ("What's the good of that to him?" says Hirth) and one of the submariners, Vogel, feels troubled enough to hand him one before compensating for his good deed by carving a swastika on the wall. The escapers take the plane, but the weight of the six of them is too much for it and they have to throw the stores overboard. One of them is killed by a rifle shot from the Eskimos. Kuhnecke (Raymond Lovell) flies the plane in an attempt to reach Lake Winnipeg, fifteen hours away, but when the fuel cuts out they are forced to crash land in the water, a well-contrived dramatic sequence in the film. Kuhnecke is killed, and from this point the dominant role among the survivors is taken by Hirth.

Played by Eric Portman, Hirth is a long way from the typical Germans of many British films, even some later ones, who were ridiculous at worst, suave at best. He is more effective even than the relatively impressive Karl Marsen of *Night Train to Munich.* Portman's northern tones freed him from the traditional school of West End acting. Francis L. Sullivan's Graum in *Pimpernel Smith* had been just a nasty version of the English gentleman. Portman, from quite a different cultural background, found the needed strength and depth. The choice of this gifted actor was exactly right for what was required, a demonstration to both British and Americans of the reality of

Nazi ruthlessness and the determination they would have to find in order to counter it.

The group finds temporary refuge in a German-speaking Hutterite settlement of "brothers and sisters in God," people existing by cooperative activity. Dialogue between visitors and hosts turns into statements of their respective beliefs. "How can he be your leader if he doesn't tell you what to do?" "We tell *him* what to do." "If someone leaves and wants to come back don't you punish him? Don't you send him to a camp or something?" "Camp?" And about the communal singing in the settlement, "Is it one of your rules to sing like this?" "We haven't any rules, we like it, it's good for the digestion," and so forth, in similar fashion. Bleakly, Hirth quotes Bismarck, "We shall leave them only their eyes to weep with." When he lectures the people on racial theory, the new Nordic wind sweeping from the east, he is rebuked by the settlement's leader Peter (Anton Walbrook), who tells him why they left Europe, to avoid poverty and persecution, while in Canada they have found the security and tolerance which Hitler is trying to stamp out. Vogel (Niall MacGinnis) is moved by the settlers' humility; he has made friends with the innocent Anna (Glynis Johns), whose mother had been drowned at sea, presumably in a torpedoed ship; and he has set about helping the community's baker. But this part of the film closes with Hirth arresting Vogel and having him executed. The episode had been introduced for very obvious reasons, as an answer to possible hostility among America's large German-immigrant population to intervention on the side of Britain.

The refugees hope to reach Vancouver and to look for a Japanese ship. They steal a car on the highway and also cover some of the distance by train, but the hunt for them is in progress, and one of the three is captured in Banff by the mounties at an Indian ceremony. Hirth and his remaining companion, Lohrmann (John Chandos), escape to the woods,

***49th Parallel.* Refugees from a sunken U-boat rest at a German settlement in Canada (Basil Appleby, John Chandos, Niall MacGinnis, Glynis Johns, and Eric Portman).**

where they go through their next encounter, this time with an English author, Philip Armstrong Scott, who is writing a book about Indian life. Leslie Howard took the part, putting forward again, as in *Pimpernel Smith,* the image of the seemingly soft and inconsequential upper-class Englishman. In his camp he shows the Germans his collection of paintings, works by artists like Picasso and Matisse who are banned in Germany, and he produces his copy of Thomas Mann's *Magic Mountain* (one of the books which the SA had been in the habit of putting on bonfires). Hirth conceals his identity until Scott compares the tribal aggression of the blackfoot with the behavior of the Nazis in Europe. Thereupon the two Germans smash Scott's collection before a quarrel among themselves causes them to separate. Scott has been freed by Canadian friends as Lohrmann, armed with a revolver, hides in a cave. Boldly Scott advances on him, ignoring his shots and taking a minor wound before he is able to seize the German. "Well, he had a fair chance, one armed superman against one unarmed, decadent democrat. I wonder how Dr Goebbels would explain that." Perhaps some Americans might have been excused for feeling that the outcome of this episode did not redeem the portrait Powell and Howard had created, conforming as it did initially to the view many of them held of British effete upper-class behavior.

Fortunately the quality of the acting in *49th Parallel,* prompted by Powell's skill as a director, just manages to rescue the film from the dangers of parody in the making of its all too obvious propaganda gestures. Even when voicing their most wooden ideological pronouncements, Portman and his opponents succeed in carrying a kind of conviction. British audiences anyway probably believed, with a vestige of truth, that the worst of the Nazis did behave like Hirth. In the final episode he is trying to cross to the United States, close to Niagara Falls, having backtracked across Canada by hiding himself in a freight car. The outcome of his flight has become a matter of national prestige for both the Germans and the allies, the award of an Iron Cross to him having been announced by Berlin radio. He meets Andy Brock, a Canadian soldier, played by Raymond Massey, who is returning to his border post after being absent without leave for eight days, another unthinkable deed in the eyes of an upright Nazi. Hirth strikes him down and steals his uniform. At gunpoint he compels Brock to stay aboard the train as it crosses the frontier. "We've beaten these dirty democracies, these weaklings," says Hirth, passing on next to eulogize the "glorious, mystical ties of blood and race." Brock's countercontribution is to assert the right of free men "to be fed up with everything we damn please and say so out loud." On the American side Hirth surrenders his gun to the customs officials. But Brock argues with them that he and Hirth are illegal pieces of merchandise and should be sent back to Canada, and the neutral Americans respond in truly Rooseveltian manner. As the train reverses across the border the Canadian soldier wades into the Nazi fanatic with simple straightforward fisticuffs.

On 7 December 1941, the Japanese attacked the United States fleet at Pearl Harbor. American indignation was so powerful that it called for a massive direction of effort across the Pacific, at the expense of immediate intervention in Europe. Hitler, with his armies already deeply and fatally bogged down in the rigors of the Russian winter, made an incomprehensible move. He issued a formal declaration of war against the United States of America.

3
Desert Victory

During the autumn of 1939, the Nazi broadcaster "Lord Haw-Haw" kept on putting a mocking question to his British listeners—"Where is the *Ark Royal?*" The Admiralty in fact had denied the confident claim of a single German airman to have made a successful hit on what was at the time Britain's largest and most modern aircraft carrier, and the truth was that an explosion caused by a very near miss had left her undamaged. Turned into a hero by Goebbels and the propaganda media and decorated with the Iron Cross, the unfortunate pilot had then to suffer the jibes of his colleagues as soon as it became clear that the *Ark Royal* was still afloat, pressure that finally drove him to suicide.[1]

The Fleet Air Arm was very much the cinderella unit of the Royal Navy. It had only recently become independent of the RAF, and it was handicapped by being equipped with slow and obsolete planes. The most famous of these, the Swordfish, known affectionately as the "Stringbag," was a biplane designed to be used for reconnaissance or for torpedo attacks, but its speed of little more than a hundred miles an hour made it extremely vulnerable. New carriers were being built, and a new fighter, the Fulmar, was being introduced in the winter of 1940–41, but even it lacked the power and the maneuverability of the RAF's best planes. The navy's chiefs for their part doubted if aircraft would be a serious threat to the dominant role played by the battleship in sea warfare.

Ealing planned their next major war film, *Ships With Wings,* as a tribute to the Fleet Air Arm, dedicated in particular to the *Ark Royal,* a name which had a unique resonance because it had been borne by Effingham's flagship at the time of the Armada. The director was the Russian-born Sergei Nolbandov, who had worked mostly as a screen writer before the war and also as associate producer for *The Proud Valley* and *Convoy.* At the end of August 1940, Roy Kellino, in charge of photography, embarked from Gibraltar with his camera crew aboard the *Ark Royal* to shoot some actuality material. The carrier was part of a force under Admiral Somerville that could be deployed either in the Atlantic or the western Mediterranean, but its particular task on this occasion was to assist the passage of stores and equipment to the isolated outpost of Malta, situated within easy bombing range of Sicily and the mainland of Italy. Kellino was able to go up in a Swordfish and he produced some useful film, though there was no action for the *Ark Royal* this time, and soon she was to join in an abortive British and Free French expedition against Dakar before returning home for a refit.[2]

The entry of Italy into the war and the surrender of France had left the situation in the Mediterranean in a state of delicate balance. The Italian navy was large and modern and included two new fast battleships. British forces were divided between Cunningham's fleet based at Alexandria and Somerville's group at Gibraltar. On land the Italian army in their colony of Libya was at least six times the size of the British forces in Egypt. Churchill realized the need to send out reinforcements, but at first dared to ship tanks only by the long and slow route round the Cape. The odds seemed to be stacked against Britain, but in practice the Italians made only a timid and limited advance into Egypt, and their fleet turned out to be shy of taking action, perhaps overawed by the long-standing weight of British naval tradition.

In November, the Fleet Air Arm launched a bold attack by night on the naval base of Taranto, tucked into the heel of Italy, a harbor where some of Mussolini's finest ships were at anchor in an apparently protected basin. A handful of Swordfish from the new carrier *Illustrious* sank one Italian battleship and crippled two others, one of them the modern *Littorio,* for a period of six months. Apart from the *Ark Royal's* strike against the *Bismarck* in the following year, it was the navy air arm's greatest triumph, an episode noted most of all by the imitative Japanese. It ought to have given Michael Balcon, keen as he was to support the war effort, an opportunity for the release of a realistic action film. *Ships With Wings* was in production throughout most of 1941, its script revised to take account of the Italian invasion of Greece and German intervention in the Mediterranean, and it was finished at about the same time as *49th Parallel.*

It was one of the films to which the observers of Mass-Observation tried to gauge public reaction by interviewing people as they were leaving the cinemas.[3] On the whole it was a case of universal approval, expressions like "wonderful" or "thrilling" being used, although some of the more thoughtful modified their verdicts somewhat after they had been given more time to reflect on them. When criticism did occur, it was directed at the plot and the sets rather than the action—judgments already made by the most respected of the press critics, even if the popular newspapers had been kinder to the film. Viewed now, *Ships With Wings* is awful almost beyond belief.[4]

Nolbandov participated in the writing of the script for the film, which, like *Convoy,* had John Clements playing a disgraced naval officer who redeems himself in death. This time he is Stacey, one of a trio of Fleet Air Arm pilots and friends—the others are Grant (Michael Wilding) and Maxwell (Michael Rennie)—who have been appointed to a new carrier in peacetime. He also wants to impress Celia (Jane Baxter), the daughter of Vice-Admiral Weatherby (Leslie Banks), to whom he has already made a sudden proposal of marriage, an impulse which she fends off with a conventional response of "I don't know what to say." Her brother Michael, performed by Hugh Burden as a young and gawky silly-ass figure, is a sublieutenant desperately keen to become a flier. Stacey takes him up in a new Fulmar and persists, for Celia's benefit, in demonstrating aerobatics that are beyond the untried plane's safety level. When it begins to break up, he bails out, unaware that young Weatherby has disobeyed his instructions and is hiding in the aircraft so that he can have a crack at landing it himself. The consequent crash causes Weatherby's death, and Stacey is court-martialed and dismissed from the service.

The scene shifts to the Greek island of Pamos, introduced with a tableau of a ruined temple and a group of costumed peasants, a piece of staging so shabby and artificial that it might have come from the primitive first decade of cinema. Stacey is flying for a disreputable local airline run by a Greek, portrayed by Edward Chapman as lazy and hysterical, perhaps what the British expected of anyone of Mediterranean origin. His fellow pilot is a German (Hugh Williams), given the not very original name of Wagner, who behaves throughout with the most predictable kind of Teutonic brutality. He tries an assault on Kay (Ann Todd), an actress and old friend of Stacey who has come out to this island paradise just for love, though she also has told him that Celia in the meantime has married Grant. With the outbreak of war, Stacey has tried to get reinstated, achieving some support from the aircraft carrier's Captain Fairfax (Basil Sydney), but the admiral remains adamant.

By the autumn of 1940 Mussolini had become impatient about his country's lack of success in the war. He was after all the senior fascist leader in Europe, and he had the most grandiose ideas for reviving the glory of the Roman Empire and for turning the Mediterranean into Italy's Mare Nostrum, but he was hurt that Hitler failed to consult him whenever Germany took a major initiative. A fascist takeover in Rumania had seen the Führer handing part of that country to the USSR, a nation that was not even a participant in the war. Italy, by contrast, had got little or nothing so far. Hitler of course supported the aims of an Italian offensive against Egypt, but for the time being he was opposed to any further moves in the Balkans. He had set his main sights instead on persuading Franco to seize Gibraltar, an intervention the Spanish dictator was able to put off. In a fit of pique, Mussolini ordered in October the invasion of Greece, his troops crossing the border from Albania, which itself had been taken by the Italians the previous year. As Hitler stepped down from his train at Florence for a meeting with the Duce, he was greeted with the words "Führer, we are marching."

Unfortunately for the Italian army, it was soon marching backwards. The Greeks put up a fierce resistance and during the winter were able to advance into Albania from both Macedonia and Epirus.[5] The enraged Hitler was forced to turn toward the Mediterranean in the spring of 1941 in order to rescue his blundering Italian allies. In the film *Ships With Wings,* the Nazis already have an agent on Pamos, in the guise of a northern English businessman. For some unexplained reason, the island is invaded by no less than the black-uniformed SS, who kill both Kay and the airline owner, the Greek rousing himself at last to make a speech about his country as the founder of democracy (though Greece in 1941 was a dictatorship run on fascist lines). Stacey manages to escape with his mechanic MacDermott, the only plebeian character in the film, played by Charles Victor as a caricature Irishman. Before being forced to crash land, they spot Italian ships laying mines in the path of an advancing British fleet.

The friends are reunited aboard the aircraft carrier, preparing now to lead a combined-operations-style attack on the island of Panteria, its main objective being the destruction of a huge dam, the set for which in the film is a sadly makeshift affair. A comical Italian general pooh-poohs the idea of any threat to the island, just as the British bombers arrive. However, the operation is jeopardized as one lone Italian aircraft succeeds in damaging the carrier's flight deck, Fairfax is wounded, and some planes are lost. Stacey now volunteers to take up a Fulmar, and MacDermott insists on joining him. Grant's torpedo attack on the dam fails, and the dreadful Wagner now appears, flying a bomber with which he is determined to finish off the carrier. In a climax of melodramatic improbability, Stacey gets MacDermott to bail out, then approaches the bomber from the rear. He is wounded by fire from the gunner, but he presses on, lowering his landing wheels until they sink into the fuselage of the enemy bomber. He contrives next to fly both planes into the dam, which is breached as the cargo of bombs explodes.

The most perceptive cinemagoers saw through the shabbiness of the sets and the absurdity of the plot of

***Ships With Wings*. Attacking the Italian dam. The shabby sets typify the superficiality of the film.**

Ships With Wings, but, if the Mass-Observation survey is to be believed, many others were not disposed to be too critical. They had gone through difficult times, with the blitz at home and the armed services having little to boast about, and perhaps the very unreality of the film was sufficient to provide them with some relief from the drabness of their day-to-day existences. Winston Churchill, though, would have liked the film not to be released at all because he felt that, if anything, it showed the Fleet Air Arm in a poor light.[6] Ealing subsequently made some amends with a documentary about the training of navy pilots, *Find, Fix and Strike,* which used substantial parts of the film shot by Kellino aboard the *Ark Royal.* Compton Bennett directed with assistance from Charles Crichton.

The Mediterranean field of operations attracted the next major collaboration of the Army and Crown Film Units in the form of a film titled *Wavell's 30,000,* made as a record of the remarkable if short-lived victory achieved by the British in Libya over the winter of 1940–41, and using material shot by both the army and the newsreels.[7] Wavell was the commander-in-chief in Egypt who, following the failure of the Italian army to follow up its initial moves, had encouraged his desert force general, Dick O'Connor, to mount a large-scale raid in December that, with unexpected success, soon became a major offensive. The film set the scene with a reminder of Britain's campaign in the previous world war, a shot of the military cemetery at Jerusalem, before making an assessment of the balance of power on land, sea, and air in the area during 1940. For this it used a high-ranking representative of each of the armed services to give a series of explanations before a map of the battleground, a device in the event likely only to confuse the viewer by impeding the natural flow of the main narrative. Later a tank officer and his sergeant-major were brought in to describe how the armored units had spearheaded the British advance.

The speed of O'Connor's victory was one of the most rapid of the war. By the beginning of February the whole of Cyrenaica, the eastern part of Libya, had fallen into British hands, and their greatly outnumbered army had rounded up many thousands of prisoners. An opportunity arose to press on to Tripoli and complete the conquest of this Italian colony, an outcome which would have left Britain in total command of North Africa beyond the Vichy French territories.[8] Hitler had a plan to rush German reinforcements there, but it is doubtful if there could have been a substantial build-up before mid-April. The chance was lost because early in March most of the British forces were moved to Greece, in hopes of starting another front there. Throughout the war, Winston Churchill was concerned with the possibility of moving forward through what he thought of as the enemy's "soft underbelly," their southern fringes, a calculation that took little account of the problems of fighting in what was mainly mountainous country. Although he began to have doubts himself about a Greek campaign, he was persuaded to attempt one by his Foreign Secretary Anthony Eden, with Wavell's concurrence.[9] In the following month, a relatively unknown German commander called Erwin Rommel was able to completely reverse the situation and drive the British out of Cyrenaica with even more speed than they had entered it. O'Connor himself became a prisoner.

By the time that *Wavell's 30,000* was finished, the desert war was being fought all over again, and the opening of the film indeed made a reference to Auchinleck, the new commander-in-chief (the unfortunate Wavell, a scapegoat for the British error of judgment and its consequences, had been packed off to India to become viceroy). The commentary was spoken by Colin Wills, an Australian journalist—some recognition of the considerable participation of Empire troops in the Middle East sector. *Wavell's 30,000* was issued almost as a belated tribute to a wasted opportunity, although Italian morale must have suffered as a result of the poor showing of their army. It was edited and directed by John Monck, and it made a lame start to what in time turned out to be a famous series of AFPU battle films.

In the same month as Rommel's advance, Hitler had made his move in the Balkans, partly to rescue his Italian allies, partly to secure his flank before his impending invasion of the USSR. Yugoslavia was quickly overrun, and the British reinforcements proved too weak to prevent the occupation of Greece. A desperate effort was made by the Commonwealth forces to hold the island of Crete. Cunningham had earlier sunk three Italian cruisers at the battle of Matapan, off southern Greece, and his fleet now was able to prevent a seaborne invasion of Crete, but it suffered terribly at the hands of the Luftwaffe, which totally dominated the skies over the Aegean. The loss of one of his destroyers was to be at the heart of the most memorable British naval feature film of the war, *In Which We Serve.* Crete was secured by the Germans after drops by parachute troops, yet another humiliating defeat for the British, remnants of whose forces succeeded in reaching Egypt. If anything at all was to sugar the bitter pill, the New Zealanders had at least given the paratroopers such a mauling that Hitler was deterred from attempting a similar air assault on Malta.[10]

The newsreels, as ever, did their best to put a brave

face on events. One isolated stronghold, the port of Tobruk, had been able to stand firm against Rommel, and it continued to do so for the rest of the year, helped by a flow of supplies and fresh troops brought round by sea. More relief came with another British advance in November, and the episode was celebrated in a short film based on the newsreel material and produced now on its own account by the AFPU. It was called *The Siege of Tobruk.* Colin Wills spoke the commentary again, an appropriate choice because the defense had owed much to the fighting qualities of the Australian soldiers. The lessons of *Wavell's 30,000* had been learned. There were no explanatory diagrams or tedious interjections by military commentators. Some of the reinforcements were Polish, and one of the sequences showed them being visited by their commander, General Sikorski, the head of the Polish government in exile who was to die in an air crash. The conclusion of the film had simultaneous attacks by the garrison from Tobruk and by the Eighth Army (as the desert force was now called) from Egypt, finishing with shots of the linkup. Unhappily the time of the film's release early in 1942 coincided with further setbacks, the most serious to date, for the British.

The desert campaign fought by the Eighth Army and the German Afrika Korps had become a seesaw of maneuvers amid large open spaces free of habitation. Following the catalogue of disasters in the spring of 1941, Churchill had appreciated the absolute necessity, in terms of both strategy and morale, of keeping Egypt and winning the struggle in North Africa. Hitler, on the other hand, was reluctant to strengthen Rommel for fear of bleeding the Russian front of men and equipment. By the autumn the British were able to build up a massive superiority in aircraft and tanks. But Rommel consistently outtricked them, and in action after action he managed in particular to tear up their armored forces. The reputedly rigid Teutons demonstrated greater flexibility and professionalism. Britain's army had been mainly a colonial force, and its officers had been educated in strict regimental codes that had the effect of repressing individuality and initiative. When Rommel adapted heavy antiaircraft guns for use against tanks, the surprised British felt that he was breaking the rules. British commanders brought up in schools of infantry tactics could not understand a new kind of warfare where their enemy coordinated different types of formations.[11] It was a mirror image on the battlefield of the immobility of the British class system at home, just as the painful evolution of the British cinema toward realism also reflected that system.

British personality, of course, does contain beneath the apparently rigid social structure a high degree of individualism, even of anarchy, and this strain found an outlet in war through the activities of commando units or, in the desert, irregular bodies operating behind enemy lines. The campaign in North Africa saw both sides behaving with a degree of respect for each other, even chivalry, if one can use that term in the context of a war each regarded as a matter of national survival. The British picked up one of the most popular of wartime songs, "Lili Marlene" from the Germans. This peculiar love-hate relationship permeated one of the most convincing of postwar films, *Ice Cold in Alex,* directed by J. Lee-Thompson in 1958. The incidents of the film were supposed to have taken place in 1942 after the eventual fall of Tobruk, with Anthony Quayle playing a German agent disguised as a South African officer who tries to reach Alexandria in a party of British soldiers and nurses.

In spite of their failures in Greece and Libya, the British at least were able to secure their rear and their eastern flank in the Middle East during 1941. The Italian East African Empire had fallen to them, and they restored to power in Ethiopia the Emperor Haile Selassie, who had been the original victim of Mussolini's imperialist aspirations. His return to Addis Ababa formed the climax of a short AFPU film called *Lion of Judah.* The British also intervened in Iraq to secure their oil supplies, and mounted with the Free French an invasion of Syria and the Lebanon, ruled at that time by the Vichy French. Fighting between the two French factions was particularly bitter and vicious. Finally, in August the neutrality of Iran was violated by both British and Russians in order to forestall German influence there. Ted Genock of Paramount was on the scene to film this first military linkup between the two new allies, and the company provoked a storm at the War Office by sending the reels not to Cairo for censorship but to New York by way of India.[12] The film was released uncensored as a world scoop. The American-owned Paramount company and its London chief, G. T. Cummins, had been the most active in trying to duck out of the rota, a situation that eventually produced an acrid meeting in October 1942 with Brendan Bracken, who had taken over as Minister of Information in the previous year. He brought them to heel by threatening to withdraw all official facilities from them.[13]

The year 1941 closed with the Royal Navy taking an unprecedented series of reverses in both the Mediterranean and the Far East. Cunningham had already lost several cruisers and destroyers around Crete. On November 10 the *Ark Royal* was torpedoed and sunk by a U-boat. The battleship *Barham* was destroyed in the same way on the twenty-fourth, an incident that

The torpedoed battleship *Barham* sinking and blowing up. Gaumont British cameraman John Turner's single reel ran out just as the vessel exploded.

produced one of the most spectacular film sequences of the war. From her sister ship the *Valiant* John Turner of Gaumont British was able to shoot the *Barham* turning onto her side and then exploding in a great convulsion of smoke and debris.[14] The *Valiant* herself was in harbor at Alexandria with the *Queen Elizabeth* on the night of December 18 when Italian frogmen, astride miniature submersible vessels designed in the shape of torpedoes, managed to penetrate the base and plant delayed-action charges beneath the two battleships. The frogmen had been taken prisoner and a couple of them were aboard one of the British vessels when the explosions put the ships out of action, for several months as it turned out. This gallant sortie became the subject of a film released in 1962 and called, appropriately enough, *The Valiant.* John Mills played the battleship's Captain Morgan, and Ettore Manni was Lieutenant Durand de la Penne, who had led the attack. The Italians awarded Penne their highest medal, and in due course it was pinned to his uniform by Morgan himself, when the Italian government had changed sides in the war.

The crippling of the only British battleships left in the eastern Mediterranean was kept secret from the public at home. However, it was impossible to conceal from them the disasters that had taken place off Malaya in the same month, although newsreel shots of the arrival of the *Prince of Wales* at Singapore had been cut out by the censor.[15] Churchill had thought that the presence of this new battleship would deter the Japanese from attempting an invasion. The Admiralty in fact had wanted to dispatch a stronger force, and the loss of the *Ark Royal* and an accident to another carrier left the British Far East squadron without naval air cover. Both the *Prince of Wales* and the battle-cruiser *Repulse* were caught at sea and sunk by Japanese aircraft, something many admirals had believed to be impossible.

By February 1942, Japanese troops had bicycled their way through the supposedly impenetrable Malayan jungle, and Singapore was surrendered to them, the most humiliating defeat in twentieth-century British history. Its effect in Asia was enormous, and the British Empire was probably doomed from that moment. In the same month, British prestige suffered a further blow when the *Scharnhorst* and the *Gneisenau,* with the cruiser *Prinz Eugen,* succeeded in escaping in daylight up the English Channel to home waters. Both battleships struck mines, but the RAF in particular failed to take the opportunity to attack them. As if this were not enough, Rommel's next offensive drove the Eighth Army back into Egypt, and in June even Tobruk fell to him. For the first time in the war, Churchill's position wavered. There was talk of replacing him with Stafford Cripps, but Parliament dissolved into hilarity when one of his critics in the Commons suggested that the Duke of Gloucester should be made commander-in-chief.[16]

The situation was most galling for the prime minister because he had spent much time trying to persuade the Americans that they should expend as much effort in trying to defeat Germany as in taking their revenge on Japan. Now Britain's participation in the war seemed to be dogged by continual failure. Cairo was in a panic, the British community making plans for an immediate evacuation. In fact Rommel, starved of resources, was on the point of exhaustion, and he was fought to a standstill at El Alamein, still sixty miles away, by Auchinleck, who had taken personal command of the battle. Churchill flew to Egypt in August, determined now to urge the Eighth Army to counterattack. He replaced Auchinleck with Alexander, who, however, like his predecessor, insisted that no attack was possible until the British had clear superiority. Bernard Montgomery was selected as army commander.

Ealing's first film of 1942, *The Big Blockade,* had nothing to say about this dire succession of defeats. It had grown from an original MOI-inspired idea for a short piece about economic warfare to a full-length feature documentary, mainly because of Michael Balcon's wish to put across something meaningful to the public that would increase their understanding of the war situation. Moreover, he brought Charles Frend from the cutting rooms to direct, a step in the right direction for Ealing toward eventually producing more authentic war movies. Frank Owen, the editor of the *Evening Standard,* narrated much of the commentary, from a screen play by Angus MacPhail. However, the basic theme was a difficult one, intended to persuade people that Britain was doing something more active than just defending itself, and, in order to communicate more easily some fairly complex arguments, the script introduced a number of comedy episodes, mingled with more straightforward documentary-style sequences.

Keeping the audience laughing had been the sole objective of a whole series of British wartime films, continuing a tradition set in the thirties.[17] For many it was in the context of catching spies, as in two of those which featured George Formby, *Let George Do It* (1940) and *Bell Bottom George* (1943). Formby's earthy Lancastrian flair found a ready response among working-class audiences. Other well known film comedians included Arthur Lucan (Old Mother Riley), Flanagan and Allen, Will Hay, Arthur Askey, and Tommy Trinder. Each in his own way presented the view of the ordinary British man in the street beating the larger and more impersonal forces of the enemy. In 1940 cheerful cockney Tommy Trinder appeared with Claude Hulbert and Michael Wilding in *Sailors Three* (U.S. title: *Three Cockeyed Sailors*), a light-hearted piece of nonsense in which the trio manage to capture a German warship. Will Hay was more of a middle-class figure, usually the bumbling schoolmaster type. Friend and foe alike were subjected to mockery in *The Goose Steps Out,* shown late in 1942, with Hay going to Germany on an espionage mission in place of his Nazi double and managing in the course of it to indoctrinate a group of Hitler Youth in the correct and ruder form of the two-fingered salute. Perhaps its style of caricature was beginning to be out of tune with the way the war was now developing, but up to that time audiences certainly had been in need of comic relief. Interludes of brief comedy were almost mandatory, too, in some more serious films, though here often with an element of condescension, because they were invariably associated with proletarian characters, who were shown as if they were capable of little else.

Will Hay contributed to the semicomic element in *The Big Blockade* as the skipper of a minesweeper, with Bernard Miles playing the mate. They start a discussion about the navy's system of granting certificates to ships with legitimate cargoes ("navy-certs" or "navvy-certs"?) and keep it up while they have to man the machine-guns as they are attacked by a German plane. It is difficult to believe that this method made the public grasp the point of the argument. Parody was carried a stage further with Robert Morley playing a Nazi official who lectures fellow European fascists on their duties in promoting cooperation in the industrial field. An Italian is treated with scorn and driven out of the room. Michael Redgrave plays a Russian visitor to Germany who wonders how the Nazis can claim to be so successful when his journey is constantly being interrupted as the RAF destroy rail communications. In company with the German industrialist Schneider, he has a miserable time in a bar which serves only alcohol-free drinks and meatless sausages. They transfer to a bus, but a puncture causes them to walk because there is a shortage of spare tyres. All this might have been intended to reassure the British viewer who had spent much of 1941 being blitzed, but it was far from a true picture of Nazi Germany at that time. In another episode, a factory director has urged his staff to double production or they will all be sent to Dachau. Later, as they go down to the shelters, one of them brightly remarks that if the factory is hit they cannot be blamed for not fulfilling their requirements. "Thank God for the British air force," the director responds. His part was taken by Alfred Drayton, another comedy actor of the period.

The first dramatized sequence in the film had a conversation in a train compartment between the industrialist Schneider and an English commercial traveller called Taylor, both returning home from Budapest in the summer of 1939. The German blames his country's collapse in 1918 on the "wicked British blockade," but now Germany is self-sufficient, helped also by her new pact with the USSR, and anyway they have since developed substitute (ersatz) products, especially in clothing. In London, Taylor, played by Leslie Banks, joins the new Ministry of Economic Warfare as the official in charge of contraband control. To assembled journalists, among them the American Quentin Reynolds, he periodically explains the principles by which Britain puts indirect pressure on the enemy. The informational nature of the film was reinforced by the introduction of the minister himself (Hugh Dalton). Unfortunately the reality was that Germany's conquest of Europe had if anything added to her self-sustaining potential, there was little or no prospect of starvation on the First World War model, and most of the assumptions behind *The Big Blockade* had become meaningless by the time the film was issued.

Using the navy for blockade, bombing the enemy's industrial installations—these were the methods propagandized as a means of striking back, given the impossibility of the army reinvading continental Europe. An air raid is directed to Hanover. Frank Owen, at the start of the film, lists the targets as an ersatz rubber factory, an oil refinery, a rail junction, a steel foundry. The film's sequence follows the plane T for Tommy, with Michael Rennie as the pilot and John Mills as the navigator, a commercial feature film version of *Target for Tonight.* They are able to make no less than three runs through the flak, and the message is the same as in Harry Watt's official film—the RAF can strike its objectives at will. In truth the aircraft itself, a Hampden, was one of their most ineffectual bombers and was destined for the scrap heap by 1941–42. The most significant part of the meandering plot of the *The Big Blockade* occurs earlier, when, at one of the ministry's press conferences, a newspaper editor argues for reprisal raids, "indiscriminate bombing" as he calls it. The British public need revenge for the blitz, and the German worker himself, as a vital unit in the production process, is a legitimate target. Taylor rejects the theory, putting the case instead for precision bombing. The moral aspect of bombing civilians is not discussed. This brief part of *The Big Blockade* is the only point in any British wartime film where there is a hint of what became the

The Big Blockade. **The issue of contraband control is explained to a group of journalists (Leslie Banks, standing, and Quentin Reynolds, seated second from right).**

great debate about British strategic bombing policy. It is put across to the public in terms that amount to deception, though there can be no question that the script writers were as much misled as the public.

In February Arthur Harris became commander-in-chief of Bomber Command. A brusque and determined man, he believed obsessionally in the ability of the bombers to win the war. He found support from Lord Cherwell, the former Professor Lindemann, the scientist who was one of the prime minister's closest confidantes. One cannot be absolutely certain that Churchill believed totally in the claims of the bombing lobby, but, having set up the RAF as the chief instrument of offensive against Germany, he seemed to be happy to let it go on as such while he argued the Americans out of a premature invasion of Europe. The facts were concealed from the public, many of whom would have supported reprisal raids anyway, but Bomber Command's policy now became saturation area bombing. The aircraft would aim for the center of cities at night, and the bombs would fall indiscriminately on installations and homes alike. It was hoped that Germany's industrial capacity would collapse, but, if sufficient number of bombers could be used, it was thought that civilian morale also might reach breaking point. Churchill's decision to help the RAF towards this end, against the counterarguments of the army and the navy, meant that the main weight of British factory production would go into turning out vast numbers of bombers, in particular the new four-engined types, and it was to remain geared up to this activity until the end of the war.[18]

The first victims were the old Hanse towns of Lübeck and Rostock, chosen because of their coastal situation and because their medieval wooden houses would burn easily, and then in May Bomber Command pulled out all the stops in a raid on Cologne. The total of more than a thousand aircraft was a convenient figure for a propaganda exercise by the press, and the spectacle of the blazing city seems to have created a sense of exultation among the fliers and the British public. Further raids followed on Essen and Bremen, and it was during one on the latter city in July that an RAF Film Unit cameraman, Pat Moyna, took the first night bombing shots, using his camera from the second pilot's seat of a Lancaster as it flew at 18,000 feet over the target.[19] The difficulties and limitations of filming from the air at night are obvious and, as the offensive developed, it became practice to fit cameras to traps cut in the floor of the aircraft. The records made of individual raids, usually little more than flashes of bomb bursts or flak and outbreaks of fire among the buildings, give some idea of the destructive force of bombing, though at a remove from the reality of the deaths and injuries being suffered by people at ground level.

The adoption of terrorization tactics by a western democracy put a new moral dimension in the Second World War. Perhaps this is the reason why, as the true nature of the British strategic bombing offensive became clear, there were no more RAF films of the *Target For Tonight* kind. One movie from 1942, Walter Forde's *Flying Fortress,* touched on the theme, but its main plot was about two American volunteers in Bomber Command. Even after the war, the only British bombing film was *The Dam Busters,* directed by Michael Anderson in 1955. Both the film and its familiar march tune attracted patriotic sentiment, but significantly, its story was of a single exceptional precision raid, on the dams controlling the Ruhr water supplies, temporarily broken in May 1943 by using the "bouncing bomb" device invented by Barnes Wallis. By the time a novel came to be written that faced the issues of bombing from both sides, Len Deighton's *Bomber,* published in 1970, it was probably still too controversial a subject for anyone to attempt a

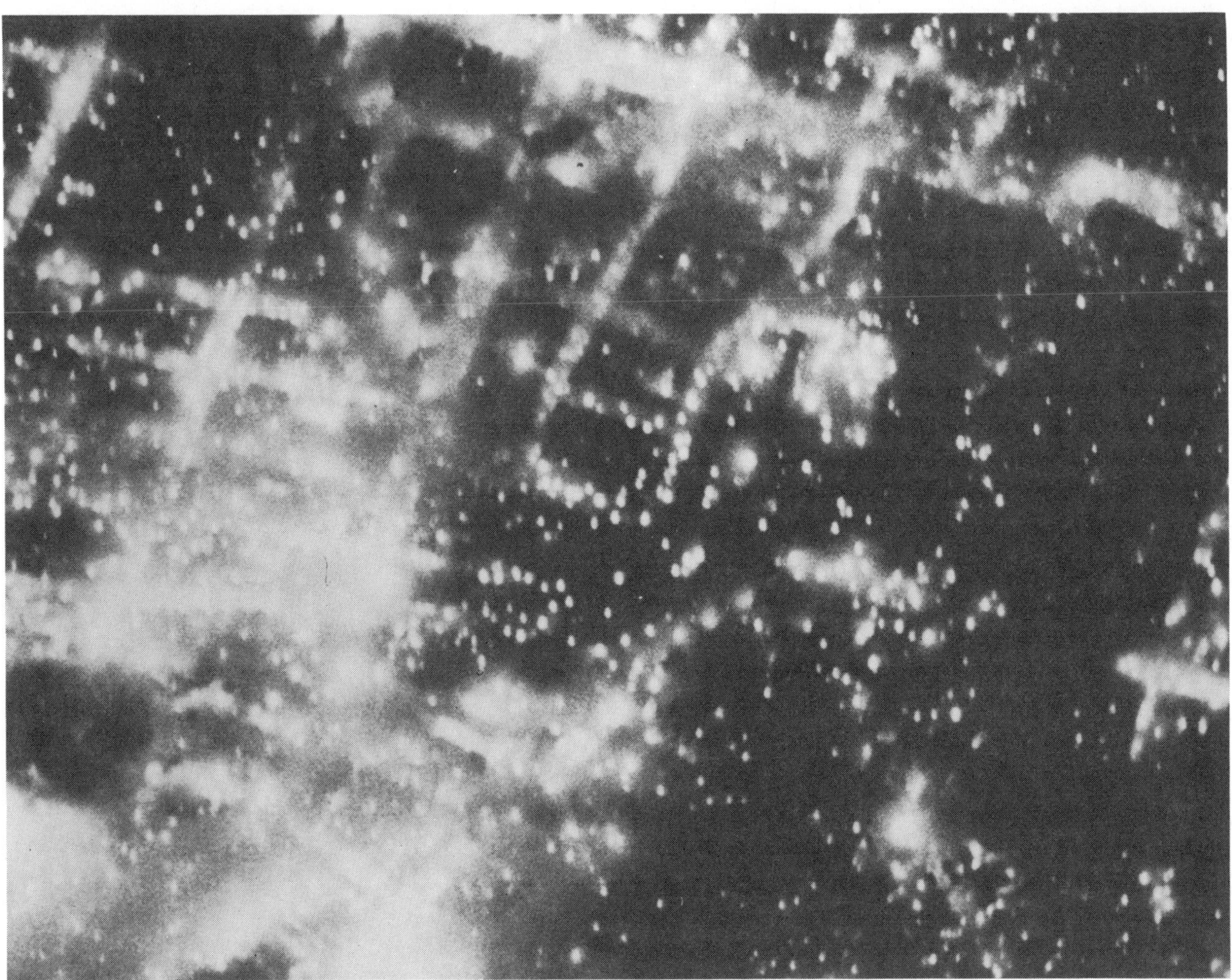

Incendiaries light up the street pattern in a raid on Brunswick, October 14/15, 1944. From footage shot by the RAF Film Unit, and typical of this type of material.

film version, even if the support had been available for one.[20] The Americans, by contrast, stuck to the principle of precision bombing, though in practice they were to depart from it in some instances (and totally in the war against Japan), and their early efforts to send aircraft from England in daylight over Germany met with disaster. In the postwar atmosphere of doubt about the strategic bombing campaign, it is impossible to imagine a British equivalent of Henry King's *Twelve O'Clock High*, produced in Hollywood in 1949, which stayed fairly frank about the level of casualties being borne by American aircrews, while keeping the ultimate aims of their kind of bombing offensive firmly in sight.

The Powell and Pressburger film *One of Our Aircraft is Missing* finished with a crew reporting for their new Lancaster, the most successful of the next generation of bombers to be used by the RAF. But its theme is a different one, looking back at an earlier episode in the life of the same men when they are forced to bail out over Holland. It has a pretitle sequence of almost surreal quality, with a Wellington flying back over the English coast, interior shots showing its abandoned controls and crew positions, until finally it crashes into a pylon and blows up. The crew of B for Bertie have in fact left the aircraft on their way back from a raid on Stuttgart, both engines having successively failed as a result of being hit by flak. While the men are drifting downwards under the parachutes, one engine picks up and carries the empty Wellington across the North Sea.

Powell directed the film with David Lean as editor. No music was used, to bring about a sense of greater naturalism, and, with the assistance of the Dutch government in exile, the landscape and architecture of Holland was faithfully re-created. The aircrew are also well characterized, even if the proportion of officers to sergeants was probably greater than the norm. The pilot John Haggard (Hugh Burden) becomes more self-effacing on the ground and allows leadership of the group to pass to his second pilot, Yorkshireman Tom Earnshaw (Eric Portman), and to the rear gunner, a middle-aged knight, Sir George Corbett (Godfrey Tearle), a seemingly unlikely volunteer, but based in fact on a real figure. The other officer, the senior in rank as it happens, is the navigator, a former actor called Frank Shelley (Hugh Williams); and the sergeants are wireless operator Bob Ashley (Emrys Jones), a Welsh professional footballer, and front gunner Geoff Hickman (Bernard Miles). Their relationship with each other is as close and friendly as it had to be in real life when fliers were on operations, though at the end of the film Hickman has to put in a hasty "sir" to a naval officer when he tries the same kind of familiarity on a service with a different tradition. All join up after the drop except Ashley, who is missing ("He's not too bright," the officers condescendingly say of him, though in fact he is bright enough to be the only one to understand German). They bury their parachutes by a canal and are soon discovered in the morning by friendly Dutch children.

The beginning of the film had a tribute to five Dutch people who had been executed by the Nazis for helping RAF crews to escape. At first, German occupation of the country had been relatively mild in character, and a large number of people either actively collaborated, some joining the Dutch SS formations, or at least went along passively with the regime. Resistance began to grow as soon as the Nazis started to remove Jews, an action that caused a short workers' strike in Amsterdam in February 1941. Many people listened to BBC broadcasts, including a service in their own language (Radio Orange).[21] These experiences were similar to those in some other parts of occupied Europe, though not in Poland, where Nazi brutality was from the outset applied in extreme measure. The plot of *One of Our Aircraft is Missing* assumes an almost universal hostility toward the Germans, although the problem of the collaborators is not evaded and is personified by the figure of de Jong, a resident of the village to which the airmen are taken on the day after their landing.

An interesting aspect of the film's production is the strength of the casting. Almost all of the players were either at the peak of their profession or later to reach it. The actors taking the parts of the airmen have already been listed. Pamela Brown is the wary schoolmistress who interrogates the fliers closely to make certain that they are what they pretend to be and not Nazi provocateurs in disguise. They put on Dutch clothing over their uniforms and cycle to church, where they notice that some of the women have concealed the parachutes, freshly dug up by the villagers, beneath their long skirts. However, Ashley's parachute has been found floating in the canal by the Germans who drive to the church to inspect the congregation. Peter Ustinov plays the priest. As a Nazi officer walks along the aisle, the organist (Alec Clunes) presses the pedals for a stealthy snatch of the Dutch national anthem, pausing as soon as the German stops. Back in the village, Hickman dresses up as a prospective bridegroom in a betrothal party. De Jong (Robert Helpmann) arrives unexpectedly and, realizing who the strangers are, is about to betray them until he is kept there by force. The small son of the mayor (Hay Petrie) has earlier attracted his father's wrath by undertaking an errand for de Jong,

***One of Our Aircraft is Missing.* Disguised RAF fliers, sheltered by the local schoolmistress, join the congregation in a Dutch church (Godfrey Tearle, Pamela Brown, and Hugh Burden).**

taking round a collection of gramophone records to the Germans. Now the sounds from the barracks indicate that he has tricked them by sticking the wrong labels on the records, which turn out to be all versions of the Dutch anthem. Naturally the Germans blame de Jong and march off in search of him. We do not discover the outcome of this episode, which already strains the credibility of the plot.

The escapers go to a football match and find the lost Ashley playing for one of the sides. They are next passed on by lorry into the keeping of the wealthy society lady Jo De Vries (Googie Withers), who is supposed to be a collaborator, a hater of the British after they have killed her husband in an air raid. In fact he is in London, a broadcaster for Radio Orange. During the night, RAF planes are heard and the sirens sound, causing the German garrison to run about in confusion, and Mrs. de Vries sermonizes about the boost the British aircraft give to Dutch morale, "hearing that steady hum night after night, noise which is oil for the burning fire of our hearts." The airmen take advantage of the diversion to slip away in a rowing boat, though they have to overpower three German officers on the way. There is a fine moment of suspense as they slide beneath a swing bridge, the only sounds being the chugging engines of the homecoming fishing fleet, the creaking of the bridge as it opens and closes, and Corbett's whispered instructions while he steers the boat. They are spotted at the last moment and Corbett is injured by rifle fire, but they manage to pull clear.

The film is vague about whether or not the airmen hope to row right across the North Sea, but in fact they board a German rescue buoy that is already sheltering two Luftwaffe fliers. The British become the captors by weight of numbers. (Rescue buoys were objects shaped like a submarine's conning tower on a broader square base with sufficient room to contain bunks, provisions, and radio equipment. They were anchored to the sea bed in shallow waters so that they might be reached by aircrew who had been forced to ditch in the sea. On both sides air-sea rescue was an organized activity, and the Crown Film Unit in fact had produced in 1941 a short film on the subject, *The Pilot Is Safe,* directed by Jack Lee.[22]) In *One of Our Aircraft is Missing,* the escapers cut loose the moorings so that the buoy will drift with the tide toward England. Eventually a British launch reaches them just before the enemy and, since Corbett is too ill to be moved, it takes the buoy in tow.

One of Our Aircraft is Missing is at its best in depicting the gallant relationship between British escapers and Dutch patriots. The Germans do not figure in it at all as individuals, only as a menacing authority of occupation that stamps permits and barks instructions over loudspeakers. The Netherlands had been neutral in the First World War and, earlier in the century, some of the Dutch kith and kin, the Afrikaaners, had fought the British in a colonial war. Anglo-Dutch amity was established as a consequence of shared experiences in the Second World War and was to thrive for many years after it. In spite of some lapses from cogency, this film probably gives a more intimate and satisfactory view of the genuine spirit of resistance within an occupied country than any British wartime production that succeeded it.

Powell and Pressburger returned to the Dutch theme with a production for their new company, Archers, a film released early in 1943 under the title *The Silver Fleet.* The designer was Alfred Junge, who also worked with the pair on *The Life and Death of Colonel Blimp* and *A Canterbury Tale.* However, *The Silver Fleet* was in fact written and directed by Vernon Campbell Sewell and Gordon Wellesley. It took the idea of resistance to another level, to the possibility of sabotage. The actual incidents have no historical parallel, but the film was lifted somewhat above the average by the main performance, that of Ralph Richardson as the shipbuilder Jaap van Leyden. His careful and restrained study in this part is one of the most distinguished in any British wartime film. Googie Withers appears again, as his wife Helene, and an interesting contribution is made also by Esmond Knight, as the SS officer Schiffer, acting that concealed from the audience the fact that he was totally blind at the time, having been injured while serving as an officer aboard the *Prince of Wales* during the *Bismarck* action. German naval officers in the film, two of them played by men from the Royal Netherlands Navy, are seen in a better light than the Nazi officials, among whom is the Protector himself (Valentine Dyall).

"Silver fleet" is a reference to the Spanish vessels seized by the national hero Piet Hein in the seventeenth century, and it is his name that Leyden uses as a pseudonym in order to organize resistance. Pretending to collaborate with the Nazis, he sets men to work on the completion of two submarines that had been under construction in his yard for the Dutch navy. Even Helene does not know the truth, and the family name is vilified in the town. Leyden contrives to have the first submarine hijacked to England by a group of his workers. He then secures the release of hostages who had been taken by the Nazi authorities. Some of the enemy suspect him, but he wins their confidence by turning over to them a cache of explosives stolen from them. In fact he is plotting to dynamite the second submarine during its trials, but, in order to achieve this, he has to sacrifice his life, by setting off the charge himself while the vessel is submerged. In the course of a dinner party for German guests the previous evening, he has found an escaped resister hiding in his house. The man commits suicide when his pursuers arrive there, but Leyden makes it appear that he has shot him. This is too much for Helene, who locks herself in her room, and Leyden is left to write the last pages of his secret journal, which she will be able to read the following day. In moving terms he describes his feelings about death and the act he is about to perform.

Although this sequence of events was not very likely perhaps in real life, the subject matter did express a need for the British people to feel that their ideals were shared by the occupied peoples of Europe. The theme had become a popular one for British filmmakers, and the exiled governments in London showed themselves to be only too willing to cooperate on productions that dealt with resistance and espionage. Since these were all basically adventure stories, audiences would respond to them. In general though, the issue of collaboration was not avoided and, even if the subject populations were shown sometimes to be more heroically active than they might have been in reality, there was no attempt to pretend that everyone was an anti-Nazi. In one episode of *The Silver Fleet,* the young nephew of a shopkeeper tried to betray both his uncle and other resisters in order to grab the family business for himself. Little perhaps was actually known by the British public of the true scale of recruitment of volunteers by the Nazis for their ethnic units or of the enthusiasm these soldiers demonstrated for an anti-

Bolshevik crusade on the Russian front. Matters of political ideology were rarely raised in the film scripts, except on the level of straightforward struggle against fascist dictatorship. There was no recognition, for instance, of the changed attitude of the European communist parties after the invasion of the USSR, a factor which was to form an important influence in the growth of resistance over 1942 and 1943.

Two of the more routine films about local resistance and British espionage were directed in 1942 by Harold French. The script for *The Day Will Dawn* (U.S. title: *The Avengers*) was based on an idea by Frank Owen, and at least its newspaper office settings are convincing enough, especially when the ace reporter Lockwood (Ralph Richardson) is present. He persuades the editor to send their racing correspondent Colin Metcalfe (Hugh Williams) out to Norway in the late winter of 1940. Metcalfe befriends a Norwegian fishing skipper, Alstead (Finlay Currie), and his daughter Kari (Deborah Kerr), and all three become involved in an incident with a U-boat on the eve of the German invasion. The plot also introduces a quisling police inspector and Francis L. Sullivan playing another pompous German. After being rescued by the British navy, Metcalfe goes to Cherbourg, where he witnesses the evacuation of part of the BEF and the death on the quay of his friend Lockwood. He is asked by naval intelligence to return to Norway in order to locate a suspected U-boat base and, with the help of the Alsteads, he succeeds in directing the RAF to it, although the father is killed by the Germans. Metcalfe and Kari are about to be executed with other hostages when a British commando unit attacks the fiord. A few shots from the AFPU's Vaagso footage were used in the action sequence and, although the film attracted praise at the time, it looks very run-of-the-mill nowadays.

49th Parallel had set the precedent of a film without a love interest, but a romantic relationship was mandatory for almost all feature films of the time. In *The Day Will Dawn* it grows between Metcalfe and Kari. For Harold French's next film, *Secret Mission,* it is the turn of British agent Peter Garnett (Hugh Williams) and a French girl from the upper classes, Michele de Carnot (Carla Lehmann). Garnett goes to France with Michele's brother Raoul (James Mason) and another

Secret Mission. **British agents land in France and kill interfering German soldiers (Michael Wilding, Carla Lehmann, Hugh Williams, and Roland Culver).**

officer called Gowan (Roland Culver) and a cockney private (Michael Wilding) whose French wife owns a café in the local village. Garnett and Gowan bluff their way into German headquarters as champagne merchants, friends of Ribbentrop, in order to photograph plans of German dispositions in the area. Michele is at first not too friendly because she believes that resistance only brings about reprisals from the Germans, and she is even more bitterly opposed to the English when her brother is killed. However, true love triumphs in the end, as of course do the British, who drop paratroopers to blow up the enemy's underground control position. Romance also flourished in George King's *Tomorrow We Live,* this time between two French patriots, played by John Clements and Greta Gynt, who finally succeed in escaping to England. The resistance has sabotaged an ammunition train, in retaliation for which the Nazis execute fifty hostages. The film was distributed in America as *At Dawn We Die,* surely one of the most strange title reversals in cinema history.

The Gainsborough film *Uncensored* was set in Brussels and took as its subject the illicit printing of a Belgian resistance news-sheet, designed to counter official German propaganda. Both its editor Victor Lanvin (Frederick Culley) and the cabaret performer André Delange (Eric Portman) who helps with its distribution pretend to be collaborators while secretly they work for the resistance. Directed by Anthony Asquith, the film is again a vehicle for the acting skills of Portman, but his performance is rivalled by that of Peter Glenville as his partner Charles Neels, who has been forced to live for most of the time in the shadow of Delange's talent. When Delange has to break up the relationship, because an invitation to make a solo tour of German military camps gives him the freedom of movement he needs, Neels becomes hysterically jealous and betrays him to the enemy. Delange escapes, but some of his colleagues, including a priest, are arrested. In a complicated and wholly incredible dénouement, they are able to avoid execution because that sentence would compromise Lanvin, still thought of as a friend of the Nazis. Copies of the paper float down from the flagpole of the Town Hall as the bewildered Germans run about trying to prevent disorder. Whereas Michael Powell's films had invited respect for a ruthless enemy, *Uncensored* followed the unrealistic path of making the Nazis seem half-witted. Phyllis Calvert plays Lanvin's daughter Julie, in love with Delange, but her acting is too staidly British to make the part believable.

Eric Portman, on the other hand, was able to display his versatility again in a film called *Squadron Leader X,* directed by Lance Comfort, though the story was too silly to have carried any likelihood of conviction. A German flier is ordered to bomb Ghent in order to put the blame on the British. While still in RAF uniform, he is found by the Belgian resistance, who "repatriate" him to England (oddly, this part fell foul of the official censor at first because details of such an escape were supposed to be secret).[23] For a time he cooperates with German spies but, as the police net closes on them, he steals a British plane, flies away, and is shot down by the Luftwaffe! Finally, from this group of spy films, *The Night Invader* had David Farrar as a British intelligence agent in Holland and Anne Crawford as an American girl he falls in love with. Herbert Mason was the director of this effort, another example of the basically escapist movie much of the industry favored throughout the war.

Ealing's *The Foreman Went to France* (U.S. title: *Somewhere in France*), on the other hand, gained more respect from critical opinion because it tackled its subject at a deeper level of seriousness and within the confines of a less improbable plot. Indeed, its story of a British factory foreman going to rescue machinery from France during the days of collapse in June 1940, conceived for the film by J. B. Priestley, had some basis in fact. There is a dedication to a real foreman, Melbourne Johns. Charles Frend had again been chosen by Balcon to direct, and he made of it his first notable screen success.

It was a clever touch to have the story told retrospectively, the opening of the film set in 1942, the year of its release, in the factory itself that is producing cannon for aircraft. The foreman Fred Carrick goes onto the roof to join the plane spotters, as an enemy bomber is chased and finally shot down by a night fighter that uses one of their own types of cannon. Later one of the spotters recalls Fred's saga of going in search of three machines loaned to the French, and so events from two years ago, which must have been very much past history to a cinema audience, are revived in a way that makes them relevant again. Moreover, the plot is dominated by the theme of collaboration, the legacy of French fascism, and the part played by the underhand forces of the "fifth column" in securing the surrender of France. If there was a lesson to be drawn, it was not that Britain might have gone the same way in similar circumstances so much as that the French situation was part of the total climate of illusion and weakness that had paralyzed the democracies in the face of the Nazi threat. "We're waking up at last," Fred says in the course of the film. "By God, it's not going to be too late."

Fred Carrick's journey is undertaken on his own initiative, against the wishes of his management, and started only after a determined battle with the bureaucrats to get himself a passport. As played by Clifford Evans, he is an epitome of the former Welsh grammar schoolboy now making a career in engineering, and one would hardly expect him to stay for long on the factory floor or even to be there in the first place except as another symbol of British class-consciousness. He has not been abroad before, he shudders with disgust when a French fellow-traveler in a crowded train compartment starts eating a sausage (garlic, no doubt), but, when he opens the window, he is quickly made to shut it again by those who do not share the British obsession with healthy fresh air. The train is halted before it reaches Fred's eventual destination of Bivry, southeast of Paris, and while he is standing in a station buffet everyone disappears, warned of a German advance in the area, except the stationmaster, who turns out to be the first of the fifth columnists. From him Fred commandeers a bicycle and carries on to Bivry.

The French factory is deserted, except for its American secretary Anne Stanford, who is clearing up documents. The part is played by Constance Cummings, an American-born actress living in England, and it is one of the curiosities of the film that at times she seems to find it difficult to recover her American accent. When the local mayor (Robert Morley) arrives with his own guarantee of the safety of the machines, she has the wit to realize that he is a fascist and has been tipped off by the stationmaster from the other town. Chance brings along a couple of British soldiers with a lorry, and Fred and Anne enlist their aid in loading the machines and making off before the collaborators can stop them. The rest of the film, much of it shot in southwest England, is concerned with their progress across France to an Atlantic port, from which they escape with the machines.

There had been some snatches of stilted dialogue in the early part of *The Foreman Went to France,* but the appearance in it of Tommy Trinder as a cockney soldier changes the tone of the film. The use of a popular comedian to represent a working-class figure was a common device in British cinema, but such was Trinder's naturalness and self-confidence, carefully guided no doubt by his director, that he made some success of the part, although his jokiness could not be entirely repressed. He is well partnered by the youthful Gordon Jackson as his Scottish companion. Jackson had been a draughtsman in an aircraft factory and had acted previously only in school theatricals and radio plays. Both of them sound unforced and unassuming as they discuss their civilian jobs and their hopes—Tommy the bus conductor from Deptford whose route runs from the underground station at Golders Green ("my brother used to be the British consul there") and along Baker Street to finish at Trafalgar Square; Jock the garage hand who is saving money to take courses in engineering. It was not a momentous breakthrough in terms of realism, but at least it was a movement toward a more credible way of representing class behaviour, and it is doubtful if it would have happened at all without the need felt by some filmmakers to come to grips with British wartime society. Cavalcanti, from a documentary background, was associate producer, and as such he was in a position to advise Ealing on ways of achieving greater naturalism.

The further adventures of the foreman and his companions lead them to encounter floods of refugees on the road, deliberately encouraged, they assume, by the fifth columnists to obstruct the movement of troops. They give a lift to a group of children just before the refugees are callously machine-gunned by Nazi fighters. Anne is looking for her sister, who works at a hospital on the route, but finds that she has been killed in an indiscriminate air raid. While she is depositing the children at a convent, the men cope with another spy, this time disguised as a British officer, and they have to shoot their way out of a chateau. They are pursued by a Stuka and, though it crashes, the pilot has succeeded in fatally wounding Jock, and they have to leave his body. In the nick of time, as German forces close in, Fred, Anne, and Tommy reach a small fishing port, from which the last vessel is about to sail for England. It is only able to take the machines aboard when the French people agree to leave their possessions behind. The skipper (Francis L. Sullivan, unrecognizable in the part) says, "We shall owe everything to your country when France lives again—one day," a rare moment of optimism in the course of Anglo-French relationships. Both the Free French and the War Office were credited with cooperating in the making of *The Foreman Went to France.*

Later in the year Ealing also completed *Went the Day Well?* with Cavalcanti taking the director's seat himself this time.[24] The opening quotes the lines—"Went the day well?/We died and never knew./But well or ill/ Freedom, we died for you." It begins retrospectively again, with a villager from Bramley End, in southern England, recalling a battle there at Whitsun of 1942, when Nazis disguised as British troops made an attempt to operate as the spearhead of an invasion that failed. It is perhaps wrong to read too much ambiguity into the title, just as the views of Cavalcanti himself a couple of decades later, about the film having a certain antiwar quality in its depiction of villagers reacting to German brutality with their own counter-

The Foreman Went to France. **Foreman and British soldiers overcome a bogus officer in a French chateau (Gordon Jackson, Clifford Evans, John Williams, and Tommy Trinder).**

violence, are essentially hindsight.[25] Fear of invasion continued to exist in Britain through 1941 and 1942, and probably only receded with news of the North African victories of the autumn, the time of the film's release. No one knows for certain how the British would have reacted to invasion and occupation, though Kevin Brownlow and Andrew Mollo tried a penetrative screen speculation on the theme in *It Happened Here,* finally completed in 1964, using amateur performers in the realist tradition of Cavalcanti as documentary filmmaker. *Went the Day Well?* suffered from some woodenness of characterization, but one of its virtues was a recognition of the level of determination needed to combat Nazi ruthlessness.

The script bears little resemblance to the Graham Greene story on which it was supposed to be modeled. Greene's *The Lieutenant Died Last* had been published during the summer of 1940, a time when a genuine invasion of England seemed to be imminent.[26] There are no disguised Germans and no collaborators. The group of parachutists who seize a village with the aim of blowing up the main railway line to the north are nervous, polite, and even inept. When a boy runs away, they shoot at him but make sure that he is only hit in the legs. The village poacher, a character re-created in the film where he is played by Edward Rigby, snipes at them with an old Boer War Mauser rifle, and those that he does not succeed in killing manage to blow themselves up with their own explosives. The lieutenant, grievously injured, begs the poacher to finish him off—which he does, with the German's own gun. It is a curious tale, not included in the volumes of collected stories by Graham Greene published after the war, and, if taken literally, its estimate of the enemy is wide of the mark and radically different from the mood of the film *Went the Day Well?*

In the film, the village harbors its own fifth columnist in the person of the local squire Oliver Wilsford, acted by Leslie Banks. It is he who has done the groundwork for the Nazis before a group of English-speaking men in British uniforms (led by officers played by Basil Sydney and David Farrar) arrive by lorry to billet themselves unexpectedly on the inhabi-

***Went the Day Well?* Nazi paratroopers masquerading as British soldiers threaten the villagers in their church (Basil Sydney, leading the enemy, Frank Lawton as a sailor on leave).**

tants. Their task is more important than that of interfering with rail communications. They have to hold their ground for forty-eight hours and dislocate British radar with their electronic equipment. Gradually the villagers begin to suspect—the newcomers write figures in the continental fashion, a boy is bullied by a soldier, a bar of chocolate made in Vienna is discovered. When the Germans realize what is happening, they lock the people in the church and, as soon as the vicar tries to ring the bells in order to raise the alarm, they shoot him. The local Home Guard is also massacred. Wilsford pretends to escape with the village policeman and murders him in the churchyard.

However, resistance soon grows. The local postmistress strikes down one of the enemy and tries vainly to phone a message before she is killed. The boy of Greene's story manages to escape and raise the alarm. Other villagers break out and seize firearms. The climactic scene of the film is the one where the vicar's daughter Nora (Valerie Taylor), aware now of Wilsford's treachery, steels herself to shoot him with a revolver after she has come upon him trying to remove part of the defenses of the manor house and admit the Germans. The female middle class responds as it did in *Miss Grant Goes to the Door,* in some ways a predecessor of this film. Another worthy lady of the parish sacrifices herself on an exploding hand grenade in order to save the children, and the only woman in the film to show hysteria springs from the lower orders. It is not simply a sudden discovery of their own potential for violence that motivates these characters, but also a translation into action of the now more commonly shared national assumption that only the methods of total and ruthless war will beat the Nazis. The armed villagers defend the manor until British troops arrive to rescue them.

During the battle for the Ardennes in 1944, a German unit did disguise itself by wearing American uniforms. The possibility of its happening in Britain was no doubt well founded, but by late 1942 the chances of betrayal from within were slight. *Went the Day Well?* was an unusual film, not liked by some critics and distributed in America under the no-nonsense title of *48 Hours*.[27] Roy Kellino was responsible for special effects, and the editor was Sidney Cole, who had worked with Thorold Dickinson on his documentaries about the Spanish Civil War. As for *The Foreman Went to France,* the music was written by William Walton.

At home, relief about the ending of Britain's isolation in the war had been overshadowed early in 1942 by the grave disappointments of the winter. The failure of the British army's initiatives in Libya, the retreat to El Alamein, and the loss of Tobruk were particularly bitter blows because of the expectations the press and the newsreels had raised about the chances of Rommel's being defeated. The morale of the people slumped at this time. The situation encouraged the first feelings of nostalgia for the brave days of the blitz, a sentiment which was destined to be repeatedly revived during many periods of crisis in postwar Britain. The blitz indeed provided the climax for the first real home front feature film of the war, *Salute John Citizen,* directed by Maurice Elvey.

The film's main character, a London clerk called Bunting, is based on the hero of a couple of novels by Robert Greenwood, and the script sets out to present the life style of an average wartime family, an intention narrated at the onset by Bunting's next door neighbor Oskey. This person is played by Stanley Holloway, rather unwisely made to speak with a northern accent that does not suit him. The Buntings husband and wife, are performed by Edward Rigby and Mabel Constanduros, who make a tolerable success of their roles as the typical lower-middle-class and middle-aged couple, renting their suburban house in the fashion of the time, before home ownership became more common. However, the players of the three children do not totally convince as members of this class—Jimmy Hanley as the elder son Ernest who does a clerical job in a laundry, Eric Micklewood as his brother Chris who runs a garage, and Peggy Cummins as their younger sister Julie. Ernest is a music-lover who plays the family piano, often to his father's discomfort, and he takes his girlfriend Evie (Dinah Sheridan) to classical concerts. He has ambitions to become a chartered accountant, but finds his father unwilling at first to raise the money for the fees. Just as Mr. Bunting is beginning to think about helping his son, he is brutally sacked from his work, after forty-eight years' service, by a new, younger head of the firm. The Bunting family have to struggle again to make ends meet.

When war comes, both boys are in reserved occupations and not eligible for immediate call-up. Ernest is a pacifist anyway, and argues in a friendly manner with his boss, who wants Germany to be bombed. Shortage of labor has caused Mr. Bunting to be reinstated in his old job. During the blitz the family take cover in an Anderson shelter in their back garden. Ernest and Evie decide to marry—they have found a suitable house to rent—but the wedding actually takes place in a roofless church bombed the previous night. Chris at last joins up and becomes a sergeant pilot in the RAF. Mr. Bunting is a warden now and, as the blitz goes on during the following year, he and Julie put on their tin hats and go out to tackle incendiary bombs, at one point climbing up to the roof of a mansion owned by a retired colonel. Ernest at first is scornful of their high spirits, but the birth of a son to Evie during a raid and the destruction of the laundry create a new sense of responsibility. He shakes off his former views and determines now to enlist, to fight for a "new and better world."

Although the execution of *Salute John Citizen* can be faulted, it still has some interest as a social document. It offered a certain challenge to the audience of 1942 in putting onto the screen a subject so seemingly mundane as the ordinary existence of a family supposedly from the terraces of suburbia, a section of society not often represented in British cinema, which preferred either the glamor of Mayfair or the abyss of the East End. It did not have quite the right players, in spite of the presence of popular performers like Stanley Holloway and the comedian George Robey, who takes a small part as Bunting's workmate, killed in the blitz. Like Elvey's previous film *For Freedom* or the Boultings' *Thunder Rock,* it did not back away from the issue of pacifism, although in all three films the idea is ultimately discredited. Nevertheless, as a family film it did not excite nearly as much attention in the mind of the public as did *Mrs. Miniver,* Hollywood's version of British domestic life in wartime.

Mrs. Miniver at least served to prove that stock ideas about the British and their hierarchy of class relationships were not confined to the British themselves. No matter how much it came to be despised by the intelligentsia, it clearly had powerful sentimental appeal for cinemagoers in 1942. Its fantasy world of middle-class respectability and lower-class comic deference suited perfectly the growing mood of self-congratulation about the preceding period of the war and also that deep-rooted conservatism of the British people which was to survive the political changes of

1945. Directed by William Wyler, it starred Greer Garson and Walter Pidgeon and, in spite of its faults, was a sincere attempt by Americans to pay tribute to Britain's stand against Nazi Germany; and indeed it did have a considerable impact in the United States.[28] It was not long before Anglo-American relationships were to move into quite a different phase.

For Americans, on the other hand, a short impression of London in the aftermath of the blitz was conjured up by a Spectator documentary called *London Scrapbook,* directed by Derrick de Marney and Eugene Cekalski. Its approach was an ingenious one, having the American actress Bessie Love, now resident in England, taking along her home movies to the Films Division of the MOI, where she has also arranged to meet Basil Radford in the corridor. He has supplied some of the ideas for the film project, all of which she disagrees with, while she hopes to sell the idea to a weary and sceptical official, played by Leslie Mitchell of Movietone. The episode is an amusing parody of MOI procedures. As they run the material in the viewing theater, Bessie Love comments throughout, making points for the intended audience across the Atlantic about the shortages and austerities being endured by British people. It includes details like the stamping of food ration books and cutting out coupons for the purchase of clothing. It is impossible to know whether or not it had the intended educational effect in America but, started as it had been before that country's entry into the war, it must have appeared somewhat outdated by the time of its release overseas, when American servicemen coming to Britain in growing numbers were experiencing at first hand the difficulties of normal life there.

Recollection of the past came also to be one of the chief features of the Crown Film Unit's documentary *Listen to Britain,* inevitable as a result of the long time span between commencement of production in April 1941 and its public premiere a year later.[29] The original idea for the film had come from Bernard Miles, as a five-minute piece about the lunchtime concerts being given in the National Gallery by the orchestra of the Central Band of the RAF (a mini-symphony orchestra, in fact) with the pianist Myra Hess, and the working title had remained *National Gallery* for some time. However, as its director Humphrey Jennings and its editor Stewart McAllister worked together on the film, it became a much broader exercise. The professional relationship of these two very different people—Jennings, the Cambridge intellectual with wide cultural horizons, and McAllister, the practical though withdrawn Scot—made of *Listen to Britain* a film which achieved a simplicity of approach often denied to well-intentioned documentaries of the British school. The distributors insisted on the addition of an intrusive verbal introduction, which was spoken by the Canadian Leonard Brockington, but otherwise there is no narration, simply a harmoniously conceived counterpoint of sound and images that offers a cumulative experience of ordinary Britons in their working and leisure environments.

Looking back now from a time when the medium of television has become such a major factor in national life, it is difficult to recapture the almost naive sense of surprise and delight that people in the forties could express when they saw themselves and locations familiar to them on the cinema screen. In some cases, it took the form of embarrassed laughter, as the researchers of Mass-Observation had noticed.[30] Unlike the newsreels, *Listen to Britain* had no aim of preaching to its audience. Within its concise range of only two reels, it presented a rapid succession of impressions of, among others, dancers at the Tower Ballroom in Blackpool, Canadian soldiers in a train singing "Home on the Range," a woman at an ambulance station in the Old Bailey accompanying herself on the piano as she sings "The Ash Grove" to her colleagues, children in a school playground, railway signalmen and coal miners, the BBC broadcasting to the world, women workers at Gillette's factory listening to a "Workers' Playtime" broadcast and singing "Yes, my darling daughter," Flanagan and Allen performing at an ordnance factory in Hayes Middlesex with "Round the Back of the Arches," the Royal Marines band marching to "A Life on the Ocean Wave," and, in what is still the climax of the film, Myra Hess touching the keyboard in Mozart's K. 453 concerto, the Queen and Kenneth Clark sitting side by side in the front row at the National Gallery. There is something in the film's visuals, photographed by Chick Fowle, and its soundtrack, recorded by Ken Cameron, that had meaning for everyone, and the very immediacy of its appeal, rather than any complex symbolism, made it a masterpiece of direct communication.

The MOI thought *Listen to Britain* worthy of reissue in many different foreign versions, some with slight variations in content and almost all with some kind of linguistic explanation. Besides areas as diverse as Spain, Turkey, and Latin America, prints were prepared later for the newly liberated territories of Europe in 1943 and 1944. Thus, this most celebrated of British wartime short documentaries was already seen as representing both British involvement in the war and the unity of the British people. The film was made at exactly the right moment in British Second-World-War history, just when from the immediate reality of the past there was emerging a new mythology that found a perfect exponent in Humphrey

Listen to Britain. **Sounds and images of British people at leisure. Two girls and an airman at the Tower Ballroom, Blackpool.**

Listen to Britain. **Senior military officer, Her Majesty the Queen, and Kenneth Clark listening to Myra Hess playing Mozart at the National Gallery.**

Jennings, with his romantic and patriotic view of British society. The dangers of this kind of vision were also recognized by a few observers who wondered if the war effort was really being helped by such a soft-centered film, and certainly the spirit behind it is far removed from the kind of hard-line propaganda put out by the enemy.[31] However, if one believes in the collective will of the British people to resist Hitler after Dunkirk, *Listen to Britain* must stand as one of its most moving and lasting memorials.

In July 1941, Duff Cooper had been replaced as Minister of Information by Brendan Bracken, one of Churchill's closest friends. He accepted the post with the traditional show of reluctance, but put such a firm hand on it that he retained it to the end of the war. In the following year, the MOI sent Sidney Bernstein to New York to negotiate for the further distribution of British films in the United States. A deal was made in October with eight distributors, each to take one feature film and two shorts and then exchange them on a rotation basis, the terms being the same for each film irrespective of merit. It caused some unease within the Films Division and more strongly expressed dissatisfaction from the MOI directorate, which had not been consulted. However, many of its critics did not fully understand how difficult it was to get any British films at all to be shown widely in America.[32]

In the meantime the MOI-sponsored program of shorter films saw during 1941 and 1942 a shift of emphasis from blitz-inspired material to the promotion of projects about industry. This effort included propaganda directed at the workers themselves, in particular the newsreel series *Warwork News,* which was made by British Paramount in association with the Ministry of Supply and shown in factory canteens during lunch breaks.[33] There were two early pilot issues, and then the first real newsreel in July 1942, with an introduction by the minister (Sir Andrew Duncan), who told viewers that the films would give workers an overall impression of what they were actually producing and how the services came to rely on what they were doing. In addition to normal news items, there was always something that came out of the shop floor itself, a description of a production process perhaps or a serviceman talking to workers about how he made use of a specific weapon or piece of equipment. The series continued to appear fortnightly until shortly after the end of the war.

The need to encourage industrial production had been emphasized by the continuing lack of success on the war fronts. The loss of Malaya had been followed by retreat in Burma and the fall of Rangoon. The Dutch East Indies and the Philippines had been taken by the Japanese and an allied squadron of cruisers and destroyers sunk off Java (one of the ships lost was the *Exeter,* of River Plate fame). Japanese air power extended as far westwards as Ceylon and forced the old battleships of the Far East command to abandon the Indian Ocean. Fears for the security of the sea route round the Cape compelled the British to undertake a combined operations expedition against the Vichy French island of Madagascar, finally captured in the face of some determined resistance in November.

At home, rationing had been stepped up, embracing not only food but also domestic fuel supplies. The growth of a black market benefited some and caused bitterness in those who could not take advantage of it. There was comment about the sacrifices being made at sea on the one hand and the activities of profiteers on the other. Gradually, the relative affluence of the American servicemen now arriving in the country was to cause further problems. It was a depressing time, and even the RAF's bombing policy seemed to be provoking a predictable response. The Luftwaffe launched in April and May a series of attacks called the "Baedeker raids" because they aimed specifically at places in England that had buildings of outstanding architectural significance—Exeter, Norwich, Bath, Canterbury, and York. It was inevitable that the British press should call for further retaliation. Criticism of the kind of terror campaign favored by Churchill and Harris, although not openly admitted to be such by the government, was voiced by only a few individuals.[34] The prime minister had won his battle against his critics, really because there was no convincing alternative leader to him, but something had to be done to persuade the Americans and the Russians that Britain could take an effective part in winning the war. A renewed initiative in the factories was part of the answer.

It may be wondered why, at a time of apparent unanimity, it was necessary to concentrate the attentions of official propaganda on the industrial sector. However, some kinds of strife in labor relations persisted throughout the war, even manifesting themselves in the form of strike action in certain industries. The legacy of prewar discontent did not disappear, and there was little general optimism that the end of the war would see a continuation of full employment or a rise in the standard of living. Many still remembered the bitter aftermath of the previous conflict. Ernest Bevin, the nation's labor supremo, had the task of meeting the new challenges created by the growing needs of wartime production. In December 1941, the first women were conscripted, either to join the services or to go into the factories. The scheme was gradually extended to take in more age groups as more men left their jobs to be enlisted in the forces. The scale of this effort was such that a higher proportion of women were mobilized for the armed services or for factory labor than in either Germany or the United States.[35] A Ministry of Production was created in February and, though Beaverbrook was offered the post of minister, he rapidly backed out of it and was replaced by Oliver Lyttelton.

In Verity's *Jane Brown Changes Her Job,* a middle-class secretary (played by Anne Firth) answers a newspaper advertisement and goes to a government training center for industry. Women of this type might have been inclined to join the more fashionable services, and so a favorable picture is painted of prospects for Jane. She becomes a skilled fitter in an aircraft factory, choosing to go there with a friend she has met in the course. The two women are given accommodation by a billeting officer. Life in the factory is not all labor, and during a meal break they are able to listen to a concert by RAF musicians. At the end of the film a finished Spitfire is wheeled out of the works, and Jane makes the point that "many more women are needed." Harold Cooper directed this recruitment piece for the Ministry of Labour. *Speed-Up on Stirlings,* produced by Edgar Anstey with Graham Tharp directing, was also shot in an aircraft factory, but the objective this time was to show the detailed procedures of assembling the components of a bomber as rapidly as possible.[36] The Stirling was the first four-engined type to be built for the RAF, but it was soon to be superseded by the most outstanding and famous RAF bomber, the Lancaster.

"This is a war of machines," the narration starts in Strand's *Mobile Engineers,* "its symbol not the sword but the motor engine, its key men not only marshals but mechanics, its battlefield the mine, the foundry, the toolshop, the assembly line, its soldiers the men who wield and the men who make the engines of total war." No time for women here, one would think, but in fact the film is about a group of travelling engineers, telling their own story, who move about the country and train the new women employees in various precision skills. It was probably inevitable in 1942 that male attitudes to women workers would still in the main be patronizing, although in other respects documentary filmmakers had been able by now to have ordinary people speaking for themselves rather than through the voices of the kind of English upper-class narrators who had been used in some earlier films. The MOI film from this year that reproduced most graphically the conditions of work for women in ordnance factories was *Night Shift,* from Paul Rotha Productions.[37]

Paul Rotha, a distinguished film historian as well as a maker of films, had been one of the most acrid critics of the ministry's early inability to work out a coherent policy of war aims. The views he held about the direction society should take after hostilities ended were soon to be put forward in his later wartime films. For the moment, however, his productions related only to immediate problems. In 1941, for instance, his *You're Telling Me!,* from a story by Sidney Gilliat, had exposed the dangers of rumor, starting with a boy throwing a stone that accidentally breaks a factory window. From a passing train a traveler imagines that a number of windows have gone, so he assumes that the place has been bombed. His secretary remarks to a waitress in a café that the factory is a "terrible mess." The waitress in turn, anxious about her brother-in-law who works there, phones her husband to say that the factory has been "gutted." He is a barber who feeds to a customer the information that his brother missed death by inches. The customer takes a train journey and talks about every man on the night shift at the factory being killed. Unfortunately, it happens that he is speaking to the factory owner who advises him to look out of the window and check the truth of the matter. *You're Telling Me!* dealt with a real problem, a potential national disease, although it exaggerated the way in which a minor rumor could be blown up out of all proportion.

Another short film from Rotha, *Essential Jobs,* with story by V. S. Pritchett, seemed to concern itself with a very minor matter, how even the least likely items contributed to war production, starting with the making of one-inch wire nails.[38] Women complain about their job as they use the nails to pack cases of cocoa. One says she might join the WAAFs, the women's branch of the RAF. At a transport café, lorry drivers moan because the cocoa has not arrived and anyway who wants the soap they are carrying about the country? In fact it is needed as a precaution against anthrax by workers who are dressing skins. For their part, the women who are turning the skins into gloves ask who is wearing these fancy gloves. Answer, the WAAFs who are helping with antiaircraft defenses. Modest film though this is, its theme represented the beginnings of a different mood in the nation from the spirit of the blitz period. "Don't you know there's a war on?" the café waitress says to the disgruntled lorry driver. This particular phrase came to be repeated endlessly and self-defensively, sometimes in genuine circumstances, sometimes as an excuse for laziness or bureaucratic inertia, when slackness and indifference spread through some areas of the war effort as soon as the likelihood of defeat began to disappear. Some of those who used it may indeed almost have regretted the end of the war and the logical redundancy of their favorite retort. These were the people who continued to strike the same kind of unhelpful attitudes through the austere late forties.

Night Shift was directed for Rotha by Jack Chambers to a script by Ara Calder-Marshall, and it was shot by Harold Young in an ordnance factory at Newport, Monmouthshire. It filmed the progress of a single night shift of women workers—two thousand of them work there, one says on the track at the beginning, women from the town and from the nearby village—to their departure early the next morning, ten hours later. A foreman explains the workings of a machine to a newly recruited woman, another male engineer helps someone out of a technical breakdown. When the meal break comes round, the women rush for their places in the canteen. Posters on the wall urge the employees to put their backs into producing weapons for the Russians. As one woman plays the piano and some use the floor space for dancing, a canteen server sings "One of These Days," and the camera stays on her afterward as she begins to clear up plates from the empty tables. Back at the benches a fitter and a woman exchange banter about their roles—"What are you trying to do, win the war on your own?" he says. Tea is brought out at four o'clock on the factory floor. As dawn breaks groups of women sing together in the bus that takes them away from the factory. Even if there are shades of self-consciousness in some of the dialogue, the film succeeds overall in putting across an impression of the working conditions of the enlisted women workers in the ordnance factory. However, the truth is that many of them, especially those who had domestic commitments, probably found this kind of labor tedious and

Night Shift. Supervisor examines a gun barrel at an ordnance factory in Wales. The background poster urges support for the Russians.

restrictive. Inevitably, absenteeism became a common feature of the working lives of a number of conscripted women.

An earlier film directed by Jack Chambers, *Battle of the Books,* had described ways by which throughout Britain the distribution of books was being improved—mobile libraries and the production of cheaper editions at popular prices. A tiny number of documentaries had begun to reflect the continuing demand for cultural activity felt by some people. Strand's *CEMA,* the title standing for the Council for the Encouragement of Music and Arts, shows music being produced both in a village church and a factory canteen, an exhibition of paintings in an industrial town, and the Old Vic on tour performing *The Merry Wives of Windsor.*[39] One of those contributing to this work was the poet Dylan Thomas, who had been recruited originally by his American friend Ivan Moffat for his *Balloon Site 568,* a short film about women from different walks of life joining the WAAFs and being assigned to training for handling barrage balloons, the operation of which they had now taken over from their male colleagues.[40]

Later in 1942, Jack Chambers assembled for Rotha a compilation of sequences previously shot by Crown and other units to produce a film called *The Great Harvest.*[41] It repeated some of the material from *Spring Offensive,* and the script, as for the earlier documentary, was by A. G. Street. However, it could now be more frank about the neglected state of agriculture between the wars, remarking on the unhappy drift of farmers and farmworkers from country to town. Only with the war did these men begin to "get back something of the proper pride that they had lost during twenty years." Farmers are seen listening to a talk by a scientist on how soil analysis worked and how they should increase their yield from each acre cultivated. British farming has become the most highly mechanized in the world, the narration says, and after a wet August everyone musters together to gather the harvest—volunteers of all kinds, schoolchildren, soldiers, some American servicemen. Already thought is being given in the film to the nature of British farming after the war has ended. Music for *The Great Harvest* was written by Francis Chagrin, and the commentary was spoken by Rex Warner.

This sense of looking forward to peacetime was gradually creeping into a few of the documentaries. *Builders,* directed for Crown by Pat Jackson, had a bricklayer, a navvy, and a cranedriver talking directly to an interviewer behind the camera.[42] Part of the purpose of the film was again to explain how these men's small contributions fitted into the total pattern of production. The example is given of the ordnance factory they have just finished and the weapons it is now turning out. The men ask, though, why we have to fight a war before everyone has a common aim. Both the interviewer and they agree that, if the job can be done now, it must be possible to keep on working together when peace has returned.

The usual flood of MOI instructional and informational films ranged from subjects like how to deal with a new and deadlier type of fire bomb to minor topics such as rodent control or the making of compost heaps. Brief food flashes tried to persuade people to eat potatoes rather than bread, or to give children cod liver oil and orange juice. Animation was used in the Halas-Batchelor production *Filling The Gap* to argue for the digging of new allotments. The final slogan says, "Dig for victory—next winter may be a matter of life or death." *Arms From Scrap,* made by British Movietone with Leslie Mitchell narrating, showed steel being recovered from bombed buildings—a modern observer cannot fail to be fascinated by the sight of traction engine and hawser being used for pulling down surviving walls—and also the removal of iron railings and gates. Private owners are asked to sacrifice these without worrying too much about compensation. The scrap goes to a foundry, and the film finishes with a montage of weapons and equipment made from it.

Responsibility for the making of military training films at this time lay with the Directorate of Army Kinematography, a separate body from the AFPU, a division of functions that created a certain amount of rivalry and some talk of an amalgamation, which never finally took place. Its director Paul Kimberley had retained his civil post as head of National Screen Service, the organization which was producing most of the feature film trailers being distributed round the cinema circuits. The rationing of film stock had inspired a suggestion that these advertizing snippets could be dispensed with, a measure Kimberley naturally was anxious to avoid, and in discussion it was pointed out that his company also produced the MOI's propaganda trailers, seen by the authorities as an important part of their informational efforts on screen. In fact, the economies that might have been made by cutting out trailers were too insignificant to be worth putting into effect.[43]

During 1941, the War Office undertook with Ealing the production of a film to deal with the vital question of security in the army, eventually growing from a two-reel short to a feature-length movie under the title *The Next of Kin,* a name selected by its director Thorold Dickinson.[44] It was derived from the standard BBC and press announcement that "the next of kin of casualties have been informed." The opening captions indeed proclaim the film's purpose—"Security—This is the story of how *you* unwittingly worked for the enemy, *you* without knowing gave him the facts, *you* in all innocence helped to write these tragic words," followed by the main title of the film. The military advisor who helped in the writing of the script was Captain Sir Basil Bartlett, himself a security officer. The treatment for it was well underway when the War Office discovered that Dickinson had been given the comical classification of a "premature anti-fascist" because of his film activities in support of the republic during the Spanish Civil War. To these blinkered bureaucrats this sounded suspicious indeed, and for a time Bartlett had to pursue some tongue-in-cheek surveillance of Dickinson while working on the film script in cooperation with Ealing's script supervisor, Angus MacPhail. At the start of the war Thorold Dickinson had not hesitated to offer his services to the military, but had been kept inactive by them for more than year, during which he had produced for the MOI his evacuation film *Westward Ho!* and a piece called *Yesterday is Over Your Shoulder,* about government training schemes in engineering. He had also turned his attention to directing *The Prime Minister,* a historical feature about Disraeli, with John Gielgud. By the time *The Next of Kin* was finished, he had been given military rank and put in charge of the production commitments of the Directorate of Army Kinematography.

Originally the plot of *The Next of Kin* had been meant to be about faulty British security at the time of a German invasion of Britain, but, as this particular threat began to diminish, it was changed to the betrayal of a commando raid on the French coast, again through careless talk on the part of servicemen. The War Office intended it only for army personnel, but in the end Michael Balcon managed to have it released to the general public. The attack shown in the film, on a submarine base in Brittany, is seen as a limited success, but at the cost of very heavy casualties. Berlin has received information about the raid a few hours before it is mounted and, although it is too late to move up heavy forces, sufficient German troops are on hand to wipe out the flanks of the British brigade as it lands. Dickinson shot these scenes around Mevagissey in Cornwall, using a group of soldiers on loan from the army and four aircraft (to represent a larger number) placed at his disposal by the RAF, and marshalling these forces proved to be a major task, especially as he had to suffer frequent changes in technical staff. For the officers, actors were used, Brefni O'Rorke as the brigadier and Jack Hawkins in an early screen appearance as the brigade major. It was the first British film to depict their own troops being mown down in large numbers and to have shots of British corpses near the end. The effect on the audience at an official preview in the Curzon cinema was predictably sensational. Thorold Dickinson himself testified to the sense of shock experienced by many of those present. Churchill insisted on some cuts in the casualty sequences and hoped that it would not be released to the general public, but he had to give in when the military themselves did not object to its distribution. It is now known that German intelligence through direct spy activity was a bungled operation in Britain, but *The Next of Kin* encouraged the reverse view, and the army authorities were anxious at all costs to maintain the secrecy that surrounded operations against the German-occupied mainland of Europe.

The first major enterprise of 1942 to be undertaken by Lord Louis Mountbatten and Combined Operations Command was an attempt in March to destroy the huge dry dock at St. Nazaire in Brittany, at the mouth of the Loire. Apart from the potential this port had as a U-boat base, the existence of the dock meant that it might be used in the future by the *Tirpitz,* sister ship of the lost *Bismarck.* Her possible presence on the Atlantic coast was a factor the navy was anxious to eliminate. The matter was resolved by taking in a British force under cover of darkness and, while groups of commandos held off the defenders, the destroyer *Campbeltown,* one of the former American lend-lease ships, was rammed into the dock gates. The Germans were puzzled. Surely the British could not expect to immobilize the dock by using a fragile destroyer? While most of the Britons who had landed were being taken prisoner and a German party was searching the *Campbeltown,* explosive charges in the destroyer's hull shattered both the ship and the dock gate. British casualties for such a successful operation had not been too heavy, but the coincidence of the raid with the completion of *The Next of Kin,* added to the fact that planning was taking place for the much larger assault on Dieppe, was responsible for Churchill's anxiety about the release of the film. It was an understandable reaction. St. Nazaire had been hailed as a bold triumph, rare enough in the early part of 1942, but there was a danger now that the public might see the operation in a different light if they made a connection between the film and the real raid.

The St. Nazaire battle itself came to be re-enacted in the final part of a feature film made in 1952 with Trevor Howard and Richard Attenborough. The lend-lease American destroyers were not popular with the navy. They rolled heavily in stormy seas, they were slow, and each had a distinctive First World War

***The Next of Kin.* Betrayed British soldiers under air attack after they have landed on the French coast.**

profile on account of their unique four funnels. The film, directed by Compton Bennett, was titled *The Gift Horse* (U.S. title: *Glory at Sea*) for these reasons. Two of the *Campbeltown's* funnels were removed for St. Nazaire so that she could try to disguise herself as a German destroyer while approaching the harbor.

German espionage is shown in *The Next of Kin* to be both widespread and efficient. One agent in London even contrives the old trick of temporarily exchanging an RAF officer's briefcase in a restaurant, so that he can borrow the "mosaics" (aerial photographs) which finally give away the brigade's operational destination. The unit has been sent to train near Westport (Liverpool), a fact first disclosed by a lovesick lieutenant to a striptease artist who has been entertaining the troops. She and her dresser are fifth columnists, though the older woman is the controlling influence, being able to exercise sway over the girl because of her addiction to cocaine. The Nazis are alerted to the fact that a special operation is being planned and parachute an agent (Mervyn Johns) into the north of England so that he can watch the camp. His pseudonym is Davis and, having lived in the country before the war, he is able to impersonate a businessman who has been bombed out of his home. In Westport his contact is a bookseller called Barratt (Stephen Murray), who had a German mother and is sympathetic to the Reich.

Davis soon attracts the attention of a security officer (Reginald Tate) who has been attached to the brigade, but he manages to slip through the net, although the cabaret girl and her dresser are arrested. Barratt blackmails his assistant, a Dutch refugee called Beppie Leemans (Nova Pilbeam), by threatening to have the Nazis imprison her parents in Rotterdam, and she discovers from her boyfriend, a soldier at the camp, the date of the brigade's departure. As soon as she realizes fully what use Barratt will be making of the information, she seizes a knife and stabs him. However, Davis returns at this moment and, after knocking out the girl, he places her near a gas fire and turns on the tap. The police assume that she has murdered the bookseller and then committed suicide. Davis knows now about the "mosaics," which will provide the final clue in the jigsaw, and, as soon as he has reported to the London spies, steps are taken to find a copy of the photographs. After the briefcases have been switched, a developed print is sent to Berlin by way of a neutral country.

In the month after St. Nazaire, Mass-Observation interviewed a small number of people who had seen *The Next of Kin* in London cinemas.[45] Almost all of them praised the film, and a large number went on to blame the officers for the careless talk, on the grounds that they should have known better and should have set a better example to their men. This prejudice against the upper classes may have been reinforced by the very end of the film where Basil Radford and Naunton Wayne appear for the first time, discussing in a train compartment the heavy casualty list which has been published in the press. What was the operation? Radford asks. Wayne says he can tell him, he knows the director of a munitions factory—he has asked him not to talk, of course—but there is another big stunt coming off in the middle of next month. As he speaks, the third person in the compartment offers him a light for his cigarette. It is Davis, the German spy.

The attack on Dieppe in August was a reconnaissance in force, a landing by six thousand troops, designed to test the defenses of a German-occupied port as a means of preparing the ground for the planning of a larger-scale invasion of France. The question of opening up a "Second Front" in Europe had become a political matter. The main burden of fighting the German army had fallen to the Russians, who were holding Moscow and Leningrad but had taken enormous losses in the face of renewed Nazi

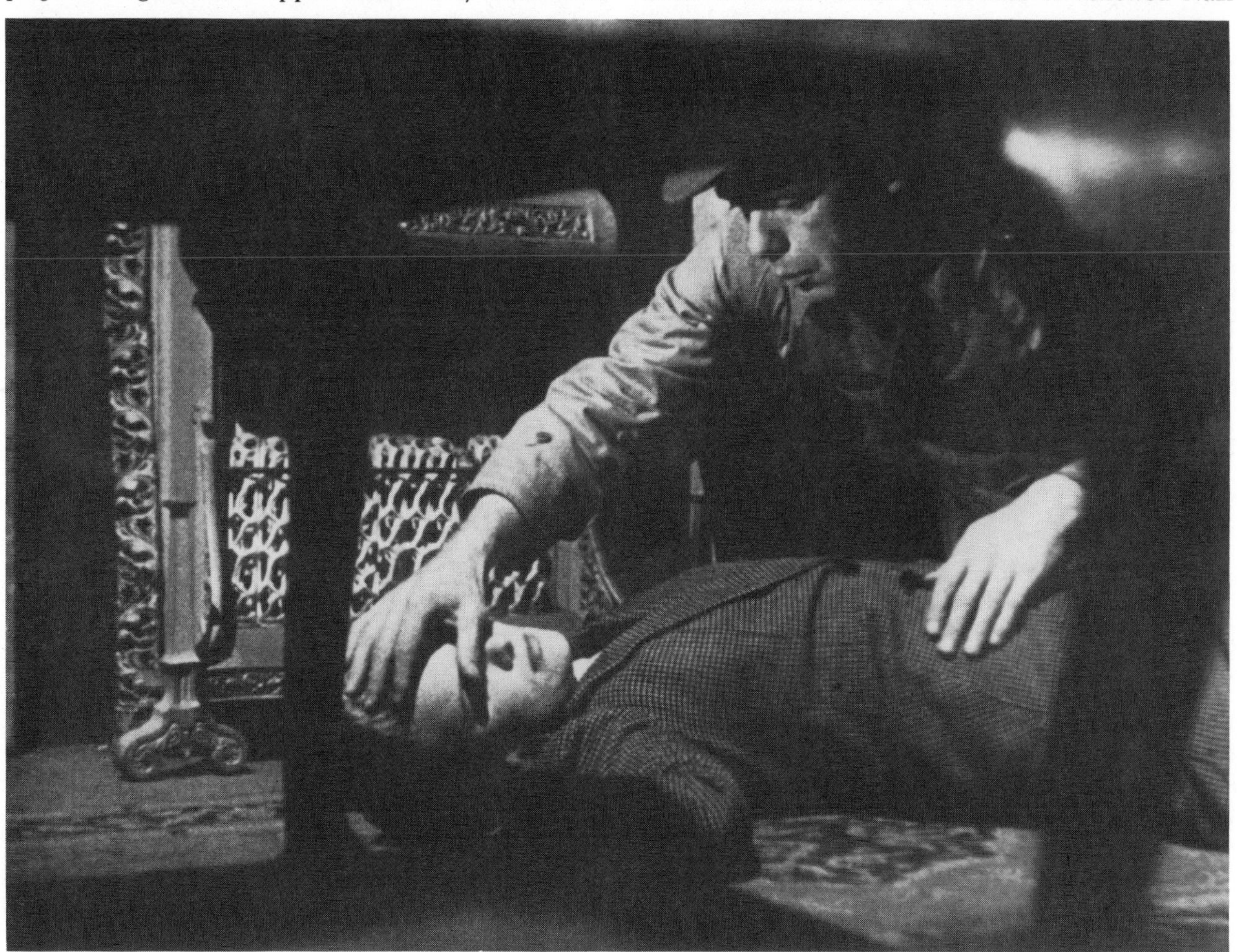

***The Next of Kin.* The spy murders his victim (Nova Pilbeam and Mervyn Johns).**

offensives over a wide area. The Americans had agreed to concentrate their main military effort against Germany, but unlike Churchill, still preoccupied with his "soft under-belly" strategy, they favored a direct invasion of northern Europe.

Dieppe was to prove how difficult it would be to undertake such an enterprise and indeed how impossible it was to seize a heavily defended coastal town. The allied forces, most of them Canadians for whom this was the first taste of war, were massacred on the beaches, few of them even reaching the sea wall. More than four thousand became casualties, the last having to surrender at midday when there was no longer any prospect of re-embarkation.[46] Overhead a titanic air battle had been taking place, and it was aspects of this conflict and the naval support that featured in the newsreels. Their commentaries admitted that there had been casualties, but blustered on about the lessons learned as if it had been a success rather than a total disaster. German film propaganda for its part, boasting of crushing an attempted invasion, was able to show to the world shots of Canadian and British bodies on the beaches, wrecked tanks, and lines of prisoners. There was talk in Britain of the real Dieppe landing, like the fictional one in *The Next of Kin,* having been betrayed to the enemy, but there was no truth in the story.

Some of those interviewed outside the cinemas felt that their intelligence had been insulted when asked what was the message of *The Next of Kin.* The Mass-Observation surveys covered only a small number of films, but there are indications that direct film propaganda often induced a feeling of weariness, a kind of "oh, here we go again" attitude. Frank Laskier, a merchant navy sailor who had lost a leg at sea, had become a sensational radio success through a number of BBC broadcasts in which he described the hardships of the men who were going through the Battle of the Atlantic. However, a clumsy attempt by the National Savings Committee to capitalize on his success by commissioning a film from Concanen in which he made a personal appearance, finishing with a savings appeal, produced a certain amount of resentment. Some people who had seen it were already buying savings certificates, and no one admitted to being persuaded to purchase more.[47] The film was called *Seaman Frank Goes Back to Sea* and, although one cannot generalize from its reception, it is bound to cast some doubt on the effectiveness of a policy of indoctrination through the cinema, especially as response to the newsreels was also so variable.[48] The physical conditions of people's lives, the bombing, and the food rationing, added to the universal conscription that affected most families, had already produced a way of thinking about the war that many needed to leave behind when they relaxed in the darkened auditoriums of the nation's screen palaces.

Although the merchant navy did not have the same glamour as the armed services, the public can hardly have been unaware of what was happening at sea. Between January and October 1942, more than a thousand merchant ships were sunk in a major new offensive by the U-boats, themselves increasing in number at a rate considerably higher than their losses. The British had to face an extra burden, that of transporting supplies and equipment to North Russia, an obligation constantly urged on them by both Stalin and Roosevelt, although the menace to them of aircraft, submarines, and heavy ships based in Norway was very considerable. The tribulations of this route came to be more realistically re-created in *The Cruel Sea* than in any wartime film. In one notorious incident an entire convoy (PQ-17) was almost totally wiped out as a result of a misunderstanding on the part of the Admiralty itself. Toward the end of the year, as more escorts went to sea, as antisubmarine devices improved, and as allied aircraft became more widely used, the balance began to be more even again. Realist made a short film, *A Seaman's Story,* directed by John Taylor, in which a Newfoundlander talked about the number of times he had been torpedoed and of how he had once spent three weeks in a lifeboat, many other crew and passengers dying before the survivors were finally rescued. Its grim mood must have been meant to remind people at home of the sacrifices constantly being made for them by these civilian sailors.

Air support for the navy was becoming a matter of some controversy by the middle of 1942. The admirals, belatedly aware of the ability of planes to spot and destroy submarines, would have liked more resources to be directed toward the RAF's shore-based branch, Coastal Command. In view of the life-or-death nature of the struggle in the Atlantic, it was a reasonable aim, but it was not to the liking of Harris and the bombing school. Churchill decided that the strategic campaign against Germany must remain the first priority, although Coastal Command would be gradually strengthened, though not to the degree the Admiralty wanted. Crown made in 1942 a film titled *Coastal Command,* an hour and a quarter long, with Jack Holmes directing.[49] Its heroes were the huge Sunderland flying boats and the slimmer American-built Catalinas. They are shown supporting convoys, attacking and sinking a U-boat, fighting off enemy aircraft, and searching for a German warship at sea. This vessel is harassed by bombers and torpedo-carrying planes operating from Iceland, all with a measure

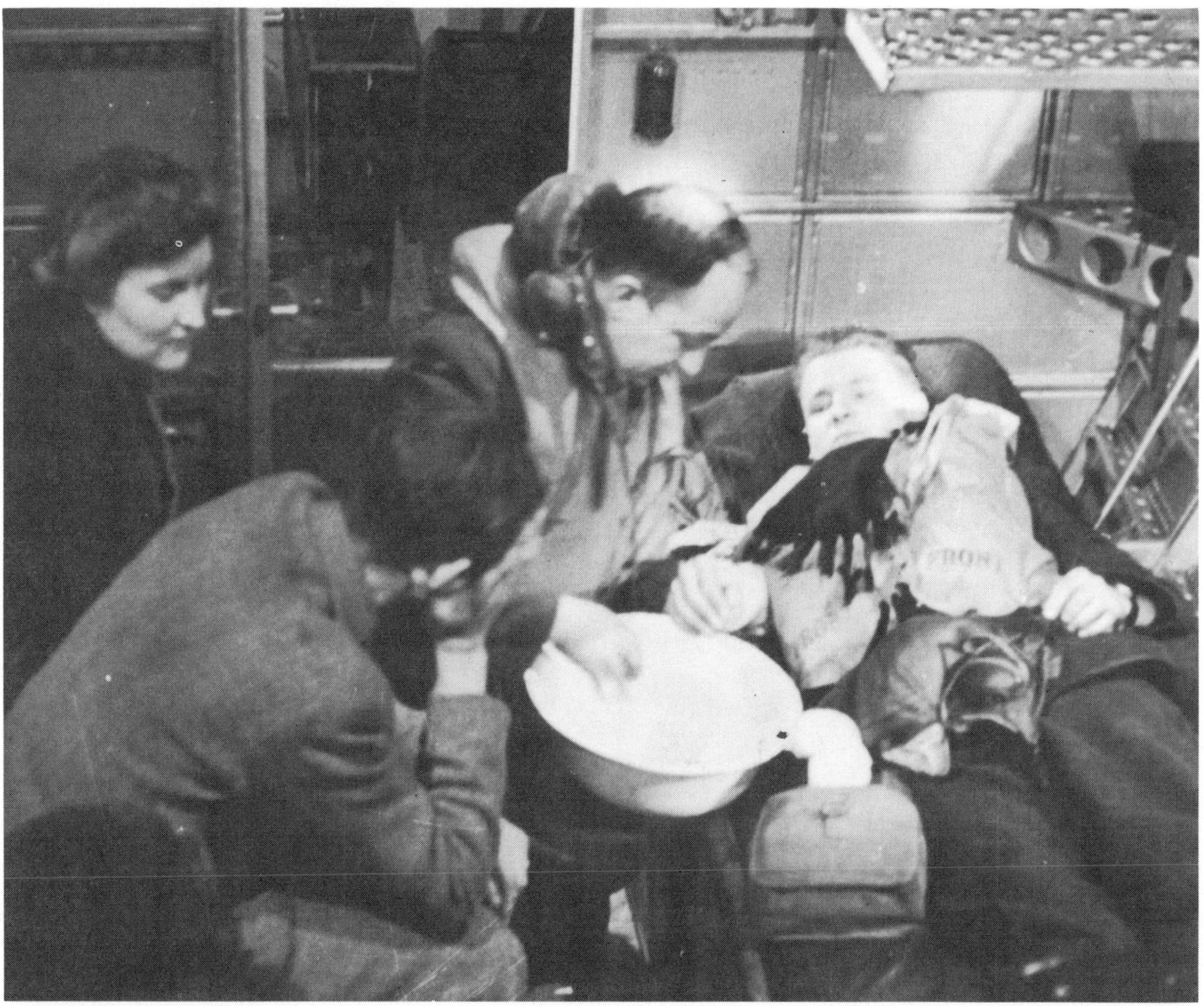

***Coastal Command.* Setting up the scene with a wounded air gunner in a Sunderland flying boat (continuity girl Isobel Pargiter and director Jack Holmes, left).**

of success that in fact was unusual for the British at that time. It is not surprising that the film put across to the public no idea of the heavy losses in aircraft that Coastal Command could take in the course of operations like this. A battle between a flying boat and a submarine on the surface, for instance, was by no means a one-sided affair. RAF personnel, including the commander-in-chief of Coastal Command, Sir Philip Joubert, played their own parts in the film, which featured also an Australian aircrew. It was a somewhat overlong production for its subject matter, but the photography of Jonah Jones proved as effective as ever. The score by Vaughan Williams was played by the London Symphony Orchestra conducted by Muir Mathieson, whose name was linked to the music for many wartime films, and it was one of the composer's best achievements for the medium, capturing superbly the feel of bleak seascapes and broad northern regions.

The crippling of Cunningham's battleships at Alexandria and the retreat of the army from Libya had left Malta in an even more exposed position than ever, and the naval operations of 1942 designed to pass supplies to the battered island became one of the epic episodes of the war. At the same time, British submarines took a toll of the enemy vessels crossing to Libya from Italy, a lifeline that was essential for the Afrika Corps. In spite of the early difficulties of covering maritime material, the newsreels had secured by now a firmer foothold in the naval camp, thanks to the initiative of Anthony Kimmins at the Admiralty. Cunningham's first reaction to the news that John Turner of Gaumont British had been able to photograph the *Barham* blowing up had been one of indignation, as if the visual evidence would be somehow more damaging than a press announcement about the battleship's loss (in fact, nothing was said about the *Barham* until January, and it was even later before the film was released). However, by February the admiral had relented sufficiently to allow Turner and his colleague David Prosser of Movietone to make a special film about submarine operations. They produced sequences of the crew of the *Thunderbolt* at their sailing stations, with the captain raising and lowering the periscope. A scene was staged in the operations room of the depot ship while the captain was being briefed on his next patrol. In order to shoot the submarine submerging, Prosser had himself tied to the radio mast, and he held his camera just above water as the *Thunderbolt* slipped temporarily below the surface. Finally, a ship that had been sunk already in shallow water was photographed being hit by torpedoes to represent an enemy vessel under attack.[50] Prosser sent back to London a cutting copy with his own commentary, and Movietone brought it out in May under the title *Submarine Patrol.* It attracted an unusual amount of praise, in spite of its faked sequences, and it still has extra interest since the *Thunderbolt* was in fact the resalvaged *Thetis,* originally lost through an accident while on her trials in Liverpool Bay in 1939. Sadly, she did not survive again for long, being sunk with all hands while on a real patrol.

In March a British move to escort four transports from Alexandria to Malta brought about one of the more extraordinary engagements of the year. The accompanying naval force was down to only four light cruisers and a number of destroyers, led by Rear-Admiral Vian, and it soon found itself fighting off first some Italian cruisers and then a much greater menace, the fifteen-inch gun battleship *Littorio.* Against her the cruisers' 5.25-inch guns were puny indeed, but Vian confused the enemy by making smoke and dodging in and out of the screen while his destroyers tried to launch torpedo attacks. Eventually the Italians withdrew, a fantastic outcome to such an uneven balance of strength. John Turner was aboard the *Euryalus* and David Prosser the *Dido* and, although wind and vibration made it difficult for them to hold their cameras steady and also inhibited them from using long-focus lenses, their record of the cruisers twisting and turning between the shell splashes and through the billowing clouds of smoke is one of the most impressive of the war, especially as any film of an actual ship-to-ship action is extremely rare.[51] Unfortunately, two of the transports were sunk next day by the Luftwaffe, which had a power and accuracy against ships at sea that their counterparts in the RAF lacked at this time. The second battle of Sirte, as the episode came to be called, was made the subject of the popular novel *The Ship* by C. S. Forester.

In April Malta received from the King the collective award of the George Cross, the normal decoration for gallantry given to civilians. A cooperative production by the Army, RAF, and Crown Film Units named *Malta G. C.* was put out as a tribute to the exceptional ordeal of the island, which only came to an end with the allied victories in North Africa at the close of the year.[52] At the worst period of the siege, the food of the islanders had been more severely rationed than in Britain. Commentary for the film was spoken by Laurence Olivier, and it had sequences of air raids (the total of nearly three thousand is mentioned), bomb damage, and civilians pluckily carrying on. From a piece of wall graffiti saying "Bomb Rome" the camera cuts to Wellingtons preparing for an attack on enemy airfields in Sicily. Some of the ships in the harbor had survived Operation Pedestal in August, one of the most savagely fought of the relief convoy passages. Although the fleet by that time could afford protection by three aircraft carriers, one of them was sunk by a U-boat and another heavily damaged by the Luftwaffe, and losses among the other warships and merchantmen were also grievous. Movietone made a separate film about the episode, *Malta Convoy,* released nontheatrically.[53] Pedestal was the biggest operation of its kind and vital for Malta's survival. Anthony Kimmins, who had been with the fleet, narrated the story of the convoy's four-day battle against constant attack by aircraft, U-boats and, torpedo boats. The American-built tanker *Ohio* was set on fire but finally brought home by her British crew to land their vital cargo, and the film showed the ship's Captain Mason at Buckingham Palace, where he received a decoration for the steadfastness of himself and his men in this critical action.

The navy had a special place in the affections of a maritime people like the British. The reputation it had built up for itself since the Napoleonic wars was as the undisputed master of the seas. In spite of the disappointing outcome of the 1916 Battle of Jutland, the only major British battleship action since Trafalgar, the navy's reputation had remained undiminished and had been augmented for the public by the spectacle of its main challenger, the German high seas fleet, coming to surrender at Scapa Flow at the end of the First World War. It was known that it would never willingly avoid combat, whatever the odds, an article of faith that episodes like the River Plate battle and the sacrifices of the *Rawalpindi* and of the *Jervis Bay* were to reinforce. The navy's prestige was strong enough to survive the loss of ships like the *Hood,* the *Prince of Wales,* and the *Ark Royal.* No one

Malta G.C. **British anti-aircraft gunners defending the besieged island.**

doubted that in the end it could not be defeated. The gradual realization that it was being outstripped by the Americans in both size and firepower, and especially in experience in the future shape of naval warfare, aircraft carrier operations, was yet to come. This universal popularity for the navy gave a head start to the Two Cities feature film *In Which We Serve*.[54]

"This is the story of a ship," the opening announces, as the destroyer *Torrin* is launched. From quick shots of her at sea on trials there is a switch to the captain and crew on the quarter-deck as the ensign is run up. The camera zooms onto the water, in which there floats a copy of the *Daily Express* (a newspaper owned by Lord Beaverbrook, who had opposed war with Germany), its headline "No War This Year," and cuts then to the caption "May 23, 1941" and the destroyer in action during the battle of Crete. The inception and accomplishment of *In Which We Serve* was almost a one-man effort by Noel Coward, as producer, director, script writer, principal actor, and composer of the score. The story was indeed that of a ship, to which the personalities of three of its sailors in particular, clearly delineated though they are, come to be almost appendages. Its original was the *Kelly*, commanded throughout her brief existence by Lord Louis Mountbatten, before he moved to Combined Operations Command and in a short time to even greater heights of glory. It is difficult to imagine a more appropriate player of the Mountbatten role than Coward. Neither Leslie Howard nor Laurence Olivier, to mention his most distinguished rivals, would have seemed absolutely right for the part of the self-confident, aristocratic, yet complex and fair-minded man Mountbatten appears to have been. Noel Coward's assumption of upper-class suavity and his special kind of theatrical flair was perfect for it. Even so, the project suffered some birth pains. In this increasingly populist era, Coward was seen by some people as an anachronistic figure. The idea of the production was also attacked in the *Daily Express,* which resented the manner of the newspaper's early appearance in the film. The MOI felt uneasy about the propaganda effect of a production that showed a British warship being sunk. However, the Admiralty managed to win official approval for it. Mountbatten helped Coward with the script, David Lean worked with him as co-director, and Ronald Neame was responsible for photography.

The *Kelly* was a flotilla leader and Mountbatten's status that of Captain (D), not only commander of the ship but also in charge of all eight destroyers of the group, the fifth destroyer flotilla. She was the first of the class to be completed, on the Tyne in the spring of 1939, and she had a distinctive and tough new style and shape with only one bulky funnel,[55] The saga of her loss was closely paralleled in the film. Captain Kinross is seen directing the destroyer's fire against enemy transports carrying German troops to Crete under cover of darkness. In the morning the destroyer is trapped by the Luftwaffe and struck twice by bombs. The *Torrin,* like the real *Kelly,* turns over with her crew still at action stations, firing her guns to the last. Kinross swims to a Carley float and is joined there by a few survivors, including the film's other two principal characters, Chief Petty Officer Hardy (Bernard Miles) and Ordinary Seaman Blake (John Mills). The bulk of the plot is then unfolded as a series of flashbacks, recollections in the minds of these three men while they struggle to stay alive in the water.

It is possible to see the characterization of Kinross, Hardy, and Blake, and their families, as a kind of stereotype of British class relationships, not so much in the way the men meet aboard ship but in the manner of presentation of their lives at home. Captain Kinross, his wife (Celia Johnson), and children

***In Which We Serve*. The crew leaps overboard as the *Torrin* sinks.**

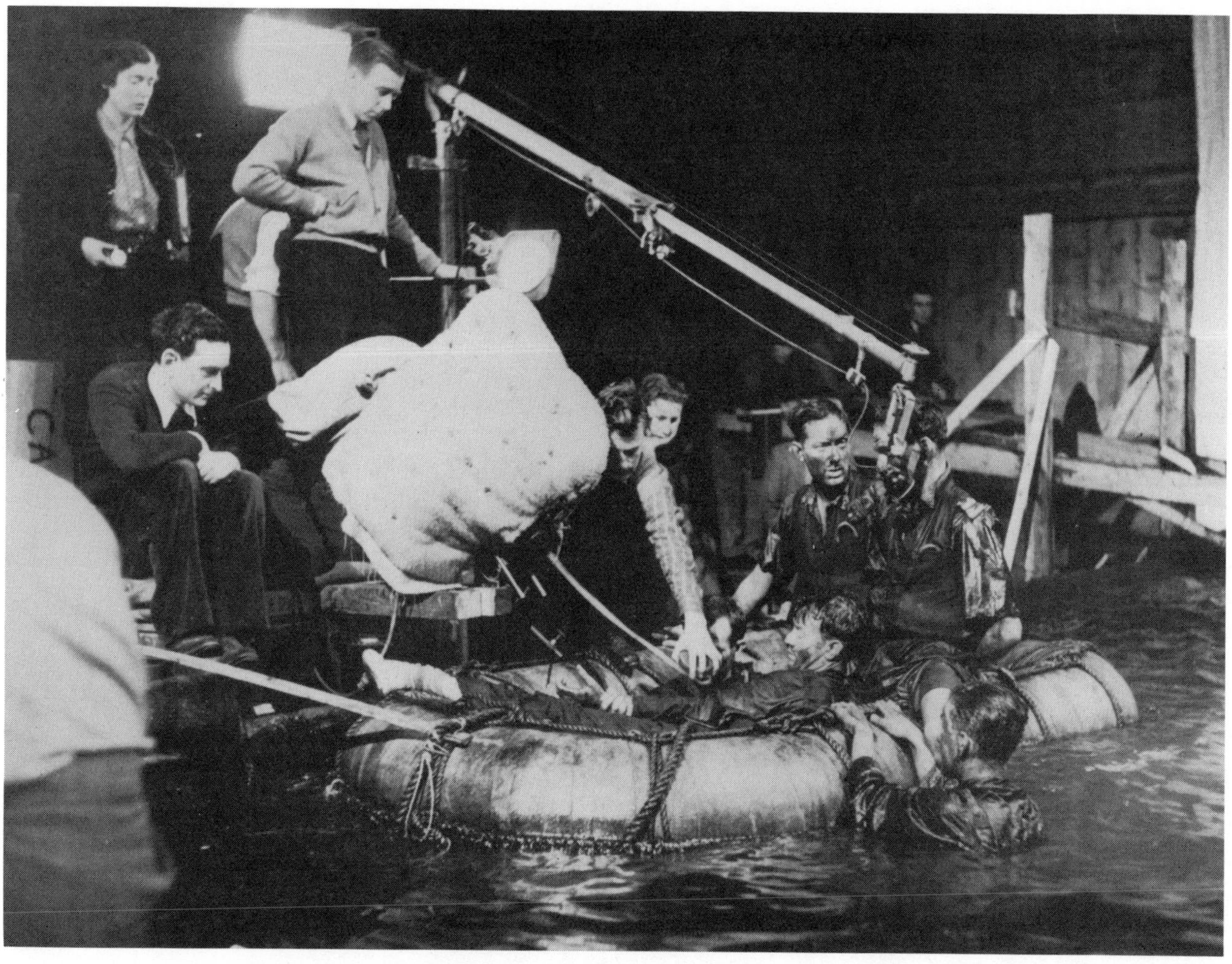

***In Which We Serve*. Setting up the sequences with the Carley float in the studio tank.**

inhabit a grand country house, they eat grouse for dinner and preside at a formal Christmas banquet. CPO Hardy's more humble table is managed by his consort Kath (Joyce Carey), who reproaches him for describing his early shore leave as "a bloody miracle," as she doesn't like "that word." In fact, "bloody" and "bastard" turn up in the film more often than they usually did in British cinema of the period, Coward's way of trying to add another touch of authenticity, though of course no film or book dared to reproduce the four-letter swear words that were in more common use on the lower decks. Watching this film, Roger Manvell noticed that the public laughed, in obvious embarrassment, at mild expressions like "bloody" and "bastard."[56] The audience was unaccustomed to even this degree of naturalism, to which a prewar censor would have objected anyway—American films had been no more adventurous in terms of language as a consequence of the influence of the Hays Office there—and Manvell rightly concluded that it was a barrier the British film in general would have difficulty in surmounting. Again it was a form of reality at odds with the fantasy life the public wanted to see on the screen.

The third character, O/S Blake, meets Freda Lewis (Kay Walsh) on a crowded train and finds out that she is a relative of Hardy, serving on the same ship. They are soon engaged and married just before the *Torrin* helps in the evacuation from Dunkirk. The real *Kelly* did not take part in this operation, and indeed was disabled at the time, so it is brought into the film almost as a history lesson for the public, a recap of a time of adversity. The symbolic value of Dunkirk to the British people is reemphasized. On the bridge the senior officer of the unit being rescued thanks Kinross and invites him to their mess some time. Army and navy counterparts unite in stiff-upper-lipped stoicism. The same kind of British endurance, at the lower-deck level, occurs later in the film when Blake has a letter from his wife to say first that she has given birth to a son and then that Kath Hardy has been killed in the blitz on Plymouth. The two women have been sharing the house with Kath's mother, a woman given to the type of wrangling traditional in this kind of family relationship on film. The pregnant Freda is the only one to survive because she has sheltered under the stairs. "Tell Walter I didn't want to leave the home," Kath says as she dies. Blake has to pass the news to Hardy who is at that moment writing to Kath. There are no visible tears. Hardy simply says he will have to take a walk on the deck for a while. He crumples up the letter and drops it into the sea.

There is, though, one incident of panic. The *Torrin* fights a night battle with German destroyers and is struck by a torpedo. One rating who is manning an ammunition hoist, played by Richard Attenborough in his first film, runs away from his post. The *Kelly* in fact had been torpedoed in May 1940 and was brought home under tow with her decks awash, a hazardous exercise. The whole of her midships section had to be reconstructed, and she was not back with the fleet again until November. Earlier in the year, a stoker had deserted his position when a mine had exploded near the *Kelly's* stern. Mountbatten's speech to his crew after that episode was re-enacted almost word for word as Kinross talks to the *Torrin's* men. He has excused this single defaulter for once, but it will be the only time he holds *himself* responsible for not getting his message across. When the *Torrin* was commissioned, he had told the crew that she must be "a happy and an efficient ship." Part of his own way of achieving that is to know each sailor personally, again a principle closely modelled on Mountbatten's own example. At the end of the film, after ninety survivors of the *Torrin* have been rescued by another of the flotilla, Kinross goes round consoling the badly injured and the dying and takes the names and addresses of their relatives. Finally, on the quay he talks to those able to walk away; he has spoken to them many times before, but now he has "run out of jokes" (Mountbatten's words, once more), and just thanks them all and shakes hands with each man in turn. A

***In Which We Serve*. The captain says farewell to the survivors (Noel Coward, John Mills, and Bernard Miles).**

hundred and thirty had died in the *Kelly*.

At the Christmas dinner Mrs. Kinross had toasted her "implacable enemy," the ship. The service and the destroyer are bigger than the men who serve in her. There is nothing remarkable about the dialogue written by Coward for the captain, the petty officer, the seaman, and their families. Indeed, it might be considered only marginally less stilted than that spoken by the characters in *Convoy* or *Ships With Wings*. However, unlike those films, *In Which We Serve* does not fall over the edge into caricature. It keeps its feet firmly grounded in real events and real experiences, seen only through the eyes of the British sailors themselves. Its very occasional use of swear words was too slight to shock the public, and its technique did not demand from them an acceptance of a kind of neorealism alien to their normal cinema-going experiences. It was finished toward the end of 1942, when remembrance of the era of Dunkirk, blitz, and retreat was already passing into mythology, and next year, while it was making more money at home than any other British feature film of 1943, it was being seen by audiences who now knew that the war had swung irreversibly in their favor.

Leslie Howard had also tried his hand again as actor-director with *The First of The Few* (U.S. title: *Spitfire*). He was joined in the cast by David Niven, another of the Britons who had returned from Hollywood to help his country. Having enlisted in the army, Niven had been specially released for this film (as he was later for *The Way Ahead*). Playing Geoffrey Crisp, an RAF station commander during the Battle of Britain, he tells his pilots the "true story" of R. J. Mitchell, inventor of the Spitfire.[57] The son of a Staffordshire schoolteacher, the real Mitchell had been apprenticed in engineering at the age of seventeen, a class background that Howard in his performance could not duplicate, but he succeeded well in portraying the man's total dedication and his obsession with work, even eventually at the expense of his own health. His main task for Supermarine Aviation in the twenties had been to design revolutionary new aircraft to win the international Schneider Trophy race, a competition undertaken, for reasons of safety, by seaplanes over water. In the film there is a semicomic episode at the 1927 race in Venice, with Filippo del Giudice as a genial Fascist party representative mouthing the words of Mussolini as Crisp races and defeats an Italian rival.[58] But in the real event only the British planes even finished that year, and the scene is introduced basically to make a political point. Inevitably the screen play, written by Miles Malleson and Anatole de Grunwald, romanticized the facts in the interests of dramatic continuity.

Mitchell visited Germany in 1934, where he became aware of the progress being achieved by Willy Messerschmidt in designing a fast monoplane fighter. In *The First of the Few*, he tries to warn a director of Vickers, which had now taken over Supermarine, of the threat from Germany. The response is that nothing can be done, the nation wants peace, and from the office window one can see a poster which says "Trust Baldwin." An earlier sequence in the film had the patriotic Lady Houston putting up £100,000 to finance the 1931 Schneider Trophy winner in place of money the government would not provide, although winning the event had become a matter of national prestige and the racing team now belonged to the RAF. The cinema public of 1942 would have appreciated these particular messages about official weakness and parliamentary lack of support for the armed forces in the thirties, and Baldwin and Chamberlain had become by now the joint scapegoats in the popular mind.

In truth, the Air Ministry itself had begun to feel that they needed to devote their estimates to genuine combat planes, not racers, and in 1930 they had put out specifications for a fast fighter. Mitchell's design, already called the "Spitfire," failed to meet them, and the contract went instead to Gloster for their Gladiator biplane. Not deterred, Mitchell went on to make an improved model, and the Rolls-Royce Merlin engine finally gave him the necessary power. In the film, William Walton's energetic fugue captures the spirit of the speed of the production process, a race against time to get the prototype Spitfire completed, though competition with Hawker's Hurricane is unacknowledged.[59] It was also a race against death for Mitchell, who in the end succumbed to cancer in 1937 at the age of forty-two. Crisp has become a convenient amalgam of a number of pilots, and he tests the first Spitfire, as well as taking part in a 1940 air dogfight sequence that finishes the film. The Hurricane had been accepted first by the RAF, and it was present in greater numbers through the Battle of Britain, but only the Spitfire had the class to outmaneuver Messerschmidt's ME109.

Arguments about appeasement on the one hand and military preparedness on the other were featured in two other films from 1942. "England has saved herself by her exertions and will save Europe by her example," says Robert Donat as the prime minister in 20th Century–Fox's historical drama *The Young Mr. Pitt*.[60] The words were genuine but the script, written by Frank Launder and Sidney Gilliat, built up a direct parallel between Britain's struggle against Hitler and her earlier stand against Napoleon, by turning the political conflict between William Pitt and Charles

The First of the Few. **Watching the Schneider Trophy race (Filippo del Giudice, center).**

The First of the Few. **The inventor alone with his creation (Leslie Howard).**

James Fox into a simple matter of the former as champion of national security through strength and the latter as leader of a peace movement. Moreover, the opening scene of the film had Pitt's father arguing for conciliation with the American rebels, a lively speech about the kinship and common language of the English and their transatlantic cousins. The lessons could not have been lost on wartime audiences. *The Young Mr. Pitt* was directed by Carol Reed, with Robert Morley as Fox and John Mills as Pitt's friend William Wilberforce.

Roy Boulting had been released by the Army Film Unit for six months to help his brother with their production *Thunder Rock,* an adaptation of a play by Robert Ardrey that had been a West End success since 1940.[61] It had Michael Redgrave as the journalist David Charleston, who, in flashback, is seen leading a passionate campaign in the thirties to wake up people to the realities of fascist expansion and to the need for collective action. However, neither his public speeches nor his book *Darkening World* have any effect. Despairing of success, he has withdrawn completely from normal life and given himself up to a hermitlike existence as a lighthouse keeper on Lake Michigan. It is 1939, and his friend Street (James Mason), an inspector for the company, vainly tries to persuade him to follow his example and to enlist with the American airmen who are helping China in the war against Japan.

Charleston is living a fantasy life, having conjured up the spirits of half a dozen people who had died when a ship carrying emigrants from Europe had sunk on the lake in 1849. Nightly he holds conversation with the captain of the vessel (Finlay Currie) and five of the passengers. Soon it seems to him that they have all been running away from something. Briggs (Frederick Cooper) from the English potteries because he cannot face the poverty and degradation of his life, Ellen Kirby (Barbara Mullen) who has been struggling for women's rights and despairs of continually going to prison for them, the Viennese surgeon Kurtz (Frederick Valk) who leaves with his wife and daughter because his use of chloroform has brought persecution upon them when one of his patients dies. With Kurtz's daughter (Lilli Palmer) Charleston has almost started a romantic relationship. But in a moment of angry impatience with them, he tells them who they really are, dead people revived only by his imagination, and they understand now that he is using them to solve his own problems. Regretting his decision to give way to mob ignorance, Kurtz says "There is no obstacle to civilization which cannot be pushed aside if only mankind has the will," and he tells Charleston that their ghosts will only leave him when he is able to summon up the strength to fight for what he believes in. The lighthouse-bound situation of the film, the dark interior shots, and the somber clothing of the emigrants create an almost claustrophobic atmosphere that is a reflection of Charleston's own dilemmas. It is doubtful, though, if the broader public much appreciated it.

Roy Boulting's return to the AFPU coincided with the critical period of the North African campaign. By this time the unit had been organized by the War Office to include a number of different sections with cinematographers and still photographers working side by side. Its members were all trained soldiers who had been selected for this special work, some with previous photographic experience, some without. The cameramen were each given the rank of sergeant and supervised by a section officer who would direct their activities and also liaise with the civilian newsreel men.[62] David MacDonald himself went out to the Middle East to lead the most important group, working at the scene of action in the western desert. One of their most experienced officers, Walter Tennyson d'Eyncourt, was lost to them when he fell into German hands at the fall of Tobruk, a fate shared by Universal's Ronnie Noble, though he was lucky enough to escape in Italy. Rushes for the material shot in the desert were processed in laboratories in Cairo before the film returned to London. Egypt was also the location for the production of a special Mediterranean newsreel series called *War Pictorial News,* compilations taken from the regular companies and distributed with a different commentary.[63]

At Pinewood the AFPU was running a training school for cameramen that was used not only by the British but also by the film units established by some of the European exiled governments. Alex Bryce had taken charge of production there after MacDonald. Hugh Stewart directed in 1942 a couple of short films, one showing life aboard a troopship and another explaining the techniques of street fighting, demonstrated by men of the Coldstream Guards. A single contribution by Harry Watt was basically an update of his earlier Dover film, now titled *Twenty-One Miles* and issued in two versions, the American one slightly longer than its British counterpart. Ed Murrow narrated the film, which, in addition to depicting the hardships of the civil population, including an obviously staged sequence of a bus being machine-gunned by a German plane, had more encouraging shots of soldiers preparing for assault landings on the enemy coast and the RAF striking back at the Nazi homeland ("a piece of cake," a raid on Cologne is described by one member of an aircrew).

Watt by now had severed his connection with the Crown Film Unit and followed his mentor Cavalcanti to Ealing, where he hoped to be able to make films of a more dramatic nature. His first effort, a short feature called *Nine Men,* sprang in its style directly from his documentary experience. It was issued at the beginning of 1943. The script, written by Watt from a story by Gerald Kersh, started as a semi-military training piece, and the first part shows recruits in various forms of exercise, a subject that was becoming a popular one for prospective screen plays at that time, with varying problems and hope of success. The AFPU had tried to produce a documentary called *The People's Army,* and some work had started with a cooperative infantry regiment until, according to Ronald Tritton's account, it had a change of commanding officer. This new broom told Tritton that he did not see why anyone would want to make a film about the British army, and anyway the title sounded as if this country was the USSR![64] Watt had more luck with his soldiers. Talking to the recruits, the sergeant reminisces to them about his own experiences in the desert, and he tells them of an incident with a patrol of which he had been a member, a recollection designed to impress his hearers with the importance in warfare of finding a little extra, *un petit peu* ("oompetypoo").

Both in the plot and in his direction, Harry Watt aimed to create a similar kind of starkness and simplicity as he had achieved in *Target for Tonight.* At Ealing he had to use actors now rather than real servicemen for the main parts, but he deliberately avoided the big screen names with their upper-class drama-school backgrounds.[65] His soldiers have genuine earthy English or Scottish accents. For the sergeant he chose the Scotsman Jack Lambert, experienced mostly as a stage actor and commissioned in the army at that time. Two other Scots characters are played by Grant Sutherland, as the burly Glaswegian who had lost his job in the police force, and the youthful Gordon Jackson, straight from *The Foreman Went to France.* He brought in Bill Blewitt, the postmaster from Cornwall who had been introduced

Nine Men. **Preparing to defend themselves against overwhelming odds and looking for that little bit extra (Grant Sutherland and Jack Lambert).**

to films by Watt in a documentary eight years previously.[66] Frederick Piper took a cockney part. Such was Watt's preference for working-class reality that he had to be reminded by Cavalcanti that other Britons were fighting the war too, and on his suggestion Watt put in a middle-class soldier, played by Eric Micklewood.

Shooting, by Roy Kellino, took place on an area of sand in Wales that convincingly simulated the dunes and distances of the desert. A patrol is attacked by an enemy plane and loses its lorry while the officer and a soldier are mortally wounded. The survivors find a stone dwelling, which they are able to hold against an Italian unit for the rest of the day, through the night, and into the next morning. They knock out an armored car with an antitank rifle, and in the darkness two of them steal food and water from a disabled vehicle. However, as their ammunition runs out they have to charge the enemy. The final hand-to-hand fight is grim and uncompromising, bayonet to bayonet, filmed in close-up. In its way it expresses the truth of war, the nasty business of man killing man. The Italians, so often derided or caricatured by the British, are treated as equal opponents. At the eleventh hour, a relieving force arrives and rescues the patrol.

Dialogue in *Nine Men* is sparse, allowing each character only so much as he needs to sketch his personality for the audience. It is as terse as it must have been in that kind of situation in the real war. The film does not aspire to the greater universality of a "patrol" film like Hollywood's *A Walk in the Sun,* directed by Lewis Milestone in 1945, and this difference marks Watt's achievement at one level, in terms of dogged realism, and his artistic shortcomings at another, a possible reason why he did not go on to make the great British Second World War film one might have expected of him. Instead he moved away from the subject altogether, directing in 1944 a musical comedy called *Fiddlers Three* with Tommy Trinder, before he created his next naturalistic film, *The Outlanders,* in Australia.

The famous Battle of Alamein that led to the decisive defeat of the Afrika Korps started on the evening of 23 October 1942. The Eighth Army had been meticulously prepared for it by Montgomery. The controversial personality of this most successful of British generals in the Second World War may be glimpsed in an item in *Warwork News No. 43,* issued in 1944, where he addresses a group of factory workers about his recent campaigns. Directness of approach without condescension, clarity of thought and speech, self-confidence, all are present there, and even a hint of the eccentricity and the vanity that were also part of his make-up. In spite of his conventional military background, Montgomery was able to reach out to the recruits of the people's army and the longer-standing regulars in a way no other British commander had done in the war to date. The men of the desert force, almost demoralized as they had been by constant setbacks, picked up their morale again in preparation for a battle that Montgomery insisted they would win.[67]

In practice of course it was not to be so easy. The Eighth Army had overwhelming superiority in numbers of infantry, tanks, and artillery, while the RAF dominated the skies. However, the defenders were dug in behind layers of minefields, and past experience had shown how difficult it was to outwit Rommel. Even Montgomery could not change overnight the outlook and the habits of some of his subordinate commanders. Knowing this, he had decided on a massive artillery bombardment by moonlight to start the operation, with a tactic then of gradually crumbling away the enemy, infantry advancing cautiously as the engineers cleared the mines, tanks brought forward with equal circumspection so that they would not be trapped by the German armor. This process of attrition lasted for eleven days. At home Churchill feared that the outcome might be yet another disappointment, but, when at last it became clear that Montgomery had broken the enemy, who was now to retreat gradually right out of Egypt and Libya, the church bells were rung in celebration on Sunday, November 15, for the first time since the war began.

David MacDonald recalled that Montgomery, like so many other generals, had shown little sympathy for the film medium. However, a chance roadside meeting with Alexander was more fruitful. Hearing about the amount of footage shot by the AFPU, the commander-in-chief suggested to MacDonald that he should return to London to set about the production of a film that would record the Eighth Army's victory.[68] In fact, at Pinewood some work had already been done on the project, but in December MacDonald, not satisfied with what Alex Bryce had assembled, decided to appoint Roy Boulting as director. The MOI tried to persuade the War Office in favor of a cooperative undertaking to cover the whole North African campaign, with the service units brought under a single central authority.[69] However, the AFPU had reached now such a stable and established position that it insisted on pressing ahead alone, although the final print of *Desert Victory* did include also a credit to the RAF Film Unit, whose material had been incorporated in the film. Completion of the hour-long documentary went ahead rapidly, backed in its later stages by Churchill's blessing—the prime minister rerecorded for Boulting at Chequers his speech made to the victorious troops at Tripoli—and it was premiered at the Odeon, Leicester Square, on 5 March 1943. The Secretary of State for War, Sir James Grigg, had insisted on viewing the print after the press show a couple of days earlier, with the option of declining to give final approval to it, but in the event all went well and *Desert Victory*'s triumphant run had started.[70]

For the public the lucidity of the film's commentary, written by the Lancastrian journalist James Lansdale Hodson, must have been one of its chief attractions. No words are wasted, beginning with an introductory few about the nature of the battleground, the desert itself, "a place fit only for war," with sand and stone, no water, plenty of flies, hot days and cold nights, and worst of all the sandstorms ("The Arabs say that after five days murder can be excused"). Auchinleck's position at Alamein, its relation to Cairo, Alexandria, and the Nile valley, is carefully explained. His successful defensive action is fought by British, Australians, Indians, and South Africans, "dogged as our infantry at Waterloo." The prime minister is seen arriving, topee on his head, fingers lifted in the familiar V sign. The new military leaders appear, and then the screen shows a copy of Churchill's directive to Alexander, to "take or destroy at the earliest opportunity the German-Italian army commanded by Field-Marshal Rommel, together with all its supplies and establishment in Egypt and Libya."

The next section is concerned with preparation for the offensive, the careful process of build-up that Montgomery thought to be so vital, introducing again factory shots already known from previous documentaries ("In no country are women so thoroughly organized for war"). The part played by America is acknowledged with a view of the tough new Sherman tanks and their powerful 75mm guns. A simple map is used to illustrate the supply routes to Egypt, round the Cape or across the heart of Africa. Landing grounds are cut in the jungle as planes assemble on the west coast before undertaking the long journey over the continent. Meanwhile Rommel has attacked and been repulsed again (the Battle of Alam Halfa), leaving behind wrecked tanks, corpses, and graves. As the Eighth Army gains its reinforcements, the enemy's supply lines are harassed by British aircraft and submarines. Training of the troops is being completed, and Alexander speaks to camera about the need for physical fitness.

Another map now lays out the disposition of forces for the battle, the forward German and Italian division, armor in the rear, the center left deliberately weak in the hope that the British will plunge into it, and on the other side Australians and South Africans in the north, Indian, Highland, and Tyne-Tees divisions below them, a London counties division in reserve and the armor backing up the front (there is no reference to the respective numbers of troops). Rommel is in Berlin; he salutes the Führer and receives from his hands a Field-Marshal's baton. Alexander confers with his RAF and naval colleagues, Tedder and Harwood, and Montgomery passes the plan of battle down to all ranks of the army. Everything is ready. Troops enjoy their final quiet moments, putting washing on a line; having haircuts, swimming in the sea, making their evening meals, writing letters. A lone piper plays beside a relaxing group of soldiers.

The central four-minute episode of *Desert Victory* was mainly shot in the studios at Pinewood. For the moonlight opening of the battle, the AFPU had been able to photograph only the flashes of the guns as the British artillery opened up on the enemy's lines. The question of faking material for documentaries or newsreel reports is a difficult one. The AFPU was certainly more scrupulous in the shooting of its record film than were the commercial companies in their somewhat differently motivated activities. There is an argument, though, that a degree of reconstruction in immediate time proximity to the real action is permissible. Unfortunately, the constant reuse of faked sequences in further compilations or nowadays television productions is likely to confuse the viewer—and the historian—about what is genuine and what is not. Throughout *Desert Victory* Roy Boulting had reversed film, so that the British appeared to move from one direction across the screen and the enemy in the opposite way (a device copied more than twenty years later by the BBC for their television *Great War* series). The well-known barrage sequence was put together in the studio for dramatic effect, and there can be no doubt that, without that particular form, it would have made a less effective climax to the film for the audience of 1943.

From a shot of a British tank, a crewman sitting on top in the moonlight, the film cuts to a totally dark screen, held while the narrator explains in a hushed voice that, as soon as the barrage begins, the sappers will go forward to clear paths through the minefields, marking the gaps with white tapes. Thirty minutes later, the barrage will creep farther into the enemy's positions, and at zero hour the infantry will advance. An officer's wrist watch comes into view, then the officer looking down at it. Men are squatting, putting on their helmets, holding the reels of tape. William Alwyn's score throughout the film had struck the expected mood, and during this section the orchestra lingers on a single, suspenseful chord. The men look

Desert Victory. **British piper encourages the troops before the offensive.**

Desert Victory. **The battle in progress and British soldiers shelter behind a disabled German tank.**

at each other, sweat on their faces. The order "Fire!" is bellowed with a sudden close-up of an officer's mouth and jaws. The AFPU's genuine artillery shots appear next; then the studio-shot sappers move out while the infantry fix their bayonets. When it is their turn to advance, a piper plays as they walk purposefully toward Rommel's lines, rifles and bayonets outstretched. The leisurely movements turn into a run, there are explosions, and a man falls as the sequence ends.

For the eleven-day slogging match, ample material was available, skilfully put together by Boulting's editors Richard Best, Frank Clarke, and John Durst. Infantry scrambling across the sand, burning tanks, crashed aircraft, wounded and dead Germans, prisoners being brought back, British armor breaking through—everything that the public expected to see. Even here though, not all is as it pretends to be, as one can see from the exposed situation of the cameramen in some sequences, and indeed a lot of the film had been restaged behind the lines. At Westminster the face of Big Ben shows it to be an hour before midnight, and Bruce Belfrage speaks on the BBC radio, "Here's some excellent news which has come during the past hour in the form of a communique from GCHQ Cairo. It says, the Axis forces in the western desert after twelve days and nights of ceaseless attacks by our land and air forces are now in full retreat." The night shift at a factory breaks into ecstatic cheering.

It is a measure of the thoughtful construction of *Desert Victory* that the remainder of the film does not shrink into anticlimax. The pursuit of Rommel is dealt with briefly, each town as it falls to Montgomery listed with its distance in miles from Alamein, ending with Tripoli on 23 January 1943. The truth is that Rommel, who had been absent during the first three days of the main battle, had conducted his withdrawal cleverly. As soon as Anglo-American forces landed in Algeria and Morocco in November, he knew that Libya was lost and, in spite of Hitler's wish that every German should stand still or die, the only realistic hope of continuing in North Africa was to fight a new campaign in Tunisia. At the end of *Desert Victory*, Churchill in RAF uniform is seen with Montgomery on the victory podium in Tripoli, taking the salute as the veterans of the Eighth Army march past.

Desert Victory attracted more enthusiasm from the press and the public than any other British documentary film which had been made in the war. Immediately after the premiere, on Sidney Bernstein's suggestion, David MacDonald flew to America and had a copy shown to President Roosevelt.[71] Its reception there was equally flattering, and, after its successful theatrical run, it was still being distributed and sold nontheatrically in the United States for a long period afterward, an unprecedented tribute to a British film.[72] On the very day of the London premiere, the press had announced that the Motion Picture Academy in Hollywood had presented a special certificate to Noel Coward for *In Which We Serve*. A year later *Desert Victory* was to win one of the treasured gold-plated Oscars as best documentary of 1943.

The making of *Desert Victory* could not have been more timely for the British people. Their army, so often in constant retreat, had won at last, seemingly on man-to-man terms, for the actual balance of forces was not appreciated at home. During the previous year and a half, Rommel had become for them the most celebrated general of the war, with a reputation for invincibility. Now Montgomery had sprung up in their consciousness as a counterhero. Churchill was happy because he could justify the British war effort to his Russian and American allies. It is likely that, for a short time, the reputation of the British army grew in America.

Desert Victory is a pivotal British film from the Second World War, both for the national expectations it embodied and raised and also for the illusions it helped to foster. The reality was that, in spite of Montgomery's determination, the army could not be so thoroughly reformed as he would have wished, as the battle for Normandy in 1944 was to demonstrate again. Even Montgomery's virtues of caution and preparedness, forged out of the cathartic cauldron of the battlefield slaughter of the First World War, were soon to be seen by the impatient Americans in a different light. Moreover, the desert campaign, important though it was for Britain, must be regarded as a sideshow in the context of the war as a whole. The truly decisive land battles were taking place on the Russian front, where the surrender of the German Sixth Army at Stalingrad had been the real turning point of the war.

For the moment though, it was clear to everyone in Britain that the allies were bound to win. Even in the Far East the march of the Japanese had been halted, with the American aircraft carrier victory at Midway, and the British could see now on their own territory the massive growth of men and material from across the Atlantic. The battle of the ocean supply lines had yet to be decisively won, and the enemy still had a number of technological tricks to pull out of the bag, as the final stages of the war were to demonstrate. But for the British public the blitz seemed now to have passed into history, and fear of infiltration and invasion had vanished forever. The audiences who watched *Desert Victory* at the beginning of 1943 did so in a new mood of confidence and self-congratulation, free at last from the anxieties of the years of struggle and hardship.

4
Looking Ahead

The feature film *The Life and Death of Colonel Blimp* (U.S. title: *Colonel Blimp*) begins with a war game.[1] Dispatch riders on motorcycles roar about the countryside, their objective to deliver the message "War starts at midnight," a signal for the opening of an exercise to capture London from the defending Home Guard. However, Lieutenant "Spud" Wilson of the Loamshires (James McKechnie) has other ideas. He starts his own move at six in the evening, a Pearl Harbor–like stroke to catch the enemy with their trousers down. His troops drive to the capital in lorries and invade the Royal Bathers' Club in Piccadilly, finding Major-General Clive Wynne-Candy, VC, DSO, in the steam room of the sauna there, naked to the waist and unprepared for hostilities. Aged, bald, and moustached, the general is commander of the Home Guard forces. His indignation has no effect on the precocious young officer, although as a final gesture Candy grapples with him and they both fall into the water.

Michael Powell and Emeric Pressburger had formed their own company, Archers, and throughout 1942 had two films in production, *The Silver Fleet,* the first to be issued, and *Colonel Blimp,* which was directed and scripted by themselves. In the original draft for the latter film "Sugar" Candy is intended to symbolize the outmoded gentlemanly traditions of the British military that have to be abandoned if the Nazis are to be beaten. Wilson, of course, stands for the new model army, eventually to be victorious from the Battle of Alamein onward. Apart from Candy's physical appearance in the sauna, there is no direct reference in the film to "Colonel Blimp," the character created by the cartoonist David Low of the *Evening Standard.* In this form, he had been in the thirties the bumbling, obtuse, and diehard figure of British conservatism, appraising the international scene in terms like "Gad, sir, there will be no peace in the east until the Japanese are driven out of China—and the Chinese too, dammit," or "Gad, sir, Mussolini is right. The dictators stand for peace—unless Russia refuses to abolish communism." However, the title alone gave away the intended analogy with Low's Colonel Blimp, and, as such, it quickly drew government disapproval.

The script attracted the baleful gaze of the Secretary of State for War, Sir James Grigg, who raised the matter of its intentions with the prime minister. At the time the country was in the deepest trough of reverse and disappointment, and talk about "Blimpery," especially as applied to the army, had been fairly common. Sweeping away such obstructive traditionalism would seem to have been in the nation's best interest, as Powell and Pressburger intended, but Churchill, in particular, happened to be unusually sensitive about anything that might appear to denigrate the military, and he clearly believed that morale would be affected if a film of this kind were shown to the public. He was persuaded, however, that it would not be in the interest of democratic freedom if the government actually tried to suppress *Colonel Blimp.* Unfortunately for him, the press heard about the controversy and, when *Blimp* finally appeared in the summer of 1943, it had the bonus of being advertised as "the banned film." Even at this stage, Churchill tried to prevent distribution overseas, in a running correspondence with Brendan Bracken, but finally he had to give in. Bracken expressed contempt for the film, but he must have known that, against the background of a war the allies were now winning, it could do no harm, and that view had been accepted also by Grigg, in a retraction of his former opposition to it.[2] It has been said that showing it in America was meant to swing audiences toward a sympathetic view of the new fighting spirit of the British army, but in publicity there, "Colonel Blimp" was represented not as a reactionary but as a swashbuckling superlover of the Douglas Fairbanks type.[3]

In fact, it would have been impossible to reproduce Colonel Blimp in the one-dimensional manner of Low's cartoons. As soon as he became a living character, he acquired a personality and style that marked him out to be an individual rather than a plastic symbol. Michael Powell had wanted Laurence Olivier to play the part, to give it some sharpness, but permission for his release from the Fleet Air Arm was refused while officialdom was still antagonistic to the film. The choice instead of Roger Livesey may perhaps have helped to bring about the appearance on screen of an essentially warm and likable character, but that is surely not the whole story. When Candy is seen in a relationship with others, especially his German friend Theo Kretschmar-Schuldorff (Anton Walbrook), he gains a human dimension that cannot be reconciled with the image of a foolish blunderer, and this ambiguity in the film has puzzled some viewers about its real intentions.

Colonel Blimp was made in technicolor at unusual length, running for almost three hours. From the sequence with Wilson and his unit, the script turned back to forty years earlier and progressed through Candy's career, on to the film's starting point again. Later shortened versions altered this structure, to its detriment, but since 1978 it has been possible to see it in its original form again, thanks to restoration by the National Film Archive in London. The use of color was itself uncommon at that time. The employment as well of a Hungarian scriptwriter (Pressburger), an exiled German designer (Alfred Junge), and a French director of photography (Georges Périnal) brought it closer to the traditions of continental cinema, French in particular. And Powell's attempt to create a more deliberately artistic kind of production indicated a further progression in his development as a filmmaker.

As a young man, Candy himself is disrespectful of authority, a trait that causes him in 1902 to go to Berlin without permission, in order to confront a German called Kaunitz, who has been spreading insidious propaganda about the conduct of the British in the Boer War. He meets the English governess Edith Hunter, the source of his original information, and in the course of his visit he manages inadvertently to cast aspersions on the honor of the German army. Although in the inevitable duel with sabers both he and his opponent Theo Kretschmar-Schuldorff wound each other, they subsequently become the best of friends and the German goes on to marry Edith. Only afterward does Candy realize that he too had fallen in love with her.

During the First World War, Candy serves in Flanders and at one point he meets a group of prisoners from Theo's regiment who have been trying to penetrate British lines. Questioning them about the circumstances of their capture, he is unable to get an answer from them. As soon as he leaves them, another officer, a South African, makes it clear that he will be employing more forcible methods to induce them to talk, the first suggestion in the film that Candy's devotion to the rules of the game is not followed by everyone. At the end of the war, won, says Candy, by "clean fighting, honest soldiering," he marries Barbara, a girl who reminds him of Edith. He finds Theo in a prisoner-of-war camp as the Germans are listening to a classical concert, a circumstance that prompts Barbara to remark on what a strange people they are, the atrocities they have committed in the war, and the way they can sit down now to enjoy Mendelssohn and Schubert. Theo at first rebuffs him but, as he is on the point of being repatriated, he relents and is invited to afterdinner drinks at Candy's town house with a group of establishment figures, many of them soldiers. The German is bitter about his postwar prospects as a member of a defeated nation. Candy tries to reassure him—Germany will not be humiliated, she will become a member of the club again. Some of his guests agree with his viewpoint but the camera reveals the expressions of others, one of them the former commandant of the prisoner-of-war camp, who obviously do not. Going home with his fellow-officers, Theo rails at the "childlike stupidity" of Candy and the other Britons who think like him.

The episode in its way hints at the fact that the allies

did not treat Germany well immediately after the war, though France was more culpable than Britain. The Versailles settlement was a factor in the rise in influence of the Nazi Party, and recognition of this allusion may have been a further reason for the dislike felt for the script by the authorities. It is possible also that Whitehall was uneasy about the portrayal of Kretschmar-Schuldorff and in fact of all the Germans, except the odious Kaunitz, the soldiers being seen as brave and honorable counterparts to the British. Candy's interwar career, finishing with his retirement in 1935, flashes by until he returns to the active service list in 1939. Theo meanwhile has become a refugee from Nazi Germany. To the sceptical panel that interviews him as an enemy alien he speaks in moving terms about his homesickness for England, the country of his now dead wife where he had spent time as a prisoner. He has called his friend Clive Candy as a witness in his favor.

Clive takes Theo to his house where, after the death of his own wife, he has lived alone with Murdoch (John Laurie), his butler and former sergeant in Flanders. The car is driven by Candy's volunteer driver Angela ("Johnny"), and Theo is surprised by her resemblance to Edith. Then, in June 1940, Candy suffers a double blow. He is about to give a postscript talk to the Sunday BBC news when he is told that he has been replaced by J. B. Priestley. Moreover, he has been retired yet again. Theo tries to explain to him that his code of conduct is useless now. In the script for his broadcast he had written that he would rather be defeated than use the enemy's methods. Candy has been educated to be a gentleman, Theo says, but now they are all fighting against "the most devilish idea created by a human brain—Nazism." In this game there is no return match. Candy is persuaded to join the new Home Guard. His house is destroyed in the blitz, and Murdoch is killed. His photograph appears a number of times on the front cover of *Picture Post,* as if he is the inspiration behind the Home Guard, the last one dated September 1942. As the film returns to its opening sequence, the viewer discovers that Johnny is the girlfriend of Wilson, who has made use of her to find out Candy's whereabouts as the war games are about to begin. In vain she rushes to warn Candy. "Gentlemen, the war will soon be over," Wilson announces to the bemused club members. "It's very fine to win the last battle. We much prefer to win the first."

At the very end Johnny gets Candy to agree not to

***The Life and Death of Colonel Blimp.* Clive Candy and the Home Guard draw up plans for an exercise (Roger Livesey, wearing cap).**

***The Life and Death of Colonel Blimp.* The new model soldier intends to thwart the old guard, while the driver vainly tries to warn Candy by telephone (James McKechnie and Deborah Kerr).**

press disciplinary measures against Wilson. The two watch as, unseen on the screen, the Loamshires march past. It is not wholly convincing because the film has made Candy into the central figure, attracting sympathy even as he is being deflated, while Wilson remains brash and unendearing, the outsider still in this traditionally upper-class world. The parts of Edith, Barbara, and Johnny are all taken by Deborah Kerr. The use of the same actress establishes both a common ideal held by Clive and Theo about the female sex and a view they share of England that the feminine personality symbolizes. The subtle differences between the three women and their respective backgrounds, somewhat beyond Kerr's abilities to fully distinguish, represent also a kind of social progression—Edith the genteel English governess; Barbara the daughter of a West Riding manufacturer, a wealthy but self-made man; Johnny the ordinary girl linked with the bumptious "Spud" Wilson, the vanguard of a potential social revolution.

Thus, *Colonel Blimp* recognizes the changed situation brought about by the war, but it does so with sadness. Its particular way of using color to increase the costume drama, the tapestry that backs the film's title sequence, the toylike appearance of the barracks in Berlin where Candy fights the duel, the similar artificiality of the Flanders settings, all these and more build up an impression of a nostalgic fantasy world that may seem to contradict the harsh realities of the film's intended message. It was a very gentle way of making the lesson stick. Even so, there is no escaping the conclusion. Banished now are memories of the sentiments expressed in Chamberlain's broadcast three years earlier, gone is the sense of going to war reluctantly in defense of simple English decencies.

No doubt it was difficult for some of those who disliked *Colonel Blimp* to face up to the implications of a new concept of warfare, the acceptability of Pearl Harbor methods, and a matching of Nazi ruthlessness with equal disregard for old-fashioned moral codes. The indiscriminate bombing of German cities by the RAF had not been officially admitted as such, and there was no British observer on hand to witness the deaths of civilian men, women, and children, soon to greatly exceed the casualties in the blitz. However, a number of other films in production over the winter of 1942–43 also came to grips with the new toughness of mood, as if the sudden change in the fortunes of war had created the means now required for pushing through victory to the end. It can be seen, for instance, in two of the earlier documentaries which were issued in 1943, Realist's *Kill or Be Killed* and Strand's *These Are The Men.*

Len Lye, the New Zealand animator, who directed *Kill or Be Killed,* had made in 1941 and 1942, also for Realist, a short account of the continuing distribution of newspapers during the blitz. Titled *Newspaper Train,* it was narrated by the American correspondent Merrill Mueller, and it stressed the value of keeping in existence an accurate, objective press that would play a part in the postwar world. Newspapers are being dispatched to Ramsgate, in spite of the problems caused by the bombing of some of London's rail junctions, a situation explained with the aid of a chart of the suburban lines south of the Thames. On the way the train is machine-gunned by a German fighter, seen only as a shadow beside the rail track. Mass-Observation interviewed people about this film, and on the whole the public was puzzled and disconcerted by Lye's use of creative montage in both sound and image.[4] His techniques made it anything but a straightforward story for them, although the details of the piece did not elude them—there were comments that the shadow of the aircraft looked more like a Hurricane than a German plane.

Kill or Be Killed, on the other hand, could not have been more explicit for the average audience.[5] As originally conceived, it was meant to be shown non-theatrically as an instructional film on techniques of stalking an enemy sniper. With a possible invasion still in the minds of the authorities, it would demonstrate how the ordinary citizen, a Home Guard perhaps, might be able to deal with individual Germans. The intention also was to highlight the personal aspect of war, the process of one man pitted against another in a life-or-death game, and in this respect it is a chilling document of a type unusual for a British propaganda film. The German sniper was played by an army captain, a former actor, with the voice of Marius Goring dubbed (not absolutely satisfactorily) onto the track to represent his thoughts. Likewise, the captain himself spoke for the British stalker, a sergeant who had been in civil life a head gillie on a game park in Scotland. The camera work was cleverly handled by Adrian Jeakins.[6] After managing to outwit and kill the German, the sergeant props up his body so that it can be a bait for the rest of the enemy patrol, and in due time he manages to dispose of five more of them with five rapid shots, a scoring rate beyond the abilities of most people. In the closing sequences of the film a flight of aircraft passes overhead, and there are cuts between the dead bodies and empty cartridge cases on the ground, giving a somewhat surreal polish to the end of this distinctive production.

Wales—Green Mountain, Black Mountain grew out of a one-reel project by the British Council to be distributed overseas.[7] Responsibility for the making and showing abroad of informational films on British life lay with the British Council, as it still does, and their established position led to a prolonged dispute with the MOI about arrangements for showing the official documentaries in America in particular—a battle the ministry was able to win because, under Bracken, it had greater faith in its own efficiency and suitability for taking on this task.[8] The MOI asked Donald Taylor of Strand to enlarge *Wales* slightly for home use. The final product was directed by John Eldridge, with a script by Dylan Thomas that had been rejected by the British Council for the earlier film. It showed a panorama of Welsh people and locations, finishing with the coal industry and some poignant reminders of the depression. "Remember the procession of the old, young men/it will never happen again" and the narrator interjects "it *must* not happen again." From being a bland travelogue *Wales—Green Mountain, Black Mountain* had become another documentary to express a mood of postwar expectation.[9]

Dylan Thomas next wrote the verse for *These Are The Men,* a film based on an idea by the novelist Robert Neumann, and edited by Alan Osbiston to include material recut from Leni Riefenstahl's *Triumph des Willens,* with some other sequences. It was not intended to be anti-German in a blanket sense, simply an indictment of the leaders of the Nazi state as the men responsible for the war, and its opening indeed had German workers of different kinds at their peaceful occupations, before moving to images of German soldiers fighting on various fronts. "Who sent us to kill, to be killed, to lose what we love?/Widowed our women, unfathered our sons, broke the hearts of our homes?/Who dragged us out, out of our beds and houses and workshops/Into a battleground of spilt blood and split bones?"

Riefenstahl's two-hour film had been put together from a mass of material shot at the Nuremberg Party

Kill or Be Killed. **Dead German sniper is used as a decoy by British sergeant.**

Wales, Green Mountain—Black Mountain. **Miners coming off their shift, an image central to Welsh folklore about the years of hardship and depression.**

Congress of 1934 to build up a cumulative messiahlike impression of Adolf Hitler.[10] Using some short extracts, *These Are The Men* placed English words into the mouths of the speakers, making Hitler for instance explain how he was "a discontented and neurotic child" who had tried various jobs and been incompetent at all of them. After coming to power with aid from sympathetic industrialists, he says he betrayed and murdered Röhm and other former friends. This was a particularly telling reference, in the light of the real context of the original film (which would not have been clear anyway to a British audience), because the 1934 rally had been held soon after the "night of the long knives," obliquely mentioned by Hitler in his real speech. Goebbels is made to describe himself as "unemployed, Jew-hating, crippled, frustrated and bitter"; Goering (in a clip from the film *Feuertaufe*) says he had been confined twice to a lunatic asylum for drug addiction; Streicher is a "torturer and murderer of Jews"; and Hess speaks of flying to Britain in 1941, "hoping to arrange a dishonorable peace between Germany and the pro-German elements I imagined I would find in England." The march-past of the SS at the rally is contrasted with newsreel sequences of German prisoners and German dead. "Where is your triumph now in the purgatories of Stalingrad?/How many of you will never return to the towns and villages you know?" However, some of the young men may survive to become comrades once the war is over, a sentiment which reemphasizes the point that the people themselves are not the guilty ones, a point many of the British at that time and for long afterwards would find it difficult to accept. At the end Hitler screams "We are the men—Sieg Heil! Sieg Heil! Sieg Heil!" The film presented the Nazi leaders as pathological maniacs, and perhaps its rhetoric was too strident for the average British cinemagoer, who hardly needed reminding of the culpability of Hitler and his gang.

This middle period of the war, 1942 and 1943, saw a gradual edging toward each other of the documentary and the commercial traditions of British cinema. The feature film industry had aimed to capture audiences by creating stories. Whatever the situation, the characters on the screen had to be dramatized in such a way that the public would believe in them, even if it did not necessarily identify with them. More evidence had to be given about themselves and their lives than would be apparent from dialogues that simply grew out of their workaday existences. The documentary, on the other hand, and its more extended form, the feature documentary, which introduced a measure of dramatization, took the opposite ideal as its cornerstone. For that school of cinema, it was exactly what people might say and do in real situations that mattered, but the penalty in artistic terms could be a presentation of people that went no further than the surface of their lives. Like all major art forms, the film can be most trenchant when it succeeds in transcending reality. The commercial cinema had the opportunity to achieve a kind of psychological insight that the documentary would not be able to imitate, in spite of the greater historical authenticity of the factual tradition. In contrast to many foreign films, the British industry in practice had rarely aspired to that level, while its classbound nature had retarded its ability so far to convincingly reflect the actuality of the British people at war.

The overlap between the two methods of approaching film was thrown into more relief by the appearance of a number of productions, from both official and commercial sources, that covered similar aspects of the war to date. Retrospectives on the blitz, for instance, emerged in Ealing's feature *The Bells Go Down* and the Crown Film Unit's feature documentary *Fires Were Started,* both based on the work of the Auxiliary Fire Service. The script for the official film was written by Humphrey Jennings, who directed it, and for him it represented a new move in his filmmaking career. It was in fact Harry Watt who suggested to Ian Dalrymple that Jennings might be interested in turning away from the style of his previous impressionistic films toward a more dramatized form.[11] The original title was *I Was a Fireman,* and a shortened version that omitted the early training sequences was called, more imaginatively, *Fires Were Started,* a name that proved to be so apt that it is now applied also to the complete film (though distribution prints still carry the other title).[12]

The Bells Go Down, directed by Basil Dearden, was named after the diary, published in 1942, of an AFS fireman called Vic Flint, who had joined at the outbreak of war after the closure of the film studio where he had been part of the scenic design team.[13] The AFS had been started in 1938 as a back-up service to the existing force in the event of war and mass bombing. It attracted people from disparate backgrounds, including a number of intellectuals who did not wish to enlist in the military, some of them for pacifist reasons, and it was their presence which provoked a celebrated jibe about progressive novelists dressed as firemen on the first page of Evelyn Waugh's *Officers and Gentlemen.*[14] Henry Green, indeed, based his novel *Caught* on his AFS experiences, and William Sansom was to play a part in *Fires Were Started.*[15] The auxiliaries at first were resented by some of the regulars and regarded as layabouts during the phony war by serving soldiers, but public attitudes to them changed dramatically as soon as the blitz began. Sansom himself had a lucky escape when a warehouse wall collapsed on him. He survived because he had been standing within the frame of one of the building's large oblong windows.[16]

Flint in his diary recorded some of these early tensions, and some even more unexpected ones, like the presence in his substation at Aldgate of a former follower of Mosley's fascists in a unit three-quarters of which were Jewish.[17] The film script avoided that particular difficulty by locating the fire station in West Ham and setting it against the backdrop of the local community, though some of its inhabitants on the screen sound as if they would be more at home in Chelsea than the East End. The only politically minded auxiliary is a man called Brooks (William Hartnell), who had fought in the International Brigade in Spain and knows what it was like when Madrid was bombed. Tommy Trinder as Tommy Turk is allowed to be more clownish than in *The Foreman Went to France,* which diminishes the effect of his performance. With Bob Matthews (Philip Friend), he joins on the first day of war and, in an exact mirror of Flint's experience, they are taken on immediately and sent to a substation, located in a school building, without the chance of going home for the night. If the blitz had started in that first week of war, as expected, they would have been thrown into the thick of it with no training at all. Trailer fire pumps were towed at that time by requisitioned taxicabs, and an early sequence in the film has a reckless race between a couple of them, another episode taken straight out of the diary.

All of the players in *Fires Were Started* were genuine firemen, and the opening of the film has them reporting for duty at the substation. Little is given about their lives, though we see Jacko, the character who eventually dies, saying farewell to his wife as he leaves his tobacconist's shop. Toward the end of the film she is shown listening to a radio bulletin about the previous night's raid, unaware that he has been killed. The first section fixes attention on the new recruit Bill

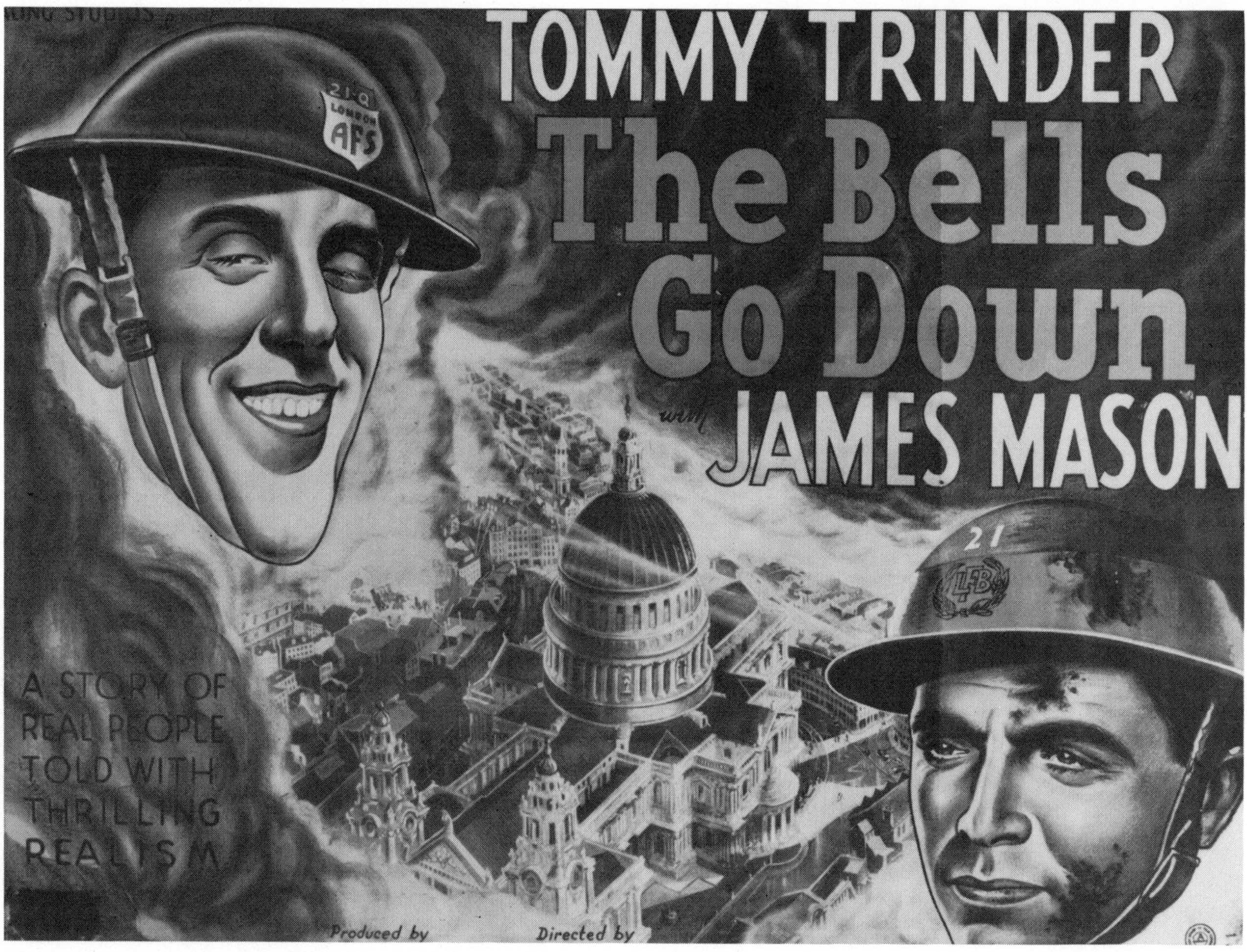

The Bells Go Down. **The poster expects the public to feel sympathetic to the depiction of realism and to identify with a representation of ordinary people on screen.**

Barrett (William Sansom), who is stared at with initial reserve by the auxiliaries already there, but is taken in hand by the cheerful, extrovert cab driver Johnny Daniels (Fred Griffiths). All we know about Barrett is that he used to write advertising copy and he has a gift for piano-playing. By contrast, *The Bells Go Down* makes a more elaborate fiction out of the lives of the firemen. Bob marries his fiancee Nan Harper (Philippa Hiatt), and the others help him to fit out his flat. Tommy races his greyhound at the track and loses money for everyone at the station, and a petty thief called Sam (Mervyn Johns), who has joined the AFS by accident, is pursued by a zealous policeman. Tommy and a supervising officer named Ted Robbins (James Mason) are also rivals for the affections of Susie (Meriel Forbes), one of the station women. In *Fires Were Started* the women at the substation and the control sites are presented strictly in work situations only. The Ealing film has them as objects of romantic interest for the males, in feature tradition (Flint's diary does refer in fact to off-duty firemen in the backs of their taxicabs with station girls).[18] However, hardly any of the main players in *The Bells Go Down* seem to be totally comfortable in their parts, whereas the amateurs of Jennings's film respond naturally to his kind of re-creation of their experiences.

Fires Were Started also followed the documentary method in the conscientiousness of its account of the operations of the Fire Service. The men at the substation are seen at practice drill with hook ladders. A fireboat starts out on river patrol, a sequence that also has barrage balloons being raised over the Thames and a memorable glimpse of the old sail barges in operation. The command structure of the service is detailed as its various substations report their equipment returns to the control center. The scene is set at the docks, where a ship is being loaded with explosives, close to the warehouse, where the firemen later have to struggle against the blaze that might spread to the vessel itself. The film was again edited for Jennings by Stewart McAllister, and its rhythms were echoed in what was probably the best of all the many scores written by William Alwyn in wartime. There are some contrived sequences, most notably the famous one where Barratt plays and Daniels sings "One Man Went to Mow a Meadow" as each fireman

***Fires Were Started*. Firemen sing around the piano at the fire station as the bombing starts (William Sansom at the piano, Fred Griffiths behind).**

enters the room in turn, the song breaking off just as the siren sounds the alert. But the strongest impression left by *Fires Were Started* is the truthfulness of its representation of the calm resolution of real London citizens in uniform as they face the capital city's ordeal by fire.

In *The Bells Go Down* the unit goes into action with the full-scale raid of 7 September 1940, and, as its men fight the fires for three nights in succession, the film continues to relate their activities to the larger life of the borough. The pub kept by Ted's parents is bombed, and they have to be dug out of the cellar. Bob's own flat is wrecked, and his pregnant wife goes to hospital to have her baby. In its turn the hospital also is blitzed. During the raid Tommy's greyhound unexpectedly wins (but he has forgotten to back it). Sam rescues from the river the policeman who has been trying to arrest him. High in a burning building Tommy and his district officer (Finlay Currie) see the floor collapse away from them, and, as they stand on a narrow ledge, trapped, they light cigarettes and watch the opposite wall swaying and then crashing down toward them. The film concludes with the christening of Nan's baby. He is to be called Tommy.

The blitz in *Fires Were Started* seems to have been modeled on the last great fire raid on London, that of 10 May 1941, when units from Essex drove to the city to assist their hard-pressed colleagues, though the original intention of the script was to set it in 1940. Throughout the film's climax, the work of the firemen is related only to that of their colleagues in the rest of the Fire Service, as the control centers monitor the progress of the attack and the extent of the fires. Photographed by C. Pennington-Richards, the blaze at the docks was restaged in an abandoned warehouse without any striving for sensational effect. Here also, men are trapped on a roof, the injured subofficer has to be lowered by cradle from a gantry, and Jacko insists on remaining, holding the rope that steadies the ladder, as Barratt goes down from the parapet. Jacko dies when the fire erupts through the top of the warehouse. There is a short and unforgettable sequence at dawn, the bedraggled firemen gathering their equipment, cloth-capped workers moving into the docks, a woman pushing a pram through the rubble, a brief exchange between Daniels and a fireman coming on duty—"Jacko's copped it," "Copped it bad?" "He's copped it, I tell you." From the funeral of the dead fireman, his colleagues bearing his coffin, the end of this extraordinary film cuts to the ship leaving the docks for the open sea, a symbol of the broader context of war, endurance, and victory.

Parallel stories about the British submarine service also appeared in 1943, with Gainsborough's *We Dive At Dawn* and the Crown Film Unit's *Close Quarters.* The feature film, which was directed by Anthony Asquith, developed a very fictional theme, the hunting by a single submarine (the *Sea Tiger*), specifically sent out for that purpose, of the "new" German battleship *Brandenburg* (though the silhouettes in the film indicate that she is an armored ship or "pocket battleship" of the prewar type). They succeed in the end only by following her into the Baltic. In fact, no British submarine during the war was able to "bag" such a prize, the largest vessel accounted for in this way being a Japanese heavy cruiser right at the war's end. The part of the film that has the *Sea Tiger* maneuvering to torpedo the enemy, with its captain Lieutenant Taylor (John Mills) raising and lowering his periscope to get the correct position while his first officer struggles to help the boat's trim, is noteworthy for maintaining an impressive atmosphere of tension.

But the rest of the production is weak in plot, relying much on the portrait drawn of the hydrophone operator, Leading Seaman Hobson (Eric Portman), a talented man who has not fulfilled himself in life and who is at odds with his wife and father-in-law. He knows German, which enables him to listen to the conversation of three German airmen picked up from a rescue buoy. In a quarrel, one Nazi injures another, and when the victim finally dies, the submariners make convenient use of his body to project it to the surface in British uniform, as well as tilting up their own stern out of the water, to give an impression to avenging destroyers that they are sinking. The *Sea Tiger* has not enough fuel for the return journey, and Hobson goes ashore on a Danish island in the Nazi's Luftwaffe uniform so that he can guide the submarine alongside a small oil tanker from which it can be replenished. Hobson holds off the Germans with a machine-gun. His heroics help toward a reconciliation with his wife when he arrives home again.

It was inevitable that a feature film like *We Dive At Dawn,* with the popular stars John Mills and Eric Portman, would overshadow Crown's extended documentary. However, *Close Quarters* is more faithful to the reality of a submarine patrol and, as scripted and directed by Jack Lee, it was a sober and competent production.[19] British submarines were never built in such great numbers as the German U-boats—they had not the same kind of strategic objectives—and their operations were always hazardous. In the Mediterranean they had inflicted heavy damage on German and Italian shipping on the route to Africa, but their own losses also had been high. The interior of the submarine *Tyrant* was actually a Pinewood studio set, realistically re-created, and the players were naval men, with Lieutenant-Commander Gregory as the

***We Dive at Dawn*. Submariners pursue a German warship (Eric Portman and John Mills).**

captain. The *Tyrant* goes on patrol in Norwegian waters. Day after day there is just the monotony of existence in that cramped and confined space, no sightings of the enemy, the submarine submerged by day and surfacing at night. Eventually they come across a U-boat and manage to sink it with gunfire. An exhaust valve has been damaged, and they are unable to dive for an uncomfortably long period in the morning. They pick up from a small boat three Norwegians who are trying to escape to England. When they do find a target for their torpedoes, it is a floating dock escorted by destroyers, a less glamorous object than a battleship. After sinking it, they have to evade the enemy's depth charges and go to the bottom for a while. The crew sit it out in some discomfort before they are able to surface again in the dark and turn toward their home base. As in *We Dive At Dawn,* the submariners survive moments of danger without visible signs of panic, which simply could not be allowed in a wartime film, at least as no more than the brief aberration of Richard Attenborough's sailor, who runs away in *In Which We Serve.*

Women in the services received their tribute with *The Gentle Sex,* a Two Cities–Concanen production, which followed the lives of seven who enlisted in the ATS. Leslie Howard directed, with Maurice Elvey, and he also appeared at the beginning, back to camera, standing on the bridge of a main London rail terminal and identifying each of the new recruits in turn as they set out on their journey to the army camp. His semi-ironic comments about the role of women are the only surviving touches of whimsy from the style of *Pimpernel Smith.* With this new film Howard had taken a huge leap toward the documentary approach. Training scenes at the camp are authentically reproduced, in almost too prolonged de-

***The Gentle Sex*. Encounter on the dance floor, the usual meeting place for men and women in the services (Rosamund John and John Laurie).**

tail. However, the service had to be made attractive for potential conscripts and, as in the documentaries, the social side of army life is also highlighted. Betty (Joan Greenwood), who has led a cloistered existence at home, is seen progressing from distress to composure. She and Gwen (Joan Gates) and the "good-time" girl Dot (Jean Gillie) are sent to an antiaircraft battery. The others become lorry drivers and take part in an exhausting day and all-night convoy move to the docks. The most remote of the seven, Joan (Barbara Waring), is gradually forced to accept the others. Czech-born Erna (Lilli Palmer) remembers her family, which has suffered at the hands of the Nazis, and so she becomes a spokeswoman for war objectives. Perhaps here the filmmakers felt that women needed more persuasion than men about what the country was fighting for. Maggie (Rosamund John) meets a Scottish corporal (John Laurie) at a camp dance—the film makes it clear that there will be a happy ending—but the RAF boyfriend of Ann (Joyce Howard) is killed. The recruits do discuss at one point the matter of the likely status of women after the war.

The last film to which Leslie Howard made a contribution before his tragic death was his production for Two Cities of *The Lamp Still Burns,* directed by Elvey. It had Rosamund John as a probationer nurse struggling against the rigid codes of behavior imposed by the matron in a country hospital. Both these films recognized the striving toward equality by a number of women at the time. It may have been a movement which was accelerated rather than initiated by the war,[20] and there can be no doubt that its treatment in film was patronizing in outlook, but it is doubtful if the subject would have found its way onto the screen at all without the incentive of these shattering events. At least women had been placed in positions, albeit temporarily, where their productive capacities had become a more essential part of national endeavor.

It was more difficult, though, to glamorize in cinematic terms factory work for women. It was often assumed that lower-class women were able to accept more easily the monotony of bench work than those who had been accustomed to more genteel lifestyles and occupations, just as it used to be believed a woman can settle more readily to routine labor than a man. Such generalizations are easily challengeable nowadays. Some women probably put a willing hand to what they were doing for purely patriotic reasons, a motivation it has become all too easy to deride in revisionist views of the British people in the Second World War. Many may have found a certain satisfaction in the communality of factory life, the opportunity given to make contact with their companions in the works and in the hostel. The organized dance held out the prospect of meeting someone from the opposite sex, very probably a serviceman away from his home and free of immediate commitments. It is possible that the unusual circumstances of the war were actually enjoyed by many whose normal domestic lives were even more boring than the disciplines brought about by mass conscription. Even if the idea of equal pay for women was still not an accepted one, most must have welcomed the chance of earning money in wartime. Nevertheless, factory labor for the most part remained a thankless task, and it was particularly hard for married women, who also had families to care for.

In the Gainsborough film *Millions Like Us,* Patricia Roc plays Celia Crowson, a young woman from a lower-middle-class family who gets her call-up and wants to join one of the services or perhaps to become a nurse. She dreams romantically about the kind of boyfriend she might be able to meet in those circumstances. However, her father (Moore Marriott) is adamant that she should go to a local factory. He has fears about the moral dangers to which his daughter might be exposed if she goes away from home, and his feelings are reinforced by seeing the example set by Celia's flirtatious sister Phyllis (Joy Shelton), who is in the ATS. Pressured also by the interviewer at the Labour Exchange, Celia gives in, though in fact she does have to leave the family and is sent to a government hostel with other women. When an RAF delegation visits the factory where she works, she is noticed by the shy young Sergeant Fred Blake, played by Gordon Jackson. Further meetings lead to courtship and marriage. But Fred is killed on duty, and at the end of the film the distraught Celia has to be encouraged by her friend Gwen to join in while everyone sings together in the canteen.

Millions Like Us was written and directed by Frank Launder and Sidney Gilliat, and it made a serious attempt to come to grips with the shifting social relationships created by the war. The title suggests a larger context than simply a factory and its women workers. In fact, the image of the Crowson family is established at the beginning by having *all* its members—father, son, son's wife, and two daughters—leaving for a holiday in the summer of 1939. Like hundreds of thousands of other working-class and lower-middle-class people, they go on the annual jaunt to the British seaside resort, staying together at a boarding house, the same one they have been using for years. Celia returns there during the war for her honeymoon with Fred. Sitting in the corridor of their train are old friends Charters and Caldicott, played as ever by Basil Radford and Naunton Wayne, both now uniformed as army officers and gloomily munching sandwiches. They have been introduced at a couple of earlier points in the film, partly to provide a bridge in the plot through the events before and after Dunkirk, but their presence, which has no other relevance to the story, is a reminder of the common tribulations of the wartime British, which even the upper classes have to accept at times.

Celia's roommate, Gwen Price (Megs Jenkins), is a Welsh university graduate, whose father was a miner and who has witnessed unemployment and deprivation in her own home, sufferings deeper than any experienced by the relatively comfortable Crowsons. She goes with Celia to a concert where the orchestra plays—what else?—Beethoven's Fifth, but Celia believes, at that early moment in her relationship with Fred, that he has jettisoned her. And so she daydreams only of him out with a girl from the services, imagines herself committing suicide, and Fred being arraigned in court for his heartlessness. The snobbish upper-middle-class Jennifer Knowles (Anne Crawford) has to share a room with a girl called Annie Earnshaw who talks with a funny northern accent—that particular inflexion was beyond British actresses of the period—and who goes to bed in her underclothes because as she says, very sensibly, she would only have to put them on again in the morning. Jennifer is idle and rebellious at the workbench and is reprimanded by the foreman, Charles Forbes, performed by Eric Portman in no-nonsense Yorkshire style.

However, an attachment soon grows between the society girl and the foreman. When an air raid alert sounds, she declines at first to go to the shelter until he picks her up and carries her down. Later he takes her to the cinema—and then at work reproves her for being too familiar with him. Even romance does not interfere with the hierarchy of the factory floor. At her job Jennifer cannot expect the privileges she has been accustomed to in her previous life. In the penultimate episode of the film she and Forbes sit on a

***Millions Like Us*. Conscripted women on the factory floor (Patricia Roc and Megs Jenkins).**

hillside overlooking the town. He talks about them "getting tied up" but remarks how domestically useless she is, to which she retorts that he is dull and morbidly suspicious. It seems he has decided they will not try marriage just yet. "The world's made up of two kinds of people," he says. "You're one sort and I'm the other. We're all together now there's a war on—we need to be. What's going to happen when it's over? Shall we go on like this or are we going to slide back?" Even with the benefit of hindsight, one feels that the filmmakers knew the probable answer to that question.

Millions Like Us, which had official approval, demonstrated that it was possible for British commercial cinema to borrow from the documentary movement and to put onto the screen characters who were at least tolerable approximations to real people. Its believable situations could indeed have been recognized by the millions it was meant for, the public who paid at the box-office, although whether all of them enjoyed something so close to their lives is another matter. It did not achieve the popularity that year of Gainsborough's *The Man in Grey,* a film set in Regency times, with James Mason and Margaret Lockwood, who also starred in a later costume drama, *The Wicked Lady,* issued after the war had finished. Mason's aggressive masculinity turned into real sadism in *The Seventh Veil,* another film from 1945. Robert Newton had also appeared as a very nasty individual in *Hatter's Castle* (1941), based on the story by A. J. Cronin, and no doubt there is a relationship between their kind of violence and the suppressed tensions and anxieties of wartime. The period pieces in particular fulfilled the audience's need for escapism and also for a different kind of relaxation, as the country wound itself down from the strains and restrictions of prolonged hostilities.[21] *Millions Like Us* had promoted a down-to-earth image of patriotic consensus, even if the final

***Millions Like Us.* Even the upper classes have to submit to the discomforts of wartime rail travel (Basil Radford and Naunton Wayne).**

scene between Forbes and Knowles cast a fleeting shadow of doubt on it. The subject was not to be repeated in that form, and the next major film from Sidney Gilliat, *Waterloo Road,* was to take quite a different view of what was happening on the home front.

It would be illusory anyway to see the better-quality feature films that had emerged over 1942 and 1943 as totally typical. The number of productions each year had fallen drastically since peacetime. Release of film stock was controlled by the Board of Trade, which dealt strictly with each film in turn. The government had requisitioned studios in as arbitrary and bureaucratic a fashion as it had seized private hotels in 1939. However, it was anxious to keep up good relationships with the producers, and, from 1942, Jack Beddington arranged a series of meetings with them, in what was called an Ideas Committee, to discuss themes for their films. If this was a form of precensorship, it was exercised lightly by the MOI, as one may judge from the instances of *Colonel Blimp* and *In Which We Serve,* films it initially disliked. It was this form of consultation that produced common agreement about the desirability of encouraging purely entertainment movies, as the public began to grow tired of war films. By 1944 a report on monopoly tendencies in the industry warned of the possible dangers to independent production posed by the growing empire of J. Arthur Rank, who now controlled half of the studios and also the Gaumont British and Odeon exhibition circuits.[22] On the other hand, Rank's capital had financed some of the more successful films, and he had cause for hoping that, when the war ended, he would be able to build on the good American reception of a feature like *In Which We Serve.*[23] Nevertheless, such ambitions had to be balanced by the increasing American penetration of the industry in Britain. Warner Brothers, for instance, had acquired in 1941 an influential interest in the Associated British Corporation, the other main film combine in the country alongside Gaumont British.

ABC had moved to Welwyn Garden City when their Elstree studios were taken over by the government and turned into a factory. During 1942 and 1943 they produced a couple of films directed by Laurence Huntington, with scripts based on plays by Vernon Sylvaine. Nothing dates more quickly than humor, and, seen now, the comedy caperings of Robertson Hare and Alfred Drayton in *Women Aren't Angels* appear decidedly unfunny. The pair play members of the Home Guard who frustrate a spy plan to blow up a bridge. The story had them putting on the clothing of their ATS wives when their own uniforms are stolen. *Warn That Man,* on the other hand, seems to have had a more serious intention, and its theme, a Nazi plot to kidnap Winston Churchill, was a clever one, to be revived in a more recent film, *The Eagle Has Landed.* The enemy attempt it by taking possession of a country mansion to which the prime minister is going for a holiday break, and they substitute for the owner, Lord Buckley, his exact double, a German actor discovered by the plotters while appearing in a Berlin production of, of all things, Shakespeare's *Othello.* Raymond Lovell plays both Buckley and his double. Unknown to the Nazis, Buckley is due to be visited by his niece Frances (Jean Kent), who expects also to meet there her RAF boyfriend John (Philip Friend). He in fact arrives with a couple of sailors who have rescued him from a crash in the sea, a captain and his mate Hawkins, played respectively by Finlay Currie and Gordon Harker, the latter introduced to provide some faint comic relief. This formidable combination succeeds in thwarting the spies, who are finally rounded up by the military. It was very much a low-budget movie, scenically confined almost entirely to the interiors of the mansion, with stock shots of a Wellington bomber used to represent the enemy's escape plane, and it prolonged the weary tradition of the most routine of prewar British films.

The ever-popular espionage theme gave James Mason the chance to perform in a more sympathetic role in *They Met in The Dark.* Without his contribution, the film, based on a novel by Anthony Gilbert and directed by Karel Lemac, might not now have much interest, except possibly for its supposed locations in Blackpool and Liverpool. Mason plays a navy lieutenant-commander, Richard Heritage, who is court-martialed and dismissed from the service because of apparently disobeying orders, an incident that has led to an unescorted ship being sunk by a U-boat. Heritage is convinced that his orders had been switched, and he goes to the northwest again to prove his innocence. The plot contains many typical thriller ingredients—a disappearing body, a sceptical police inspector, a mind-reader, spies hiding under cover of a theatrical agency and a dancing academy, and also—one of the most common attributes of such films—an elaborate system for passing messages to other members of the network, in this case by transmitting secret information through a code based on musical notation, performed on a harmonica by Ronald Chesney. Heritage's "meeting" is with Laura Verity, played by Joyce Howard, who accidentally gets herself caught up in the tangle. Finally, it seems that he is being used as bait by naval intelligence, represented by his former friend and prosecutor Lieutenant-Commander Lippinscott (David Farrar), and of course the spies are arrested at the end. Before the close of 1943, James Mason had appeared in yet another espionage melodrama, *Candlelight in Algeria,* produced and directed by George King, with Carla Lehmann as an American girl who helps him to frustrate a Nazi plot.

The famous Herbert Wilcox and Anna Neagle team also filmed on a similar subject in their *Yellow Canary.* It is distinguished mostly by having Anna Neagle skilfully play the part of an upper-class girl who, like the real Unity Mitford, is infatuated with the Nazis and their leader. Sally Maitland appears on the top floor of an office block, signaling by torch to German bombers as they raid London. When the police arrive, they find only the body of a man, killed by a revolver shot. In the meantime, Sally has gone to a night club, where she bears with dignity a chilly reception from the diners and a series of jibes about her by the comedian Cyril Fletcher. In the morning, at breakfast, the Maitland family read about Buckingham Palace being bombed. Sally is leaving for Canada, for her own good, and much of the action takes place aboard ship. The liner is carrying a number of passengers, including children being evacuated overseas—an option open to wealthier parents—and these include the supposed Polish officer Jan Orlock (Albert Lieven), who becomes attached to Sally, and a shadowing British intelligence officer, Jim Garrick (Richard Greene). Neagle keeps up the fiction for two-thirds of the film, until she can disclose that in fact she is also a British agent. The deception is meant to put her in touch with the enemy, though what benefit they would gain from such an openly pro-Nazi figure is a mystery. After shooting in London the spy who had been trying to signal to the Luftwaffe the whereabouts of the royal family, she had herself directed the planes to the palace because the King and Queen that night are staying out of town!

They Met in the Dark. **The girl tries to persuade the police inspector that the man is up to no good (James Mason, Brefni O'Rorke, and Joyce Howard).**

The film has some fascinating impressions of Halifax, Nova Scotia, and its position as the vital terminus and starting point for allied convoys; and these are of more lasting interest than the Nazi spy story, which is, if anything, even more absurb than in most movies of this type. Jan is an enemy agent, and the leader of the Nazi group in Halifax is disguised as his disabled mother. The plan is to blow up the harbor and all its shipping, by moving out of an incoming convoy a ship manned by fifth columnists and putting in its place another with a German crew and which is packed with explosives. This substitution is achieved under cover of a convenient fog, not thick enough, though, to stop the RCAF from bombing the ship once Sally has unmasked the plot. She survives an attempt to shoot her and goes home to her family as a heroine, in the uniform of the Wrens, and also brings back Garrick as a newly wedded husband. She tells them how her original resolve to do what she could for her country had dated from hearing Ribbentrop remark to Hitler on how Britain would be too spineless to fight, to which her mother, Lady Maitland, responds with the film's final line—"not bloody likely." Even the language of the Wilcox and Neagle world had not been entirely unaffected by the war.

The title of the film refers to the delivery on two occasions to Sally Maitland of a parcel containing a model yellow-colored canary accompanied by a rude note about her dedication to the Führer. In fact the sender had been Jan Orlock, and it was a device meant to put to the test her continuing loyalty to the cause. In overall artistic terms, *Yellow Canary* is a minor piece but, if taken as characteristic of all these wartime thrillers, it represents at a level of undemanding film entertainment a number of themes present in the minds of the public at the time. Even the issue of "careless talk" is still raised through the personality of a garrulous middle-aged passenger on the ship, played by Margaret Rutherford. When a German warship stops the liner in order to search for Garrick, the leader of the boarding party is performed by Valentine Dyall as a straight-backed, barking Hun, the public's normal and expected image of the enemy. From the historical observer, if not the film critic, slighter movies like these may merit nearly as much attention as the better-known productions.

The American actress Ann Dvorak appeared in a couple of British war spy thrillers, first *This Was Paris,* issued at the beginning of 1942 and set in the French capital just before the surrender, and then *Escape to Danger,* made in 1943. In the latter she is a Danish teacher of English who poses as a collaborator so that she can be sent as a spy to Britain. On the way she finds herself on a raft with Eric Portman, after the ship carrying them from Lisbon has been torpedoed. He turns out to be a British intelligence officer, and together, following their rescue, they prevent the Germans from detecting the destination of an allied invading force. MGM's *Adventures of Tartu* (U.S. title: *Tartu*) was set in Czechoslovakia, with Robert Donat playing an agent who has the task of blowing up a poison gas plant. Valerie Hobson and Glynis Johns also starred in this film. None of these productions gave any evidence of radical rethinking of the industry's approach either to subject matter or technique. If there was indeed a kind of renaissance of British commercial cinema during the war, a common critical assessment,[24] it was confined to a very limited number of titles.

The Two Cities production *The Flemish Farm,* directed by Jeffrey Dell, was certainly not one of these, in spite of its promising theme, supposedly based on a real incident. It had Clifford Evans as Jean Duclos, a Belgian airman, returning to his country to find the flag of his squadron, which had been hidden during the blitzkrieg of 1940. Duclos is told in England by his colleague Fernand Matagne (Philip Friend) that he has buried it in the ground close to a farm where his wife Tresha (Jane Baxter) lives. Matagne's death in the Battle of Britain causes Duclos to go back alone, to try to persuade Tresha to reveal the exact location. He is also helped by his former commander Major Lessart (Clive Brook), who lives in Brussels in retirement and who finally sacrifices his life in order to save hostages by pretending to have been himself the assassin of a collaborator. The mission is successful, but Duclos has to avoid a Nazi pursuit, right up to his crossing of the river that separates occupied and Vichy France. By the time the film was released, this border in fact had disappeared, the Germans having invaded the southern zone as soon as Anglo-American forces landed in Algeria and Morocco.

The execution of *The Flemish Farm* suffered from being enclosed within the theatrically derived traditions of most British cinema. The same was true of Ealing's *Undercover* (U.S. title: *Underground Guerrillas*), a production about guerrillas in Yugoslavia, although a great deal of the shooting was not in the studio but took place in Wales, a location with a somewhat gentler landscape than the one it was supposed to simulate. However, the use of this environment was carried a stage further, with some of the players talking in Welsh accents as they represent local peasants. The Petrovitch parents, better-off farmers, are played by Tom Walls and Rachel Thomas (who had been the mother of a Welsh mining family in *The Proud Valley*). The young Stanley Baker makes his debut as a schoolboy who sees some of his friends executed by the Nazis and goes off to join the guerrillas. Putting foreigners onto the screen had always been a problem, especially when they were rural characters, and in this case the film fell back on the convention of taking a familiar ethnic group and using it to stand in for the earthy Slavs, folk dances and all. Unfortunately, the result was a disaster, worsened by the employment as the Petrovitch sons of upper-middle-class actors like John Clements and Stephen Murray. To be fair, Murray's performance as the doctor Stevan, continuing to practise in Belgrade and secretly helping the resistance under cover of being a collaborator, is a sound one. But Clements as Milosh, the army officer who takes to the hills and leads the guerrillas, is too like the British navy types he portrayed in *Convoy* and *Ships With Wings,* and he is wholly empty as a Yugoslav national hero.

Directed by Sergei Nolbandov, the production was originally meant to be called *Chetniks,* after the name of the first resistance group in Yugoslavia to attract attention in London. The situation in this country was extremely complicated, a consequence of the tribal divisions that had not been healed by unification after the First World War. In Croatia, for instance, a nationalist sect actively cooperated with the Germans and tried ruthlessly to exterminate minorities within the area. The cetniks (as they are more usually spelled) were basically royalist and Serbian, a group of former army officers, with Colonel Mihailovic at their head, leading armed bands drawn from villages and farms and attired in traditional fashion. As far as this, the script of *Undercover* kept close to historical accuracy, but in fact Mihailovic had pursued a policy of organizing his groups only in preparation for eventual allied intervention. He was wary of military activity, for fear of inviting retaliation by the Germans

***Undercover*. Yugoslav guerrilla meets his surgeon brother (John Clements and Stephen Murray).**

on local populations. However, more serious resistance was soon to be mounted by Tito and his communist forces, and indeed their actions did bring about the expected reprisals. Soon fear of communism was to turn many of the cetnik leaders against Tito. During 1941 and 1942, a muddled impression of events was received in London, but by the middle of 1943 it had been decided to switch the main Anglo-American support behind Tito's partisans.[25]

The hasty change of title for the film was a response to these different circumstances, although it was later in the year before the British decisively gave recognition to the communists as the main resistance force. The guerrillas in *Undercover* appear garbed as cetniks—not a red star in sight—and they undertake sabotage and witness Nazi retaliation. The German governor, General von Staengel (Godfrey Tearle), at first tries reasonableness, until an assassination attempt on him. Milosh is identified as the man who fired the shot, and his schoolteacher wife Anna (Mary Morris) is interrogated by Staengel's grim subordinate, Colonel von Brock (Robert Harris). However, she manages to escape, with the help of her pupils, and joins her husband and the guerrillas in the hills. Ironically, Stevan has saved the general's life by performing the hospital operation on him, and he is sent now on a mission to try to persuade his brother to stop his activities. During the journey, both he and the Petrovitch father give up their lives when they contrive to blow up an ammunition train, and the final episode of the film has Milosh and his group defending their village, while elsewhere the main guerrilla forces start an offensive. The filmmakers had received help from the exiled monarchist government in London, before it became clear that events in Yugoslavia were to move in the direction the communists wanted. In spite of its weaknesses, *Undercover* is still worth viewing, if considered in the light of British misinformation about Yugoslavia, an instance, of course, of a larger lack of comprehension by an island people of European nationalities in general. The playing of the Nazi governor by Godfrey Tearle not as a totally rigid figure is also an interesting element.

A Welsh setting was used for the Crown Film Unit's documentary *The Silent Village,* an imaginary transposition to a small mining community of the real tragedy of the people of Lidice in Czechoslovakia.[26] In September 1941, Bohemia had acquired a new Protector in Reinhard Heydrich, at that time second only to Himmler in the SS. He was a savage and ambitious man, who saw his ultimate destiny as being ruler of all the Reich's eastern territories, inhabited for the most part by Slavs, whom the Nazis despised as subhumans. At once, he set in motion a policy of terrorization in his province. However, in May 1942 he was mortally wounded in an attack on his car by Czech agents sent from Britain. Hitler ordered immediate reprisals, and a campaign of executions culminated the next month in the total destruction of the small village of Lidice, chosen for purely arbitrary reasons. All adult males—nearly two hundred—were shot in batches, women sent off to concentration camps, and the children also taken away, a few to be selected for re-education as German citizens, but the majority eventually gassed on the orders of Adolf Eichmann. The event was not concealed in any way, but instead was well publicized by the Nazi media, which took photographs of their soldiers smiling amid the burning houses. The news caused worldwide indignation, a fact that had no effect whatsoever on future Nazi extermination policies.

The Silent Village was directed by Humphrey Jennings, with the assistance of the Czech government in exile. To have attempted a reconstruction of the Lidice episode by imitating Czech backgrounds, with English-speaking players taking the parts of Czech working-class people, would have invited failure. In fact Jennings had Welsh people play themselves in the small village of Cwygiedd. The film's opening moments establish the environment of such a place, the

***The Silent Village*. Welsh miners are lined up to be executed by the Nazis.**

Before the Raid. **Nazi authorities close in to confiscate the catch of Norwegian fishermen.**

chapel, the mine, the school, the miners' cottages, colliers in the pit baths, the cinema, the pub. Life is ordered and peaceful. When the enemy arrives suddenly, they are seen at a distance, in the form of a car with a loudspeaker, the occupants invisible. Proclamations appear on walls. Normal rights and activities are suspended. The miners react with a strike, with some sabotage, until repression forces them back to work. The teaching of Welsh is banned in the schools.

Is the film really saying what might have happened if Britain had been occupied? Probably not, for the Welsh background is in many ways only incidental. With the aid of his collaborators, Chick Fowle and Stewart McAllister, Jennings adopted a cerebal method of detachment from the story. *The Silent Village* fell short of being a drama, using only such few words as were necessary to move the action forward. In the plot the Protector's death incriminates the village, and the Germans take their revenge, but these incidents are shown dispassionately rather than realized in emotional terms, a technique which makes the film's tribute to the Lidice victims a more composed one than might have been the case in a production conceived so soon after the real events.

A very different style was chosen by the exiled Czech director Jiri Weiss for *Before the Raid,* a Crown film about not his own country but the occupation in Norway.[27] It starts with commandos setting out across the North Sea, British and Norwegians together. As they talk to each other, a picture emerges of the plight of the fishing village from which the Norwegians came. Confiscation of their fish stirs up resistance, reaching its climax at sea with the fishing boats closing round a German armed launch and attacking it. The village quisling is caught in a net and thrown overboard. This literal account was on a different level of narration from the more surreal structure of Jennings's film.

Another sort of exile was featured in the Spectator film *Lift Your Head Comrade,* directed by Michael Hankinson. The title came from a song written by an Austrian concentration camp prisoner, and this short documentary was concerned with the work of one of the companies of the Pioneer Corps formed from aliens in Britain. Ian Dalrymple had been unable to make a film on the subject in 1940, but, nearly three years later in a more relaxed climate, Spectator's producer Basil Wright had more success. The script was written by Arthur Koestler, the Hungarian author and thinker who had escaped from France just before that country's collapse and after a short period of internment had been able to join the pioneers. Most of those appearing in the film were German and Austrian antifascists. Koestler has explained how their

***Lift Your Head Comrade.* Anti-Nazis from Central Europe are trained to join the allied forces.**

stance was met with incomprehension by most British working-class people whom, in his experience, he found to be badly informed about war objectives.[28] The pioneers are shown performing building and forestry tasks, all that these aliens were allowed to do at first, jobs for which many of them were ill suited. At the end they undertake arms training, and in time some were able to join more active fighting units, although certain death awaited them if they were caught by the Nazis. Koestler himself went on to become an army lecturer for a time before moving to the MOI's Films Division, and it was then that he produced the draft for *Lift Your Head Comrade.*[29]

Koestler had been anxious to have some of the refugees talk about their tribulations in the concentration camp and, although this was done to a small extent—a former Austrian boxing champion demonstrates how he was hung up by the wrists in Dachau—he was persuaded by the MOI that this aspect of the film should not be overemphasized. It was felt that at this stage of the war the British public would find it difficult to accept the truth about these places. This attitude is a reflection of a certain caution following the admitted excesses of First World War propaganda, and there was indeed a general reluctance to come to terms in official films with the precepts and effects of Nazi ideology. *These Are The Men* had been something of an exception, but even *The Silent Village* had preferred to describe an actual atrocity in allusive rather than in direct fashion. It is instructive to contrast this approach with that of a documentary made by the Polish Army Film Unit in Britain, *Calling Mr. Smith,* directed by the artists Stefan and Franciszka Themerson, an interesting piece technically in its use of dufaycolor, superimpositions, and freeze-frames, but also an emphatically didactic film that called on the average Briton, the Mr. Smith of the title, to stop complaining about having too much propaganda pushed at him and instead to face the facts about the consequences of Nazi persecution and destructiveness. Its views are very similar to those which Koestler wanted to express and which, according to his own account, he had also found it difficult to communicate in army education classes. The real truth about Nazism perhaps only came home to many of the British after publicity given to the liberation of the concentration camps in 1945.

The apathy Arthur Koestler had encountered among his audiences at an early period of the war was a factor the Army Bureau of Current Affairs (ABCA) came into existence to counter from 1941 onward. Units were required to allocate some time in training to the organization of discussion groups. The AFPU made a film about its work in 1943 that emphasized how solid information had been needed to replace rumor about the war and other world events. It also showed an Anglo-American question-and-answer team, or "brainstrust" as it was called then, dealing with contemporary topics. ABCA helped to raise the consciousness of some soldiers about social concerns at a period in the middle of the war when more attention was being turned to the need for change afterward, in particular an end to the poverty and deprivation that had been suffered by the poorer classes in the nation. Naturally, this tendency soon became disliked by many conservatives, to the extent that Sir James Grigg at first even tried to discourage ABCA from discussing the Beveridge Report.

The appearance of this document in December 1942 was a watershed in the British social history of the Second World War, not so much for the reforms it proposed, which fell far short of outright socialism, but for its reception by the public. There was certainly no inertia here. An opinion poll discovered that almost everyone in the country had heard of the report and that most people favored its recommendations for providing schemes of social insurance for everyone. About two-thirds of a million copies of it were sold.[30] It even produced one slight film, *Two Good Fairies,* made by the Co-operative Society from a story by Dr. C. E. M. Joad, the most celebrated member of the BBC's radio "brainstrust" team during the war. A young soldier reads the report and dreams of the benefits he will receive when he is released from the services—a retraining scheme for a new job, hostel accommodation, allowances for his wife and baby, social care for the child's grandparents (the other "good fairy" alongside the welfare state was the Co-op itself).

It has already been observed that a number of films like *Wales—Green Mountain, Black Mountain* had begun to take up the theme of the kind of Britain that was expected after the war. One of the few able to handle with confidence an English regional situation was Spectator's *Tyneside Story,* directed by Gilbert Gunn and cast from members of the People's Theatre, Newcastle-on-Tyne.[31] It described the rerecruitment of shipyard workers who had been laid off in the thirties. "What a nerve," the wife of a shopkeeper says. "You'll be daft if you went back." One man remarks how they had been thrown out and, as soon as the war is over, out they will go again. However, the men do return (to the background music of the popular local song "The Blaydon Races") and a ship is launched. The call-up for the forces has created a demand for more labor, and women are brought in to be trained for heavy jobs like welding. The narrator says, "As long as Britain calls for ships the call will be answered by the ring of steel on steel in the shipyards of the Tyne." One of the shipyard workers, facing the camera, has the last and arguably more prophetic words in the long term—"Remember, five years ago, idle, derelict, men forgotten. Will it be the same again five years from now?"[32]

A British National feature, *The Shipbuilders,* also made in 1943, took as its subject the struggle to keep open the Clydeside yards in the thirties, carrying the story up to the outbreak of war. Its director, John Baxter, had specialized in comedies, making some during the war, for instance, for Flanagan and Allen and another with Radford and Wayne as Charters and Caldicott. But his populist method also had its more serious side and, in *Love on the Dole* and *The Common Touch,* both from 1941, he had presented with sympathy the subcultures of society that the prewar censors preferred to have kept away from the screen. In 1942, *Let the People Sing,* loosely adapted from J. B. Priestley, had Edward Rigby as a music-hall comedian and Alistair Sim as an exiled Czech professor, both running away from the law for different reasons and coming to the aid of a community that wants to keep its town hall to use for popular entertainment. They have to defeat some industrialists who would prefer to turn it into an exhibition space and also a group that wishes to convert it to a local history museum. The latter are presented as a gang of diehards and reactionaries trying to force their views down the throats of the public. Eavesdropping on their meeting, Patricia Roc, as the daughter of the family sheltering the two fugitives, mockingly calls out "Heil Hitler!" Finally, a drunken arbitrator, played by Fred Emney, turns the meeting into a farce but comes down in favor of the community. The film's

***The Harvest Shall Come*. Farm laborer and wife face up to the reality of harsh times (John Slater).**

final montage mixes the ordinary people with the armed forces, uniting them with a sense of democratic aspiration and optimism in wartime. Reaction among the servicemen against the Conservative party may have been the decisive factor in giving Labour its landslide victory of 1945.[33]

In 1940 the GPO Film Unit's *Spring Offensive* had only barely hinted at the truth about British agriculture between the world wars. Now in 1943, Realist could deal with the problem more historically in an extended film, *The Harvest Shall Come,* by using a method of semidramatization, with John Slater playing the Suffolk farm laborer Tom Grimwood. It was scripted by H. W. Freeman and directed by Max Anderson, and genuine farmers and laborers took part in it alongside the players. Tom joins a farm at the start of the century. Conditions are bad, but at least they are better than those experienced by his father. He marries, and he and his wife bring up three children. There are improvements during the First World War, but suddenly from 1921 the support for the price of wheat is dropped, and the farmer has to cut wage levels. As imports pour into the country, the situation worsens. With other laborers, Tom endures a couple of decades of hardship and unemployment. Both work and remuneration are restored with the Second World War. Listening to the radio, Tom and his wife hear Bruce Belfrage say, "Never again must we neglect our land and the men and women who live by it." She comments, "They said all that in the last war," and Tom responds, "Well, this time it's got to be different." The film had been sponsored by ICI, and John Taylor of Realist remembered that some of their board of directors reacted to it as if it had been communist propaganda![34]

The best-known film about postwar hopes was Rotha's *World of Plenty,* which dealt specifically with the need to rearrange the existing inequitable system of world food resources.[35] The idea for it had originated with Eric Knight, a writer and film journalist in America, who had emigrated there from England before the First World War and had become famous for his imaginative stories of Yorkshire life. Now he had joined Capra's scriptwriting team for the *Why We Fight* series. The outline for a British film about a world food strategy was discussed in London by Knight with Rotha and with Arthur Calder-Marshall of the MOI, which undertook to finance it. It soon grew from its original short-span concept to become a larger project, intended at first for American audiences, to appeal to the spirit of the New Deal and to the sentiments of the Atlantic Charter. Sir John Boyd Orr, author of a notable book about prewar nutrition levels, was consulted for specialist advice, and Lord Woolton, the Minister of Food, agreed to appear in the film. Knight was able to return to the United States to fulfill his official duties there with two-thirds of the script written, the rest to be finished by Rotha.[36]

The film was intended to shock by its rhetorical style, the calm statistics spoken by E. V. H. Emmett interrupted by dissident voices—"laugh that one off with that diagram," one says in order to qualify America's status as the wealthiest nation in the world by the fact that a third of its people had been ill-nourished. Rotha's clever use of isotype charts escalated the budget, to the dismay of the MOI bureaucrats, until Arthur Elton persuaded them of the effectiveness of the method. The making of *World of Plenty* also went through other uneasy patches. The United States Department of Agriculture disliked references in the script to the dumping of surplus produce (pork and cotton "mountains," they would be called now) to keep up prices. In addition to the considerable cutting-in of stock material, Rotha needed specially filmed sequences in America, for which he had to make use of an American crew. The *March of Time* team was selected, but Rotha was to protest that Sidney Bernstein, representing the MOI's interests in New York, had not passed on to them his detailed shooting instructions and also had failed to consult Eric Knight. For his part, Bernstein, feeling that the content of the film was too controversial, suggested that it be cut down to a more factual account of how rationing and food distribution worked, advice which was rejected by Jack Beddington at the MOI. The difficulties of coordinating the British and American ends of the production helped to delay progress on it.

The sequences about Britain dealt with the neglect of agriculture between the wars, while people were suffering from diet-related illnesses like rickets and turberculosis. War had at least stimulated more concern about national health, with food rationing organized on a fair and sensible basis. However, the main message of *World of Plenty* was the necessity of

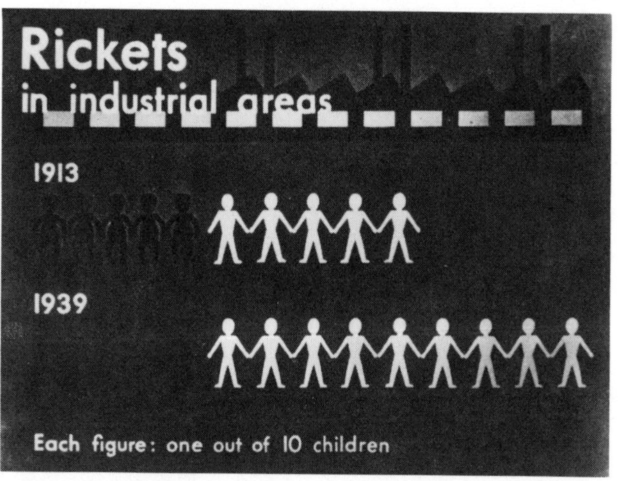

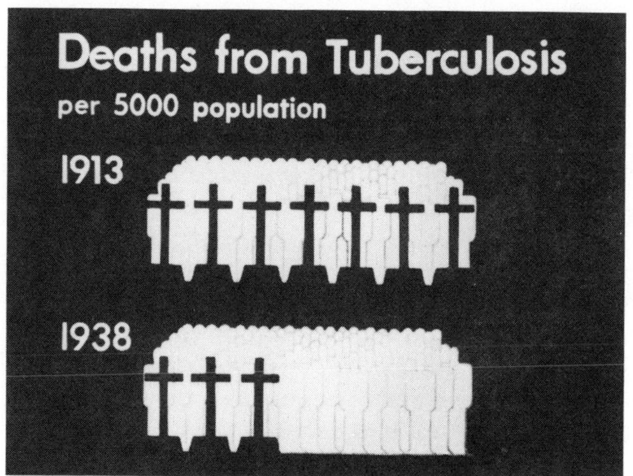

World of Plenty. **Paul Rotha and Eric Knight put forward the statistics about prewar health.**

organizing postwar resources in such a way that surpluses passed to the poorer nations, on the lend-lease model. The film asks, is this a revolutionary plan? "What are we fighting for if not for something revolutionary?" says Sir John Boyd Orr. The Ministry of Agriculture was unhappy about the emphasis on distribution at the expense of production, thinking more realistically perhaps that such an idealistic scheme was unlikely to be carried out in practice. Nevertheless, Beddington was able to counter most of their objections, and the minister (Sir Donald Vandepeer) finally came round to praising the completed film, which at an earlier stage he had described in a letter to Elton as "dangerous, and all the more so because of its technical excellence."

Unhappily, Eric Knight did not survive to see *World of Plenty* finished. He was killed in a plane crash in January 1943. The film was shown to a world food conference in the United States in May and attracted considerable enthusiasm from the delegates there and from the press. Naturally the thesis put forward could not be wholeheartedly embraced by advocates of a purely market economy, but the climate of the film accurately represented the mainstream feelings of people at the time, dominated as they were by a sense of Anglo-American idealism as the inspiration of postwar international harmony. The track at the end carries the words of the American vice president, Henry Wallace, as he talks about "the century of the common man." It would have been untimely to forecast political differences, in particular the coming gulf between the western allies and the USSR that was to frustrate many of these hopes and to substitute the Cold War for them.

Enthusiasm for the Soviet stand against Hitler was widespread throughout Britain during 1942 and 1943, and it reached a climax with news of the heroic battle over Stalingrad and the decisive defeat inflicted there on the Nazi invaders. The twentieth anniversary of the foundation of the Red Army on 23 February 1943 was celebrated in many British cities with rallies and marches, the biggest pageant of all taking place at the Albert Hall in London, with an address by Anthony Eden, the Foreign Secretary. The Internationale was sung by solid dignitaries of all political persuasions. These events were filmed by the newsreels and later put together for the MOI in a short compilation called *Salute to The Red Army,* edited by Raymond Perrin and distributed overseas.

The Communist party, which originally on instructions from Moscow had not approved Britain's entry into the war, now gained more support, though not enough to shake the leadership of the left by Labour. Many intellectuals in the thirties had swallowed uncritically the euphoric views of the Soviet regime that had been put out by George Bernard Shaw and Sidney and Beatrice Webb. Little was known of the horrendous repression and coercion in the USSR, and those glimmerings of information that did come through were either disbelieved by the left or ignored on the principle that a few excesses on the path to socialism were excusable because the end justified the means. Conservatives in Britain, for their part, including that indefatigable anti-Bolshevik warrior Winston Churchill, were willing to suspend their dislike of the USSR so long as Hitler's legions were destroying themselves in the east. For the bulk of the population though, with Russia as remote from them as another planet, there had emerged a sense that, as they were beginning to hope for a better era after the war, a genuine period of the "common man", their aspirations were not so dissimilar from what had been achieved already in the USSR, vaguely seen as a society where everything was run by the people for their own benefit under the benevolent tutelage of "Uncle Joe" Stalin. Admiration for the determination and the boundless sacrifices of the Russian people was a sentiment that carried opinion before it and that was stronger at the time than any reservations about the fundamental nature of Soviet society, the truth of which was appreciated only by a very few.

In the light of postwar political developments, it is more surprising perhaps to witness how far this pro-Soviet feeling extended itself also in the United States. It has been argued that Roosevelt was more apprehensive about future British imperialist ambitions than about Soviet aims in Europe.[37] To many Americans, even more cut off from an appreciation of the rest of the world than their British counterparts, Russia must also have seemed like a nation where, as in the United States, the ideals of the "common man" were the legacy of the twentieth century. Britain by contrast, with its empire, its monarchy, its social heirarchy, and its straitlaced conventions, belonged to another age. America's *Why We Fight* films, produced in the first place for the education of American servicemen about war aims, included the remarkable *Battle of Russia,* directed by Anatole Litvak, a vigorous and generous tribute to the Soviet Union, its history, people, and achievements. The Hollywood feature *Mission To Moscow* went so far as to discredit the victims of the purge trials. It also criticized Anglo-French appeasement policies, a fact which caused the Conservative party in 1943 to ask for a ban on its screening in Britain, a request refused by Brendan Bracken.[38] *Mission to Moscow* was a foolish film, but its uncritical admiration for Stalin and his regime represented a mood that was beginning to alarm those on the right in Britain, who now saw this movement as a possible threat to their own interests once the war was over.

The script for the Two Cities feature *The Demi-Paradise* was written by a Russian exile, Anatole de Grunwald, and was seemingly designed to mirror this stage of Anglo-Soviet amity. The Russian engineer Ivan Kuznetsov, inimitably played by Laurence Olivier, visits England first in 1939 to persuade a shipyard to build a vessel that will employ his own patent propeller design for breaking up pack ice. Returning next year, he has the opportunity to see the British at war. "I don't understand the English," he tells the firm's managing director Runalow (Felix Aylmer), who answers, "My dear fellow, who does?" Runalow has an encyclopedic knowledge of world railway timetables. The local middle-class community expends time and effort on a ghastly historical pageant, Margaret Rutherford in the lead. Runalow's

The Demi-Paradise. Discussion about a blueprint and a clash of cultures between the British industrialist and the Russian engineer (Felix Aylmer and Laurence Olivier).

granddaughter Ann, played by the ever-smiling Penelope Dudley Ward, takes Ivan to see a comedy performance by Leslie Henson, which the Russian rightly thinks unfunny. During an air raid, Beatrice Harrison plays her cello to the nightingales. Ivan almost gives up on the British until finally he senses the steel beneath the surface, and, when his invention works at last, he gives his verdict on this curious people who have found a "practical religion—making the best of things." In the meantime, with the USSR now at war, the locals turn their next pageant into a celebration of Kuznetsov's home town. Ann has joined the Wrens and declares her love for Ivan (it is hard though to imagine a postscript with them in postwar Moscow).

Directed by Anthony Asquith, *The Demi-Paradise* was not only myopic about the USSR but also complacent about England, the real subject of the film's title. Runalow is a figure dear to English folklore, the self-made industrialist who does not commit the indecency of being too totally engaged in his work. The film's impressions of lovable English dottiness were to be re-enacted, most particularly in the postwar Ealing school of production, which created charming and accomplished films that were yet symbolic in their way of the growing inertia of British society as traditional codes and frozen class relationships began to reassert themselves.[39] Apart from the modest political reforms brought about by the Labour government immediately after the war, there was little change in Britain until the social and sexual emancipations of the sixties. Even these were achieved in the context of a decade that now looks to have been illusory and escapist, inevitable perhaps as Britain abandoned its imperial straitjacket, but also clearly a prelude to a harsher period of national decline. *The Demi-Paradise* was released in America under the less provocative title of *Adventure for Two*, and demonstrated there a view of British life even more absurd than anything dreamed up by Hollywood in the likes of *Mrs. Miniver.* At a time when Churchill still hoped that Britain would come out of the war as an equal partner of the United States, it was not a triumph for home-grown propaganda.

The first test of Anglo-American military cooperation took place with the campaigns in North Africa. As soon as the Americans had been persuaded, not without some difficulty, that an invasion of northern Europe was not a feasible operation for 1942, it was agreed instead to occupy the French territories in Africa. The allied forces were brought in two convoys, one from Britain and one directly across the Atlantic from America, and the landings in November resulted in a rapid seizure of Algeria and Morocco. The French military put up some resistance, but gradually they started to change sides, especially after Hitler made his decision to move into the south of France. Rommel in the meantime had retreated from Libya, and German and Italian reinforcements in strength were rushed across the narrow passage from Italy to Tunisia. There a bitter struggle commenced in the mountains and continued through the winter until May 1943, when the allies drove the enemy back toward the sea and finally forced the surrender of many thousands of their troops. The local French and African populations in all these areas greeted their liberation with enthusiasm.

A film on the theme of this new victory was already being projected in London before the campaign was finished. The unexpected success of *Desert Victory* had been observed, not without a degree of jealousy, by the MOI's Films Division and, if a successor was to be made, the Crown Film Unit wished to have a hand in it. There was objection even to the AFPU's proposed title *Tunisian Victory,* because it might appear to be treading too closely in the footsteps of their box-office winner.[40] The MOI wanted a more comprehensive approach, to cover all the services and also the background work of people at home; and, though the AFPU put up a certain amount of resistance to the idea, it had to give in to pressure from Brendan Bracken, who was anxious to see the production pushed through as quickly as possible. Crown took on the main burden of costs for the film, to be a cooperative effort between them and the service units, and Jack Holmes was dispatched to Birkenhead to take shots at the docks of troops embarking on ships. An elaborate treatment had been devised to include a lengthy prelude to the operation, with a number of re-enacted or semifictionalized sequences, and it was clear at this stage that the MOI was aiming to make a large and prestigious movie. However, in the interest of speedier production, this plan was gradually whittled down, and most of the Holmes material was scrapped. In Tunisia Hugh Stewart, having landed with the first allied forces at Algiers, was leading the AFPU's unit at the front, and Roy Boulting began the assembly of some of the returned film at Pinewood. Requests for American film so far had proved to be fruitless, and it was decided that coverage of the actual military operations would be largely British, with acknowledgment given to the American contribution in the field. On returning from Africa, Stewart took up direction of the film, to be titled *Africa Freed,* and, in spite of a running battle with the Air Ministry, who constantly complained that the RAF was not being adequately represented in the script, he had it ready in a rough cut by August 1943.

Although the finished version of *Africa Freed* has survived to the present day, it was destined never to reach wartime cinemas. As soon as American representatives saw the previews in London, they passed the message home to Washington that the British had made a film about North Africa that undervalued American involvement. The MOI for its part had believed that complementary projects were being prepared in the United States. Indeed, before the campaign was even over, Darryl Zanuck, using material mostly shot by John Ford with the U.S. Army Signal Corps, had released a technicolor production called *At the Front in North Africa.* Throughout the war, the Americans were able to make more use of 16mm color stock than anyone else. However, the name of Frank Capra had also been mentioned in connection with a film that would draw on the 35mm black and white records. In August, a proposal was made by the U.S. War Department that the Capra material should be amalgamated with the British film, a plan that found immediate favor with Brendan Bracken, eager to make the most of the American relationship with Britain. Bracken went so far as to suggest, probably on American promptings, that the rough cut of *Africa Freed* should be sent to Hollywood for Capra to re-edit, incorporating his own sequences, an idea greeted with derision and dismay by the filmmakers in London. Finally, after Capra had made a personal visit to England, it was settled that he and Stewart would collaborate at Pinewood on a joint production, now to be called *Tunisian Victory* and credited to the service film units of both countries. There was to be no further involvement by Crown, although responsibility for distribution of the film remained with the MOI. American sensitivities stayed high, Capra having to show the film to General Marshall, the chief of staff in Washington, and then take it to Hollywood for completion. Stewart also traveled to America to safeguard British interests as well as he could, but the consequence of these maneuvers was that *Tunisian Victory* was not released finally until 1944, by which time the African campaign had become a matter of past history.[41]

As for *Desert Victory,* the commentary for *Africa Freed* had been written by J. L. Hodson, with Leo Genn as the main narrator. Genn's voice was transferred to the British sections of *Tunisian Victory,* but the text was much simplified, as were the explanatory diagrams, on the grounds no doubt that American audiences were even less informed than British and unlikely to be captured by too much detail. As with all these documentaries, the political background was skated over, and there could be no hint of any dissension between the allies. In fact, the planning and the operation itself had been unusually disputatious. Both films explained the need for victory in Africa as motivated by fear of the Germans linking up in the Middle East and moving toward India—a preoccupation on the part of the British that many Americans suspected was caused mainly by concern about the future of the Empire. The situation regarding the French was even more complicated. The legacy of actions by the British at Mers el Kébir, Dakar, Syria and Madagascar was considerable hostility to them in the French military and, to overcome this problem, the landings were represented at the time as a mainly American effort. Pétain's deputy, the anglophobe Admiral Darlan, was in Algiers, and it was he who ordered the French to cooperate as soon as southern France was invaded by the Germans. Moreover, General Giraud, who had escaped from a German prisoner-of-war camp, had now arrived to take over command of the forces. Soon Darlan was to be assassinated, rather to the relief of the British, who detested him, and *Tunisian Victory* showed Giraud meeting de Gaulle, who was himself intent on being recognized by the French as the real leader of their new war against Germany. De Gaulle was distrusted by the Americans, who looked instead to an accommodation with Vichy, while Churchill's own relationships with the prickly French patriot had become severely strained.

Tunisian Victory took on a snappier style than its predecessor, a style more reminiscent of the *Why We Fight* films. Only vestiges of Alwyn's score were kept, and new music was produced in America by Dmitri Tiomkin, much of it directly pilfered from Rachmaninoff. One of the major differences in content between the two films was the introduction into *Tunisian Victory* of a long and sentimentalized section about the troops at Christmas, which was not even mentioned in the British film. When Capra brought his rushes to London, Stewart and Boulting objected that they were almost all concerned with one single episode, the taking of Hill 609 by the Americans, and even that had been entirely faked in California. In fact, the *Why We Fight* films had made indiscriminate use of contrived material, and clearly Capra saw no reason why this should not be done again. However, in spite of the authenticity of most of the AFPU film, *Africa Freed* had also contained some reconstructed sequences, notably a lengthy exposition of the night crossing of Wadi Zigzaow, one of the assaults by which Montgomery had broken down Rommel's Mareth Line defense in the south. This episode was severely shortened in the final joint production. The end-caption of *Tunisian Victory* contained an acknowledgment that use had been made of some stock shots and re-enacted material where original film was not available—a new degree of honesty in an endeavor of this kind.

Although the British in the final stage of the campaign contributed most of the ground troops, overall command had been given to the American General Eisenhower (with Alexander in charge of the armies), a sensible decision that eased susceptibilities in the United States and was anyway justified by his common sense and tact. Such qualities were needed when the relatively raw Americans took a severe hammering from Rommel at the Kasserine Pass, while the reputation of the British soldiers, both of the Eighth Army in the south and the new First Army in the north, probably now reached their highest point in the entire war. An ordinary British private is represented on the track of *Tunisian Victory* by the voice of Bernard Miles, with occasional (and acceptable) swear words, and, in the concluding section of the film, he and the American actor Burgess Meredith discuss in simple terms the destructiveness of war and their hopes for a future world. "You and me, Joe," says Miles, "we may not always think alike but we do think." A montage of faces reveals that the thinking people are all allies, including Russians and Chinese, and it is they who will have the job of reconstruction afterward. The moralistic ending does not fit too easily into the structure of the film—it would have been unthinkable in the more factual *Africa Freed*—but one should not assume that it was necessarily an unwelcome American imposition on a joint production. In fact Capra and Stewart worked it out together, and it was not a surprising development in a film made at that period of the war, when the end was beginning to come into sight. The hopeful Anglo-American sentiments it expressed were not basically different from those put forward in *World of Plenty.*

Nevertheless, the story of the production of *Tunisian Victory* illustrates the kind of rivalry between British and Americans that had emerged with the campaign itself and that was to continue until the end of

***Tunisian Victory.* Restaged for the camera. British and American troops meet in Tunisia, an early moment of accord in their dealings with each other.**

the war. In the film context, it is likely that the Americans, confident about the technical resources of Hollywood and indifferent to the British documentary tradition (though the Oscar win for *Desert Victory* must have surprised them), simply expected as of right to be assigned the dominant role. Ronald Tritton recorded that when another joint production was planned in 1943 and 1944, on the Italian campaign, tension rose as it became clear that the Americans wanted to make the film entirely in the United States and on their own terms.[42]

During the battles around the Mareth Line, Rommel had brought into action some of the new and formidable Tiger tanks, but the Eighth Army had been able to repulse them by using their own recent acquisitions, seventeen-pounder guns. The race to produce an efficient antitank weapon that would be an effective counter to the Tigers was the ingenious subject of the AFPU's *A Date with a Tank,* a quarter-hour film directed by Donald Bull and finished in 1944. Most of it was shot in the armaments factories that were making the gun, and the story narrated the urgency of the process, as the War Office demanded speedier production schedules. German footage of tanks being tested was cut in, and the film developed a lively sharpness of rhythm, up to the climactic moments when the seventeen-pounders were fired at the enemy.

Meeting at Casablanca, Churchill and Roosevelt decided that, since an invasion of northern Europe was still not a likely prospect for 1943, some further action should be taken in the Mediterranean, partly in the hope that Italy could be driven to make peace. The allied landing in Sicily in July was the largest seaborne operation of its kind in the war, and conquest of the island took just over a month. The vital objective was the port of Messina in the northeastern corner, and Alexander had intended that the main thrust toward it would be made by the British Eighth Army, with the U.S. Seventh Army acting only as a shield for it. Predictably, the Americans resented this subordinate role and, when Montgomery ran into heavy opposition before he could pass Mount Etna, the flamboyant General Patton charged off instead toward Palermo at the western end of Sicily before turning along the northern coast, a move that enabled him to enter Messina ahead of the British. By this time, Mussolini had been overthrown, and his successor Badoglio was undertaking covert negotiations with the allies.

One observer of the Sicilian landings had been Humphrey Jennings, who was hoping at this time to make a film about the Royal Marines. He had done some work with them and their commandos in Scotland, and he accompanied a unit aboard ship as it prepared to go into action. Apparently a large amount of material was shot by Jonah Jones, but the project was never completed (the film does not seem to have survived),[43] and Jennings turned instead to another story that had grown out of the Mediterranean war, the way in which the German song "Lili Marlene" had been picked up by the British troops in the desert and modified with their own words. *The True Story of Lili Marlene* was narrated by Marius Goring, and Jennings himself made a brief appearance, reading the original German words.[44] Almost all of it was reconstructed, to show the German broadcasting station in Belgrade that first put out the song in a program directed to their soldiers in the field, and the way in which it was later used by the British, for BBC propaganda and simply as a theme tune by the Eighth Army.

The collapse of fascism in Rome and the rapid allied success in Sicily created an irresistible momentum toward a crossing to the mainland of Italy, although the Americans originally had not welcomed such a development, arguing that it would divert attention from the main aim of invading northern Europe. Four years to the day since Britain entered the war, British and Canadian soldiers of Montgomery's Eighth Army disembarked in Calabria and started a slow trek northward, meeting only light opposition on the way. Five days later, the surrender of Italy was announced, although Badoglio and his government, as well as the Italian royal family, had to flee to the protection of the allies as soon as the Germans reacted to the news by occupying Rome. Mark Clark's U.S. Fifth Army, made up initially of one American and one British corps, landed around Salerno and soon found itself bogged down against heavy resistance. For a time it seemed as if he might have to re-embark his troops. One of the many killed at Salerno was Harry Rignold, the War Office's original cameraman. The death of this popular figure caused sadness throughout the film industry. During his AFPU career, he had tried to be as close to the action as possible, and he was posthumously decorated with the Military Cross for his contribution.

British units had landed in Apulia, on the Adriatic side of southern Italy, and, as Montgomery made his cautious approach to Salerno on the other coast, the Fifth Army gradually was able to consolidate its position, and the Germans were forced to withdraw. The allies entered Naples, finding a wrecked city, heavily bombed as it had been before the Italian surrender and now also devastated by German actions. The Nazis had even planted delayed action explosives, causing heavy civilian loss of life in a tragic incident when the post office was blown up. Deprived of food and water and any source of power, the million inhabitants of Naples found themselves on the verge of starvation. This situation and its aftermath were described in a short film, *Naples is a Battlefield,* produced by the RAF and Army Film Units in 1944 and jointly edited by Roy Boulting and Peter Baylis. It made up an impressive record of the first major city in Europe to be rehabilitated by the allies, both in terms of physical reconstruction and political re-education. The citizens at first are in a state of near panic, worsened by the outbreak of an epidemic of typhus. They have to be evacuated before the American engineers who have restored the power lines dare even to turn on the electricity, for fear of more explosions. Supplies are brought in by sea, and the people struggle through to a state of survival. Shops open and begin to attract customers from the ranks of allied servicemen. However, the commentary makes no reference to some of the more dire consequences of the war for Neapolitans, like the inevitable growth of widespread prostitution caused by desperate economic need. Its concluding section is understandably more concerned with the rebirth of democracy in Italy and its acceptance by the population after their own disillusionment with fascism.

Churchill still hoped that the Italian campaign might help his favorite scheme for infiltrating the Balkans, a plan which Roosevelt and his advisors had rejected. They saw no profit in trying to reach eastern Europe before the Russians and, unlike the British leader, they were not concerned yet about Soviet intentions on the continent. Churchill had been keen to impress on his military commanders the need for them to imitate the boldness of the likes of Clive of India, and they responded by trying to seize the

Dodecanese islands in the Aegean. However, the aeroplane had not been invented in Clive's day, and the Germans still had superiority in the skies in that part of the Mediterranean. The British expedition ended disastrously, and one of its immediate consequences was that Turkey, a nation Churchill had wished to prompt into joining the allied side, decided instead to remain neutral. There was to be no way into Europe from the southeast, and the allied armies in Italy were soon to be starved of men and equipment as the plan was evolved for the invasion of France in 1944.

Anglo-American expectations in Italy were anyway to be disappointed when Hitler decided to turn down the advice of Rommel, who wanted to withdraw to the north, and to accept instead the judgment of Kesselring that the road to Rome should be defended for as long as possible. Mussolini had been rescued from captivity high in the Abruzzi by SS troops who made a bold and difficult landing by glider, and it would be possible now to reconstruct under his leadership the semblance of a new fascist republic in Italy. By the end of the year, the Fifth and Eighth armies, nudging forward in worsening weather conditions and having to fight for peak after peak in the Italian mountains, had ground themselves to a halt. Their left flank had come up against the dominant heights of Cassino. Alexander was still in command on the ground, but Eisenhower and Montgomery had returned to England to prepare for the cross-Channel invasion.[45] The AFPU section on this front was headed by Geoffrey Keating, one of its most experienced officers, who had been a stills photographer.

The Casablanca conference had also pointed to the need to unify the British and American air offensives against Germany in order to cripple the enemy's industry as a prelude to invasion. However, American daylight raids in 1943 were still restricted in range because of the lack of fighter protection, and the RAF continued to put its main resources into night bombing of urban areas. In July the city of Hamburg was subjected to a series of terrifying attacks that created uncontrollable fire storms. The number of civilians killed in a week equaled the total number of those killed in the bombing of Britain to date. Harris confidently told Churchill that, with sufficient support from the Americans, he could devastate Berlin from end to end and finish the war at a stroke. In fact the assault on Berlin remained mainly a British operation and, at the end of that winter, Bomber Command had lost a further thousand aircraft, while Germany was still functioning in spite of the heavy damage to its cities.[46]

On film, advocacy of the bombing campaign was presented almost entirely by the newsreels. When Movietone made a short documentary for the Ministry of Aircraft Production called *Sky Giant,* it began with scenes of the factory assembly of a Lancaster and moved on to some of the RAF Film Unit's stock footage of night raids, showing unbroken lines of fires on the ground.[47] The tone of Leslie Mitchell's commentary is revengeful, implying that the enemy is now receiving the medicine he had handed out to Warsaw, Rotterdam, and London, but nothing is said directly about civilian casualties. The aim is that of "paralysing German war effort, the overthrow of German armed might, the elimination of Nazism." The Crown Film Unit's *Workers' Weekend,* on the other hand, was wholly shot in a factory, to show how a bomber was being produced in record time, in this case just over twenty-four hours.[48] At the end, the employees hand over their bonuses to Red Cross Aid for Russia.

However, one short MOI film did come close to admitting the indiscriminate nature of British bombing. Alexander Korda had returned to Britain on a number of occasions during the war, partly for business reasons and partly in pursuit of his undercover intelligence activities. The latter had aroused some suspicion in American isolationist circles before Pearl Harbor, just as there had been antagonism from the same people to the pro-British patriotic stance of his feature on the life of Lady Hamilton. Korda was knighted in 1942, a recognition as much of his work for the government as for the film industry, and he returned to England in the following year, the first American reports indicating that he was about to take up some high post in the propaganda field. In fact, he had come to amalgamate London Films with MGM-British and, with this new company, he hoped to set out again on a series of spectacular movies.[49] A number of filmmakers were promised contracts, among them Ian Dalrymple, who left Crown partly for that reason,[50] but the only feature to emerge eventually was *Perfect Strangers,* finished in 1945 and directed by himself. In the meantime Churchill had put to him the idea for the documentary *The Biter Bit,* which would justify the allied bombing campaign by looking retrospectively at the actions of the Luftwaffe.[51] It starts with a re-enactment of the episode at the German embassy in Oslo when *Feuertaufe,* with its sequences of the bombing of Warsaw, was shown to an invited audience of still neutral Norwegians, to impress them with the might of Nazi air power. There are reminders also of the ordeals suffered by Rotterdam, Belgrade, and London and a quotation from Churchill's "finest hour" speech, the narration eloquently delivered by Ralph Richardson. "The biter is

***The Biter Bit.* Bomb damage in England, destruction which is used as an excuse for massive retaliation against Germany.**

bit," the prime minister had said about the allied counteroffensive.

Aerial photographs demonstrate how much greater an area has been devastated in cities like Düsseldorf and Cologne than in Coventry. After the bombing of the Ruhr, the German propaganda machine has changed to a plea, Richardson says, to "humanise warfare, think of the historical monuments, the terrible scenes of fire and destruction, think of the sanctity of human life," but in fact they are putting on this "whining tone" only because retaliation is falling on them. The film was made under the cloak of "Coombe Productions," and the commentary was written by Michael Foot. Any thoughtful person who saw it should have been able to draw the correct conclusions about the suffering of German civilians in the bomber offensive, but there would be another couple of winters of war before a few British consciences were touched by the implications of the strategy Harris and Churchill had agreed upon.

There had been one small advance from the assumptions of the *Target for Tonight* period, in that there was more recognition now on screen that flying over Germany was a perilous job and might end in death. Features like *Millions Like Us* and *The Way to the Stars* had leading characters killed in action while serving in bombers, and there were other examples. In Strand's short film *There's a Future in It,* Johnny O'Connor, pilot of a Stirling, goes missing for a time with his aircraft before finally he reaches base, bringing home a wounded man.[52] At the pub Johnny meets his girlfriend Kitty. A Canadian airman remarks of him, "There goes a guy who's part of the future of the world." Outside, Johnny tells Kitty that really he hates the operations, he likes comfort, not being shot at, but he dislikes even more what "they"

***There's a Future in It.* A moment of repose for a weary RAF flier (Ann Dvorak and Barry Morse).**

are doing—"sometimes I think we need more hatred." Kitty has been having difficulty at home over Johnny, but, in an outburst to her father, she says that there is a future for them all because of men like him, and she even repeats the message out of her bedroom window. In spite of some distinguished contributors, a script by H. E. Bates, the American actress Ann Dvorak as Kitty, photography by Georges Périnal, editing by Alan Osbiston, and music by William Alwyn,the overall handling of the theme by director Leslie Fenton is heavy-handed, and Barry Morse is so smooth and complacent as Johnny that one might have preferred to feel the future should not be left to people like him.

From Archers came an extended film about the Fleet Air Arm, *The Volunteer,* scripted and directed by Michael Powell and Emeric Pressburger.[53] Ralph Richardson plays himself as an officer in the service, meeting up with his former theater dresser Fred (Pat McGrath), who has progressed from prewar clumsiness in his old occupation to confidence and skill as an aircraft engineer aboard a carrier, in which role he manages to win a medal. Powell took his unit aboard ship in the Mediterranean, and the film showed how far the navy's air arm had come since the early days, with newly completed carriers and modern planes like the Seafire, a nautical adaptation of the Spitfire. *Operational Height,* from the RAF Film Unit, looked at a more obscure area of the war in a documentary account of how barrage balloons were being operated at sea from the decks of drifters to protect incoming convoys and minesweepers from air attack.[54] Ealing followed in 1944 with *For Those in Peril,* a featurette directed by Charles Crichton about air-sea rescue. The plot had a resentful RAF officer called Rawlings (Ralph Michael) drafted to the service on medical grounds and taken in hand by Murray (David Farrar), a former merchant navy sailor. While rescuing a ditched aircrew, their launch has to engage a German armed trawler. Murray is killed and Rawlings finally

***The Volunteer.* The actor meets his dresser in the Royal Navy, aboard an aircraft carrier (Ralph Richardson and Pat McGrath).**

appreciates the value of the work he is doing. Credit is given for the story to Richard Hillary, a pilot who had been badly injured by burns in the Battle of Britain and who attracted much attention with his book *The Last Enemy,* an account of his training and of his recovery in hospital that was seen by contemporaries as expressing responsible and humanistic attitudes by a representative of his social group of university-educated volunteers in the RAF.[55] Hillary tried to fly again, against advice, and was killed in January 1943 while on a practice. To use his name in the film was no doubt a device to bring it a measure of publicity, for the only part of *The Last Enemy* that in any way resembles it is Hillary's fall into the sea after bailing out from his plane. The beginning of *For Those in Peril* had a pilot parachuting into the Channel in 1940, though in this case a lifeboat fails to reach him—hence the necessity of building up a new service with high-speed launches so that a similar tragedy need not be repeated.

At home the output of informational films had somewhat slackened during 1943, as pressures on civilian morale began to diminish. Even so, isolated air raids continued to take place, and there were still some projects of a civil defense nature, as for example one by Shell on techniques for rescuing people who had been buried beneath bombed buildings. The same company also made *Control Room,* directed by Geoffrey Bell, shot in Bristol to demonstrate how central procedures operated in a blitz.[56] Its producer was Edgar Anstey, the original founder of the Shell Film Unit, who subsequently had been British editor for *The March of Time.* During the war, he produced a very large number of short films for the MOI, made by various independent companies. For Realist, John Halas and Joy Batchelor created their most humorously inventive animated film of the time, *Dustbin Parade,* a plea for the collection of scrap materials, with the various items themselves mustering for public duty.[57] *We Sail at Midnight,* a longer film from Crown, had as its theme the operation of the lend-lease program.[58] It was directed by Julian Spiro, and it was made with the cooperation of the American and Canadian authorities. A tank is being tested in the dark, the silhouetted figures of officials shown as they watch its trials. All that will be needed to complete the

***Dustbin Parade*. Scrap materials put themselves at the service of the war effort.**

***We Sail at Midnight*. Lend-lease supplies for Britain are driven along Broadway, a fantasy world of light for British audiences.**

model are some special gear machines from the United States. The decision is taken, after some discussion of the pros and cons, by the lend-lease committee in Washington. There is hasty activity at the factory in Connecticut before the heavy cases can be dispatched by road to the docks in New York. They must arrive by nine o'clock so that the British freighter can sail at midnight to join its convoy. The trucks drive down Broadway, ablaze with neon light, a glimpse of a remote and magical world for British wartime viewers. The ship's Welsh skipper explains the perils of the Atlantic route that have to be negotiated before the vital parts finally arrive in Britain, diverted for convenience from Glasgow to Liverpool, a shift of destination that allows the film to show another wartime committee in operation.

A number of the MOI trailers were made by Richard Massingham, whose wit and ingenuity in the production of miniature films were much admired by his contemporaries, including such an important figure in French cinema history as Henri Langlois. Massingham was a master of visual symbolism through the use of rapid cutting between carefully chosen close-ups, usually of objects rather than people, and he employed sometimes this technique with the most seemingly ungrateful material, as in the quarter-hour film *Believe It or Not,* scripted by Lewis Grant Wallace, on the work of the War Organisation of the British Red Cross and St. John. Their activities are seen being put into graphic form by the cartoonist Ripley of the *Daily Express,* accompanied by more explicit film sequences. An earlier Massingham production from the war, *Fear and Peter Brown,* had a headmaster calming the nervousness of one of his scholars, ingrained in him since childhood and illustrated in the film by the shadows of his toys on the wall of his nursery. His parents, kind people though they are, have been unable to comprehend his anxieties. The schoolmaster persuades him that there is nothing wrong with being afraid under certain circumstances. The war is being fought for freedom and justice and "with fear in its proper place we can look forward to the future." A shorter film, *Dangers in the Dark,* tells a motorist, a lorry driver, a dispatch rider, a cyclist, and a pedestrian who have been involved in an accident in the blackout that they might have prevented it with more care on the part of each of them. Of the trailers, *The Five-Inch Bather* won most appreciation for its clear, humorous, and also satirical manner of presenting a needed propaganda message. The portly Mas-

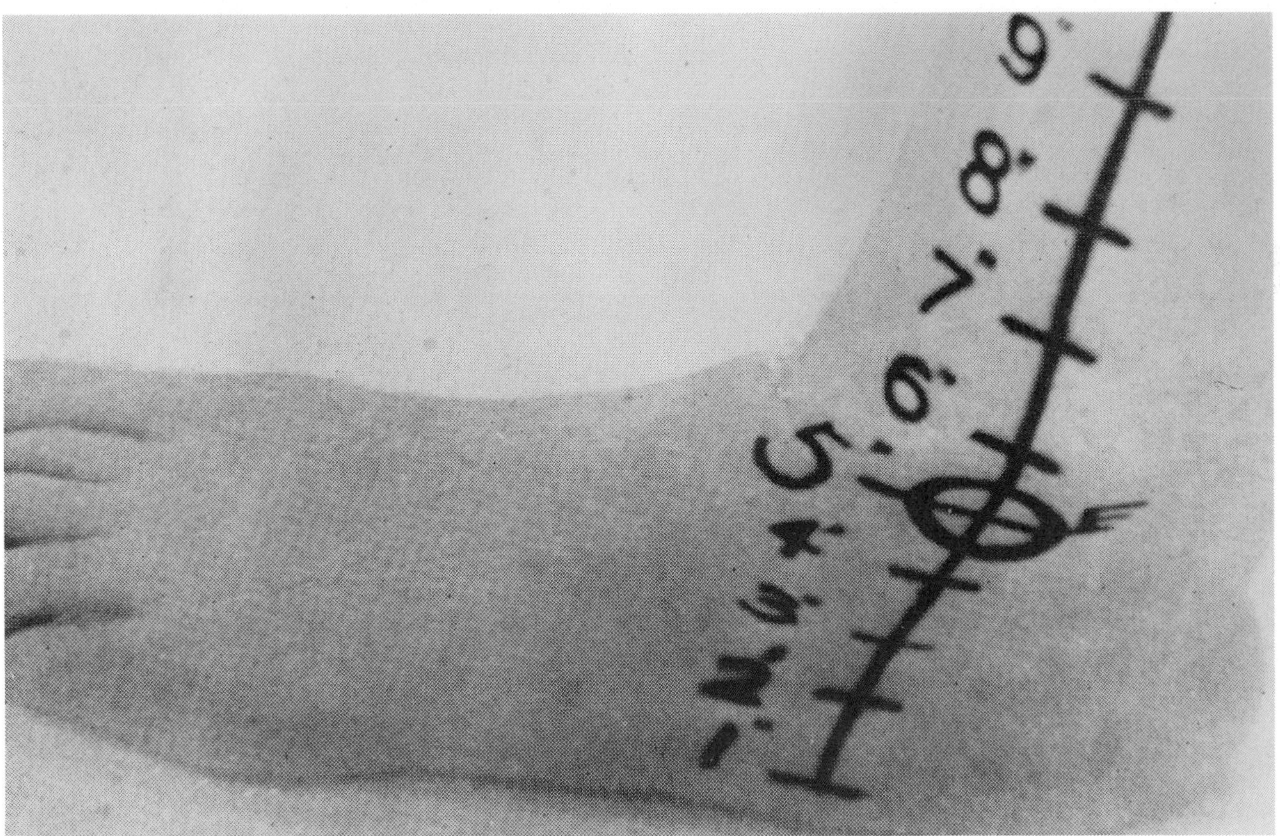

***The Five-Inch Bather.* Richard Massingham takes care to observe the wartime bathing regulations to the letter.**

singham himself copes with the problem of having a bath in the regulation economy amount of five inches of water. He has drawn a measurement on his ankle so that he is certain not to exceed the rule. The film was shot in a cramped bathroom at the London Fever Hospital where Massingham had worked at one time. One of his last productions from the war, *Down at The Local,* was made specifically to remind the troops in Burma of the pubs at home. Reviewing it, Humphrey Jennings commented on its imaginative selection of shots, showing for instance not so much the pub drinkers themselves as the beer they are consuming, while the track carries the sounds of their conversation. The film "is saved from cleverness by being really human."[59] Like Jennings himself, Massingham was not destined to live for long after the war.

It had become common again to issue lengthier documentaries, running for around half an hour, and in this field Paul Rotha, after *World of Plenty,* had turned his attention definitively towards postwar developments. *Power for the Highlands,* directed by Jack Chambers, dealt with the production of hydroelectric schemes in Scotland, discussed by a couple of Scottish soldiers who happen to come across two American enlisted men; and they in turn tell them how their own Tennessee Valley scheme works.[60] Another Rotha film set in the same country, *Children of the City,* directed by Budge Cooper for the Scottish educational authorities, was concerned with juvenile delinquency and the kind of social improvements and organization that would be needed to overcome the problem.[61]

A singular film from the period, nearly an hour and a half in length, was Strand's *Battle for Music,* produced and directed by Donald Taylor. It reconstructed the true story of the London Philharmonic Orchestra, the future of which had been jeopardized when its founder Sir Thomas Beecham had departed for America at the beginning of the war. Players themselves, like Thomas Russell and Charles Gregory, re-enact their roles as the orchestra turns itself into a self-governing body and makes its own bookings for concerts. They are supported by J. B. Priestley, who, in a witty and ironic speech at the Albert

***Battle for Music.* Adrian Boult conducts the London Philharmonic Orchestra, saved from the threat of wartime dissolution.**

Hall in July 1940, makes an appeal on behalf of the players, implying also that the government is indifferent to their fate. Times are still hard though, and ultimate security only arrives with the intervention of the popular impresario Jack Hylton, when he engages them to play in a series of regional theaters. There are interesting glimpses of musicians of the period, including Moiseiwitsch, one of the old school of pianists who is the soloist in the fashionable Rachmaninoff Second Concerto, and Malcolm Sargent conducting Beethoven's Fifth Symphony through an air raid on Newcastle. Sargent goes on to speak to the audience about how Hitler has been unable to destroy the performance of music in Britain.

Len Lye's next film for Realist, *Cameramen at War,* was a short tribute to the activities of the newsreel and service cinematographers, showing many of them at work and identifying them by name.[62] Its commentator, Raymond Glendenning, talks about the hazards of the job, as some of the war's more effective action sequences are reproduced. The careful though brief selection of material constitutes a useful visual guide to the methods used by the cameramen. Jack Ramsden of Movietone, for instance, is seen fixing his camera to a door in an American B-17 bomber before a high-level raid. An electric blanket is fitted to prevent the motor from freezing up. A shot of Fred Baylis of Paramount is cut into his own photography of final preparations for the Sicilian landings, where

Cameramen at War. **Jack Ramsden of Movietone sets up his camera before a B-17 daylight raid by the USAAF over Germany.**

***Cameramen at War.* A Paramount camera team operating on the English coast.**

he was killed. In order to put the techniques into context, there is also some retrospect on the previous world war, with the famous episode of the great American filmmaker D. W. Griffith at the front with the British army, and a glimpse of the present General Alexander as a junior officer in the trenches.

By the middle of 1943, the navy was gaining the upper hand in the Battle of the Atlantic. Shipping losses had been heavy in the earlier part of the year, but the use of coordinated escort groups, the presence of new frigates and special small aircraft carriers, and above all the efforts of the code-breakers who were able to listen to the signals sent out by U-boats, guaranteed in the end that the enemy was sliding toward defeat. At this stage of the war, service in a U-boat was beginning to mean almost certain death. It was a victory won almost entirely by the British and Canadians, because the Americans had withdrawn most of their vessels to the Pacific, except for those being used in the invasion of Europe, and, undramatic though it might have seemed to be, it ensured the survival of Britain and so of the western cause. In the use of their surface ships, Dönitz's navy had become surprisingly unenterprising. Germany's most powerful battleship, the *Tirpitz,* was crippled in harbor by a daring attack from British midget submarines, and, when at last the *Scharnhorst* attempted a foray against a convoy bound for Russia, it was caught and sunk on Boxing Day by Admiral Fraser's flagship, the new *Duke of York.*

Early in the war, the merchant seaman could have been able to complain with some justification that not enough was known about the dangers of his unrewarding job, and a film like *Neutral Port* might have done more harm than good, but by 1942 and 1943, fewer members of the public would have been ignorant of the stark nature of the Battle of the Atlantic. The official volume *The Saga of San Demetrio* by F.

Tennyson Jesse, published in 1942, told the true story of a tanker that had been part of a convoy returning home in November 1940 when attacked by the German armored ship *Admiral Scheer.* Their only protector was the armed merchant cruiser *Jervis Bay,* a converted liner. As soon as the *Scheer* opened fire, Captain Fegen of the *Jervis Bay* turned directly toward her in an effort to save the convoy. It was a heroic and doomed gesture. After a quarter of an hour, the *Jervis Bay* was blazing from end to end and when she sank, Fegen and most of his crew went down with her. Although in the gathering darkness most of the merchant ships were able to escape, a few were singled out as targets by the *Scheer.* The *San Demetrio* was hit and set on fire and, since her storage tanks were full of petrol, she was abandoned at once. However, she remained afloat and, after a couple of nights of struggling in a boat against galelike weather, a number of her crew, led by the second officer and the chief engineer, decided to reboard her. They managed to put out the fires and restore power and, by using a primitive method of steering her, they finally succeeded in navigating her home without aid from compasses or charts, all of which had been destroyed in the flames.

Ealing's feature film *San Demetrio–London* was directed by Charles Frend, assisted by Robert Hamer, and, in spite of obvious embellishments in the script that gave a more personal side of the participation of the main characters, it was remarkably faithful to the original book. In this respect, as a conscientious reproduction of a real incident, it was unique among British commercial films of the Second World War, and its documentary-derived style was more in the tradition of *Nine Men* than in that of *In Which We Serve,* another film with a foundation in fact. Although it was entirely studio-shot, it was made to seem almost totally authentic, thanks to the level of accomplishment now developed by Balcon's team, though the lifeboat scenes have not escaped criticism, especially when set beside those in *Western Approaches.* The very fact that the story was selected at all by a studio like Ealing presupposed at least some of the public's acceptance by now of a film that would be completely unglamorous and had no major stars. There was of course no hint of love interest, and women were referred to only in the context of presents being bought for them in America before the ship sailed. Nevertheless, recognition of the existence of a family life at home was not forgotten in the script, and this aspect of it was built around the the personalities of the engine-room greaser Boyle and the young messroom boy Jameson, played respectively by Mervyn Johns and Gordon Jackson, who were, in the film, related to each other, one with a wife and the other a girlfriend in Britain.[63]

Much of the appeal of *San Demetrio* rests on an invitation to its audience for sympathy with the individual small acts of improvisation the crew are forced to make. The sober styles of performance by Ralph Michael as Second Officer Hawkins, Walter Fitzgerald as Chief Engineer Pollard, and Frederick Piper as bo'sun Fletcher arouse confidence in these men's calm professionalism. There is still some sense of public underestimation of their value beside that, for instance, of fighting servicemen. Pollard says the British merchant seaman is "the most neglected beggar in the world," and Fletcher speaks with some bitterness about civilians at home enjoying too thoughtlessly the luxuries brought to them by the sacrifices of the men at sea. Although the sailors themselves are unified in their own endeavors, apart from one grumbler who complains about reboarding the ship, they are clearly not 100 percent confident about the backing they have in the nation, and this faint tinge of disillusionment is an interesting element in the script. Robert Beatty takes the important part of the Canadian seaman Oswald Preston, known to everyone as "the Yank," who has joined the ship in Texas to work his passage to England. He is reluctant to exert himself, and he is made by Fletcher to repaint the funnel, but during the crisis he shows his true worth, working round the clock and keeping the men's spirits alive with his good humor. Pollard has damaged his thumb while he was abandoning ship and, when the wound swells and goes septic, Preston employs the old crude method of opening it up with his knife and releasing the pus. Boyle has suffered more serious injuries and, though he carries on without complaint, he is forced in the end to give up, and he dies aboard ship. His place in the engine room is taken by Jameson.

Because the *San Demetrio* had been brought home entirely unaided, refusing even the help of a tug, the crew were able to receive salvage money. By a unanimous vote, the tattered red ensign was handed to Oswald Preston, but, sadly, he was killed shortly afterward in the blitz on London. Although the *San Demetrio* was repaired and went back to sea, she soon fell victim again, this time to a U-boat, which torpedoed and sank her. Two Hebridean seamen, MacNeil and MacLennan, returned with their prize money to Barra for a month's respite. MacLennan was being married and had expected a dry wedding, but in fact it turned into one well lubricated with whisky, thanks to the wrecking on the island of a vessel laden with many cases of the spirit, an episode celebrated in print by Compton Mackenzie and made into a well known postwar Ealing film, *Whisky Galore.*[64]

***San Demetrio–London.* Part of the crew adrift in their lifeboat, a scene shot in the studio tank (Robert Beatty, Barry Letts, Ralph Michael, Walter Fitzgerald, and Frederick Piper).**

The realism and the method of *San Demetrio–London* have often been contrasted to those of the Crown Film Unit's *Western Approaches,* directed by Pat Jackson.[65] Although the later film was not finished until late in 1944, it had been started two years previously, a tempo of production that would have been unacceptable in a commercial movie. The slowness of completion was due in part to the decision to follow Crown's established tradition of location shooting. It had been planned at first as a convoy film, and Jackson intended to accompany a group of ships from America for some of his photography. However, his first and most difficult task was the filming of the sequences of men in a lifeboat, for which he and his unit based themselves for some months at Holyhead, with a number of seamen employed as actors. Moreover, the film was to be in technicolor and the MOI had hired Jack Cardiff from the industry to handle the color cinematography. The large and heavy triple-negative camera and its operators and the sound apparatus had to go into the lifeboat with the seamen. Jackson and his other assistants worked first from a launch and then, after his request for better facilities, from a drifter. Weather conditions in the Irish Sea were frequently bad—they needed to be made to look like those in mid-Atlantic—and the photography and the sound recording were completed only after several weeks of trial and stress. Studio work commenced at the beginning of 1943, and the sequences on the convoy followed at the end of the summer. Even so, it was January 1945 by the time that *Western Approaches* was generally released.

The reward for the grueling weeks of photography off Holyhead can be seen in the bleak opening of the film, with its impressions in color of towering waves, water splashing on the faces of the exhausted men at

***Western Approaches*. Survivors of a torpedoed ship, photographed in a real lifeboat on a real sea.**

the oars, a hand pump being used for bailing out, and instructions and encouragement from the captain of the torpedoed ship (the part was played by a real merchant navy skipper, Captain Pycraft). A switch of scene to a control room on land establishes the fact that the *Jason* had dropped out of a convoy and had been picked off by a U-boat. Back in the boat, the captain hands out rations. One man, Rawson, has been injured and, when he asks what happened, another seaman named Banner, a native of Merseyside like many of the crew, explains at length how their vessel had been sunk and how the U-boat had come up to fire at them with a machine-gun as they were abandoning ship. As the sea grows calmer, the crew raise the boat's mast and set a sail, hoping now to reach the coast of Ireland. There is next a change of location to New York, with preparations for another convoy, scenes shot at the docks as ships are loading, in particular the *Leander,* which is to play a prominent role in the plot. Pat Jackson himself takes the part of a junior officer aboard the ship. In the dramatization of a convoy conference, all those participating are genuine master mariners. They are addressed by the commodore (Admiral Fullerton) and by the comander of the naval escort, with the usual warnings about keeping station, and Captain Kerr of the *Leander* points out that, if there has to be a drastic reduction in speed, he will have difficulty in controlling his heavily laden ship.

Thereafter, *Western Approaches* alternates sequences between the *Jason's* lifeboat on the one hand and the convoy and the *Leander* on the other. Among the men in the boat is the real journalist Tosti Russell, British-born but an American citizen now and the son of an operatic impresario, and while talking to the sailors he questions them on their motivation for returning to the sea, to take up such a lonely and difficult job. They try to maintain their spirits by singing, and the wireless operator continues to send out distress signals, although the batteries of his set are fading. During the night they think that they hear a U-boat on the surface, and Rawson, delirious now, has to be quieted.

In the meantime, a sluggish French vessel has delayed the convoy and, as its speed is lowered, the *Leander* begins to yaw out of control. The commodore agrees that she should go ahead alone and rejoin later. However, a report of U-boats in the vicinity causes the convoy to change course, and it is realized that there is no way, since wireless silence must be kept, that the *Leander* can be warned.

Pat Jackson was remarkably successful in the quality of performance he drew from his amateur actors, though some obviously needed more coaching than others. At the central point of the drama, he brought in a further and, for a few critics, more controversial element by introducing scenes aboard a U-boat itself. The interiors were shot in the studio, but, for the climax of the film, he had been able to make use of a Royal Navy submarine on the surface. It was rare in a feature production to present the enemy's viewpoint directly, and moreover Jackson had the actors (actually officers in the Netherlands Navy) speak in German with subtitles in English, a device employed in no other British movie of the war period and a solution to the linguistic problem of accurately portraying Germans that helped to bring to *Western Approaches* another degree of naturalism.

On the fourteenth day of being adrift in the lifeboat, with supplies running out and the sick Rawson growing weaker, the survivors are spotted by the U-boat. Hearing also the wireless SOS messages, the German commander decides to lie in wait for a rescuing vessel. In fact, the *Leander* has picked up the signal, and the smoke from her funnel is seen by a cockney sailor, Walden, who is leaning against the mast as the others rest. At that moment, Rawson sees the U-boat's periscope and, although there is an argument about the matter for a while, the stubborn Banner is finally convinced when he too sights the submarine. In vain they try to warn the *Leander,* but the U-boat manages to hit her with a torpedo, and the crew abandon ship, an episode which Jackson and the unit had been able to record in reality while the vessel was in convoy. However, Kerr has remained aboard,

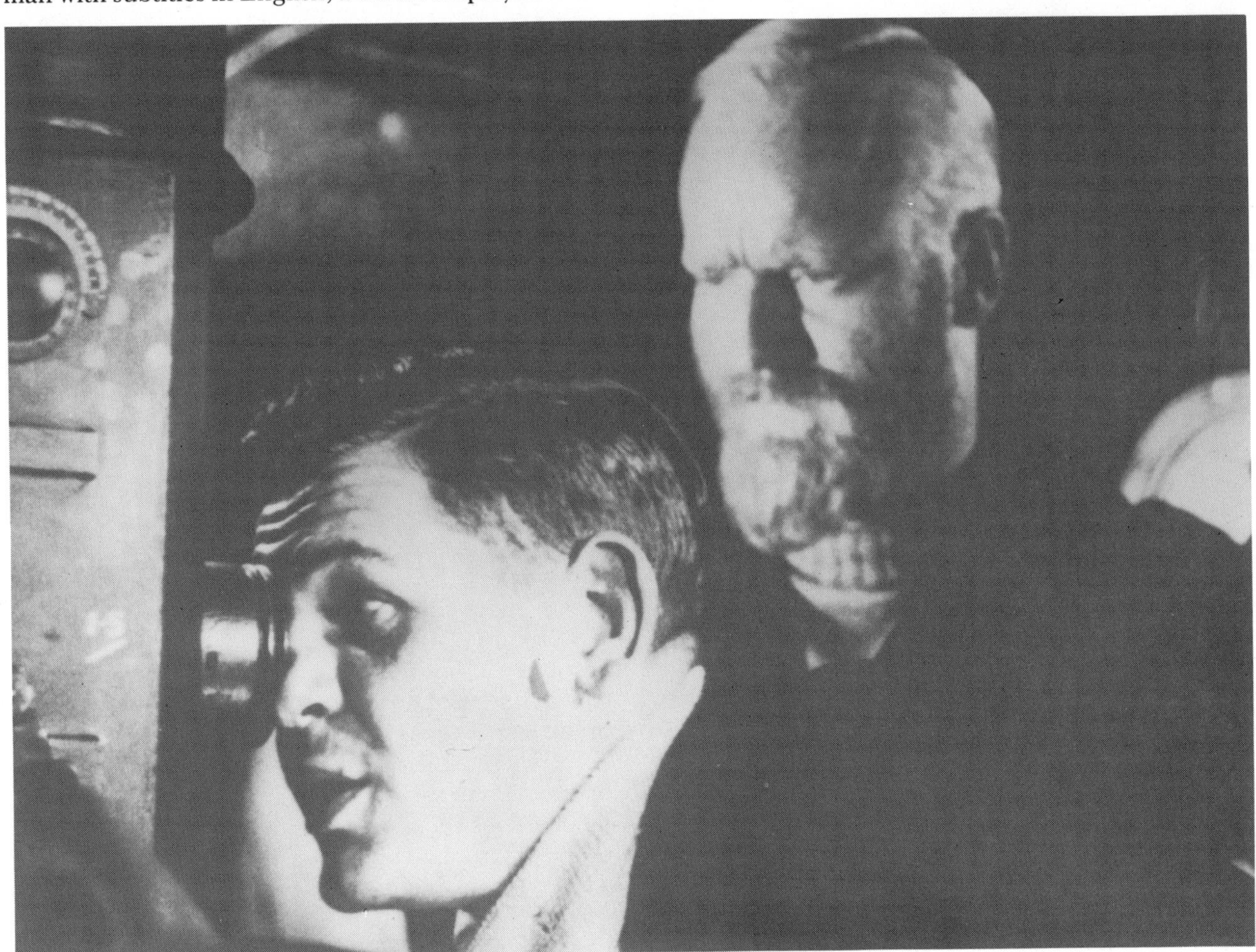

***Western Approaches*. U-boat officers, watching the lifeboat through their periscope, use it as a decoy.**

and the first officer has gone in search of a missing naval gunner who has been trapped below decks. The U-boat surfaces to finish off the *Leander* with gunfire when it refuses to go down, but the Germans are surprised to be engaged by the ship's four-inch gun. In the action which follows, the British naval rating is killed, and the *Leander*'s first officer succeeds in landing a shell on the U-boat, penetrating her hull and sinking her. At the end of the film, Pycraft and his men are picked up, though there is no further reference to the fate of the submariners, some of whom had been struggling in the water, and a final long shot shows the abandoned lifeboat receding into the distance. *Western Approaches* was the only British realistic feature documentary of the war to be shot in color, and its rugged evocation of the atmosphere and actuality of the Battle of the Atlantic was a decisive vindication of all the time and effort Crown had expended on making it.

The winter stalemate in Italy caused Churchill to put pressure on Roosevelt to delay the transfer of some landing craft from the Mediterranean to England in order to attempt a seaborne invasion south of Rome. Reluctantly the American president let him have his way, but the enterprise itself, in which soldiers of both nations went ashore at Anzio, was not pressed home with sufficient vigor and quickly came to a halt against growing German opposition. Farther south, British, Americans, New Zealanders, and Indians had all in turn been bloodily repelled from the heights of Cassino. Reports, which turned out to be untrue, that the Germans were occupying the ancient monastery brought about the regrettable decision to destroy it by bombing. The event was photographed for Movietone by Paul Wyand, and, in the newsreel issue itself, Leslie Mitchell speaks of its "absolute military necessity," forced on the allies by irrefutable proof of the enemy presence.[66] However, the only consequence of the bombing was the real occupation of the ruins by the Germans, who made ideal defensive territory of them, and the film sequences showing tremendous explosions tearing apart the walls and structures of the historic building can be looked at now rather as a positive indictment of the violence and nihilism of war.

The attrition was not halted until May, when French North African troops managed to take the neighboring hills, and the enemy had already started to withdraw when a Polish unit reached the summit of Cassino at last. Alexander had asked Mark Clark to make his first priority the cutting off of the retreating German forces, but, as soon as the Anzio front began to move again, the American general decided instead to drive directly toward Rome. Most of Kesselring's soldiers escaped to fight another time, and on 4 June 1944, two days before the Normandy landings, American troops of Clark's Fifth Army entered the first European capital to be liberated from fascism. Americans had come into the war against Nazi Germany, and they meant to prove to the public at home that they were not going to be put in the shadow by Churchill and the British. Their march into Rome was a symbolic gesture, but it represented also a growing sense of reality about the present balance of relationships in military terms between the two major western allies. The American-made film on the campaign, *The Liberation of Rome,* was produced for Britain in a version with an English narrator. It was modest and factual in spirit, and it acknowledged the help of the British service film units. Possibly the public, more concerned now with war events elsewhere, was made to realize the difficulties that had been faced by the allied armies in Italy.

As soon as *In Which We Serve* had been finished in the autumn of 1942, Brendan Bracken had appreciated the desirability of a single feature to boost the image of the army just as Noel Coward's film had been successful in doing for the navy. It was not an easy task, and Coward himself declined the assignment. The army, up to Alamein, had not distinguished itself, whereas the navy had seemed to come out creditably, even from episodes like Dunkirk and Crete. It happened that in 1942 the Directorate of Army Kinematography had produced a dramatized training film directed by Carol Reed and called *The New Lot,* at the request of military psychiatrists, to show to a fresh wave of recruits, many of them now older men who had been in reserved occupations, as a way of calming their anxieties about joining the army.[67] Unfortunately, the script by Eric Ambler, who had been assisted by Peter Ustinov, was disapproved by the more blinkered of the military authorities, unable to accept the kind of conflict between a regular sergeant and the civilians-turned-soldiers that was written into it (the film was not used and no copies of it survive). However, Two Cities took up the idea of a longer feature on the same subject, with encouragement from David Niven, himself a serving officer, although it needed persuasion by Jack Beddington to convince the War Office that a production about conscripts from different walks of life eventually becoming an efficient fighting unit had any likelihood of success at that time. Eric Ambler produced the treatment, chose the title *The Way Ahead,* and worked again with Peter Ustinov on the script.[68] When the film was completed and released in mid-1944, just as the final phase of hostilities was starting, it proved to be one of the most accomplished

***The Way Ahead*. Garage owner turned territorial officer with his wife (Penelope Dudley Ward and David Niven).**

feature films of the war.

In direction it was also the first great success for Carol Reed, who, in the immediate postwar years, was to gain greater prestige than any other British film-maker of that period, with productions like *Odd Man Out* and *The Third Man.* David Niven, the main star, was still contracted in Hollywood to Samuel Goldwyn, who had released him for *The First of the Few* but now made a fuss about being given favorable distribution rights for the new film in the United States. Niven's role in *The Way Ahead* was that of the platoon commander, Lieutenant Jim Perry. In civil life he has run a garage, and he has trained with the Territorials. At first he has difficulty in getting across to the recruits, who are especially resentful of the authority of Sergeant Fletcher (William Hartnell). They respond badly to Perry's appeal for volunteers for a camp concert. When they deliberately wreck an exercise, he goes to their hut and lectures them on the regiment's traditions and its past glories in battles like Talavera and Salamanca. This history is also symbolized in the film by brief appearances from a couple of Chelsea pensioners who reminisce about how the Duke of Glendon's Light Infantry (the DOGs) "formed squares" in the Sudan, and complain how nowadays modern soldiers don't train hard but look after their "fancy battle suits"—a scene cut against sequences of the real hardships the recruits are undergoing. This aspect of military training was handled with more polished humor than in any previous film, and it was meant to be enjoyed by sympathetic audiences.

The script directs attention to seven of the recruits, and each is drawn in a lifelike way. The store manager Davenport (Raymond Huntley) is disconcerted when he and his junior employee Parsons (Hugh Burden) are called up together. It is "thoughtless of the

***The Way Ahead*. Startled recruits arriving at the camp are greeted by a drill instructor (Jimmy Hanley, Leslie Dwyer, Stanley Holloway, Raymond Huntley, and James Donald).**

powers that be to let this situation arise," Davenport says, but he decides that they must disregard their differences in status. At the camp, Davenport complains about the sanitary arrangements. Parsons is noticed by Perry and Fletcher to be troubled by something and later, after he has gone absent without leave for a short time, he admits that his wife is being harassed by hire-purchase debt collectors. Perry reassures him and grants him leave, a privilege which leads Davenport, who is unaware of the background, to remark of him to the others, "cunning little beggar, sucking up." Stainer (Jimmy Hanley) is a braggart, a former car salesman, who has clashed with Fletcher in the station buffet at Crewe on the way to the camp and thinks the recruits are being victimized by the sergeant as a result. However, he leaves it to Lloyd (James Donald) to complain to Perry. In fact, Fletcher tells Perry he thinks the recruits will all make good soldiers in the end. Luke (John Laurie), a Scottish farm laborer, overhears Perry saying to Fletcher that things are going to be "very different now" and, misunderstanding the reference—Perry is actually talking about the war situation—he reports to the others that the sergeant is being reprimanded. Next morning, Fletcher drives them harder than ever.

Lloyd, who had been a rent collector at home, is the ringleader when the platoon decides to abort the exercise, a move which embarrasses both Perry and the company commander, Captain Edwards (Leo Genn). The former travel agent Beck (Leslie Dwyer) wants to take part in the camp concert, but he is held back by the soldiers' hostility to Perry and Fletcher. The group is invited by Marjorie (Renee Asherson), who works in a mobile canteen, to her home, where they meet her mother, have tea, and enjoy the luxury of a bath. Brewer (Stanley Holloway), who had been a

***The Way Ahead*. Officer, sergeant, and men dig in to wait for a German attack (William Hartnell, James Donald, David Niven, Stanley Holloway, and John Laurie).**

stoker at the Houses of Parliament, attends to the boiler in the house. Unexpectedly one day, Perry turns up there, and recruits and officer for the first time begin to relax with each other. Suddenly everyone discovers an enthusiasm for the camp concert. At the end of the training period as they are going on leave, Perry meets his wife (Penelope Dudley Ward) at Crewe station. Seeing the soldiers, she asks, "Are they the awful men?" "No, different lot," Perry answers.

The troops are directed to take part in the North African landings, the destination kept secret from them until after embarkation. Lloyd now has been promoted to corporal. However, the troopship is torpedoed, and the heavy equipment has to be pushed overboard before it is finally decided that everyone must abandon the vessel. Fletcher has been trapped below decks, and Perry and Luke together manage to free him. The troopship's captain is the last to leave over the side. The Admiralty gave full cooperation to Two Cities for these scenes, and Clan Line Steamers provided models of their ships to help construction of the sets. The incident itself was purely fictional, for there were no losses from the original convoys, a remarkable rate of success under the circumstances. Nevertheless, it affords the film an excuse to return the soldiers to Gibraltar and to defer further their date of joining the war.

It is March 1943 now, and the Chelsea pensioners lament that the press has made no reference yet to the DOGs. In fact they are arriving at a village in Tunisia where the surly café owner (Peter Ustinov) dislikes the idea of having British troops there, at least until they teach him how to play darts. This final part of the film was starkly shot by cameraman Guy Green in North Africa itself, with soldiers and Arabs standing in as extras.[69] At first, there is an atmosphere of inactivity. The unit is in reserve, and it digs in at the side of a hill. The action is distant from them, sampled at night only in the form of gun flashes on the horizon. However, in the morning the Germans attack, shelling them first and then sending in tanks with infantry following, forcing the British to fall back to the village. Even in the battle, the film concentrates almost totally on the nine selected characters—the lieutenant, the sergeant, and the seven recruits. The only outsider is the café owner, who obliges Brewer by pouring wine over his overheated machine-gun. When the Germans, under cover of a white flag, ask the British to surrender, Beck tries to respond in their own language, "Go to hell," but he temporarily forgets the word for "hell." The village is bombed, and from the smoke and the dust the soldiers rise to march forward, bayonets fixed, in a counterattack.

In Which We Serve had been about a service and a ship, with the lives of its three main characters adding little to its central thesis. But in *The Way Ahead,* the individuals matter more, because they have been introduced to reinforce the image of democratic consensus the authorities were anxious to maintain in wartime. In this sense, the film is the military equivalent of a production like *Millions Like Us.* It is evident that this selected group of nine soldiers contains too high a proportion of recruits from the middle classes, even though some of them are supposed to have come from reserved occupations. Only Brewer and Luke and possibly the regular soldier Sergeant Fletcher appear to have pronouncedly proletarian origins. One may quibble indeed that Niven, convincing enough as an officer, hardly seems to fit the part of a civilian garage owner (nor of course does Penelope Dudley Ward look a likely consort for one). Nevertheless, the largely working-class cinema audience would be invited to laugh at the fastidiousness of a man like Davenport and then to sympathize with his abandonment of social inhibitions, as he has to merge his personality with the collective aims of the unit, and so with those of the country. The truculent Stainer goes through a civilizing process as he is brought into closer contact with his fellow men. The discipline imposed by Fletcher and the feeling of regimental pride preached by Perry are a microcosm of a greater sense of national endeavor and unity.

The method employed by the script of *The Way Ahead,* starting with the middle class and working downward, was radically different from the assumptions that had guided Harry Watt in the making of his *Nine Men.* Watt had tried to bring to the commercial industry some of the dissatisfaction that he and his colleagues in the documentary movement had expressed about the depiction of ordinary people in British film. The documentary filmmakers had been a dedicated group, and a few of their works, especially those by Rotha, had been able to offer prospects of a different kind of society after the war. The vision of the New Jerusalem had begun to dominate the domestic political scene, and for a time Bracken and the MOI accepted the theme of social reform with muted approval, perhaps as a way of appeasing the public, though with victory in sight they were to grow less enthusiastic about it.[70] Hardly any of the feature filmmakers, on the other hand, with the possible exception of a lesser-known figure like John Baxter, had done more than build up that impression of unanimity cherished by the government and by the conservative establishment in general (and which, ironically, was endorsed in a romanticized fashion by a documentary director like Humphrey Jennings, although he too looked for a different kind of future). The best of their productions, a selected few only, had managed at last to represent real people on the screen in a way that was not a caricature. It was to be a short-lived achievement in British film, one that would vanish again for a couple of decades as soon as the war was over and there was no longer reason for keeping up the same facade of togetherness in the nation.

The end-title of *The Way Ahead* was "The Beginning." At the time of the film's issue the allies were breaking away from their beachhead at Normandy, Paris was being liberated, and it looked as if the war with Germany might be over by Christmas. For the British, it would be a victory brought about by the common people, the workers of the home front who had been celebrated in *Millions like Us* and the citizens turned into the soldiers of *The Way Ahead.* In the final sequence of Carol Reed's film, the nine men move steadily forward side by side through the haze, bayonets at the ready, symbolic of the most basic and fundamental method of grappling with the enemy. The Chelsea pensioners nod their approval. The DOGs have done it at last.

5
Winning Together

Cinematically, the D-Day landings of 6 June 1944 have become known worldwide from repeated screenings, now mostly on television, of the 1962 Hollywood epic *The Longest Day,* a film that characterized the various national participants in the battle in predictable fashion. The Germans are cool and efficient and immaculately dressed, their defense measures frustrated mainly by their fear of waking up the sleeping Führer. The Americans are macho heroes—John Wayne leading his group of paratroopers in his own familiar western cavalry style, Robert Mitchum rallying his men on Omaha Beach, the most bloodily contested of the landing zones. The British part in the action is understated almost to the point of extinction. The seizure of the Orne bridges is carried off with phlegmatic composure. Trevor Howard as a beachmaster defeats the failures of modern technology by giving a recalcitrant vehicle a good, hard thump in the guts. Richard Burton follows buttoned-up British tradition in his portrayal of a shot-down RAF pilot who is forced to miss out on the main events. A lesser-known film from 1975, made in Britain, *Overlord* (the code name for the operation), directed by Stuart Cooper, used archive material to brilliant effect, especially the sequences of preparations for the landing, including the testing of the special devices employed to overcome the obstacles laid out by the enemy on the beaches. Unfortunately, it was handicapped by a lame script, based on scanty historical knowledge, which tried with little subtlety to transfer contemporary viewpoints about war to the events of thirty years before.

The British Second Army, landing on the left, aimed to take the city of Caen on the first day, to establish a commanding and threatening position in the face of German counterattacks. It failed in its objective, and the next six weeks were spent in a grim battle of attrition reminiscent of the First World War. The American First Army on the right also found itself unprepared for the reality of struggle in the Norman hedgerows, but it was able gradually to turn into the Cotentin peninsula and reach the port of Cherbourg.

For the British Normandy was a chastening experience. The people's army was lined up against some of the most experienced and fanatical of the SS and panzer units. Even Montgomery's desert veterans fared badly and, in spite of superiority of numbers and total command of the air, neither they nor the fresher British and Canadian troops could make headway. When in desperation an armored assault ("Operation Goodwood") was tried, it turned into almost as costly and futile an affair as the Charge of the Light Brigade. Weaknesses of leadership, inferior equipment (especially tanks), lack of initiative, all played a part but they were compounded by the war

Uneasy allies Montgomery, Eisenhower, and Bradley during the battle for Normandy. From the AFPU's record footage.

weariness of the British after nearly five years of conflict. Montgomery, like many other British generals who had gone through the previous war, was anxious to avoid heavy casualties, a factor never understood by the Americans, who had larger reserves of manpower and who were more willing to sacrifice numbers in a "do or die" spirit. Montgomery's own self-engrossment alienated likable Americans like Eisenhower and Bradley (he was already hated by the anglophobe Patton) and even some of his British colleagues like Eisenhower's deputy Tedder. However, at home he was still a popular hero, although the public, looking day by day at maps of the front in the newspapers, was puzzled by the British lack of progress, just as the soldiers themselves became mortified by reports in August of the breakout by the Americans. In fact, the British and Canadians had held at bay the bulk of the Nazi formations, enabling their American allies, some of whose units had also performed only modestly, to sweep away to the west and south.[1]

In 1950 Two Cities made the first British feature based on the campaign and its aftermath, *They Were Not Divided,* scripted and directed by Terence Young. Its two principal characters, serving in the Guards Armoured Division, are an Englishman (Edward Underdown) and an American volunteer (Ralph Clanton). As they die side by side in the winter of the Ardennes, toy British and American flags set in the snow droop toward each other, a symbol of the blood brotherhood of the two nations at war. The film had continued to prop up the myth of equally shared effort and achievement, an article of faith dear to the hearts of Winston Churchill and the British people. In reality, it concealed a deeply felt inferiority complex about the dominance of the United States in the final stages of the war. The American volunteer was to surface again in another film directed by Young, *The Red Beret,* made in 1953, which had Alan Ladd in the uniform of a British paratrooper, and this craven submission to the needs of a transatlantic market reflected only too clearly the bankruptcy of Britain's immediate postwar situation as a crumbling imperial power and a satellite of America.

British actuality filming of D-Day and the subsequent campaign was also overshadowed, at least in numbers of cameramen put into the field, by the American effort. It had been decided by the allied high command (SHAEF) to impose a central direction and censorship on photography of the invasion, and this degree of cooperation was to produce at the end a jointly made film, *The True Glory,* which took the story up to the fall of Germany. Both of the allies had learned how to organize their respective photographic teams after their experiences in North Africa and Italy. Hugh Stewart returned from America to command the AFPU's unit (No. 5) that was preparing to work in France. The sergeant cameramen had been meticulously trained at Pinewood, and they could use now a British-made camera (the Vinten) that had been designed specially for use in battle. Although its lenses were excellent, it proved to be temperamental mechanically, and no allied model could compare with the superb Arriflex that was the property of the Germans.

One of the most commonly shown British sequences of D-Day, of troops moving forward to the ramp of their landing craft, one soldier seen to reassuringly pat the back of the man in front of him, had been shot by a camera mounted at the rear end of the vessel and operated automatically. Stewart had planned for similar footage from other craft, but in the excitement of the moment it is probable that no one found the time to start the cameras rolling.[2] Several members of the AFPU landed on that first day, and one of them, Ian Grant, has written at length about his experiences with the commandos who made the link-up with British paratroopers.[3] The cameraman Desmond O'Neill, going ashore on Sword Beach, had been told by his officer, Derek Knight, to meet him in the middle of the afternoon on the steps of Caen Town Hall. Soon he saw British bodies, which he was advised not to photograph, and German prisoners, which it was permissible to record. Before he could go inland, he was wounded in the elbow while the soldier next to him was killed instantly.[4] Of the two other AFPU cameramen in that section of the beach, one was also wounded and another forced to hide for half of the day as he found himself surrounded by the enemy. These instances were not untypical of the hazards faced by the allied combat cameramen, a number of whom became casualties in the campaign. By the time they reached Caen, later in the summer, the ancient city was in ruins, a circumstance faithfully recorded for posterity by the army photographers. It had been devastated by the RAF in an assault as unnecessary as the destruction of Cassino.

Ronald Tritton had become the British secretary of a committee formed to coordinate planning for joint British and American productions. At times this body seemed to exist mainly as a vehicle for airing the various rivalries between the two allies and their individual services. David MacDonald had returned to supervise production at Pinewood, and originally it was intended that the final campaign film would be made by him and the American director George Stevens, who was also active with an American photographic unit in France, but cooperation between them sometimes proceeded on a less than happy note.[5] The two groups did turn out a preliminary film, *Eve of Battle,* which detailed the preparations for the landing and used especially fine film material of the air offensive. Music by William Alwyn was to be reused later for *The True Glory.* It was finished in June, shortly after the invasion had taken place, but progress on a second and entirely British film, *A Harbour Goes to France,* was slower on account of censorship difficulties. One of the outstanding engineering feats of the Overlord operation had been the transfer of sections of a mobile floating harbor (Mulberry) to the beaches off Arromanches, a device intended to overcome the supply problems that would be caused by the allies' inability to capture a genuine port intact. On the thirteenth day, a gale sprang up with unusual strength for the time of year, and some of the installations were severely damaged. The AFPU secured the assistance of the Admiralty for the making of the film, but it was not completed until the end of the year.

The American breakout decisively ended the stalemate in Normandy. British and Canadians battered their way through to Falaise as the remnants of the shattered German forces, constantly harassed from the air, made their withdrawal to the east. The rest of the summer became a matter of pursuit. Roy Boulting had followed the British forces to France, seemingly with the intention of devising his own film project on the campaign, and, though in the end it came to nothing, he was responsible for one notable coup when he led a group of photographers into Paris with the liberating French troops. They had been afraid that the episode might be scooped by the Americans, but in fact they were able to film the triumphant arrival of de Gaulle followed by the sudden moments of panic among the crowds as shots were heard, fired apparently by French fascist collaborators.[6] In the meantime the British Second Army had made a spectacular dash into Belgium, to be greeted by rejoicing crowds in Brussels at the beginning of September.

David MacDonald's last production on the campaign for the AFPU, *Left of the Line,* was a concise account of the British and Canadian contribution up to that stage of the war, drawing upon photographic material taken by the official units of both Commonwealth countries (unhappily, the original Canadian film records have been lost in a nitrate fire). Canada had developed its own documentary tradition under the influence and leadership of John Grierson, and during the war some notable newsreel and informational series were produced there. One of the most moving passages in the film is the sequence where Canadian soldiers pray beside the mass graves of their fellow countrymen at Dieppe, followed by scenes of their march-past to pipe music in the town. Before this production had been completed, further bickering had broken out among the members of the joint committee, which decided in July to make a fresh start on the final campaign film, a move which caused MacDonald to withdraw from the project.[7] To this point the British had seen the affair as a rerun of their difficulties with *Tunisian Victory.* However, by the end of the month Carol Reed, on the strength of his public success with *The Way Ahead,* had been approached to take over the direction, and eventually with a new American colleague, Garson Kanin, he was able to push ahead on a more amicable basis with the making of *The True Glory.*

Victory in France had been made possible by allied dominance of the skies. The squabbles between the various air commanders and with their other service counterparts have become a legendary feature of the history of the Second World War. Although by the beginning of 1944 the belief of Harris that he could defeat Germany by bombing alone had been exploded, both he and the American Spaatz continued to resist the direction of their forces toward the tactical objective of assisting the Overlord operation. Command of the air had in fact been won by the deployment of the long range Mustang fighter, using drop fuel tanks, in support of the USAAF over Germany, a factor which had compelled the Luftwaffe to come up and fight a battle it was doomed to lose. Spaatz was determined to press home his new advantage with a campaign of precision bombing of German oil objectives, but in the spring and summer both he and Harris were instructed to submit to Eisenhower's needs and to concentrate on tearing up enemy communications in France.

The RAF Film Unit had grown in strength since its early days so that its cinematographic coverage had now become as comprehensive and efficient as possible, given the considerable difficulties of filming from the air and normally from cramped situations within the aircraft themselves. The use of synchronized 16mm automatic cameras, designed to operate whenever a fighter used its guns, was always a hit-or-miss affair, only a minority of sequences providing adequate definition in the end. However, operations in daylight by fast fighter-bombers produced some very satisfactory material, one of the earliest being the record of the low-level attack on the Philips factory at Eindhoven in December 1942.[8] It became practice to mount an automatic 35mm camera in the nose of these planes and for a hand held model to be operated by a cameraman from within the aircraft. These techniques were seen at their most successful in the filming of the daring and well-planned attack by Mosquitoes on the prison at Amiens in February 1944.[9] The aim of this unusual enterprise was to breach the walls in order to help the escape of a large number of French members of the resistance who were being imprisoned there. It was achieved with minimal loss to the RAF, but one of their pilots who crashed and lost his life was Pickard, the man who had flown F for Freddie in *Target for Tonight.* During the preliminaries and immediate aftermath of D-Day, further impressive film footage was obtained as rocket-firing

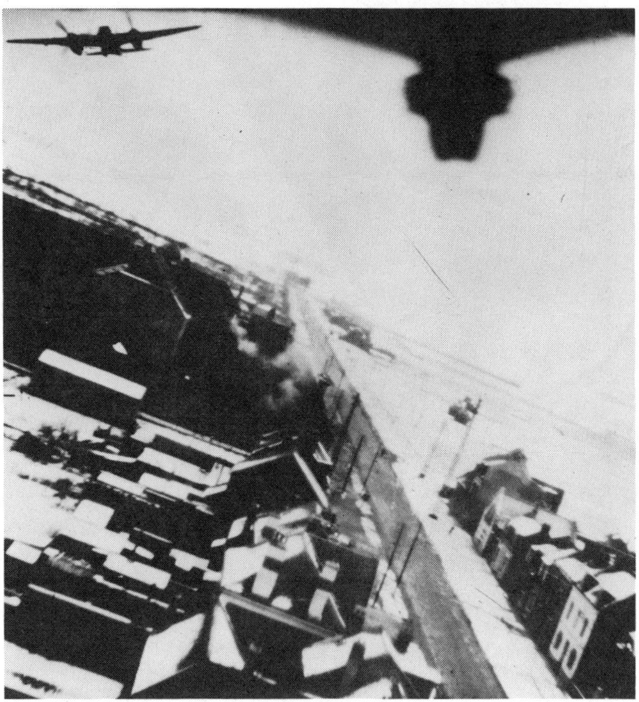

Mosquitoes attack the prison at Amiens, recorded in action by the RAF Film Unit.

Typhoons made repeated attacks on German transport in the narrow French lanes.

This actuality material was incorporated in a number of RAF documentaries, unfortunately somewhat dull in general presentation, like *Towards the Offensive,* which dealt with the allied build-up for the invasion of Europe; *The Big Pack,* which was about the work of Maintenance Command in keeping up a flow of supplies; and *The Air Plan,* on the British and Commonwealth contribution to D-Day, emphasizing attacks on communications. The last film recruited Eric Portman as narrator,but it is amusing to hear how this Yorkshireman, normally so natural in acting roles, obviously felt that he had to adopt in this case a "posh" accent, a temptation too easy for educated north-country people at a period when the London region held a position of total cultural hegemony over the rest of England.

The RAF Film Production Unit also set out in 1944 to make a film about one of the most clandestine areas of activity in the war, the operation of special agents in France in support of the resistance, a role they could carry out only with the cooperation of the air force pilots who parachuted them to their destinations and kept them supplied with arms and explosives.[10] There have been some disputes about how effective resistance was in practice, but its advocates have claimed that the French succeeded in helping the disruption of enemy transport after D-Day and also delayed the transfer of some vital Nazi units to Normandy. Resistance was also an important political factor in the period of the decline of the Vichy regime. It was intended that the film would use real people who had been active in the field, and two British agents, Harry Rée and Jacqueline Nearne, were chosen to take the leading parts and to play out some of the duties they had performed in France—organizing resistance groups, keeping up communications with London, and preparing the French for the allied invasion. One episode in Rée's career was not reproduced in the script. In a bizarre encounter with a Gestapo agent, he had been shot a number of times but had still managed to defeat his foe and to escape. In this case a real-life event perhaps had been

School for Danger/Now It Can Be Told. Real agents Jacqueline Nearne, third from left, and Harry Rée pass through a French checkpoint.

too unbelievable for the cinema.

Sequences showing the training of the selected officers were shot in Scotland in the autumn, and then at the end of the year the unit traveled to the south of France, now liberated from the enemy, for more location work. In the plot the two agents (with the codenames "Felix" and "Cat") have been dropped by parachute. They meet friendly French contacts and proceed to set up resistance groups, Felix traveling around by bicycle and Cat keeping in touch with London by wireless. The resistance sabotages several locomotives and tries to set fire to a factory, although in the end they have to call in the RAF to finish off the job. A wounded man is taken to England by air, but there is a more difficult problem when they have to return the whole crew of a shot-down Lancaster. By this time the Germans are closing in, some of the resistance have been arrested, a British agent is shot. Felix has to arrange for a Hudson to land in the only appropriate field in the area, and London also orders him to return with the Lancaster crew.

The film was being directed by Edward Baird, of the RAF Film Unit, who clearly lacked the ability of the more experienced documentary filmmakers to draw more than moderately convincing performances from amateur actors. When it began to snow in Provence, he decided to return to London with the reels that had been shot already, and on the way the Hudson was fired on from La Rochelle, still held as an isolated outpost by the Germans, forcing it to make an emergency landing on a small island. Work on the film resumed later with another aircraft. The important final part shows the Hudson unable to take off because rain has made the ground soggy and its wheels have sunk into the mud. The resistance calls out the inhabitants of the nearby village from their beds in order to free the aircraft. Although more shooting at Pinewood was finished before the war had ended, nothing further was done until June 1946, when the Central Office of Information (as the MOI had been retermed) called in a private company to complete the assembly and the dubbing. It was released to the cinemas as *School for Danger,* but a longer version, designed for nontheatrical issue, was titled *Now It Can Be Told.* Many critics commented on the film's understatement and on how unfortunate it was that it came so late, after a couple of Hollywood productions on a similar theme had been distributed in Britain.[11]

Frank Launder wrote and directed the Gainsborough feature *2,000 Women,* which had a more unusual setting in France, a chateau being used by the Germans to keep under guard women who have been interned. Their ordered existence is disturbed when three RAF airmen from a crashed plane take refuge there, and efforts to hide them from the Nazis at times border on the farcical. The cast included Patricia Roc, Phyllis Calvert, Jean Kent, Anne Crawford, Flora Robson, Muriel Aked, Renee Houston, Thora Hird, and Dulcie Gray, all of them worthy of a better film. In the end this clever band of Englishwomen succeed in outwitting the incompetent Germans. Patricia Roc agrees to do a cabaret performance that will divert the attention of the guards, the fliers depart disguised in Nazi uniforms, and the triumphant ladies join together in a rousing rendition of "There'll Always Be an England." A blossoming romance between Roc and one of the airmen was another predictable element in this thoroughly conventional plot, which had little to say about the real psychological and social problems of women held captive in such circumstances.

D-Day and victory in France were celebrated in the Two Cities technicolor production of *Henry V,* in preparation at the time, with outdoor shooting taking place in Ireland. It was issued at the beginning of 1945, and a caption dedicated it to the men who had taken part in the allied landings. Laurence Olivier's vigorous playing of the king is a major achievement, supported by a distinguished cast of British performers, and he also showed considerable imagination in this adaptation of the Shakespeare play, directing it himself, with a splendidly contrived opening in the Globe theater before the action moves to the fields of France. Perhaps it was unfortunate that the enemy happened to be the French, but the most brutal lines of mockery from the play had been cut out, and anyway it ends with reconciliation and marriage between Henry and the daughter (Renee Asherson) of the French king. Much of the film's style, especially in the battle scenes, seems to have been influenced by Eisenstein's *Alexander Nevsky,* which had appeared in Britain with a friendly introduction by Molotov, the Soviet foreign minister, and which had featured the historical Teutons as the menace to the Russian homeland. Prokofiev had written one of his best scores for the Soviet film and, if not quite rising to the same level, William Walton also produced effective music for *Henry V,* best remembered for a lament on the death of Falstaff and for the agitated accompaniment to the charge of the French knights at Agincourt, dramatically interrupted by the whirlwind sound of the arrows as the English archers fire on the advancing enemy. Shakespeare for a mass audience was a daring development for British cinema, perhaps only made possible even with this aptly chosen play by the circumstances of the war itself (although Olivier was to repeat the experiment in 1948 with *Hamlet*); and for many it may have been made palatable by its sequences of the battle, the comedy episodes with Ancient Pistol (Robert Newton), and the film's outright jingoism, which captured the exultant mood of victory in Europe in 1945.

For the previous year the top money-making release had been the Two Cities feature *This Happy Breed,* also in technicolor, directed by David Lean after the play by Noel Coward, who was the film's producer. The project had been started shortly after the completion of *In Which We Serve,* some of the values of which it went on to reinforce in a different setting. Robert Newton and Celia Johnson took the leads in this story of an average suburban family between the wars, a social environment similar to that attempted in *Salute John Citizen.* Although the life of the Gibbons family is not undisturbed by personal tragedy, the main picture drawn in the film is one of order and improvement, though not of course total emancipation for its female characters. It was a complacent view of British society that on the whole seems to have been well received by the public, a fact which may be interpreted in two ways—either the government had been successful in preaching its sermon on national unanimity and people believed in it, or the drama was seen as an image of a tolerably comfortable existence for all British citizens that could be further consolidated as soon as the war was over. Many cinemagoers may have held both views simultaneously. Mass-Observation's Leonard England, in giving an overall impression of the British film and family life, decided that the audience wanted to avoid the presentation on screen of unpleasant facts (a film like *Love on the Dole,* which had tried to face up to them, had not been such a box-office success).[12]

British people at home had grown accustomed by now to the presence in their country of large numbers of Americans. Those allies who had come from Europe or from the Empire had been accepted gratefully but, to a degree, with condescension, as if they were either refugees or dependents. But Americans were very different. The pay and standard of living of United States servicemen (and women) so outstripped what was available to their British counterparts that some tension was inevitable, especially when it was a matter of competing for the attention of girls, just as the frank and easy manners of Americans were bound to conflict at times with the more reserved habits of their hosts. The sources of misunderstanding were recognized on screen, but the overriding objective of the filmmakers (on both sides of the Atlantic) was to reconcile the differences and emphasize the shared aspirations of these English-speaking allies.

Cinema produced, to this end, some unlikely romantic liaisons, more in the tradition of *Pygmalion* than of real life. In British National's *Welcome Mr. Washington,* directed by Leslie Hiscott and issued in 1944, Lieutenant Johnny Grant, USAAF (Donald Stewart) has to cope with the prejudices of the local villagers as soon as he falls for Jane Willougby (Barbara Mullen), who owns the land; but all is resolved when he calls in his men to bring home the harvest. The Associated British production, *I Live in Grosvenor Square* (U.S. title: *A Yank in London*), from 1945 and directed by Herbert Wilcox, has Anna Neagle as Lady Pat Fairfax, granddaughter of a cheerful duke (Robert Morley). She prefers John Patterson, an American air gunner who had been an engineer in civil life, played by the Hollywood actor Dean Jagger, to the man she should have favored, smooth and staid English Guards officer, Major David Bruce, impersonated by Rex Harrison. The film's climax, anticipating the ending of *The Way to the Stars,* has Patterson helping the wounded pilot of their crashing B-17 Flying Fortress to steer clear of the west-country town close to their base, thereby saving many British civilian lives but giving up their own. Bruce is last seen departing on a paratroop operation, in which perhaps he too is killed, to balance the sacrifice made by his American rival and comrade in arms. This film also has another interesting element, a by-election in which Bruce as the National Government candidate is defeated by an independent—a recognition of what had occurred in some constituencies, as public opinion started to veer away from confidence in the government's capacity to handle postwar Britain. In the local pub, though, the verdict is not a popular one, the film here not concealing its sympathy with the status quo.

Anxious as they were to avoid misunderstandings between the two allies, the MOI cooperated readily with its opposite number, the U.S. Office of War Information. A film titled *A Letter from Ulster* described the condition of American servicemen in Northern Ireland, the first to land in the United Kingdom, and, although its acting was clumsy, it still gives some interesting impressions of that province at the time.[13] (In general, film coverage of Ulster, isolated as it was from the main events of the war and concerned also with internal problems, was relatively scarce. *Kinematograph Weekly,* in a grim article from January 1944, noted that even the cinema managers there carried revolvers).[14] The most ambitious production to outline Anglo-American social differences, in the form of a guide for United States troops, was commissioned from Strand, called *A Welcome to Britain,* and directed by Anthony Asquith.[15]

***A Letter from Ulster*. American soldiers are shown the press on which were trained the apprentices who printed the Declaration of Independence after emigrating from Ireland.**

The main burden of narrating the argument was carried by Burgess Meredith, posing as a uniformed reporter and intervening at points along the way by talking to the camera in confidential close-up as he makes his survey of the English scene and its effect on Americans. Inevitably, the starting place is the pub, where, of course, the American enlisted man will find neither cold beer nor ice. Instead he behaves brashly at the bar, throwing his weight about, mocking a kilted soldier, until he is told of the need to respect British decorum and reserve. In a typical home, he learns about food rationing and about the way citizens have had to bear the ordeal of being bombed. Many of the older men have returned to work, a fact quaintly represented by having Felix Aylmer appear in gown and mortar board in a "Mr. Chips" imitation. A more explosive topic is touched upon with a scene of a black soldier being invited to tea. The United States services were still segregated on color lines, and the extent of racial feeling was not appreciated in Britain, a country relatively free at the time from that kind of prejudice, at least in the minds of ordinary people (although, with what foreigners may see as characteristic British hypocrisy, racial distinction was the order of the day in the colonies). This conflict was also highlighted in John Schlesinger's feature *Yanks,* made in 1979, as a retrospect of Americans in Britain during the war. Anthony Asquith's film from 1944 had somewhat superfluous appearances by Bob Hope and Beatrice Lillie, before Meredith could wind up his exposition with a few final remarks about what he had not found the time to say—"Sorry I can't finish the picture—that's up to you."

While they had been working on *World of Plenty,* Eric Knight and Paul Rotha had put forward in 1942 another scheme, to produce a documentary that would explain America to the British public. Knight wanted to pull no punches in his analysis of the virtues and failings of his adopted country, especially in the matter of race relations in the south, but again Sidney Bernstein from New York tried to persuade Jack Beddington that it would be tactless to approach the subject in that way. In this case the objections were more successful. Even after *USA, The Land and its People* was previewed in February 1944 to British and American officials, it became necessary to rewrite the script and to start again.[16] The film was not finally released until March 1945. It provided a wide panorama of the American people and regions, and it still at least hinted at the fact that the good way of life was not being shared by all. It also corrected a common misapprehension held in Britain, that most Americans were of British stock, and it told the viewer that even those who did have Anglo-Saxon roots were not necessarily more pro-British than the others.

Tradition and historical continuity had come to be familiar ingredients of the more patriotic films made in Britain during the war. The opening of the Powell and Pressburger feature *A Canterbury Tale* establishes the link between Chaucer's pilgrims and those who have been brought to this part of Kent by present-day hostilities.[17] One of those to arrive, accidentally in his case, at the small town of Chillingbourne is the American sergeant Bob Johnson, who has gotten out at the wrong stop in the blackout. Now he has no alternative but to spend the night there. The part is played by a real American sergeant, John Sweet, whose gentle manners in the role are at a remove from what had become in Britain the commonplace assumption about the personal attributes of American troops. He meets a British sergeant, Peter Gibbs, an intelligent man who had trained as an organist but had used his talents in civilian life only by playing in cinemas, and the middle-class land girl Alison Smith—these parts performed by Dennis Price and Sheila Sim. Within minutes the trio is startled when a figure from the dark dumps a pot of glue over Alison's hair. At the end of a remarkable section, photographed in darkness by cameraman Erwin Hillier, they come upon the local magistrate, Thomas Colpeper, sitting in his office at the Town Hall, the tilting angle of the camera identifying him for the audience as the likely culprit, before the victims themselves begin to realize it.

As in the other collaborations between this pair of filmmakers, Emeric Pressburger was responsible for the script, the ambiguities of which puzzled and even enraged contemporary critics. Michael Powell's direction, aided by the talents of Hillier and the designer Alfred Junge, produced his most singular film from the war period. At one level it is indeed difficult to reconcile the glue-throwing exploits of Colpeper, impressively played by Eric Portman, with his dedication to the continuity of English culture. He rationalizes his apparently sadistic acts in harassing the local girls as a means of preventing fraternization with the British troops at a nearby camp, which in turn will drive the soldiers to look for alternative ways of diversion—specifically, attending Colpeper's lectures on local history and archaeology. Acting together, Smith, Gibbs, and Johnson manage to unmask him but, in the end, after all four have journeyed to Canterbury in the same train compartment, they come to a reconciliation with his point of view, even the British sergeant dropping his intention of reporting Colpeper to the police.

The clue lies in an appreciation of the sense of the miraculous that attaches itself to the film. Perhaps only those who are antipathetic to British cinema can fail to recognize the ways in which Powell, in *A Canterbury Tale,* anticipates the surrealism of Italian filmmakers like Fellini and Antonioni. Contact with Colpeper works individual miracles for each of the three other characters. Bob Johnson, who has noticed little about England except its cinemas, becomes aware of the antiquity of the land and the cathedral at Canterbury, and simultaneously news arrives of his American girlfriend at home, from whom he has heard nothing in months. Peter Gibbs abandons his own cynicism about life when he is allowed to play the cathedral organ, and the sounds of a Bach toccata reverberate around the great building. Alison Smith discovers that her supposedly lost fiance is in fact alive, a moment brilliantly illuminated by Powell and Hillier as the sun breaks through the dust-laden atmosphere of the garage where Alison's caravan has been laid up for the duration. The feeling of magic in the film is heightened by the wordless chorus (by Allan Grey) that accompanies distant shots of the cathedral.

A Canterbury Tale is a celebration of England and, in particular, of that rural part of it whose ancient culture Michael Powell was familiar with from childhood, a damaged England in 1944, as the shots of heavy bomb destruction in Canterbury make evident. Its romantic, arguably parochial and certainly conservative, vision of the kind of country and society the British had been fighting to preserve from fascism is allied to the disturbing eccentricity and misogyny of a man like Colpeper, defender of the faith against the uncaring materialism represented by the military he has to educate at all costs. The era of *Colonel Blimp's* "Spud" Wilson and his followers has brought a new threat to traditional beliefs and values. These modern

A Canterbury Tale. The American sergeant shocks the stationmaster, the land girl, and the British sergeant by breaking the blackout regulations (Charles Hawtrey, Sheila Sim, John Sweet, and Dennis Price).

pilgrims have not come to worship at the shrine; so they must be taught to submit to its influence. Esmond Knight, a war victim himself, speaks the Chaucerian words at the beginning, plays a sergeant in Colpeper's audience, and acts the village idiot in one of the more mysterious episodes of a film the stature of which has continued to grow over the years. The subtheme of Anglo-American relationships also had peculiar interest for Powell and Pressburger and, following a suggestion by Jack Beddington, they were to explore it again in their fantasy *A Matter of Life and Death* (U.S. title: *Stairway to Heaven*), completed immediately after the war.

1944 in general was a bleak year for the British feature film industry, but there was a universal mood of turning away now from war plots. Even the masters of realism were working in unusual areas, Cavalcanti directing Tommy Trinder in the musical *Champagne Charlie* and Harry Watt following suit with *Fiddlers Three.* The postwar world also merited little direct attention, the only real exception being Ealing's transference to screen of the West End cast of J. B. Priestley's *They Came to a City.* An assorted group of individuals find themselves lost but at the border of a city of the future, to which they are temporarily admitted and then given the choice of remaining or leaving. The film version was directed by Basil Dearden, with John Clements unexpectedly successful in a working-class role and Googie Withers and Raymond Huntley also making their mark. Priestley's "city" is not seen, but is clearly meant to be the ideal socialist welfare state that is accepted by the most deprived and the most public-spirited of the characters and rejected by the more self-centered. However, it is not a polemical script. If *They Came to a City* is a film of the left and *A Canterbury Tale* is one of the right, both productions follow a moderate path, which anticipated the political consensus of the three decades

***They Came to a City*. The poster for the film depicts the brave new world in stark and geometrical style.**

following the war's conclusion.

The atmosphere of calm that had by now settled over southeast England was shattered in mid-June 1944 by the unexpected launching toward London of a new and frightening Nazi weapon, the pilotless aircraft, or V1, which ran for as long as its fuel lasted and, when its engine cut out, plunged down into the city, carrying a load of explosives with it. Hitler had boasted of technological marvels that would swing the war in his favor again, and the V1 seemed to be the first of these. It was totally indiscriminate, and it arrived by day, when few of the population were in shelters. To the Germans it appeared a just retribution for the RAF's terror bombing of their homeland. For a while indeed, it did shake the morale of Londoners. The stoical defiance of the blitz days was now a matter of memory, and people had to rally themselves in order to cope with this final ordeal. By August, the V1 firing sites had been overrun by the allied armies, but occasional missiles were still launched from piloted planes. In the following month, the Nazis started to use another device, a rocket or V2, pioneered by Wernher von Braun, who later achieved fame in America as a leader of that country's space program. The V1's engine could be heard and, for those beneath it, there was a terrifying period of tension as soon as it stopped. But the V2 arrived without any kind of warning. Some nine thousand people were killed in these raids.

During the summer Crown started to make a film about the V1 attacks, with Humphrey Jennings directing and a commentary spoken by Ed Murrow, the CBS correspondent. A shorter version was meant primarily for release in America under the title *V1,* but the British issue was called *The Eighty Days,* the duration of the main offensive.[18] A small amount of official record material was used, but for most of it Jennings preferred to shoot his own film. It follows the progress of the V1s from flashes signaling their launching across the French coast, through an antiaircraft barrage over the cliffs of southern England, meeting RAF fighters, and on (for those not destroyed) to the capital itself. As ever, the selection of images by Jennings is striking; tin-hatted girls on the

***The Eighty Days.* Servicewomen on the English coast watch out for the firing of Vls across the Channel.**

lookout on the Sussex coast, observers in action near Hythe, a V1 exploding as it is caught by the gunfire, another blowing up in front of a fighter (a real camera-gun synchronized shot), watchful faces turned upward, city buildings and city streets foregrounding the rising plume of smoke made by one of the devices landing. Murrow's words mention the tiredness of Londoners at this stage of the war, and, in a Bastille Day scene from a French town, he says that the battle of London was also part of the battle for France. The home front had given birth to a whole series of short and noteworthy documentaries of the *Britain Can Take It* kind—in sum, an enduring legacy of historical images of British citizens at war—and *The Eighty Days,* at war's end, was one of the best and most concise of them.

Gainsborough's feature *Waterloo Road* starts with a Lambeth general practitioner, Dr. Montgomery, played by Alistair Sim, reflecting on the years of endurance suffered by Londoners, while shots of bomb sites reinforce his point. It finishes with him thinking about the future, a touch of optimism here as he hopes that these sacrifices will not have been in vain. Scripted and directed by Sidney Gilliat, the film was released early in 1945, but the events it deals with look back to the blitz winter of 1940–41, and in a subtly different spirit from that of earlier home front productions. It was, for instance, the first major movie to admit that not everyone had been pulling his weight at the time, and a strong element in the film is its representation of the underworld of petty criminals, black marketeers, and "spivs," as they came to be called. In terms of location, there is a convincing sense of moving out to the streets, and the style of *Waterloo Road* foreshadowed the neorealism attempted by British cinema in the late fifties and the sixties. Gilliat was able to capitalize on the progress made by the best British features of the war years and to introduce a theme it had become possible to depict on the screen without embarrassment now that the real crisis of the conflict was over.

However, it is an interesting sidelight on this topic that Sidney Gilliat, together with Frank Launder, had already made for Gainsborough in 1942 a short film called *Partners in Crime,* which finishes with a judge, played by Robert Morley, sentencing both petty thieves and those profiting by the black market.[19] The example given is of a woman who receives some extra meat from her butcher, and Morley points out that, if everyone behaves in this way, the nation will soon be starving. It was rare for a British production during the war to deliver this kind of propaganda message acknowledging the existence of black marketeers.

In *Waterloo Road,* scripted by Val Valentine, the principal "spiv" character is Ted Purvis, played by Stewart Granger. When he is not dodging military service, his main preoccupation at present is how to seduce Tillie Colter (Joy Shelton) while her husband is away at the war. Tillie has been flattered by the attentions of Purvis, a popular local figure who has been a prizefighter at the Blackfriars ring, and she quarrels about him with her in-laws, Mrs. Colter (Beatrice Varley) and daughter Ruby (Alison Leggatt). In a flashback to her wedding, Tillie is seen leaving Waterloo station with her groom Jim Colter, played by John Mills. From the train window they have a glimpse of the house they hope will be their future home. Instead, the war has set back their expectations, so that the couple are living with Jim's family, and he has declined for the time being to have children. Tillie feels frustrated and neglected, one cause of her restlessness, and, although she struggles with her conscience, she has agreed to meet Purvis beneath the clock at the station.

In the meantime, Ruby has sent a message to Colter, a member now of the Royal Armoured Corps, who decides to go absent without leave in order to sort out his affairs. He is put back onto his train at Waterloo by the military police, but, jumping out onto the track, he ducks into the YMCA, where he finds a Canadian who has gone missing from his unit for six weeks. This character helps Jim to escape from the station, and he is able to make his way to his mother's house nearby, at least until the civilian police come looking for him and he is compelled to run off again. From Ruby he learns that Purvis might be at his pintable club. In fact he is not there, but Jim does encounter some of Purvis's shady friends and, in a fight with them, he takes a blow on the head. He has to go for aid to Dr. Montgomery, who talks about Purvis as a man who wants to have his cake and eat it, the type who should not be allowed to reap the benefits of what the soldiers are fighting for.

Purvis has persuaded the initially reluctant Tillie to go to a pub for drinks and lunch, and then to an afternoon dance. Eventually, Jim also arrives at the dance hall, after he has evaded the police once again, having been directed there by one of Purvis's jealous girlfriends, the hairdresser Toni (Jean Kent). There is a disturbance when the police arrive in search of petty criminals—Jim even manages to give the law a helping hand—and he is only able to catch sight of Purvis and Tillie getting into a cab. Purvis has lured Tillie to an apartment above his club on the pretext of having a birthday party. Jim takes shelter temporarily during an air raid alert, but in the end, on Dr. Montgomery's advice, he reaches the right place just as Tillie has virtuously rejected the advances made by Purvis. The two men fight and, when the scrimmage ends badly for the ex-boxer, he is told by Dr. Montgomery that his pretext for evading the army is indeed correct—he is in medical trouble. The last words of the film rest with the doctor, and Jim's reconciliation with his wife is conveyed by a scene of her with their baby. Although neither Mills nor Granger were absolute naturals as cockney characters, *Waterloo Road* succeeded in combining what for the period was an acceptable amount of local flavor with a plot that was a refreshing deviation from the normal portrait of upright and unified effort.

Even so, the film stayed true to the prevalent morality of the time, which the cinema industry had shown itself anxious to maintain. Inevitably, the war had in reality caused more freedom in sexual relationships, and the problem of the husband away from home and the wife confined to the domestic hearth was one that sometimes produced a different outcome from that which society in general, as represented by *Waterloo Road,* continued to uphold, with a degree of what nowadays would be regarded as self-righteousness. In fact, the divorce rate escalated during the war.[20] It was rare for any film to deal with sex, except in the conventional "love" context, and unusual for one to depart from a formula that forbade people to take an interest in each other when one or both of the participants is already married to someone else (there were, of course, exceptions, like the incident of the captain's wife in *Convoy* who runs away with the lieutenant, but the film condemns the frolic as unacceptable behavior even for the upper classes).

The temptations of adultery do come to light in *Perfect Strangers* and *Brief Encounter,* both released in 1945, although in neither film are the liaisons carried through. It is possible that these particular plots would have not been filmed had the war not imposed appreciable strains on family life or drawn attention to the independent aspirations of what may have been a minority of women. Korda's *Perfect Strangers,* with Robert Donat and Deborah Kerr, deals directly with the question of separation, as a married couple who have led a restricted life in peacetime both join the

Waterloo Road. The would-be seducer lures his victim to his flat (Joy Shelton and Stewart Granger).

Royal Navy. In the end, they each benefit from the emancipatory effect of their experiences and, after some early alienation from each other, they finally come closer together. *Brief Encounter,* a popular success directed by David Lean from a play by Noel Coward, has Celia Johnson as dowdily dressed, middle-class Laura Jesson furtively meeting Trevor Howard, playing a doctor called Alec Harvey, in the spartan surroundings of a minor railway station refreshment room, an environment that aptly evokes the austerity and misery of wartime provincial England. The dialogue sags under the burden of Christian guilt and repression as decency wins the final battle. When Laura goes at last to Alec's flat, the rendezvous is aborted by the arrival of one of his friends and the audience can breathe again, happy that she will return contrite to her dull, safe husband. The family has been preserved, and woman is back in her traditional place at home, a commitment shared equally by the middle-class Laura Jesson of *Brief Encounter* and the working-class Tillie Colter of *Waterloo Road.*[21]

By 1944 and 1945, the future of British documentary was coming to be actively debated by members of the movement, all of whom now hoped that the extension of their role in society would receive further acknowledgment when the war was over. They had some cause for anxiety in the light of Brendan Bracken's apparent desire to have the MOI dissolved as soon as hostilities had ended. They could point to the success in attracting new audiences of the nontheatrical scheme, which by this time had been responsible for almost one hundred and fifty projection units working in twelve areas of Britain, with regular shows being given in factory canteens, village halls, and other similar venues. The only major gap was in schools, where 16mm projectors had not yet become mandatory equipment and where it took time to break down the conservatism of traditional teaching methods.[22] Internal distribution (with the Central Film Library acting as an important loan source) was complemented by overseas activity. Following a plan devised by Thomas Baird, distribution points in major cities throughout America had been set up by the British Information Services there and, although none of their efforts could make more than a shallow dent in the overwhelming dominance of the market by native American products, they did gain a limited amount of recognition. The MOI also continued to produce foreign-language versions of its films for other countries and, to increasing degree as Europe began to be liberated, the topics covered were postwar reconstruction and rehabilitation.

Much of the discussion took place at Film Centre and through its journal, *Documentary News Letter.* Originally Film Centre had been set up before the war to coordinate the work of the documentary film units and to find sponsors and outlets for their productions. At the end of 1944, Arthur Elton, one of its founders, returned there from the MOI, while Basil Wright progressed in the reverse direction, taking up the leadership of the Crown Film Unit, which had virtually lain dormant since Dalrymple's departure. As one would have expected with a group basically left-wing in sympathy, the documentary filmmakers hoped to be able to pursue a radical political and social line in tune with a national mood that now seemed uneasy about the record of the prewar government and that was moving in the direction of reform on matters like housing, health, and education.

Nevertheless, the methodology employed by the documentary school had varied greatly, from, for example, the romantic impressionism of Humphrey Jennings on the one hand to the pungent directness of Paul Rotha on the other. The Jennings influence

***Our Country.* A merchant sailor looks at the symbol of survival, St Paul's Cathedral, amid the ruins of the City of London.**

can be felt in Strand's *Our Country,* directed by John Eldridge, a lengthy portrait of Britain, held together by the trick of having a merchant seaman undertake a journey through different areas of England, Wales, and Scotland.[23] It provoked widespread disagreement among critics, and its release was delayed until mid-1945 in spite of the fact that it ended with the D-Day operations. Today its discursive style, a series of fine images photographed by Jo Jago and wedded to verse by Dylan Thomas, may still divide opinion between those who see it as rambling and pretentious and those who feel it to be a genuinely poetic statement. Certainly many of its sections arouse interest, if only for their historical value—sequences for example of a harvest folk dance in a Kentish village, black American soldiers in an English pub, and West Indian tree fellers in Scotland.[24]

During the winter of 1944–45, Humphrey Jennings had begun work on *A Diary for Timothy* for Crown, although perhaps without a fully-worked-out conception of how the film would develop, and Paul Rotha was setting up the documentaries that in time became *Total War in Britain* and *Land of Promise.* Rotha's production company was now called Films of Fact, and it had been responsible for a series of newsreels, starting in May 1942, which were issued under the title *Worker and Warfront.*[25] All of them were intended to reflect the social background of the war, especially as it affected ordinary men and women at their place of work. There were also appearances in the newsreels by popular performers like the "Hi Gang" cast, Tommy Handley and his ITMA team, and Fred Astaire and Bing Crosby at a London stage door canteen. The last issue appeared in January 1946.

Thoughts about the end of the war were traumatically derailed by the sudden setbacks to allied military hopes in the autumn and winter. Montgomery, seemingly throwing aside his habitual caution, had wanted Eisenhower to concentrate all his forces for a decisive drive through Holland, catching the enemy off balance and pushing him back across the Rhine before he could recover. Such a move would have allowed the British to form the spearhead of an advance into Germany, and Churchill no doubt would have been happy to see them reach Berlin before the Russians. However, it was hardly surprising that Eisenhower equivocated or that Patton had his own ideas for an offensive thrust, into the center of Germany. In the end though, a bold move into Holland was undertaken, with parachute units landing near a number of river and canal bridges and the British Second Army pushing forward to link up with them. Eindhoven and Nijmegen were taken by American paratroopers, but the third stage at Arnhem was a costly failure for the British, who landed too far from the bridge and came up against elite SS troops. Moreover, the Second Army could not complete its forward drive and, after eight days of severe fighting, the operation was abandoned.

The British have a peculiar facility for turning a defeat into an epic of endurance, and Arnhem has become one of the most celebrated of such episodes from the Second World War. Although Mike Lewis of the AFPU had parachuted onto the battlefield with the soldiers and two other cameramen landed by glider, they found little opportunity for photography under the conditions of siege imposed on them almost as soon as they started. The material they did shoot was incorporated in an immediate-post-war production, *Theirs is the Glory,* the major part of which was made under the direction of Brian Desmond Hurst as a re-enactment of the battle on its real location and with some of its participants. One of these was the Canadian broadcaster Stanley Maxted, who had sent out vivid accounts of the ordeal as it was in progress. Its raw kind of re-creation is closer to the spirit of what happened on the ground than Richard Attenborough's glossy *A Bridge Too Far* from 1977, a production that featured Sean Connery as Urquhart, commander of the British first airborne division, and Dirk Bogarde as his senior, General Browning, whose unflattering representation in the film aroused a measure of protest.

Until the Arnhem debacle, public opinion anticipated a swift conclusion to the war, but expectations were deferred again in December when the Germans made a surprising counterattack through the Ardennes in an attempt to reach the port of Antwerp. The furious struggle known as the "Battle of the Bulge" finally ended with the Americans holding the line and Hitler's forces backing away, but it put a stop to hopes of finishing hostilities by the beginning of 1945. It began to look as if Germany would be turned into an impenetrable fortress that would be defended to the last and as if this final stage of the war could cost the allies enormous losses before victory was realized.

This is the context of the most controversial phase of the RAF bombing campaign. The striking power of the Lancaster, in terms of bomb load, was now devastating, and its effectiveness was demonstrated in the autumn with the three daylight attacks, all filmed for the records, that were made against the *Tirpitz* in its Norwegian refuge.[26] The great battleship capsized and sank. Air power had brought to an end the long history of the big-gun warship that had lasted since Tudor times. Bomber Command's Arthur Harris, still

A Lancaster takes a 22,000-pound "Grand Slam" bomb to the Arnsberg Bridge, 19 March 1945. Filmed by the RAF Film Unit from the nose of an accompanying plane.

confident that a "thunderclap" blow against German cities could bring the Reich to surrender without the heavy bloodshed which many now felt inevitable, turned his attention again to a resumed area offensive. The allied air forces had been directed to concentrate on oil targets, and some Germans were in fact to express surprise after the war that the Allies delayed so long in attacking such a vital part of Nazi economy. The authority of Harris in the RAF at the time was so strong that even his chief, Portal, could not turn him in the required path. The destruction of Dresden in February 1945 is the incident that has become symbolic of this obsessional policy, which was then beginning at last to attract a limited amount of protest.[27] Again these final assaults, both night and day, were extensively photographed by the RAF Film Unit, some of whose members, like its commander Pat Moyna, were decorated for their work in this part of the campaign.

Bombing did wreck German industry and communications beyond the possibility of recovery in 1945, but, when the task might have seemed completed, the Americans, rather than leave their aircraft idle, now joined in the indiscriminate area attacks. Such by this time was the terrible momentum of remorseless war. Mute sequences of acres of flattened buildings, a view like a weird lunar landscape, finished the Seven League Productions documentary *Target Germany,* produced by Hans Nieter, which had detailed the preparations and the execution of a typical RAF raid (on Mannheim).[28] It was possible for the film's commentary to admit now that Bomber Command's losses over the course of campaign had been heavy. In fact some 55,000 aircrew were killed—the decimation of an exceptional group of men that John Terraine has suggested was parallel to the casualties among the officer class in the First World War.[29]

The Way to the Stars (U.S. title: *Johnny in the Clouds*), the big feature so often cited as doing for the RAF what *In Which We Serve* and *The Way Ahead* had done already for the other two services, was not released until after the German surrender.[30] But it is more than an RAF Film, for the USAAF secures some parallel attention, and the Anglo-American aspect of its plot is important. Indeed, it was the main reason for the promotion of the idea by the MOI, which at first had tried to encourage the making of a Hollywood film with a script by Terence Rattigan. Only when this fell through was the initiative passed to Two Cities. The film's director, Anthony Asquith, displayed here a consistent sureness of touch that had eluded him in his previous wartime productions. He had made for Crown a short film called *Two Fathers* (from a story by V. S. Pritchett), which had Bernard Miles and Paul Bonifas as an Englishman and a Frenchman sharing a hotel room and exchanging information about their respective children, one an RAF pilot and the other a girl in the resistance. The theme again was mutual understanding, and a similar quality may have attracted Asquith to the script of *The Way to the Stars,* written by Rattigan with Anatole de Grunwald. However, as in *The Demi-Paradise,* supposedly about Britain and Russia, the film turned into a panegyric, albeit more subtly expressed, of England and English upper-middle-class virtues.

There is no military action on the screen, everything being witnessed entirely on the ground. The opening shots are sharply conceived to suggest the postwar dereliction of the airfield; windows boarded up, an abandoned control tower, the crew room empty with its graffiti on the wall, in one place the scribbled name "Johnny." Out of doors the sheep are returning to this "halfpenny field" that had been mentioned in the Domesday Book. Then the film moves back to 1940 and a Luftwaffe raid on the station. The squadron is joined by Peter Penrose, a former schoolmaster, played by John Mills, a man who has had only fifteen hours' flying experience. He is cockily confident until harshly reprimanded by David Archdale, an experienced officer (Michael Redgrave), for his shaky landing in a Blenheim. The squadron goes out to attack German barge concentrations at Calais, and the commanding officer, Carter (Trevor Howard), is killed, leaving Archdale to take over. His own wedding is interrupted by another raid. The bride is "Toddy" Todd, proprietress of the local hotel (Rosamund John), and the main speech at the reception, broken by the alert, is made by one of the older squadron members, the controller "Tiny" Williams (Basil Radford). About Carter's death, Toddy has remarked to Archdale that, if someone she knew had been killed, she would like to hear of it at once rather than have him listed as "missing" for a while, a conversation that prompts Archdale to produce a poem he has been writing on that very subject.

On next to 1942 and the arrival of the first American officer at the field, which is to be taken over by the USAAF. The RAF squadron is flying American-built Bostons now, and Penrose is a pilot with forty-three missions behind him, a total that leads Archdale to persuade him against his will to stand down and go on a controllers' course. At the hotel—the only other major location in the film apart from the airfield—Toddy is looking after her baby and coping with the niggling complaints of the cantankerous resident Miss Winterton (Joyce Carey), who stays there with her niece Iris (Renee Asherson). In fact, Penrose is paying court to Iris and hints to her that he will be

***The Way to the Stars*. Officer pilots and their mechanic (Michael Redgrave, John Mills, and Charles Victor).**

making a proposal of marriage after he has returned from his last mission with the squadron. As the aircraft land, the camera has a close-up of Archdale's cigarette lighter, which he has left in the mess, and then a man's hand reaching for it comes into vision. However, the hand belongs to Penrose. He has the task now of going round to the hotel to tell Toddy that her husband has been killed. The meeting is stoical and tearless in the most British, emotion-starved tradition ("I don't know what to say," Penrose confesses, when he has to offer comfort). There is no question of Archdale being just "missing." Penrose has found among Archdale's belongings a poem he assumes his friend copied from somewhere:

Do not despair
For Johnny-head-in air;
He sleeps as sound
As Johnny underground.

Fetch out no shroud
For Johnny-in-the-cloud;
And keep your tears
For him in after years.

Better by far
For Johnny-the-bright star,
To keep your head,
And see his children fed.[31]

Archdale's death has convinced Penrose that marriage in wartime is wrong, and in the corridor he rebuffs the eager Iris.

When the Americans arrive, Williams, Penrose, and another RAF officer remain for a while as the plot wallows in the clichés of Anglo-American cultural misunderstandings—baseball versus cricket, warming the pot before tea is made, talking in hushed voices in restaurants, and so forth. Bonar Colleano plays Joe

***The Way to the Stars*. British and Americans at the local hotel (John Mills, Bonar Colleano, Douglass Montgomery, Rosamund John, and Joyce Carey).**

Friselli, the brash type of American who boasts of how the USAAF will win the war overnight, but Douglass Montgomery, with the decently Anglo-Saxon name of Johnny Hollis, is restrained and sensitive. He soon strikes up a platonic friendship with Toddy. By 1944, the Americans have grown to appreciate the grim realities of bombing operations over Germany, and even Friselli has become tamed by his new understanding of the English way of life. Penrose is flying again, as pilot of a Lancaster, and at the eleventh hour Toddy persuades him to snatch up Iris, who is about to leave, having finally rejected her aunt. Miss Winterton indeed has complained about her bottle of Worcester sauce once too often, and Toddy is happy to accept her notice of giving up her room in the hotel. Just before going on his final mission before returning to the United States, Johnny Hollis has written his name on the wall of the mess, at the spot where his dart throw had landed underneath the board. His B-17 comes back damaged, one bomb still wedged in the racks, and, though the rest of the crew bail out, he declines to crash the plane into the town, trying instead to bring it onto the airfield. On the ground, the Flying Fortress explodes. "Uncle Johnny" is unable to preside at the children's party run by the vicar (Felix Aylmer), and Friselli instead speaks a few words. Afterward, Toddy shows him the "Johnny in the Cloud" poem. The verse itself is heard over the final sequence of the film, the surviving principals watching aircraft passing overhead, a conclusion that invites the cinema audience to give way, as well they might have done at the time, to a handkerchief-clutching display of sentiment the players themselves had been intent on stifling in the interests of keeping up that tight-lipped show of British doggedness which characterizes the plot throughout.

The Way to the Stars still impresses by the confidence and accomplishment of its style. However, its values are very forcibly those of the British ruling classes, barely touched by any real sense of the democratization brought about by the war, and, just as the Russian in *The Demi-Paradise* comes to accept these values, so do the American characters here. The British for their part loosen up only in superficial ways—Williams joins in a baseball game, and some of them manage to pick up the transatlantic jitterbugging habit on the dance floor. The RAF pilots are all officers, and the only noncommissioned flier to have any words is Penrose's observer Nobby Clarke (Bill Rowbotham, an actor better known in later years as Bill Owen), who is at least invited to drink with his betters, but who exists only on the fringes of the script. Mr. Palmer, the barman at the hotel, tells bad jokes and sings "Macnamara's Band," and he is played, predictably, by Stanley Holloway, while, as in other wartime films, Charles Victor, cast this time as an RAF mechanic, looks morose and trampled upon, a fitting fate for the lower ranks. The world it creates is that of a Terence Rattigan drama, a cozy, insular outlook on British life that survived the war for more than a decade. Powell and Pressburger, in *A Canterbury Tale,* at least had understood the potential power of the upheaval in Britain that the war had stimulated, and they had tried to absorb it into the common stream of English culture. In fact, the real and limited revolution was to lie dormant until the sixties. The box-office acceptance by viewers of *The Way to the Stars* in 1945 is not surprising, in view of how little discernible change there had been in the structure and assumptions of British society, in spite of some popular reaction against the Conservative party, as evidenced by their general election defeat that year.

Johnny Frenchman. **Anglo-French reconciliation on the Celtic fringes (Françoise Rosay and Tom Walls).**

From Ealing in the summer of 1945 came *Johnny Frenchman,* directed by Charles Frend, a feature built around relationships between the British and the French, specifically between fishing people from Cornwall and Brittany, regions of their respective countries that each have strong traditions of independence. They have been rivals before the war and, even when some of the Bretons take shelter in England after their homeland has been occupied, their reception is not overfriendly. "I'll have ruddy froggies for grandchildren," says Nat Pomeroy (Tom Walls), when he hears that his daughter Sue (Patricia Roc) has secretly married Jan (Paul Dupuis) instead of the local young man Bob (Ralph Michael) who has been courting her. Jan is the son of the formidable Mme. Florrie (Francoise Rosay), the scourge of the Cornish fishermen in prewar days, but now she becomes the main advocate of reconciliation and settles the matter when she goes out in her own boat to catch and explode a mine drifting toward the harbor. Jan and Bob are able to have a drink together in a pub, and the film ends with Mme. Florrie making a speech about friendship. In spite of its good intentions and some fine location photography by Roy Kellino at Mevagissey in Cornwall, it missed being more than a somewhat artificially conceived production, the main characters failing to carry any kind of conviction as genuine fisherfolk.

By the beginning of 1945, the Italian campaign was little more than a sideshow in the eyes of the public. Rehabilitation in the south of that country was the subject of *Stricken Peninsula,* a joint AFPU and Seven League production, which showed peasants returning to their battered homes.[32] As the European war rolled on to its conclusion, allied troops broke into the Po valley, and Italian partisans themselves rose against the enemy in the northern towns. Mussolini and his mistress were seized and murdered in the last days of hostilities. Communist movements were the most powerful elements in the Italian and Balkan resistance and, following a cynical deal between Churchill and Stalin, British troops were to become actively engaged against them in Greece. However, British support for Tito remained unqualified, and the situation in his country was responsible for a couple of interesting documentaries, *The Star and the Sand,* about the settlement of Yugoslav refugees in Egypt, a story written by Arthur Calder-Marshall,[33] and *The Nine Hundred,* which used material shot by allied service units to narrate an account of the battle fought by one corps of the partisans, cut off in the mountains and supplied by air from Italy.[34] American policy had frustrated Churchill's hopes of the western allies' having more say in the political settlement of eastern Europe, and his intervention in Greece also aroused wrath in his left-wing adversaries, although his Labour successors in fact were to be no more accommodating to the designs of Greek communists to gain power in their country.

None of the films made in 1945 recognized the growing political tensions of the period and, so long as the unity of the allies was still being promoted, to the end of the war, it seemed inappropriate to think about the kind of totalitarian societies that communists, encouraged by the USSR, were aiming to create in central and eastern Europe. The chief instrument for the defeat of Nazi Germany on land was, after all, the Red Army, which started its final assault on the Reich from Poland in January 1945. A number of Soviet-made films had been distributed in Britain by the MOI, and Paul Rotha made his own tribute, using Russian newsreel material, in the short production *A Soviet Village,* which described the liberation of Boutovka near Moscow, presented scenes of the devastation caused by the retreating Germans, and re-created the participation of the villagers themselves in guerrilla-type operations.[35] A Soviet documentary that covered various fronts on a single day of warfare appears to have inspired an MOI project titled *Morning, Noon and Night,* a British effort on a comparable theme. But after much planning and discussion, it became one of the many productions abandoned before completion.[36] The last decisive battle of the war against Germany was fought by Soviet forces for Berlin in April and early May, ending four years of unparalled sacrifice by the Russian people. Hitler's suicide was followed a few days later by total German capitulation.

The joint Anglo-American committee responsible for production of the final film on the western campaign intended that it should be made and issued as rapidly as possible, so that its impact would not be diminished when audiences became more involved with topical news about the war against Japan. Rightly, they recognized the danger of simply repeating what had become familiar already from the newsreels. Carol Reed and Garson Kanin made it their aim, during the early months of 1945, to bring the film to a completed stage, leaving only a last reel to be rushed through after the fall of Germany had taken place. The title *The True Glory,* proposed by General Burnham, Director of Public Relations at the War Office, was chosen only at the final meeting late in May and after much discussion of a number of more prosaic alternatives.[37] The quotation came from Drake's prayer—"O Lord God, when Thou givest to thy servants to endeavour any great matter, grant us also to know that it is not the beginning, but the

***The Nine Hundred*. Young Yugoslav partisans cut off by Nazi forces.**

continuing of the same, until it be thoroughly finished, which yieldeth the true glory." It was accepted because the words seemed to sum up the sense of idealism and endeavor the allied nations then felt both about carrying through to victory and looking forward to a peaceful postwar world.

Movietone made their own series about the ending of the war, a set of films titled *From Italy to D-Day, From Paris to the Rhine,* and *From the Rhine to Victory,* edited by Raymond Perrin.[38] But *The True Glory,* whose production was credited to all the allied service units, was meant to be more than a conventional documentary. It was to be a tribute both to the fighting men themselves and to the democratic aspirations of the western allies, and this dual purpose defined its style of narration, carried forward by the spoken words of what were assumed to be real soldiers, sailors, and airmen (though many were actors in civil life) and linked by passages of blank verse that supplied brief but factual comment, on the model of the Chorus in *Henry V.* A number of script writers worked on it, the main British contributors being Eric Maschwitz, Peter Ustinov, and Frank Harvey, together with the American team of Guy Trosper, Harry Brown, and Saul Levitt, all actually serving in their respective armies at the time. The verse, spoken by Robert Harris, came from Gerald Kersh, and the introduction of this element into the film was not universally approved by its critics, even in 1945. Whatever one may feel today about its high-flown sentiments, it is instructive to recall their motivation. The matter had been much discussed by the joint committee, many of whose members expressed unease about the device of having "real" servicemen tell the story of the film. The verse seemed to satisfy the need to project a more elevated perspective. A spoken introduction by General Eisenhower, on the theme of teamwork winning wars, also presented some of the broader objectives of the allied enterprise.

It is extraordinary that Reed and Kanin were able

to produce such a well-integrated film as *The True Glory* from the kind of directives they received from the Anglo-American committee. Its members included few people with cinema experience (Jack Beddington and Sidney Bernstein were notable exceptions), and most of them represented the interests, to each of which they were individually sensitive, of the British and American services, SHAEF, and the Canadian military. It was inevitable that many of them would look at a script as if it were simply a treatise that should try to say everything possible of significance about the details of the operation being described, regardless of the concision required by the confines of a nearly ninety-minute film. It was also difficult for some to understand that the amount of camera material available varied from event to event, so that a documentary, to a degree, is structured around what film it is possible to use, a limitation the makers did not intend to circumvent by putting in faked or reenacted sequences. On the other hand, the strict authenticity of *The True Glory* was inspired by the thoroughness of these committee discussions.

The need, therefore, to be lucid, comprehensive, and fair, and yet to turn out a film that would carry the audience with it and not be overlong, was responsible for the distinctively fast-moving style of this feature-length production. The AFPU editors at Pinewood worked under the supervision of Robert Verrall, whose collaboration with Reed and Kanin was of central importance. The voices of the anonymous narrators, expressing immediate reactions to their own situations, were married to rapid cutting from shot to shot, a technique that, while making the argument easy to follow for the average cinemagoer, at the same time bombarded him with a swift succession of carefully chosen images. The urgency of William Alwyn's score further emphasized the mood of the film. In spite of the reservations about it, the blank verse

***The True Glory.* The British enter Brussels to the acclamation of the liberated populace.**

was not too obtrusive in the overall context of such a forward-thrusting production, and it was used to accompany graphics that gave a diagrammatic explanation of the next area of territory to be fought over.

The True Glory was first shown in August 1945, and soon it was to carry off a Hollywood Oscar, celebrated with some justification as the outstanding campaign documentary of the war. Its final part illustrated the allied crossing of the Rhine in March, the Americans helped by the lucky capture of an intact bridge at Remagen. The weary British had gone through a heavy slogging match in the Reichswald forest. British colonel: "Every German killed on our side of the Rhine was to make it easier for us on the further bank and a lot of the Boche were killed, I can tell you. Reichswald was the bloodiest show I've seen in this war." As ever, Montgomery carefully laid down a tremendous artillery barrage before his troops went across the river. British sailor: "They lugged the assault boats onto trucks and sent us across Belgium by road. Talk about silent service. I've never been sick at sea but I was sick as a dog on the road. When we reached our destination I was feeling lousy, longing for a breath of sea air, and we found the whole bloody landscape under a stinking smokescreen. Like London, it was. The next day we crossed the Rhine. It was good to get back on the water again." British soldier: "We'd got across OK and everything was going fine when suddenly I gets detailed to guard some German prisoners. I'll never forget their faces when them airborne blokes started to come over. They just stood there looking up at them and then after about half an hour of it one of them looks at me, looks up at the sky and says 'Huh, propaganda!'" Scottish soldier: "We came across a POW camp. . . . Yanks mostly. They went mad when they saw us, screeched Red Indian war cries . . . asked what the news was. It seemed a shame to tell them when they

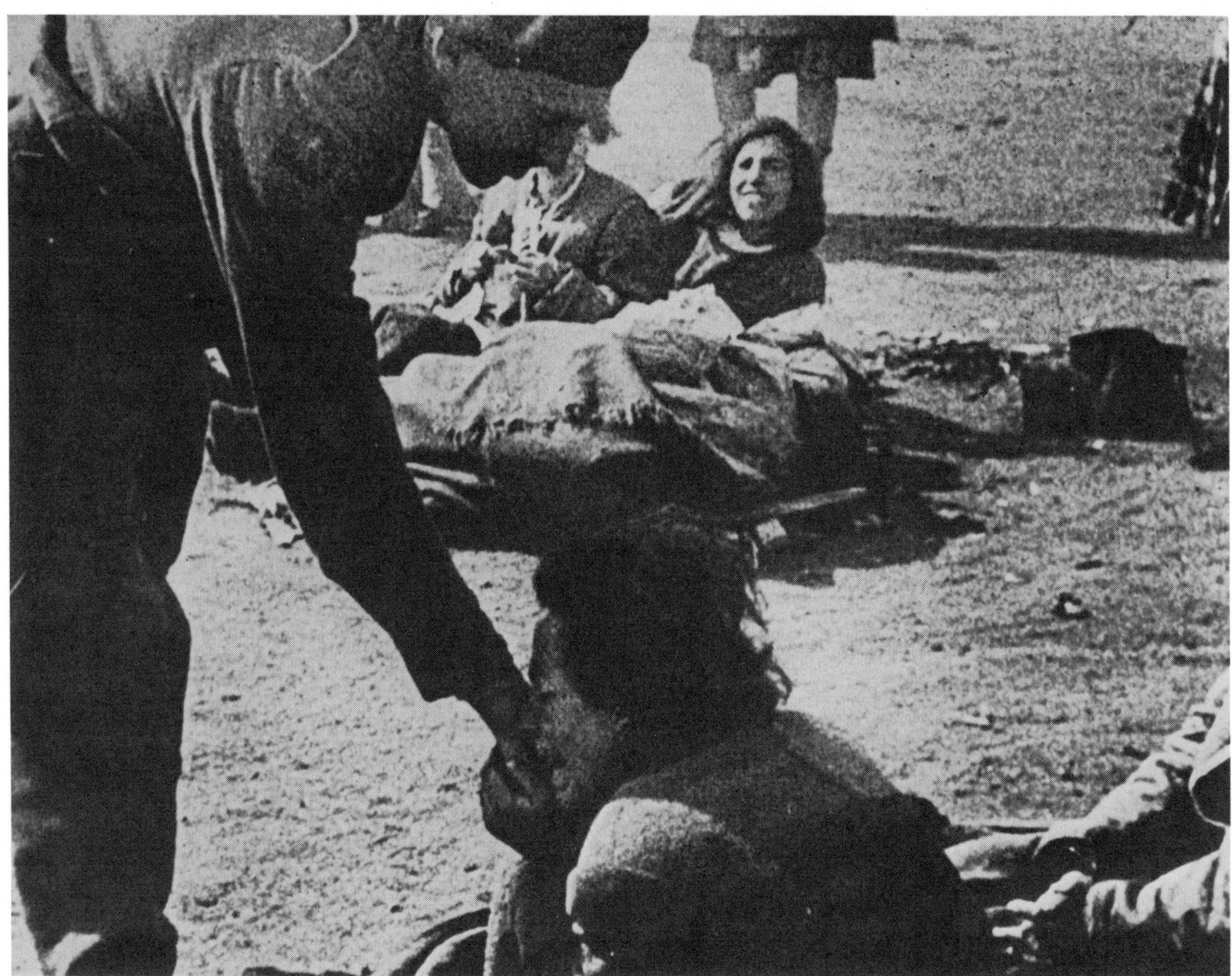

The True Glory. **The liberation of Bergen-Belsen concentration camp. An inmate expresses her feelings to an AFPU photographer, Lieutenant Wilson.**

were so happy but, well, there was nothing for it. . . . 'President Roosevelt died yesterday afternoon,' I said. You should have heard them quieten down."

Shortly after they entered Germany, some military units began to come across concentration camps. At Bergen-Belsen, liberated by the British, thousands already had died, and thousands more, their bodies emaciated beyond belief, were succumbing to typhus, neglect, and cruelty. The film taken in the camps had a startling and horrifying impact at home when it was first shown in the newsreels. The rhythm of *The True Glory* slows momentarily at this point. It reproduces one of the most moving shots of the war, taken by Mike Lewis, showing a woman inmate on her knees, tearfully pressing to her head the hand of a British lieutenant (in fact an AFPU stills photographer). British medical orderly: "I don't know any words big enough to make you understand what we all felt. All I can say, and I'm proud of this, is that I had to fall out and be quietly sick in the courtyard. As I say, I'm not squeamish but, well, I'm human and thank God for it." United States Congressman at Dachau: "I talked to some of the prisoners, those that had the strength to talk. Their offences were the usual Nazi crimes—wrong religion, wrong race, belonging to a union or the wrong political party. . . . it was the worst thing I ever saw in my life, and I wouldn't have missed it for anything."

In addition to his duties in the MOI, Sidney Bernstein had become head of the film section of the Psychological Warfare Division of SHAEF and, as soon as evidence grew of the scale of Nazi atrocities, he devised a project for the making of a documentary film on the subject, the intention being to distribute it both in the allied countries and in Germany itself, where hopefully the defeated population might be brought to a recognition of the evil consequences of the Hitler regime. The AFPU and its American counterpart, helped by the newsreel companies, set about making a careful record of the scenes within the liberated concentration camps. The MOI seems to have shrewdly appreciated the fact that postwar attempts might be made to deny the truth of the scale and the nature of these Nazi crimes. Bernstein was especially anxious that material should be shot that would demonstrate the complicity of German industry in the campaign of extermination under which Europe's Jews in particular had suffered so grievously.

In fact, the Americans soon withdrew from the joint scheme, only a few days before the dissolution of SHAEF, although they were to make their own short film on the topic for use in Germany, *Die Todesmühlen (The Wheels of Death),* directed by Billy Wilder. Treatments were prepared in London by the Australian journalist Colin Wills and by Richard Crossman, who had been in charge of propaganda for Germany at the Psychological Warfare Division, and a script for a six-reel production emerged as the film material was being assembled.[39] It would fall into two sections; an opening part on Bergen-Belsen, to be edited by Stewart McAllister, using AFPU film shot by Mike Lewis and Bill Lawrie, with some sound inserts of interviews made by the Movietone team; and a more summary account of various other camps to be put together by Peter Tanner, drawing on material mostly from American sources, with some Russian film for the final reel that would deal with Auschwitz and Maidenek. Sidney Bernstein found it more difficult to settle the matter of a director, but his final and perhaps favorite choice was Alfred Hitchcock, the best known internationally of all British-born filmmakers.

It seems in retrospect a curious decision, to enlist the services of a man distinguished mainly for a subjective brand of direct creativity with the camera and to ask him to structure a collection of actuality material shot outside his personal control and supervision. Hitchcock had in fact made two short films already for the MOI, in January and February 1944, during a visit to London.[40] Throughout the war he had suffered from a sense of guilt about being a British exile in Hollywood, and sometimes his best intentions had been misunderstood (the ending of his *Foreign Correspondent,* made in 1940 to stir up sympathy in America for Britain, with its scene of London being bombed, had been harshly criticized by Paul Rotha and others in a letter to *Documentary News Letter*).[41] Sidney Bernstein had invited him, toward the end of 1943, to produce a couple of films in French on the resistance, using the talents of an exiled French acting group called the Molière Players. The results, brief pieces titled *Bon Voyage* and *Aventure Malgache,* were undistinguished and not recognizably Hitchcockian, and they were screened neither in Britain nor in France. Hitchcock's second crossing of the Atlantic led to a stay of about a month in July 1945, during which time he and Bernstein discussed arrangements for setting up a feature production company after the war, and some kind of advice, although it is no longer clear exactly what, was passed to McAllister and Tanner about the completion of the concentration camp film. In any case, it is certain that the editors had already assembled the basic material from the finished script. From this point the project began to fade, to be abandoned altogether by September. The probable reason is that the allied authorities, having shown atrocity film to Germans through the newsreels (a German language series titled *Welt im Film* was being distributed in the western zones),[42] felt now that a longer documentary on the subject might be counterproductive. Rehabilitation was to be the main objective in postwar Germany.

Five of the reels (the sixth was lost) were deposited in their rough-cut state in the Imperial War Museum, London, in 1952. There is still some fascination in studying Stewart McAllister's construction of the Bergen-Belsen section—a growing sense of accumulating horror as the camera passes from the innocent faces of children at the beginning to the tragic situation of the camp inmates, and later from the happiness of the survivors as they are able to clean themselves and be fed to the mass graves where the SS guards are compelled to move the skeletonlike frames of the dead.[43] What remains from the project is silent except for comments by an ordinary British soldier and a military chaplain and a speech in German over the graves by an officer to an audience that includes sad-faced dignitaries from the local town. In recent years, these remnants of an unfinished production have attracted considerable attention, much of it journalistic, but they have little or no relevance to the film career of Alfred Hitchcock.[44]

Of films made about the aftermath of war in Europe there are no better examples than the two directed by John Ferno for the MOI and the Netherlands government, *Broken Dykes* and *The Last Shot.*[45] The first was concerned with the flooding in the autumn of 1944 of the island of Walcheren as a result of allied action against German forces trying to contain the port of Antwerp. Much of it dwelt on the rescue of Dutch families from the area. The second film depicted destruction in other parts of Holland, and drew attention to the shortage of food and fuel in the country, and to the problems caused by the presence of displaced persons and returning prisoners of war. On a different topic, Crown produced a film called *Channel Islands 1940–1945,* directed by Gerald Bryant, a recollection, largely through re-enactments by the islanders themselves, of the tribulations suffered by the only British population that had directly

***The Last Shot*. Feeding starving Dutch children in the aftermath of liberation.**

***A Diary for Timothy.* Humphrey Jennings, standing by the piano, directs the film as Myra Hess prepares to play.**

experienced Nazi occupation during the war.[46]

When Basil Wright took up his new post in charge of Crown on New Year's Day 1945, one of the projects in progress that he had to examine was *A Diary for Timothy,* another very personal creation by Humphrey Jennings. It had started with an idea about the birth of a baby—Timothy James Jenkins, in a nursing home at Oxford—on 3 September 1944, the fifth anniversary of Britain's entry into the war. It would then chart a "diary" of his first few months of life, as Europe became liberated and victory was gained, so that the new child became a symbol for a fresh feeling of hope in the world. Some of it had to be improvised and reconstructed according to the way that events proceeded during that final period of the war. The first screening of the rough cut at the MOI provoked complaint from many of the Films Division officials—ominously, "waste of public money" was given as a reason for opposition—but Jack Beddington supported Basil Wright and insisted on the film's being completed. E. M. Forster came in at a late stage to write the commentary.[47] He may have wanted the message of the film to be more radical and, in a letter to Wright, he criticized Jennings's choice of such a privileged child as the centerpiece of his argument.[48] The words were delivered by Michael Redgrave, and contact with the events of the war was intermittently maintained by using the voices of BBC announcers.

There are passages in *A Diary for Timothy,* photographed by Fred Gamage and edited by Alan Osbiston, that reveal Jennings at his most masterly in handling the association of vision, words, and sound. From the face of a wireless set as Stanley Maxted talks about Arnhem, the film cuts to the child's mother listening, a farmer smoking his pipe as he also attends to the broadcast, then to the hands of Myra Hess as she begins Beethoven's Appassionata Sonata, a pan across the audience at the National Gallery, finishing on a girl who puts up a hand to touch her hair, back briefly to the pianist, and Maxted's voice drifting in again with his story of the soldiers collecting rain water in their capes, and at once there is a shot of a London water tank, followed by battered house roofs and men working to repair them, Redgrave's voice as Beethoven flows on—"Some of us think it is the greatest music in the world, yet it is German music and we're fighting the Germans—That's something you'll have to think over later on"—and more images of water and rain through the episode of the child's baptism. Again, sequences of John Gielgud playing Hamlet in the scene with the gravedigger, switching over to Civil Defence workers in their canteen discussing how long it takes for a V2 to arrive, then ducking as one actually explodes, and finally the men working in the dark to delve into the rubble in search of survivors. At other points, though, it misfires, the wooden presence and dialogue of an injured fighter pilot, and the conversation of a Welsh miner with his wife about fears for the future, which is too incidental to be meaningful. At the end Redgrave asks, "Are you going to have greed for money or power ousting decency from the world as they had in the past or are you going to make the world a different place—you and the other babies?" There is a deep ambiguity at the heart of *A Diary for Timothy.* It is possible to detect a psychological as well as a literal gloom from the picture presented of London in that depressing winter of 1944–45 when the war seemed to be dragging on for longer than expected. After finishing it, Jennings traveled to the former enemy country to make *A Defeated People,* a compassionate view of Germans in their first few months since the collapse of the Nazi regime.[49] Before his early death by accident in 1950, he failed in his last documentaries to rediscover his distinctive touch, almost as if he had some awareness that the Second World War had been an enterprise that, for the British people, could not be repeated or emulated.

Paul Rotha's *Total War in Britain* was written by Ritchie Calder and Miles Tomalin, and spoken by John Mills.[50] It again used isotypes to demonstrate the scale of the British war effort and the remarkable mobilization of labor that had taken place in the country. Its objective was to demonstrate that central planning could also win the peace. By the sixth year of war, the narration says, less than half of 1 percent, many of them invalids, were still unemployed, a statistic which, however, omits reference to the number enlisted in the armed services. Production of aircraft is said to have increased sixfold since 1939 and, in spite of its losses, most of the merchant fleet had been replaced, an overview of British industrial achievement that sounds too praiseworthy now, in the light of later evidence.[51]

Rotha's other film, *Land of Promise,* was concerned with the particular problem of housing, which opinion polls had identified as the top priority in the minds of the people in 1945.[52] Five million homes had been destroyed or damaged in the course of the conflict, but the film also stressed the inadequacies of housing provision before the war. "No power on earth can stop the British people once we have the will," the narrator says. Left and right both, in different ways, had fostered a sense of national unity. Unfortunately, victory created not the required will to change, but for the most part a sense of complacency that would follow the election of 1945 and in time undermine the regeneration of Britain. Acceptance of either the nation's diminished status in the world or the need to come closer to her European neighbors would be a painfully slow process for British people. But the more militant among the working classes did feel a fresh confidence and a determination not to be set back again, as they believed they had been in the twenties (the mood was captured by an extraordinary short film made by the Co-operative Society, *Song of the People,* a piece which was in fact sung, almost like an opera). Although the reforms introduced by Attlee's new Labour government did not go so far as some on the left wanted, they succeeded in establishing at last the concept of the welfare state, which was to go virtually unchallenged in the postwar consensus until the late seventies.

As a medium for instruction, information, and propaganda, the British cinema documentary reached its highpoint during the Second World War. Thereafter, the movement was to gradually crumble. The expectations of Paul Rotha that the documentary would continue to lead in the field of social commitment were to be disappointed.[53] Labour took as little interest in this area as it had done before the war. However, the MOI was rescued, with the downgraded title of Central Office of Information, and, when the Conservatives were re-elected in 1951, they allowed it to continue although the Crown Film Unit was closed down. In fact, government needs were adequately served by the kind of bland informational films the COI could commission from private companies. The austere late forties and the dreary fifties saw most classes in the nation discovering a vested interest in propping up the existing structures of a society that seemed to have survived the war in tolerably good state, and in time the tradition of British documentary was to pass over to television and there gain a new measure of pragmatism and investigative zeal, which owed something both to the pioneering initiatives of John Grierson and his followers and to transatlantic models like *The March of Time.* The British cinema newsreel was also doomed to fall beneath the competition of television.

The last British feature production from 1945 that was directly about the Second World War, *Journey Together,* came from a surprising source.[54] The RAF Film Unit to date had hardly excelled in the making of completed films, but for this large-scale endeavor on the training of aircrew, it enlisted from the ranks of the service John Boulting as director. In fact, almost all of the actors and technicians were at that time members of the RAF. The plan for it had started as early as 1943, and a script was eventually written by Terence Rattigan after a basis had been established in discussion with Boulting. Since it contained no domestic drama and was almost entirely concerned with action, the scenario turned out to be less cliché-ridden than the script for *The Way to the Stars* (although it did not avoid spotlighting yet another transatlantic culture clash, when the British trainees fail to understand that their American hosts eat cheese with their apple pie!). Its plot follows the progress, on both sides of the Atlantic, of two young RAF airmen in training, working-class David Wilton and public school John Aynesworth, played respectively by Richard Attenborough and Jack Watling, both relatively unknown to the public at the time. More familiar faces appear in some other roles, among them John Justin, who had starred in *The Thief of Bagdad,* now impersonating the British flying instructor, as well as future celebrities like George Cole, who is seen as the bomb aimer of Aynesworth's Lancaster crew. The cast originally drawn up included Rex Harrison, Alistair Sim, Miles Malleson, and Sheila Sim, but in the end their parts were dropped, and possibly the documentary qualities of the film were enhanced by the omission of better-known British players (Sheila Sim was in fact still seen in one form, in a photograph, as Wilton's fiancee). However, for the part of the American flying instructor in Arizona, *Journey Together* did use one of Hollywood's biggest names, Edward G. Robinson, who consented to come to London on payment of traveling expenses only, at a time when the capital was being subjected to V-bomb attack. Bessie Love, already resident in England, plays his wife in the brief scene where they entertain Wilton and Aynesworth at their home.

Wilton, an RAF ground staff corporal, is reprimanded for going up in an aircraft without authority, but this does lead him to be interviewed for flying training (one of the officers on the board is played by Derek Twist, the first head of the RAF Film Unit). He is passed and, at a reception center in a requisitioned greyhound stadium, he meets Aynesworth, straight from undergraduate life. Thereafter, the various stages are carefully detailed, first the initial training, for which they are billeted in Aynesworth's Cambridge college. Wilton is seen to be scrupulous and hard-working, while Aynesworth dodges the routines of theoretical learning. But at the flying training school it is a different story. Aynesworth is a natural pilot, while Wilton finds difficulty in landing his Tigermoth without bumping it. Nevertheless, at the aircrew distribution center, both are posted to Arizona for further training. Some of the American scenes, including that of the cadets arriving at the town of Mesa and being greeted by a band and flag-waving citizens, were shot on location by an American crew under the supervision of George Brown, the production manager, but flying sequences were skilfully cut into shots featuring the actors, none of whom left Pinewood. In the plot, Edward G. Robinson's Dean McWilliams persists with Wilton as far as letting him fly solo, but, when the trainee crashes his Stearman biplane on landing, fortunately without injury to himself, the American decides against him. Wilton has no judgment of height, and he will never make a pilot.

Deeply disappointed, he has to revert to training in Canada to be a navigator, a task that visibly bores him. He is only made to recognize his responsibilities in an incident, partly contrived by a sympathetic RCAF pilot, when he has to guide down an aircraft in bad weather. Aynesworth, a visitor to the station, has witnessed the episode, and he is not overenthusiastic when in time Wilton joins the same Lancaster squadron in England. He is even less so when, after a long period in reserve, Wilton is ordered to substitute for a wounded navigator and go with Aynesworth on a mission over Berlin. Their former British flying instructor also accompanies them in the bomber. The raid is completed, but the Lancaster has been damaged and the crew's bomb aimer is wounded. Finally, they have to ditch in the North Sea and take to the dinghy and in time, after some hours of doubt, they are spotted by an aircraft that will direct the rescue launch toward them. Wilton's navigation has been flawless after all, for it was his fix that the radio operator had been able to transmit to base.

In *Journey Together,* Aynesworth and his crew are all sergeants, as are most of the other men at the briefing. The officer instructor who accompanies them is an equal, united with them by common danger. Put beside its contemporary, *The Way to the Stars,* the film is a more truthful statement about the RAF in 1944, the year in which both productions set their climax. The script was not completely free of the awkwardness that had dogged the British film for many years, and yet it made an honest attempt to recognize what had been achieved by working and winning

Journey Together. The American flying instructor discusses the progress of the trainees with his British colleagues (Edward G. Robinson, Sebastian Shaw, and Ronald Adam).

Journey Together. For one pilot in training the course has an unhappy ending (Richard Attenborough).

together during the war. Its style also was a fruitful amalgam of the legacies of the feature and the documentary in British cinema. The sequence of the Lancaster crashing is one of the most realistically fashioned in any British Second World War film—the pilot crisply speaking his ditching instructions, the altimeter needle swinging downward, crewmen blowing up their lifejackets, the wireless operator tapping out his messsage until the last second, canvas flapping in the empty fuselage, the sound of the wind as the plane glides down, water appearing beneath the nose, and the bomber rocking as it hits the surface. *Journey Together* could hardly be called a great movie, but it was a summation of the lessons learned by the best of British filmmakers as they mustered themselves in the service of the nation while it passed through its greatest test of survival in modern times. Again apart from a neorealistic interlude in the early sixties, this tradition was to wither until the more recent revival of a factual movement in British television and film.

The presence in *Journey Together* of Edward G. Robinson owed much, without doubt, to the wish that the film be well received in the United States. Much has been said and written about the differences and the conflicts between British and Americans during the war. However, what was more important in the end was the unity of their effort, an achievement *The True Glory* had rightly recognized. Without British resistance to Hitler in 1940 and 1941, there would have been no base from which to launch the liberation of western Europe, and, without the vast resources mobilized by America, there would have been no way of attempting it. There could have been no Marshall Plan to provide the means to set the European states on their feet again, and no restoration of democracy on the continent, which would have been left instead under the control either of Nazi Germany or of the Soviet Union. Whether intended or not, the "togetherness" in the title of *Journey Together* embraces also this spirit of cooperation between these two English-speaking countries in the Second World War.

The defeat of Germany did not end the war. Victory over Japan was almost entirely an American affair, with the USSR intervening briefly at the end, and the British contribution was limited in the main to the struggle to recover Burma. However, this was an area in which people in Britain did take an interest, even if the Fourteenth Army that operated there had deserved the title "the forgotten army." Mass-Observation had discovered that *War in the Pacific,* a Shell Film directed by Graham Tharp in 1943, was well received by the public.[55] It had given a clear explanation of the strategy of the allied counteroffensive and, as well as outlining the island-hopping tactics of the Americans in moving their forces back toward the Philippines and toward Japan itself, it had brought in also an account of the important campaign by the Australians in New Guinea. However, the tide in Burma did not turn until the middle of 1944. British sensibilities were offended in the summer of 1945 by the short-lived issue in Britain of the notorious Hollywood production *Objective Burma,* with Errol Flynn. It was not resented because it showed Americans fighting there—the American part in air support and in engineering was vital, and there was American infantry in the north working with the Chinese—but because in a theater where paratroopers were not used, it invented a fictitious American parachute regiment that was seen in the final stages of the film to be dropping over the jungle and winning the decisive battle on its own.[56]

The record was put straight by the completion of *Burma Victory,* the last of the campaign films to be produced by the Army Film Unit.[57] Southeast Asia was also to be the last great area of operation for the AFPU, whose film section in the field, commanded by Derek Knight, was known as the SEAC (Southeast Asia Command) Film Unit. It recorded the aftermath of Japanese surrender in Malaya, Indonesia, and Vietnam. Churchill had wanted Alexander Korda to be in charge of film affairs there, an assignment the War Office successfully resisted, but that had been an attempt to bring in a glamorous name on a par with that of SEAC's commander-in-chief, Lord Louis Mountbatten, who was appointed in October 1943.

The task undertaken by Mountbatten was one of the most difficult and daunting of any taken up and eventually mastered by an allied commander in the Second World War. British prestige had been shattered by the fall of Singapore, and the morale of the troops had sunk to zero as a result of defeats in Burma in 1942 and 1943. It was generally believed that the Empire soldiers could not face the Japanese on equal terms in the jungle, an environment that had contributed also to the spread of malaria and other tropical ailments among the British. There was the ever-present possibility of insurrection in India, and indeed large numbers of Indian troops captured by the enemy had been induced to join the Indian National Army, formed to fight alongside the Japanese. The situation was complicated by the sympathetic views of Roosevelt and most other Americans to Indian independence, and their consequent reluctance to feed Churchill's ambitions to restore the British Empire exactly as it had been before the war. America placed exaggerated hopes on the participation of Chiang Kai-shek and the nationalist Chinese, and it was significant that the American general, Joe

Stilwell, who had been sent to liaise with them, was a dedicated anglophobe who felt nothing but hatred and contempt for British imperialism, British snobbery, and what he believed to be British military incompetence. Stilwell was made Mountbatten's deputy, but, before the war had finished, he was recalled when Washington finally became disillusioned with the Chinese.[58]

Mountbatten was both a film enthusiast and an advocate of the pursuit of harmonious Anglo-American relationships, and the promotion of a joint production on the Southeast Asia campaign soon became one of his main hopes. Frank Capra was proposed as its director, and work on the film commenced in the United States. David MacDonald arrived at SEAC headquarters at the end of 1944, with War Office approval to initiate the British side of the project. He received the firm message from Mountbatten that any work would have to proceed in the context of Anglo-American collaboration, that MacDonald should take his instructions from Mountbatten and not from the War Office, that he would be required to stay on the task as long as the commander-in-chief required, and, if he did not like all this, he should return to Britain immediately and hand over control of the film production solely to the Americans. However, after this unpromising start, Mountbatten soon made a retreat when it became clear that Washington regarded American and British political aims in the area as being irreconcilable. There was no possibility of the American authorities collaborating in a film that might appear to endorse British imperialism. For their part, British observers who viewed Capra's rough cut objected that it was concerned only with the question of aid to China. Moreover, the American film was to be a two-reeler, whereas the British wanted a longer production. In a message to Field Marshal Wilson, leading the British joint staff mission to the Combined Chiefs of Staff, Mountbatten relayed his hopes that General Marshall would prevent "a rabid all-Stilwell film being put over on the American public, to the detriment of Anglo-American relations." The matter was settled amicably when MacDonald flew to Washington in May 1945; it was agreed that the British would proceed with their own separate and longer production, with Capra supplying them with material on American participation in the campaign. *Burma Victory,* directed by Roy Boulting, who also wrote the script with Frank Harvey, was rapidly finished and released in October. After an American screening it was reported that General Marshall was happy about the film and that Warner Brothers (ironically, the producers of *Objective Burma*) had secured wide distribution for it in the United States.

The opening of the film, studio-shot to represent a couple of British soldiers sheltering in a tent from the tropical rain, vividly establishes the atmosphere and the travails of fighting a war in the monsoon climate of Burma. One of them is reading from a guidebook: "Burma—there is romance in the very word, recalling a vision of white pagodas on the Irrawaddy gazing out across the peaceful countryside, a land of light-hearted laughing people, lovers of flowers and bright colours, and women, dainty and self-possessed, ascending the pagoda steps, the morning sunshine beating down through paper parasols on the delicate beauty of their gay silks." He tosses the book into the mud outside. The film moves immediately to actuality shots of the jungle and the troops, and the narrator explains the nature of the monsoon—four months of rain, bringing behind it malaria, dysentery, and typhus: "enemies more deadly than the Jap." The difficult topography of Burma is described, a jungle plain enclosed by a horseshoe of mountains, with three rivers flowing into the sea. Mountbatten is seen addressing his men with words chosen to bolster their self-confidence: "Somebody started the story that the Jap was a kind of jungle superman. I can assure you that he's nothing of the sort. He's an unintelligent slum-dweller, with nothing worth fighting for except a fanatical belief that his Emperor is a kind of god."

By the beginning of 1944 the Japanese were ready for an advance into India.[59] In spite of their reverses elsewhere, they intended to encourage a general rebellion there against the British, a scheme much to the liking of their ally, the Indian nationalist leader Subhas Chandra Bose. It would have brought a huge territory into their sphere of influence, and the idea of a march on Delhi was energetically advocated by Mutaguchi, the most ambitious of the Japanese generals in Burma. Understandably, neither of these personalities is mentioned in *Burma Victory* (nor indeed is the matter of Gandhi and passive resistance in India), and the only people acknowledged are the allied commanders, occasionally seen in somewhat self-conscious appearances at restaged briefings. Prominent among them is William Slim, the general then in charge of the Fourteenth Army, a man who came to be revered as second to none among the leading soldiers of the war. He knew what the Japanese objectives would be, and he had worked out his plan in advance. The key lay in the holding of Imphal, a town in the border Indian state of Manipur, and its northern neighbor Kohima. Here, between March and June, there developed one of the epic battles of the Second World War, while a second field of activity blossomed in the Arakan, close to the Burmese coast. The allied forces on these fronts were a mixed bunch: British, Indian, Gurkha, and African infantry, with

***Burma Victory*. Mountbatten gives a morale-boosting talk to soldiers of the Fourteenth Army.**

the British and American air forces securing command of the skies. The defenders held their ground, and the Japanese, worn down by malnutrition and disease, pulled away from them. In the interior, a diversion had been created by the air-supplied columns of British "chindits," led by the unorthodox and controversial Wingate, who was killed in a plane crash in the middle of the operation. From the north, Stilwell and his Chinese and Americans made their own push to secure the most important airfield in Burma and to open up a road that would solve the formidable problems of bringing in supplies to the armies. *Burma Victory,* was silent about the exhaustion and demoralization that affected these units, but it sang the praises of one of the heroes of the campaign, the American Dr. Seagrave, who with his helpers performed up to a hundred operations a day on the wounded.

Mountbatten had emphasized that there would be no stopping this time for the monsoon. The retreating Japanese continued to fight back with ferocity, preferring death to surrender. Again the allied soldiers had to cope as well with the jungle and the climate, and *Burma Victory* creates unforgettable impressions of the men struggling against the perils of malaria and against the heat, the dampness, the leeches, and the mosquitoes. Another studio sequence reproduces a typical situation at night where Japanese voices speaking in English ("Where are you, Tommy?") try to get the British to reveal their positions. With the monsoon over, air supply becomes possible again. One of the items dropped is the soldiers' own newspaper, SEAC, which was edited from Calcutta by Frank Owen as part of the morale-building strategy carefully fostered by Mountbatten.

In the last stage of the campaign, engineers brought up an improvised bridge to span the Chindwin and, as more territory was liberated from the enemy, the AFPU film material had villagers celebrating in festive mood, General Slim looking uneasy with a garland of flowers round his neck. On the whole, the Japanese had managed to alienate most local sympathies. The crossing of the Irrawaddy, this time possible only with boats, was one of the great achievements of the war, and there was further record film of the battle for the ancient capital of Mandalay, a severely fought contest with the Indian divisions winning a full share of the glory. Although Slim tried to respect the historical monuments, he was compelled to call in the RAF to dislodge the Japanese from a number of them. The capture of Mandalay opened up the road to Rangoon, but the Japanese had already moved out when forces which had traveled down the coast made a landing from the sea, just as the Second World War was ending.

The dropping of the atomic bombs on Hiroshima and Nagasaki in August 1945 put the final seal on the disintegration of Japan's war effort. The campaign in Burma was not a significant factor, although (except only for the quick victories of the Russians at the very last stage) it had seen the heaviest defeat of Japanese land forces in the field. It was, therefore, something of a military curiosity. The British did not even have time to reconquer Malaya, an operation that had been planned, although they rushed to take the surrender at Singapore, the scene of their original humiliation. Self-respect had been restored: "In twelve months," the narrator of *Burma Victory* said, "The men of the Fourteenth Army . . . had made a fighting advance of over one thousand miles across the worst country in the world"—but it was too late to rescue the Empire. Its many millions of inhabitants had realized that their masters had feet of clay.

Burma Victory's modesty of means and methods marks it as a fitting conclusion to the various productions made by the British service film units during the war, groups that were rapidly disbanded as military cinema needs soon reverted to the making of training pieces only. The last sounds of the film are of silence, its final images the slow lowering of artillery gun muzzles, a symbol of the sudden peace that had arrived in the world.

Notes

Introduction

1. The Imperial War Museum, London (IWM), holds unedited 35mm film shot by the British service units in its entirety, silent rushes of material shot on the war fronts by the various newsreel companies and submitted for military censorship, and additionally 35mm newsreel issues from Gaumont British and Paramount. The rights to both of the latter are owned by Visnews. Pathé (now owned by Weintraub) and Movietone continue as newsreel libraries.

2. Betts, *The Film Business,* 82.

3. The dominance of Hollywood in Britain has been discussed by many writers. For a recent view, see Peter Stead, "The people and the pictures," in Pronay and Spring, *Propaganda, Politics and Film,* 77–97. Anthony Aldgate in his BBC/Open University series, *British Cinema of the 1930s,* has challenged some of these assumptions, for which see Richards and Aldgate, *Best of British,* 29–39.

4. For a summary table of British cinema admissions 1935–80, see Patricia Perilli, "Statistical Survey of the British Film Industry," in Curran and Porter, *British Cinema History,* 372.

5. The percentage was dropped from 22½ percent to approximately 14 percent, *Kinematograph Weekly,* 11 July 1940.

6. Stevenson and Cook, *The Slump,* is a general account of the period that balances the facts against what had been a long-standing myth of the thirties.

7. See Jeffrey Richards, "Patriotism with profit: British Imperial Cinema in the 1930's," in Curran and Porter, *British Cinema History,* 245–71.

8. *Kinematograph Weekly,* 14 January 1943.

9. Surveys in 1928, 1932, 1934, and 1937. The Mass-Observation Archive (see n. 15) has a report on the 1937 survey that compares it with the previous ones, Box 2/A (Films). It confirms, from nearly 160,000 returns, the popularity of Hollywood stars for British audiences. In 1937, for example, out of sixteen most popular male stars only one, Charles Laughton, is British and of the top sixteen female stars four are British, Jessie Matthews, Merle Oberon, Gracie Fields, and Madeleine Carroll. Another interesting aspect of the survey is that among the most disliked stars there is a high proportion of comedians.

10. See Jeffrey Richards, "The British Board of Film Censors and Content Control in the 1930s: Images of Britain," *Historical Journal of Film, Radio and Television* 1 (October 1981): 95–116, and Nicholas Pronay, "The political censorship of films in Britain," in Pronay and Spring, *Propaganda, Politics and Film,* 98–125, and also James C. Robertson, *The British Board of Film Censors: Film Censorship in Britain 1896–1950* (London: Croom Helm, 1985).

11. For comments on *The Proud Valley* see Barr, *Ealing Studios,* 19–22, and Peter Stead, "Wales in the movies," in Tony Curtis, ed., *Wales: The Imagined Nation* (Wales: Poetry Wales Press, 1986), 159–80.

12. The progress of the British documentary movement is chronicled by Rotha, *Documentary Diary,* and Watt, *Don't Look at the Camera,* writing as participants, as well as by Sussex, *Rise and Fall of British Documentary;* Eva Orbanz, ed., *Journey to a Legend and Back: The British Realistic Film* (Berlin: Volker Spiess, 1977); and Rachael Low, *The History of British Film 1929–39: Documentary and Educational Films of the 1930s* (London: George Allen and Unwin, 1979), 48–170. See also Stuart Hood, "John Grierson and the documentary film movement," in Curran and Porter, *British Cinema History,* 99–112, and Paul Swann, "John Grierson and the GPO Film Unit, 1933–39," *Historical Journal of Film, Radio and Television* 3 (March 1983): 19–34.

13. Soviet films were screened in Britain by the influential Film Society, founded in 1925, in which Ivor Montagu was the guiding spirit, for which see Rotha, *Documentary Diary,* 10. Later Turin's *Turksib* was to have a profound effect

on British documentary filmmakers (Rotha, 38).

14. For an aspect of this criticism, see Richards and Aldgate, *Best of British,* 2–3.

15. Mass-Observation (M-O) was started in 1937 by the anthropologist Tom Harrisson with the poet Charles Madge and filmmaker Humphrey Jennings in order to research public attitudes to a number of social topics. Their papers are located in the Mass-Observation Archive at the University of Sussex. See Angus Calder and Dorothy Sheridan, *Speak for Yourself: A Mass-Observation Anthology 1937–49* (London: Jonathan Cape, 1984).

16. M-O Archive; Leonard England's report "Uses of intelligence for the film," 9 October 1940, Box 8/B (Films).

17. In only a few cases, viewing prints of feature films are not available at the National Film Archive, London (NFA), because master material has not been made. For those films it was not possible to view at the NFA and for those very few that could not be found elsewhere, summaries only of the plots have been given, based on information in the British Film Institute's *Monthly Film Bulletin.*

18. Film is still a neglected part of the available evidence for twentieth-century historians. The field is surveyed in, Paul Smith, ed., *The Historian and Film* (Cambridge: Cambridge University Press, 1976).

19. Channel Four in Britain has taken the lead in screening documentaries in their original form. Flashback Productions have made for the same channel some interesting films that use larger documentary sequences than normal to place them in their historical context. The same techniques were first developed by the BBC/Open University for educational purposes, including the *War and Society* series conceived by Arthur Marwick. Thorpe and Pronay, *British Official Films,* is an invaluable catalogue of the nonfiction films produced by the British Government during the war, and it lists the archives in Britain, the United States, and Canada that hold prints of them. Although a few films have disappeared, the majority of British documentaries from the period can be viewed, especially at IWM and NFA in London. The Library of Congress, in Washington, D.C., has a number of 16mm prints.

Chapter 1. The First Months

1. Events leading up to the outbreak of war, the appeasement factor, and the effect of the Nazi-Soviet Pact are concisely discussed in Michel, *Second World War,* 1–23.

2. For a list of his own works on mechanized warfare, see Liddell Hart, *Second World War,* 767.

3. Stanley Baldwin addressing the House of Commons, 10 November 1932, as quoted in Hastings, *Bomber Command,* 43. For the growth of a bombing policy in Britain, see Hastings, 37–58.

4. See Don Macpherson, ed., *Traditions of Independence: British Cinema in the Thirties* (London: British Film Institute, 1980) and Bert Hogenkamp, *Deadly Parallels: Film and the Left in Britain 1929–39* (London: Lawrence and Wishart, 1986).

5. Production details and correspondence relating to many of the official films are deposited at the Public Record Office, Kew, London (PRO). However, these records vary a great deal from film to film in terms of the amount of information they provide. *Do It Now,* INF 6/349.

6. *The First Days,* INF 6/983.

7. For the most informative account of the work of the MOI Films Division, notably the way in which it was established, see the introduction to Thorpe and Pronay, *British Official Films,* 1–56. See also Arts Enquiry, *The Factual Film,* 63–106.

8. Watt, *Don't Look at the Camera,* 125–29.

9. INF 1/867. Reproduced in full in Christie, *Powell, Pressburger and Others,* 121–24.

10. See. T. J. Hollins, "The Conservative Party and film propaganda between the wars," *English Historical Review* 96 (April 1981): 359–69.

11. Ian Dalrymple, "The Crown Film Unit 1940–43," in Pronay and Spring, *Propaganda, Politics and Film,* 209–10.

12. M-O Archive, reports by Leonard England and from members of the viewing panel, Box 1/A, 1/C, 4/B, 4/C (Films).

13. Deutsche Wochenschau 514/29/1940, IWM copy GW/167. Possibly the use of this sequence was the origin of the occasionally repeated but unlikely story that *The Lion Has Wings* was shown in Berlin for public amusement.

14. Jackson, *Before the Storm,* 53–56.

15. Ibid., 65–69.

16. See n. 12. The public seems to have become bored in particular with the factory sequences and with the film's ending.

17. "As a statement of war aims, one feels, this leaves the world beyond Roedean still expectant," Graham Greene, *The Spectator,* 3 November 1939. The review is reprinted in Graham Greene, ed. John Russell Taylor, *The Pleasure Dome: The Collected Film Criticism 1935–40* (London: Secker and Warburg, 1972), 249–50.

18. For an account of this period, see Turner, *Phoney War.*

19. "This was the first time in history that a blacked out city had been put on the screen," Michael Powell in interview with Kevin Gough-Yates, quoted in Christie, *Powell, Pressburger and Others,* 27.

20. See Pope, *River Plate,* for a full account.

21. Michael Powell wrote his own semifictionalized account of the battle to coincide with the film's release, *Graf Spee* (London: Hodder and Stoughton, 1956).

22. Pope, *River Plate,* 236–37.

23. The subject of the famous propaganda film *Olympische Spiele,* directed by Leni Riefenstahl. See Glenn B. Infield, *Leni Riefenstahl: The Fallen Film Goddess* (New York: Thomas Y. Crowell, 1976), 113–55.

24. For a history of this war, see Anthony F. Upton, *Finland 1939–40* (London: Davis-Poynter, 1974).

25. For the production of *Let George Do It,* see Aldgate and Richards, *Britain Can Take It,* 76–95.

26. See J. L. Moulton, "Hitler strikes north," in Liddell Hart and Pitt, *Second World War,* 1: 147.

27. For evacuation and its effects, see Calder, *People's War,* 35–50.

28. *Documentary News Letter (DNL),* published monthly from January 1940 by Film Centre, 34 Soho Square, London.

29. Thorpe and Pronay, *British Official Films,* 34–35. For what Kenneth Clark describes as the "inexplicable choice" of himself, see Clark, *The Other Half,* 10–14.

30. *Now Your're Talking,* INF 6/527.

31. *All Hands,* INF 6/524.

32. *Dangerous Comment,* INF 6/525.

33. *Spring Offensive/Unrecorded Victory,* INF 6/351.

34. For the prewar state of agriculture and government wartime intervention, see Calder, *People's War,* 411–18.

35. Watt, *Don't Look at the Camera,* 129–34.

36. *War Illustrated,* 26 January 1940.

37. Watt, *Don't Look at the Camera,* 144.

38. *Men of the Lightship,* INF 5/66–8, 6/353.

39. For *Men of the Lightship,* see Vaughan, *Portrait of an Invisible Man,* 46–53.

40. J. L. Moulton, "Conquest of Norway," in Liddell Hart and Pitt, *Second World War,* 1:158–67.

41. For Niemöller's life, see Davidson, *Pastor Niemöller.*

42. Roy Boulting describes the making of *Pastor Hall* in IWM Department of Sound Records interview, no. 4627/06, transcript, 3–7.

43. Fest, *Hitler,* 449–80.

44. The subject is comprehensively covered by Peter Hoffman, *The History of the German Resistance,* trans. Richard Barry (London: Macdonald and Jane's, 1977).

45. Public support for Chamberlain or Churchill seems to have been evenly divided in March and April 1940, for which see Addison, *Road to 1945,* 80.

Chapter 2. Britain at Bay

1. For a concise account, see Robert Jackson, *The Fall of France May–June 1940* (London: Arthur Barker, 1975).

2. These political changes are comprehensively covered in Addison, *Road to 1945.*

3. Noble, *Shoot First!,* 24–33.

4. For newsreel cameramen in France with the BEF, see Ronnie Noble, IWM Department of Sound Records interview, no. 5392/07, transcript, 1–30.

5. The main types used by British cameramen at this time were the Newman Sinclair and the Bell and Howell Eyemo. The Newman was a heavy camera, normally only suitable for use with a tripod, and it took a magazine of two hundred feet, i.e., two minutes' filming. It had to be wound during running, and a bag had to be used for changing the reels. The Eyemo was smaller and could be more easily hand-held, and it took one hundred feet of film. Later, under the lend-lease agreements, the American De Vry became available and was widely used. For some interesting comments on these cameras and the various technical problems of filming, see Gerald Massy Collier, IWM Department of Sound Records interview, no. 3897/09, transcript, 33–35 and 87–93.

6. For the MOI's relationships with the newsreel companies, see Nicholas Pronay, "The news media at war," in Pronay and Spring, *Propaganda, Politics and Film,* 173–208.

7. M-O Archive, letter to Tom Harrisson from a member of the film viewing panel in Watford, Herts., 4 May 1941, Box 1/B (Films).

8. Pronay in *Propaganda, Politics and Film,* 188.

9. Original dope sheets from the newsreel companies, with censorship markings, are held by IWM Department of Film.

10. Tom Harrisson, "Films and the home front—the evaluation of their effectiveness by Mass-Observation," in Pronay and Spring, *Propaganda, Politics and Film,* 234–45.

11. M-O Archive, various newsreel reports, Box 7 (Films). According to the result of these surveys popularity of newsreels with the public dropped from 62% in 1939 to 25% in 1940.

12. *Channel Incident,* INF 6/425.

13. ". . . a flaming insult to the men of Dunkirk and to the men and women of the little boats," from "Films and a People's War," *DNL* 1 (November 1940): 3.

14. The battle of Britain has been chronicled by a number of writers. For one of the most recent accounts, see Len Deighton, *Fighter* (London: Jonathan Cape, 1977).

15. Clark, *The Other Half,* 14–15.

16. Thorpe and Pronay, *British Official Films,* 35–36.

17. Dalrymple, "The Crown Film Unit, 1940–43," in Pronay and Spring, *Propaganda, Politics and Film,* 211–12.

18. INF 1/205–6.

19. *Kinematograph Weekly,* 31 October 1940.

20. M-O Archive, report by Leonard England on MOI short films, 10 October 1940, Box 8/B (Films), and reports from members of the film viewing panel on the poor distribution of MOI films, Box 8/C (Films).

21. For nontheatrical distribution by the MOI, see Arts Enquiry, *The Factual Film,* 76–83, and Helen Forman, "The non-theatrical distribution of films by the Ministry of Information," in Pronay and Spring, *Propaganda, Politics and Film,* 221–33.

22. 13th Select Committee on National Expenditure. Report published by His Majesty's Stationery Office, 21 August 1940. The MOI's Films Division was able to resist pressure to stop the production of documentaries, a fortunate circumstance in the light of British wartime film history.

23. *Sea Fort,* INF 6/433.

24. Dalrymple in *Propaganda, Politics and Film,* 211.

25. *Merchant Seamen,* INF 6/332.

26. For the general subject of music in British wartime films, see John Huntley, *British Film Music* (London: Skelton Robinson, 1947).

27. Calder, *People's War,* 88 and 100–103.

28. *Welfare of the Workers,* INF 6/356.

29. *Behind the Guns,* INF 6/430.

30. Calder, *People's War,* 234.

31. *The New Britain,* INF 6/430.

32. Calder, *People's War,* 138–39 and 246–47.

33. For a concise account, see Norman Longmate, *The Real Dad's Army* (London: Arrow Books, 1974).

34. *Miss Grant Goes to the Door,* INF 6/429.

35. In fact *Miss Grant* seems to have been favorably received by the public, a conclusion reached by Mass-Observation after six viewings in London, M-O Archive, report by Leonard England, 13 August 1940, Box 8/A (Films). It clearly had appeal as a mini-drama, and note was taken of its security lessons, inadequate though one might feel them to be now, with hindsight about genuine Nazi military efficiency.

36. *The Front Line,* INF 5/70, 6/354.

37. Watt, *Don't Look at the Camera,* 135–37.

38. Calder, *People's War,* 140.

39. *Dawn Guard,* INF 6/442.

40. Boulting, IWM interview, 7–9.

41. *Goodbye Yesterday* had taken a real group of individuals and showed how the war had changed their lives. According to Basil Wright, they were invited to view the film and to make comments, at a meeting chaired by the Australian journalist Colin Wills, for which see Basil Wright, IWM Department of Sound Records interview, no. 6231/08, transcript, 42–44. John Taylor, IWM interview no. 7259/06, transcript, 9–15, recalls little about the film but says that the decision to withdraw it was taken after a viewing by Cyril Radcliffe, the MOI's Director-General.

42. *Home Guard,* INF 6/446.

43. For this phase of the bombing of Britain, see Calder, *People's War,* 163–227.

44. *London Can Take It,* INF 6/328.

45. Watt, *Don't Look at the Camera,* 137–43. See also Vaughan, *Portrait of an Invisible Man,* 63–64.

46. Americans also had difficulty with the British accents. This gave rise to reports that Hitchcock had been commissioned to re-edit and redub some films, but it has been difficult to confirm that this was ever done, INF 1/600.

47. *Christmas Under Fire,* INF 6/329.

48. *The Heart of Britain,* INF 6/331. The logo at the beginning incorporated both GPO and Crown, as the name of the Unit was being changed.

49. Vaughan, *Portrait of an Invisible Man,* 72–74.

50. For views on class-consciousness and morale during the blitz, see Marwick, *Home Front,* 68–75.

51. *Neighbours Under Fire,* INF 6/1036.

52. *Ordinary People,* INF 5/76, 6/330.

53. Marwick, *Home Front,* 60–66.

54. *Living with Strangers,* INF 6/448.

55. *When the Pie Was Opened,* INF 6/490.

56. *Night Watch,* INF 6/457.

57. *Machines and Men,* INF 6/931.

58. *Ack-Ack,* INF 6/436.

59. *Words for Battle,* INF 5/79, 6/338. See Vaughan, *Portrait of an Invisible Man,* 74–76.

60. *The Times,* 18 June 1940. Reprinted, with the newspaper's editorial and some illustrations, as *An Airman's Letter* (London: Putnam, 1940).

61. Hastings, *Bomber Command,* 94–99.

62. *Target for Tonight,* INF 1/210, 5/81, 6/335. See Watt, *Don't Look at the Camera,* 145–52.

63. M-O Archive, report by Leonard England, 27 September 1941, Box 8/A (Films).

64. Hastings, *Bomber Command,* 106–22.

65. *Ferry Pilot,* INF 5/83, 6/334.

66. *Health in War,* INF 6/984.

67. For recollections of filming with Rignold in France in 1939 and 1940, see Massy Collier, IWM interview, 37–59.

68. Ronald Tritton, IWM Department of Sound Records interview, no. 4626/04, transcript, 8–9.

69. Information from the unpublished wartime diary of Ronald Tritton, extracts from which have been made available to IWM Department of Documents, entry for 8 March 1941, and David MacDonald, IWM Department of Sound Records interview, no. 4654/03, transcript, 14–15.

70. IWM Department of Film has a complete set of AFPU dope sheets, usually handwritten by the cameraman. W. Tennyson d'Eyncourt's record of shooting this sequence is included in the Lofoten group, part of the A/69 series.

71. Tritton, diary, 10 March 1941. See also *Kinematograph Weekly,* 17 April 1941.

72. Robert Verrall, IWM Department of Sound Records interview, no. 7335/02, no transcript. There is no confirmation from any other source that Jennings worked on *Lofoten.* Verrall speaks of him as being a background figure. With the Crown Film Unit being involved, it is conceivable that Jennings was asked to put the material into shape as a routine piece of work.

73. Memo from D. Anderson, MOI Newsreel Section, to newsreel editors, 10 March 1941, copy filed with IWM dope sheets A/69.

74. *DNL* 2 (July 1941): 128–29.

75. See Harry Watt, "Notes on Vaagso," in *DNL* 3 (February 1942): 23.

76. The making of *The Gun* is described by its producer Lieutenant E Terrell, RNVR, in Edward Terrell, *Admiralty Brief* (London: George C. Harrap, 1958), 116–28.

77. Guy Morgan, *Red Roses Every Night; An Account of London Cinemas under Fire* (London: Quality Press, 1948), 36.

78. Calder, *People's War,* 176–77.

79. For the production of *Pimpernel Smith,* see Aldgate and Richards, *Britain Can Take It,* 44–75.

80. MacIntyre, *Naval War against Hitler,* and Roskill, *Navy at War,* give comprehensive single-volume accounts of the war at sea.

81. Kulik, *Korda,* 245–53.

82. For the production of *49th Parallel,* see Powell, *A Life in Movies,* 343–84, and Aldgate and Richards, *Britain Can Take It,* 21–43.

83. *Kinematograph Weekly,* 14 November 1940. It was also the only feature film for which the MOI provided actual production funds. Thereafter, the ministry, following the recommendatons of the 13th Select Committee on National Expenditure, took a more distanced view of the industry, though it could give more active encouragement when needed, as in the cases of *The Way Ahead* and *The Way to the Stars.*

Chapter 3. Desert Victory

1. Jameson, *Ark Royal,* 29–32.

2. Ibid., 194–95.

3. M-O Archive, reports from members of the film viewing panel, Box 10/D-J (Films).

4. For comments on the class-based theatricality of *Ships With Wings,* see Barr, *Ealing Studios,* 25–26, and for audience reception, Jeffrey Richards, "Wartime British Cinema Audiences and the Class System: The Case of *Ships With Wings,*" *Historical Journal of Film, Radio and Television* 2 (June 1987); 129–41.

5. Edwin Packer, "Italian Fiasco: The Attack on Greece," in Liddell Hart and Pitt, *Second World War,* 1: 341–55.

6. Perry, *Forever Ealing,* 61.

7. *Wavell's 30,000,* INF 6/342.

8. John Connell, "Wavell's 30,000," in Liddell Hart and Pitt, *Second World War,* 1: 393–411.

9. For the relationship of prime minister and foreign secretary in general, see Barker, *Churchill and Eden at War.*

10. See Alan Clark, *The Fall of Crete* (London: Anthony Blond, 1962).

11. For single-volume accounts of the desert campaign, see W. G. F. Jackson, *The North African Campaign 1940–43* (London: B. T. Batsford, 1975) and Warren Tute, *The North African War* (London: Sidgwick and Jackson, 1976).

12. Tritton, diary, 19 August 1941.

13. Tritton, diary, 26 October 1942.

14. John Turner, IWM Department of Sound Records interview, no. 005438/04, transcript, 26–27.

15. Dope sheets held by IWM Department of Film, Movietone B 205/D, Gaumont British B 205/E.

16. Addison, *Road to 1945,* 190–210.

17. For a general discussion of the role of comedy in wartime, see Anthony Aldgate's chapter "Raise a Laugh," with particular reference to *Let George Do It,* in Aldgate and Richards, *Britain Can Take It,* 76–95.

18. Hastings, *Bomber Command,* 123–40.

19. Ibid., 146–54. Moyna's dope sheet, IWM Depart-

ment of Film, Ops 2, 2–3 July 1942.

20. Len Deighton, *Bomber* (London: Jonathan Cape, 1970).

21. For Dutch resistance, see Werner Warmbrunn, *The Dutch under German Occupation 1940–45* (Stanford: Stanford University Press, 1963).

22. *The Pilot Is Safe,* INF 6/336.

23. James C. Robertson, "British Film Censorship Goes to War," in *Historical Journal of Film, Radio and Television* 2 (March 1982): 61–62.

24. For the production of *Went the Day Well?,* see Aldgate and Richards, *Britain Can Take It,* 115–37, and also Barr, *Ealing Studios,* 29–33.

25. Elizabeth Sussex, "Cavalcanti in England," in *Sight and Sound* 44 (Autumn 1975); 205–11.

26. Reprinted in Hugh Greene, ed., *The Pirate of the Round Pond* (London: The Bodley Head, 1977).

27. C. A. Lejeune, *The Observer,* 1 November 1942, felt that presentation of the enemy as so totally brutal cheapened the effect of victory.

28. *Mrs. Miniver* was a huge popular success in the United States, and it won six Academy Awards. President Roosevelt expressed his gratitude for the fact that its effect would diminish opposition to his lend-lease program of aid to Britain. See Colin Shindler, *Hollywood Goes to War: Films and American Society 1939–52* (London and Boston: Routledge and Kegan Paul, 1979), 48–49.

29. *Listen to Britain,* INF 5/82.

30. The M-O reports confirm anyway an impression of a higher degree of participation and comment than one would expect now of a cinema audience.

31. See the discussion between Elizabeth Sussex and Edgar Anstey, in Sussex, *Rise and Fall of British Documentary,* 144–46.

32. INF 1/632. The MOI was worried that the deal might prevent the full exploitation of a real "hit," a box-office winner. However, no British film during the war qualified for such success in the United States.

33. IWM Department of Film has a complete set of *Warwork News,* two pilot issues and eighty-one full issues, from 1942 to 1945. See Thorpe and Pronay, *British Official Films,* 256–62, for details.

34. Hastings, *Bomber Command,* 170–78.

35. Calder, *People's War,* 267–70. Even so, the scale of British production lagged behind that of both Germany and the United States, a fact attributed by Correlli Barnett to the characteristically British combination of amateurish management and union restrictiveness, for which see Barnett, *Audit of War,* 143–83.

36. *Speed-up on Stirlings,* INF 6/482.

37. *Night Shift,* INF 6/457.

38. *Essential Jobs,* INF 6/473.

39. *CEMA,* INF 6/471.

40. *Balloon Site 568,* INF 6/452.

41. *The Great Harvest,* INF 6/503.

42. *Builders,* INF 5/84, 6/340.

43. *DNL* 4 (March 1943): 194.

44. *The Next of Kin,* INF 6/1043. For the production of this film, see Aldgate and Richards, *Britain Can Take It,* 96–114.

45. M-O Archive, film viewing reports, Box 9/D (Films).

46. See R. W. Thompson, "Massacre at Dieppe," in Liddell Hart and Pitt, *Second World War,* 3: 1093–1101.

47. M-O Archive, film viewing reports, Box 9/G (Films).

48. *Seaman Frank Goes Back to Sea,* INF 6/559.

49. *Coastal Command,* INF 5/86, 6/24.

50. David Prosser, IWM Department of Sound Records interview, no. 4844/09, transcript, 56–63.

51. Prosser, ibid., 48–51, and Turner, IWM interview, 30–31.

52. *Malta G.C.,* INF 6/348.

53. *Malta Convoy,* INF 6/480.

54. For the production of *In Which We Serve,* see Aldgate and Richards, *Britain Can Take It,* 185–217.

55. For the story of HMS *Kelly,* see Poolman, *The Kelly.*

56. Roger Manvell, "They Laugh at Realism," *DNL* 3 (March 1943): 188.

57. For Mitchell and the development of the Spitfire, see Vader, *Spitfire.*

58. Filippo del Giudice, a refugee from fascist Italy, was better known as a producer for Rank and as the founder of Two Cities Films.

59. However, the Vickers-Supermarine management is described as "incompetent" by Correlli Barnett in his withering criticism of the British aircraft industry, in Barnett, *Audit of War,* 138–40.

60. For the production of *The Young Mr Pitt,* see Aldgate and Richards, *Britain Can Take It,* 138–67.

61. For the production of *Thunder Rock,* see Aldgate and Richards, 168–86.

62. At this time the AFPU sections were: no. 1 Western Desert, no. 2 Tunisia, no. 3 Home Forces, and no. 4 Airborne Division, "Film Progress in the Services," *DNL* 3 (May 1943): 210–12.

63. IWM Department of Film has an almost complete set of *War Pictorial News* and its successor *World Pictorial News* (1945–46). See Thorpe and Pronay, *British Official Films,* 241–77, for details.

64. Tritton, diary, 27 July 1942.

65. Harry Watt, "Casting Nine Men," in *DNL* 3 (February 1943): 179–80.

66. *The Saving of Bill Blewitt* (1936).

67. The standard biography of Montgomery is Nigel Hamilton, *Monty,* 3 vols. (London: Hamish Hamilton, 1981–86). For the general reader, see Alun Chalfont, *Montgomery of Alamein* (London: Weidenfeld and Nicolson, 1976). There are several accounts of Alamein, one of the most recent being James Lucas, *War in the Desert: the Eighth Army at Alamein* (London: Arms and Armour Press, 1982).

68. MacDonald, IWM interview, 18.

69. Jack Beddington's proposal was supported by Anthony Kimmins (Admiralty) and Derek Twist (Air Ministry), according to Tritton, diary, 11 December 1942.

70. Boulting, IWM interview, 18–28.

71. MacDonald, IWM interview, 22–23.

72. See J. P. Williams, "Status of the British Documentary and Distribution in the USA," in *DNL* 5 (June 1945): 66–69.

Chapter 4. Looking Ahead

1. For the production of *The Life and Death of Colonel Blimp,* see Richards and Aldgate, *Best of British,* 61–74.

2. PRO, PREM 4/14/15. The correspondence between Churchill and Bracken is reproduced in Ian Christie's account and discussion of the matter, in Christie, *Powell, Pressburger and Others,* 105–20.

3. Nicholas Pronay and Jeremy Croft speculate that Bracken secretly approved of the film and encouraged its American distribution, for which see "British Film Cen-

sorship during the Second World War," in Curran and Porter, *British Cinema History,* 155–63. Nevertheless, the American publicity book for the film contained posters which presented Blimp in terms like "a rogue with a roving eye" and "a fighting fool about women," arguably not the most obvious way of suggesting that he was an obsolescent figure, for which see British Film Institute Press Book.

4. M-O Archive, film viewing reports, Box 10/A (Films).

5. *Kill or Be Killed,* INF 6/479.

6. In order to make a tracking shot more realistic as it follows the marksman crawling forward, Lye and Jeakins had the camera slung from a rifle. For the episode of the German patrol being shot, they arranged a mask to simulate the rifle's sights in front of the camera and jerked it slightly as the rifle is supposedly being fired.

7. *Wales—Green Mountain, Black Mountain,* INF 6/483.

8. INF, 1/598.

9. *Wales—Green Mountain, Black Mountain* was released nontheatrically. The original British Council film *Wales,* made by Merton Park Studios, remained in existence. It had been meant to parallel a film called *Ulster,* produced by Strand in 1941. Martyn Howells (Welsh Arts Council) has investigated the curious fact that *Wales* was shown in cinemas in Cardiff and Rhyl to invited Welsh audiences in a Welsh-language version, as late as July 1944. Even more curious, it was denounced by Rhyl Council as "an insult to the Welsh nation," and it was agreed that representation should be made to the British Council, MOI, and BBC for it not to be shown overseas, where it had been meant to be seen wherever there were groups of Welsh-speaking people. It was a short factual film, with much about the war effort in Wales, and, with the end of hostilities in sight, the likely explanation is that the viewers thought it to be too brief to do justice to Welsh culture and life for peacetime audiences. *Kinematograph Weekly,* 24 August 1944, and *The Cinema,* 27 September 1944.

10. See Infield, *Leni Riefenstahl,* 73–112.

11. Dalrymple in Pronay and Spring, *Propaganda, Politics, and Film,* 217.

12. *Fires Were Started,* INF 6/985. For the production of this film, see Aldgate and Richards, *Britain Can Take It,* 218–45.

13. Published anonymously. "The bells go down" is a reference to the signal that calls out the firemen.

14. Evelyn Waugh, *Officers and Gentlemen* (London: Chapman and Hall, 1952).

15. Henry Green, *Caught* (London: Hogarth Press, 1943).

16. Wallington, *Firemen at War,* 145.

17. [Flint], *Bells Go Down,* 7–8, 23–24.

18. Ibid., 5.

19. *Close Quarters,* INF 6/25.

20. Calder, *People's War,* 331–35.

21. For Gainsborough films, see Robert Murphy and Sue Aspinall, eds., *BFI Dossier 18: Gainsborough Melodrama* (London: British Film Institute, 1983).

22. Betts, *The Film Business,* 209–14.

23. See Robert Murphy, "Rank's Attempt on the American Market, 1944–9," in Curran and Porter, *British Cinema History,* 164–78.

24. See, for example, Jeavons, *War Films,* 97.

25. F. W. D. Deakin, *The Embattled Mountain* (London: Oxford University Press, 1971) gives a British liaison officer's view of working with Tito's partisans. The accepted gospel of the Titoist liberation of Yugoslavia from the Nazis has been challenged recently in a controversial book by Nora Beloff, *Tito's Flawed Legacy: Yugoslavia and the West, 1939 to 1984* (London: Victor Gollancz, 1985).

26. *The Silent Village,* INF 5/90, 6/1916.

27. *Before the Raid,* INF 5/91, 6/357.

28. Arthur Koestler, IWM Department of Sound Records interview, no. 5393/03, transcript, 7–9.

29. Ibid., 12–15.

30. Marwick, *Home Front,* 128–30.

31. *Tyneside Story,* INF 6/598.

32. For a characteristically scathing view of the failures of the British shipbuilding industry, see Barnett, *Audit of War,* 107–24.

33. Addison, *Road to 1945,* 263–69.

34. Taylor, IWM interview, 17–18.

35. *World of Plenty,* INF 1/214, 6/561. This is one of the most complete of PRO production records. See also Manvell, *Films and the Second World War,* 165–67.

36. Rotha, *Portrait of a Flying Yorkshireman,* 194–224.

37. In Wilmot, *Struggle for Europe,* and other works.

38. INF 1/178. For an account of *Mission to Moscow* as an American propaganda film, see David Culbert's introduction to the published screenplay (Madison: University of Wisconsin Press, 1980), 11–41.

39. For the most perceptive accounts of this school of British film, see Barr, *Ealing Studios,* and Durgnat, *A Mirror for England.*

40. Information on the production of *Africa Freed* and *Tunisian Victory* from INF 1/223 and from a file held by IWM Department of Film. See also Clive Coultass, "*Tunisian Victory*—a film too late?," in *Imperial War Museum Review,* no. 1 (1986): 64–73.

41. Capra's account is given in his autobiography, Frank Capra, *The Name above the Title* (New York: Macmillan, 1971), 351–55, and Stewart's in Hugh Stewart, IWM Department of Sound Records interview, no. 4579/06, transcript, 17–23.

42. Tritton, diary, 8 February 1944.

43. This is a little-known episode in Jennings's career. Part of a letter from him to Cicely Jennings, 3 September 1943, is quoted in Mary-Lou Jennings, ed., *Humphrey Jennings,* 36. Although the film has disappeared, four stills from it are held by IWM Department of Photographs, listed as FLM 1730, 1731, 1735, and 1736.

44. *The True Story of Lili Marlene,* INF 5/100, 6/360.

45. For general accounts of the Italian campaign, see W. E. F. Jackson, *The Battle for Italy* (London: B. T. Batsford, 1967) and Dominick Graham and Shelford Bidwell, *Tug of War: The Battle for Italy 1943–45* (London: Hodder and Stoughton, 1986).

46. Hastings, *Bomber Command,* 178–88 and 251–68.

47. *Sky Giant,* INF 6/481.

48. *Workers' Weekend,* INF 6/359. For the production of this film, see Ralph Elton, "Shooting *Workers' Weekend,*" in *DNL* 6 (June 1943): 229.

49. Kulik, *Korda,* 282–83.

50. Dalrymple had become critical of some aspects of MOI policy, for which see Sussex, *Rise and Fall of British Documentary,* 151–52. It is interesting that one of the things he wanted was to keep MOI material for historical use in the future. The idea was rejected and both the MOI, and its successor the COI made a practice of junking their off-cuts.

51. *The Biter Bit,* INF 6/564.

52. *There's a Future in It,* INF 6/611.

53. *The Volunteer,* INF 6/600.

54. *Operational Height,* INF 6/1034.
55. Richard Hillary, *The Last Enemy* (London: Macmillan, 1942).
56. *Control Room,* INF 6/530.
57. *Dustbin Parade,* INF 6/472.
58. *We Sail at Midnight,* INF 6/346.
59. *Our Time,* July 1945, quoted in the memorial program of Massingham films, 27 and 28 March 1955, attached to Basil Wright et al, *Richard Massingham: a Tribute by His Friends and a Record of His Films* (London, Hertford, and Harlow: The Shenval Press, Simson Shand, 1955).
60. *Power for the Highlands,* INF 6/591.
61. *Children of the City,* INF 6/1247.
62. *Cameramen at War,* INF 6/575.
63. For comments on the significance of *San Demetrio* to Balcon and the studio, in the context of war propaganda, see Barr, *Ealing Studios,* 35–38.
64. MacNeil, *San Demetrio,* 123–24.
65. *Western Approaches,* INF 1/213, 5/103–9, 6/370, one of the most complete of PRO production records. For the making of this film, see Aldgate and Richards, *Britain Can Take It,* 246–76.
66. Copy held by IWM Department of Film, NMV 773/01.
67. Ambler, *Here Lies,* 182–88.
68. *The Way Ahead,* INF 1/224. For the production of this film, see Vincent Porter and Chaim Litewski, "*The Way Ahead:* Case History of a Propaganda Film," in *Sight and Sound* 50 (Spring 1981): 110–16.
69. Green used smaller apertures than usual to obtain greater depth of focus, to take in all the characters, and to add to the severity of the background, for which see *Kinematograph Weekly,* 2 September 1943.
70. Addison, *Road to 1945,* 164–89. See also Barnett, *Audit of War,* 11–37. A succinct account of the MOI's attitudes to social reform is given in Yass, *This is Your War,* 57–60. A view of the way in which prospects for the future were presented by the documentary filmmakers is put forward by Nicholas Pronay, "'The Land of Promise': the Projection of Peace Aims in Britain," in K. R. M. Short, ed., *Film and Radio Propaganda in World War II* (London: Croom Helm, 1983), 51–77. However, this account does not make it clear that only a small minority of documentaries were concerned with the theme, and its listing of the films contains some errors.

Chapter 5. Winning Together

1. Hastings, *Overlord.* See also D'Este, *Decision in Normandy,* which is particularly critical of Montgomery's strategy.
2. Hugh Stewart, IWM Department of Sound Records interview, no. 4579/06, transcript, 34–35.
3. Grant, *Cameramen at War,* 42–59.
4. Desmond O'Neill, IWM Department of Sound Records interview, no. 3971/04, transcript, 30–37.
5. Tritton, diary, 8 March and 16 May 1944.
6. Grant, *Cameramen at War,* 111–16.
7. Tritton, diary, 17 and 18 July 1944.
8. Eindhoven Raid, IWM Department of Film, Ops 20, 6 December 1942.
9. Amiens raid, IWM Department of Film, Ops F68, 18 February 1944.
10. Information on this production from a file in IWM Department of Film. This includes the transcript of a BBC talk by Harry Rée.
11. Dilys Powell, for example, wrote ". . . it seems a pity to reserve it till now, when so many romantic fictions have intervened, and when the truth is already in danger of looking remote," in *The Sunday Times,* 9 February 1947.
12. M-O Archive, report by Leonard England, "British film and family life," 13 June 1944, Box 3/I (Films).
13. *A Letter from Ulster,* INF 5/87, 6/347.
14. *Kinematograph Weekly,* 13 January 1944.
15. *A Welcome to Britain,* INF 6/601.
16. *USA, The Land and its People,* INF 6/1249.
17. For the production of *A Canterbury Tale,* see Richards and Aldgate, *Best of British,* 43–60.
18. *The Eighty Days,* INF 5/111, 6/362.
19. *Partners in Crime,* INF 4/460.
20. Calder, *People's War,* 311–15.
21. For a view of the effect of the war on the presentation of women in British feature films, see Sue Aspinall, "Women, Realism and Reality in British Films, 1943–53," in Curran and Porter, *British Cinema History,* 272–93.
22. For a summary, written at the time, of the needs of education, see Arts Enquiry, *The Factual Film,* 105–35. At the end of this section, reference is made to the work of the Colonial Film Unit, founded by the MOI in October 1939 to make films for use in Africa, an aspect of documentary production more fully covered by Rosaleen Smyth, "Movies and Mandarins: the Official Film and British Colonial Africa," in *British Cinema History,* 127–43.
23. *Our Country,* INF 6/630.
24. For favorable advocacy of this film, see Wright, *The Long View,* 203–4.
25. IWM Department of Film holds an almost complete series of *Worker and Warfront.* See Thorpe and Pronay, *British Official Films,* 262–63, for details.
26. *Tirpitz* attacks, IWM Department of Film, Ops 228, 241, 242, September–November 1944.
27. Hastings, *Bomber Command,* 327–45.
28. *Target Germany,* INF 6/783.
29. Terraine, *Right of the Line,* 682.
30. For the production of *The Way to the Stars,* see Aldgate and Richards, *Britain Can Take It,* 277–98.
31. Original poem by John Pudney, "For Johnny," in *Dispersal Point and other air poems* (London: John Lane, The Bodley Head, 1942).
32. *Stricken Peninsula,* INF 6/664.
33. *The Star and the Sand,* INF 6/663.
34. *The Nine Hundred,* INF 6/655.
35. *A Soviet Village,* INF 6/634.
36. Ironically, the progress of this abortive production is one of the best documented at the PRO, INF 5/92–97.
37. Information on the making of *The True Glory* from a Pinewood Studios file handed to IWM Department of Film by Robert Verrall. Production and editing notes are included.
38. *From Italy to D-Day,* INF 6/689. *From Paris to the Rhine,* INF 6/1263. *From the Rhine to Victory,* INF 6/690.
39. INF 1/636. For an account of this project, see Elizabeth Sussex, "The Fate of F3080," in *Sight and Sound* 53 (Spring 1984): 92–97, and also Moorehead, *Bernstein,* 164–69.
40. Donald Spoto, *The Life of Alfred Hitchcock: The Dark Side of Genius* (Boston: Little, Brown, 1983), 270–72.
41. *DNL* 1 (December 1940): 19. The letter was signed by Rotha, who quoted support from, among others, Michael

Balcon, Ritchie Calder, Cavalcanti, Michael Foot, and Dilys Powell. Their indignation was directed at the final scene of *Foreign Correspondent,* where Joel McCrea says, "America! Hang on to your lights, they are the only lights left in the world!" Even John Grierson, who had gone to Canada and who was rumored (wrongly) to have had something to do with this scene, did not escape what now reads like misplaced fury. In truth, the film was trying to shake Americans out of indifference to events in Europe, not to suggest that Britain was incapable of doing anything.

42. Copies of the *Welt im Film* series, neither fully complete, are held by IWM and NFA. See *Microfiche Film Catalogue no. 1, Welt im Film 1945–50* (London: Imperial War Museum 1981), and, for an account of the making of the newsreel, Roger Smither, "*Welt im Film:* Anglo-American Newsreel Policy," in Nicholas Pronay and Keith Wilson, eds., *The Political Re-education of Germany and Her Allies after World War II* (London: Croom Helm, 1985), 151–72.

43. Vaughan, *Portrait of an Invisible Man,* 153–57.

44. IMW Department of Film has called the reels *Memory of the Camps* in response to a number of requests for the material to be screened. However, there is no historical justification other than convenience for this title.

45. *Broken Dykes,* INF 6/642. *The Last Shot,* INF 6/650.

46. *Channel Islands,* INF 6/26.

47. Wright, IMW interview, 55–58. See also Lindsay Anderson, "Only Connect: Some Aspects of the Work of Humphrey Jennings,"in Mary-Lou Jennings, ed., *Humphrey Jennings,* 55–57.

48. Forster to Wright, 15 May 1945, a letter lent by Basil Wright to IWM Departments of Film and Art for their exhibition "The Screen Goes to War," June–September 1982. *A Diary for Timothy,* INF 6/1917.

49. *A Defeated People,* INF 6/374.

50. *Total War in Britain,* INF 6/671.

51. In fact, British shipbuilding had failed to reach its wartime targets and had proved itself incapable of adopting American mass production and prefabricated methods, for which see Barnett, *Audit of War,* 120.

52. Calder, *People's War,* 579.

53. Rotha, *Documentary Diary,* 285–86.

54. Information on the production of *Journey Together* from a file held by IWM Department of Film.

55. *War in the Pacific,* INF 6/599. M-O Archive, film viewing reports, Box 12/D (Films).

56. The case of *Objective Burma* and British reactions to it is fully documented by I. C. Jarvie, "Fanning the Flames: anti-American reaction to *Operation* [*sic*] *Burma* (1945)," in *Historical Journal of Film, Radio and Television* 1 (October 1981): 115–37. (The film is titled correctly in the body of the article). In both the popular and the historical context, British criticism of *Objective Burma* was far from "niggling," as it is described by Bernard F. Dick, *The Star-Spangled Screen: The American World War II Film* (Lexington: University Press of Kentucky, 1985), 226–29, a misjudgment also made by Jeavons, *War Films,* 135–36.

57. Information on the production of *Burma Victory* from a file held by IWM Department of Film.

58. Thorne, *Allies of a Kind,* describes in full the issue of Anglo-American relationships and the war against Japan.

59. See Barker, *March on Delhi,* for the Japanese plans and their failure. Allen, *Burma,* is the most recent and comprehensive history of the campaign. With regard to the two most controversial characters involved in it, he defends Wingate and denigrates Stilwell, views that no doubt will continue to be argued by other historians.

Select Bibliography

Addison, Paul. *The Road to 1945: British Politics and the Second World War.* London: Jonathan Cape, 1975.

Aldgate, Anthony, and Jeffrey Richards. *Britain Can Take It: The British Cinema in the Second World War.* Oxford: Basil Blackwell, 1986. *See also* Richards, Jeffrey, and Anthony Aldgate.

Allen, Louis. *Burma: The Longest War 1941–45.* London: J. M. Dent, 1984.

Ambler, Eric. *Here Lies: An Autobiography.* London: Weidenfeld and Nicholson, 1985.

Arts Enquiry, The. *The Factual Film.* For Political and Economic Planning. London: Geoffrey Cumberlege, Oxford University Press, 1947.

Balcon, Michael. *Michael Balcon Presents . . . A Lifetime of Films.* London: Hutchinson, 1969.

Balfour, Michael. *Propaganda in War 1939–45: Organisations, Policies and Publics in Britain and Germany.* London: Routledge and Kegan Paul, 1979.

Barker, A. J. *The March on Delhi.* London: Faber and Faber, 1963.

Barker, Elisabeth. *Churchill and Eden at War.* London: Macmillan, 1978.

Barnett, Correlli. *The Audit of War: The Illusion and Reality of Britain as a Great Nation.* London: Macmillan, 1986.

Barr, Charles. *Ealing Studios.* London: Cameron and Tayleur, 1977.

Betts, Ernest. *The Film Business: A History of British Cinema 1896–1972.* London: George Allen and Unwin, 1973.

Boyle, Andrew. *"Poor Dear Brendan": the Quest for Brendan Bracken.* London: Hutchinson, 1974.

Brown, Geoff. *Launder and Gilliat.* London: British Film Institute, 1977.

Calder, Angus. *The People's War.* London: Jonathan Cape, 1969.

Christie, Ian, ed. *Powell, Pressburger and Others.* London: British Film Institute, 1978.

Clark, Kenneth. *The Other Half.* London: John Murray, 1977.

Curran, James and Vincent Porter, eds. *British Cinema History.* London: Weidenfeld and Nicolson, 1983.

Davidson, Clarissa Start. *God's Man: Pastor Niemöller.* New York: Ives Washburn, 1959.

Davis, Kenneth S. *The American Experience of War 1939–45.* London: Secker and Warburg, 1967.

D'Este, Carlo. *Decision in Normandy: The Unwritten Story of Montgomery and the Allied Campaign.* London: Collins, 1983.

Durgnat, Raymond. *A Mirror for England: British Movies from Austerity to Affluence.* London: Faber and Faber, 1970.

Fest, Joachim. *Hitler.* Translated by Richard and Clara Winston. London: Weidenfeld and Nicolson, 1974.

Fitzgibbon, Constantine. *The Blitz.* London: Macdonald, 1957.

[Flint, Vic]. *The Bells Go Down: The Diary of a London AFS Man.* London: Methuen, 1942.

Frankland, Noble. *Bomber Offensive: The Devastation of Europe.* London: Macdonald, 1969.

Gifford, Denis. *The British Film Catalogue 1895–1970.* Newton Abbot: David and Charles, 1973.

Grant, Ian. *Cameramen at War.* London: Patrick Stephens, 1980.

Hastings, Max. *Bomber Command.* London: Michael Joseph, 1979.

———. *Overlord: D-Day and the Battle for Normandy 1944.* London: Michael Joseph, 1984.

Jackson, Robert. *Before the Storm: The Story of Bomber Command 1939–42.* London: Arthur Barker, 1972.

Jameson, William. *Ark Royal.* London: Rupert Hart-Davis, 1957.

Jeavons, Clyde. *A Pictorial History of War Films.* London: Hamlyn, 1974.

Jennings, Mary-Lou, ed. *Humphrey Jennings: Film-maker, Painter, Poet.* London: British Film Institute, 1982.

Jesse, F. Tennyson. *The Saga of San Demetrio.* London: His Majesty's Stationery Office, 1942.

Kulik, Karol. *Alexander Korda: The Man who Could Work Miracles.* London: W. H. Allen, 1975.

Liddell Hart, Basil. *History of the Second World War.* London: Cassell, 1970.

Liddell Hart, Basil, and Barrie Pitt, eds. *History of the Second World War.* 6 vols. London: Purnell, 1966–68.

Lysaght, Charles Edward. *Brendan Bracken: A Biography.* London: Allen Lane, 1979.

MacIntyre, Donald. *The Naval War against Hitler.* London: B. T. Batsford, 1971.

McLaine, Ian. *Ministry of Morale: Home Front Morale and the Ministry of Information in World War II.* London: George Allen and Unwin, 1979.

MacNeil, Calum. *San Demetrio.* London: Angus and Robertson, 1957.

Manvell, Roger. *Films and the Second World War.* South Brunswick, N.J., and New York: A. S. Barnes; and London: J. M. Dent, 1974.

Marwick, Arthur. *The Home Front.* London: Thames and Hudson, 1976.

Michel, Henri. *The Second World War.* Translated by Douglas Parmée. London: Andre Deutsch, 1975.

Moorehead, Caroline. *Sidney Bernstein.* London: Jonathan Cape, 1984.

Noble, Ronnie. *Shoot First! Assignments of a Newsreel Cameraman.* London: George Harrap, 1955.

Perry, George. *Forever Ealing: A Celebration of the Great British Film Studio.* London: Pavilion/Michael Joseph, 1981.

Poolman, Kenneth. *The Kelly.* London: William Kimber, 1954.

Pope, Dudley. *The Battle of the River Plate.* London: William Kimber, 1956.

Powell, Michael. *A Life in Movies: An Autobiography.* London: Heinemann, 1986.

Pronay, Nicholas, and D. W. Spring, eds. *Propaganda, Politics and Film 1918–45.* London: Macmillan, 1982.

Rhode, Eric. *A History of the Cinema: From its Origins to 1970.* London: Allen Lane, 1976.

Richards, Jeffrey and Anthony Aldgate. *Best of British: Cinema and Society 1930–1970.* Oxford: Basil Blackwell, 1983. See also Aldgate, Anthony and Jeffery Richards.

Roskill, S. W. *The Navy at War 1939–45.* London: Collins, 1960.

Rotha, Paul. *Documentary Diary: An Informal History of the British Documentary Film 1928–39.* London: Secker and Warburg, 1973.

———. ed. *Portrait of a Flying Yorkshireman: Letters from Eric Knight in the USA to Paul Rotha in England.* London: Chapman and Hall, 1952.

Stevenson, John and Chris Cook. *The Slump: Society and Politics during the Depression.* London: Jonathan Cape, 1977.

Sussex, Elizabeth. *The Rise and Fall of British Documentary.* Berkeley and Los Angeles: University of California Press, 1975.

Taylor, A. J. P. *The Second World War.* London: Hamish Hamilton 1975.

Terraine, John. *The Right of the Line: The Royal Air Force in the European War 1939–45.* London: Hodder and Stoughton, 1985.

Thorne, Christopher. *Allies of a Kind: The USA, Britain and the War against Japan.* London: Hamish Hamilton, 1978.

Thorpe, Frances and Nicholas Pronay. *British Official Films in the Second World War.* Oxford: Clio Press, 1980.

Toller, Ernst. *Pastor Hall.* Translated by Stephen Spender. London: John Lane, The Bodley Head, 1939.

Turner, E. S. *The Phoney War.* London: Michael Joseph, 1961.

Vader, John. *Spitfire.* London: Macdonald, 1970.

Vaughan, Dai. *Portrait of an Invisible Man: Stewart McAllister.* London: British Film Institute, 1983.

Wallington, Neil. *Firemen at War: The Work of London's Firefighters in the Second World War.* Newton Abbot: David and Charles, 1981.

Watt, Harry. *Don't Look at the Camera.* London: Paul Elek, 1974.

Wilmot, Chester. *The Struggle for Europe.* London: Collins, 1952.

Wright, Basil. *The Long View.* London: Secker and Warburg, 1974.

Yass, Marion. *This is Your War: Home Front Propaganda in the Second World War.* London: Her Majesty's Stationery Office, 1983.

Zuckerman, Solly. *From Apes to Warlords 1904–46.* London: Hamish Hamilton, 1978.

Film Title Index

General Index